Mary Clemmer

Ten years in Washington

Mary Clemmer

Ten years in Washington

ISBN/EAN: 9783742892560

Manufactured in Europe, USA, Canada, Australia, Japa

Cover: Foto ©Thomas Meinert / pixelio.de

Manufactured and distributed by brebook publishing software
(www.brebook.com)

Mary Clemmer

Ten years in Washington

TEN YEARS IN WASHINGTON.

LIFE AND SCENES

IN

THE NATIONAL CAPITAL,

AS A WOMAN SEES THEM.

BY

MARY CLEMMER AMES,

Author of "EIRENE, OR A WOMAN'S RIGHT," "MEMORIALS OF ALICE AND PHŒBE CARY,"
"A WOMAN'S LETTERS FROM WASHINGTON," "OUTLINES OF MEN,
WOMEN AND THINGS," ETC.

Full Page Illustrations.   Steel Plate Portrait of the Author.

[PUBLISHED BY SUBSCRIPTION ONLY.]

HARTFORD, CONN.:
A. D. WORTHINGTON & CO., PUBLISHERS.
A. G. NETTLETON & CO., CINCINNATI, O., AND ST. LOUIS, MO.
1875.

LIST OF ILLUSTRATIONS

(iii)

CONTENTS.

CHAPTER XIV.

A VISIT TO THE NEW LAW LIBRARY.

CHAPTER XV.

THE HEAVEN OF LEGAL AMBITION—THE SUPREME COURT ROOM.

CHAPTER XVI.

THE "MECCA" OF THE AMERICAN.

CHAPTER XVII.

THE CAPITOL—MORNING SIGHTS AND SCENES.

CHAPTER XXV.

THE WHITE HOUSE NOW ITS PRESENT OCCUPANTS.

CHAPTER XXVI.

MRS. GRANT'S RECEPTION—GLIMPSES OF LIFE.

CHAPTER XXVII.

INAUGURATION DAY AT WASHINGTON.

CHAPTER XXVIII.

THE NEW PRESIDENT—THE INAUGURATION BALL.

CHAPTER XXIX.

THE UNITED STATES TREASURY—ITS HISTORY.

CHAPTER XXX.

INSIDE THE TREASURY—THE HISTORY OF A DOLLAR.

CHAPTER XXXIII.

THE GREAT CASH-ROOM—THE WATCH-DOG OF THE TREASURY.

CHAPTER XXXIV.

WOMAN'S WORK IN THE DEPARTMENTS—WHAT THEY DO AND HOW THEY DO IT.

CHAPTER XXXV.

WOMEN'S WORK IN THE TREASURY.

2

CHAPTER XLV.

CHAPTER XLVI.

CHAPTER XLVII.

CHAPTER XLVIII.

CHAPTER XLIX.

Ten Years in Washington.

CHAPTER I.

FROM THE VERY BEGINNING.

The Young Surveyor's Dream—Humboldt's View of Washington—A Vision
of the Future Capital—The United States Government on Wheels—
Ambitious Offers—The Rival Rivers—Potomac Wins—Battles in Con-
gress—Patriotic Offers of Territory—Temporary Lodgings for Eleven
Years—Old-Fashioned Simplicity—He Couldn't Afford Furniture—A
Great Man's Modesty—Conflicting Claims—Smith Backs Baltimore—A
Convincing Fact—The Dreadful Quakers—A Condescending Party—
A Slight Amendment—An Old Bill Brought to Light Again—The
Indian Place with the Long Name—Secession Threatened—The Future
Strangely Foreshadowed—A Dinner of Some Consequence—How it was
Done—Really a Stranger—A Nice Proposal—Sweetening the Pill—A
" Revulsion of Stomach "—Fixed on the Banks of the Potomac.

MORE than a century ago a young surveyor, Captain
of the Virginia troops, camped with Braddock's
forces upon the hill now occupied by the Washington
Observatory, looked down as Moses looked from Nebo
upon the promised land, until he saw growing before his
prophetic sight the city of the future, the Capital of a
vast and free people then unborn. This youth was George
Washington. The land upon which he gazed was the undreamed of site of the undreamed of city of the Republic,
then to be. This youth, ordained of God to be the Father
of the Republic, was the prophet of its Capital. He foresaw it, he chose it, he served it, he loved it; but as a
Capital he never entered it.

Gazing from the green promontory of Camp Hill, what was the sight of land and water upon which the youthful surveyor looked down? It was fair to see, so fair that Humboldt declared after traveling around the earth, that for the site of a city the entire globe does not hold its equal. On his left rose the wooded hights of Georgetown. On his right, the hills of Virginia stretched outward toward the ocean. From the luxurious meadows which zoned these hills, the Potomac River—named by the Indians Cohonguroton, River of Swans—from its source in the Alleghany Mountains, flowing from north-west to south-west, here expanded more than the width of a mile, and then in concentrated majesty rolled on to meet Chesapeake Bay, the river James, and the ocean. South and east, flowing to meet it, came the beautiful Anacostin, now called Eastern Branch, and on the west, winding through its picturesque bluffs, ran the lovely Rock Creek, pouring its bright waters into the Potomac, under the Hights of Georgetown. At the confluence of these two rivers, girdled by this bright stream, and encompassed by hills, the young surveyor looked across a broad amphitheatre of rolling plain, still covered with native oaks and undergrowth. It was not these he saw. His prescient sight forecast the future. He saw the two majestic rivers bearing upon their waters ships bringing to these green shores the commerce of many nations. He saw the gently climbing hills crowned with villas, and in the stead of oaks and undergrowth, broad streets, a populous city, magnificent buildings, outrivaling the temples of antiquity—the Federal City, the Capital of the vast Republic yet to be! The dreary camp, the weary march, privation, cold, hunger, bloodshed, revolution, patient victory at last, all these were to be endured, outlived, before the beautiful Capital of his future was reached. Did the youth foresee these, also? Many toiling, struggling, suffering years bridged the dream of the young surveyor and the first faint dawn of its fulfillment.

After the Declaration of Independence, before the adoption of the Constitution of the United States, its government moved slowly and painfully about on wheels. As the exigencies of war demanded, Congress met at Philadelphia, Baltimore, Lancaster, York, Princeton, Annapolis, Trenton, and New York. During these troubled years it was the ambition of every infant State to claim the seat of government. For this purpose New York offered Kingston; Rhode Island, Newport; Maryland, Anapolis; Virginia, Williamsburg.

June 21, 1783, Congress was insulted at Philadelphia by a band of mutineers, which the State authorities could not subdue. The body adjourned to Princeton; and the troubles and trials of its itinerancy caused the subject of a permanent national seat of government to be taken up and discussed with great vehemence from that time till the formation of the Constitution. The resolutions offered, and the votes taken in these debates, indicate that the favored site for the future Capital lay somewhere between the banks of the Delaware and the Potomac—"near Georgetown," says the most oft-repeated sentence. October 30, 1784, the subject was discussed by Congress, at Trenton. A long debate resulted in the appointment of three commissioners, with full power to lay out a district not exceeding three, nor less than two miles square, on the banks of either side of the Delaware, for a Federal

town, with power to buy soil and to enter into contracts
for the building of a Federal House, President's house,
house for Secretaries, etc.

Notwithstanding the adoption of this resolution, these
Commissioners never entered upon their duties. Probably the lack of necessary appropriations did not hinder
them more than the incessant attempts made to repeal
the act appointing the Commissioners, and to substitute
the Potomac for the Delaware, as the site of the anticipated Capital. Although the name of President Washington does not appear in these controversies, even then
the dream of the young surveyor was taking on in the
President's mind the tangible shape of reality. First,
after the war for human freedom and the declaration of
national independence, was the desire in the heart of
George Washington that the Capital of the new Nation
whose armies he had led to triumph, should rise above
the soil of his native Dominion, upon the banks of the
great river where he had foreseen it in his early dream.
That he used undue influence with the successive Congresses which debated and voted on many sites, not the
slightest evidence remains, and the nobility of his character forbids the supposition. But the final decision at-
tests to the prevailing potency of his preferences and
wishes, and the immense pile of correspondence which
he has left behind on the subject, proves that next to the
establishment of its independence, was the Capital of the
Republic dear to the heart of George Washington. May
10, 1787, Massachusetts, New York, Virginia and Georgia
voted for, and New Jersey, Pennsylvania, Delaware and
Maryland against the proposition of Mr. Lee of Virginia,
that the Board of Treasury should take measures for

erecting the necessary public buildings for the accommodation of Congress, at Georgetown, on the Potomac River,
as soon as the soil and jurisdiction of said town could be
obtained.

Many and futile were the battles fought by the old
Congress, for the site of the future Capital. These battles doubtless had much to do with Section 8, Article 1,
of the Constitution of the United States, which declares
that Congress shall have power to exercise exclusive legislation in all cases whatsoever, over such district (not exceeding ten miles square,) as may, by cession of particular
States and the acceptance of Congress, become the seat
of government of the United States. This article was
assented to by the convention which framed the Constitution, without debate. The adoption of the Constitution
was followed spontaneously by most munificent acts on
the part of several States. New York appropriated its
public buildings to the use of the new government, and
Congress met in that city April 6, 1789. On May 15,
following, Mr. White from Virginia, presented to the
House of Representatives a resolve of the Legislature of
that State, offering to the Federal government ten miles
square of its territory, in any part of that State, which
Congress might choose as the seat of the Federal government. The day following, Mr. Seney presented a
similar act from the State of Maryland. Memorials and
petitions followed in quick succession from Pennsylvania,
New Jersey and Maryland. The resolution of the Virginia Legislature begged for the co-operation of Maryland, offering to advance the sum of one hundred and
twenty thousand dollars to the use of the general government toward erecting public buildings, if the Assem-

bly of Maryland would advance two-fifths of a like sum. Whereupon the Assembly of Virginia immediately voted to cede the necessary soil, and to provide seventy-two thousand dollars toward the erection of public buildings. "New York and Pennsylvania gratuitously furnished elegant and convenient accommodations for the government" during the eleven years which Congress passed in their midst, and offered to continue to do the same. The Legislature of Pennsylvania went further in lavish generosity, and voted a sum of money to build a house for the President. The house which it built was lately the University of Pennsylvania. The present White House is considered much too old-fashioned and shabby to be the suitable abode of the President of the United States. A love of ornate display has taken the place of early Republican simplicity. When George Washington saw the dimensions of the house which the Pennsylvanians were building for the President's Mansion, he informed them at once that he would never occupy it, much less incur the expense of buying suitable furniture for it. In those Spartan days it never entered into the head of the State to buy furniture for the "Executive Mansion." Thus the Chief Citizen, instead of going into a palace like a satrap, rented and furnished a modest house belonging to Mr. Robert Morris, in Market street. Meanwhile the great battle for the permanent seat of government went on unceasingly among the representatives of conflicting States. No modern debate, in length and bitterness, has equalled this of the first Congress under the Constitution. Nearly all agreed that New York was not sufficiently central. There was an intense conflict concerning the relative merits of Philadelphia and Germantown; Havre de

Grace and a place called Wright's Ferry, on the Susquehanna; Baltimore on the Patapsco, and Connogocheague on the Potomac. Mr. Smith proclaimed Baltimore, and the fact that its citizens had subscribed forty thousand dollars for public buildings. The South Carolinians cried out against Philadelphia because of its majority of Quakers who, they said, were eternally dogging the Southern members with their schemes of emancipation. Many others ridiculed the project of building palaces in the woods. Mr. Gerry of Massachusetts declared that it was the hight of unreasonableness to establish the seat of government so far south that it would place nine States out of the thirteen so far north of the National Capital; while Mr. Page protested that New York was superior to any place that he knew for the orderly and decent behavior of its inhabitants, an assertion, sad to say, no longer applicable to the city of New York.

September 5, 1789, a resolution passed the House of Representatives "that the permanent seat of the government of the United States ought to be at some convenient place on the banks of the Susquehanna, in the State of Pennsylvania. The passage of this bill awoke the deepest ire in the members from the South. Mr. Madison declared that if the proceedings of that day could have been foreseen by Virginia, that State would never have *condescended to become a party to the Constitution.* Mr. Scott remarked truly: "The future tranquillity and well being of the United States depended as much on this as on any question that ever had or ever could come before Congress;" while Fisher Ames declared that every principle of pride and honor, and even of patriotism, was engaged in the debate.

The bill passed the House by a vote of thirty-one to nineteen. The Senate amended it by striking out "Susquehanna," and inserting a clause making the permanent seat of government Germantown, Pennsylvania, provided the State of Pennsylvania should give security to pay one hundred thousand dollars for the erection of public buildings. The House agreed to these amendments. Both Houses of Congress agreed upon Germantown as the Capital of the Republic, and yet the final passage of the bill was hindered by a slight amendment.

. June 28, another old bill was dragged forth and amended by inserting "on the River Potomac, at some place between the mouths of the Eastern Branch and the Connogocheague." This was finally passed, July 16, 1790, entitled "An Act establishing the temporary and permanent seat of the government of the United States." The word temporary applied to Philadelphia, whose disappointment in not becoming the final Capital was to be appeased by Congress holding their sessions there till 1800, when, as a member expressed it, "they were to go to the Indian place with the long name, on the Potomac."

Human bitterness and dissension were even then rife in both Houses of Congress. The bond which bound the new Union of States together was scarcely welded, and yet secession already was an openly uttered threat. An amendment had been offered to the funding act, providing for the assumption of the State debts to the amount of twenty-one millions, which was rejected by the House. The North favored assumption and the South opposed it. Just then reconciliation and amity were brought about between the combatants precisely as they often are in

our own time, over a well-laid dinner table, and a bot-
tle of rare old wine. Jefferson was then Secretary of
State, and Alexander Hamilton, Secretary of the Treasury. Hamilton thought that the North would yield and
consent to the establishment of the Capital on the Potomac, if the South would agree to the amendment to assume the State debts. Jefferson and Hamilton met acci-
dentally in the street, and the result of their half an
hour's walk "backward and forward before the President's
door" was the next day's dinner party, and the final,
irrevocable fixing of the National Capital on the banks
of the Potomac. How it was done, as an illustration of
early legislation, which has its perfect parallel in the legislation of the present day, can best be told in Jefferson's
own words, quoted from one of his letters. He says:
" Hamilton was in despair. As I was going to the President's one day I met him in the street. He walked me
backward and forward before the President's door for
half an hour. He painted pathetically the temper into
which the legislature had been wrought; the disgust of
those who were called the creditor States; the danger of
the secession of their members, and the separation of the
States. He observed that the members of the administration ought to act in concert . . . . that the President
was the centre on which all administrative questions
finally rested; that all of us should rally around him
and support by joint efforts measures approved by him,
. . . . that an appeal from me to the judgment and discretion of some of my friends might effect a change in
the vote, and the machine of government now suspended,
might be again set in motion. I told him that I was
really a stranger to the whole subject, not having yet

informed myself of the system of finance adopted . . . .
that if its rejection endangered a dissolution of our Union at this incipient stage, I should deem that the most
unfortunate of all consequences, to avert which all partial and temporary evils should be yielded.

"I proposed to him, however, to dine with me the next
day, and I would invite another friend or two, bring them
into conference together and I thought it impossible that
reasonable men, consulting together coolly, could fail by
*some mutual sacrifices of opinion to form a compromise
which was to save the Union.* The discussion took place.
. . . . . It was finally agreed to, that whatever importance
had been attached to the rejection of this proposition,
the preservation of the Union and of concord among the
States was more important, and that therefore it would
be better that the vote of rejection should be rescinded
to effect which some members should change their votes.
But it was observed that this pill would be *peculiarly
bitter to Southern States, and that some concomitant measure should be adopted to sweeten it a little to them.* There
had before been a proposition to fix the seat of government either at Philadelphia or Georgetown on the Potomac, and it was thought that by giving it to Philadelphia
for ten years, and to Georgetown permanently afterward,
this might, as an anodyne, calm in some degree the fer-
ment which might be excited by the other measure alone.
So two of the Potomac members, [White and Lee,] but
White with a revulsion of stomach almost convulsive,
agreed to change their votes, and Hamilton agreed to
carry the other point . . . . and so the assumption was
passed," and the permanent Capital fixed on the banks
of the Potomac.

CHAPTER II.

CROSS PURPOSES AND QUEER SPECULATIONS.

Born of Much Bother—Long Debates and Pamphlets—Undefined Appre-
hensions—Debates on the Coming City—Old World Examples—Sir
James Expresses an Opinion—A Dream of the Distant West—An Old-
time Want—A Curious Statement of Fact—" Going West "—Where is
the Centre of Population—An Important Proclamation—Original Land
Owners—Well-worn Patents—Getting on with Pugnacious Planters—
Obstinate David Burns—A " Widow's Mite " of Some Magnitude—
How the Scotchman was Subjugated—" If You Hadn't Married the
Widow Custis "—A Rather " Forcible Argument "—His Excellency
" Chooses "—The First Record in Washington—Old Homes and Haunts
—Purchase of Land—Extent of the City.

AS we have seen, the Federal City was the object of
George Washington's devoted love long before its
birth. It was born through much tribulation. First
came the long debates and pamphlets of 1790, as to
whether the seat of the American government should
be a commercial capital. Madison and his party argued
that the only way to insure the power of exclusive legislation to Congress as accorded by the Constitution, was
to remove the Capital as far from commercial interests as
possible. They declared that the exercise of this authority over a large mixed commercial community would be
impossible. Conflicting mercantile interests would cause
constant political disturbances, and when party feelings
ran high, or business was stagnant, the commercial capital would swarm with an irritable mob brim full of
wrongs and grievances. This would involve the necessity of an army standing in perpetual defense of the·

capital. London and Westminster were cited as examples where the commercial importance of a single city
had more influence on the measures of government than
the whole empire outside. Sir James Macintosh was
quoted, wherein he said "that a great metropolis was to
be considered as the heart of a political body—as the
focus of its powers and talents—as the direction of public opinion, and, therefore, as a strong bulwark in the
cause of freedom, or as a powerful engine in the hands
of an oppressor." To prevent the Capital of the Republic becoming the latter the Constitution deprived it
of the elective franchise. The majority in Congress opposed the idea of a great commercial city as the future
Capital of the country. Nevertheless when a plan for
the city was adopted it was one of exceptional magnificence. It was a dream of the founders of the Capital
to build a city expressly for its purpose and to build it
for centuries to come. In view of the vast territory now
comprehended in the United States their provision for
the future may seem meagre and limited. But when we
remember that there were then but thirteen States, that
railroads and telegraphs were undreamed of as human
possibilities—that nearly all the empire west of the Potomac was an unpenetrated wilderness, we may wonder
at their prescience and wisdom, rather than smile at their
lack of foresight. Even in that early and clouded morning there were statesmen who foresaw the later glory of
the West fore-ordained to shine on far off generations.
Says Mr. Madison: "If the calculation be just that we
double in fifty years we shall speedily behold an astonishing mass of people on the western waters. . . . .
The swarm does not come from the southern but from

the northern and eastern hives. I take it that the centre of population will rapidly advance in a south-westerly direction. It must then travel from the Susquehanna if it is now found there—*it may even extend beyond the Potomac!*"

Said Mr. Vining to the House, "I confess I am in favor of the Potomac. I wish the seat of government to be fixed there because I think the interest, the honor, and the greatness of the country require it. From thence, it appears to me, that the rays of government will naturally diverge to the extremities of the Union. I declare that I look upon the western territories from an awful and striking point of view. To that region the unpolished sons of the earth are flowing from all quarters—men to whom the protection of the laws and the controlling force of the government are equally necessary."

In the course of the debate Mr. Calhoun called attention to the fact that very few seats of government in the world occupied central positions in their respective countries. London was on a frontier, Paris far from central, the capital of Russia near its border. Even at that early date comparatively small importance was attached to a geographical centre of territory as indispensable to the location of its capital. The only possible objection to a capital near the sea-board was then noted by Mr. Madison who said, "If it were possible to promulgate our laws by some instantaneous operation, it would be of less consequence where the government might be placed," a possibility now fulfilled by the daily news from the Capital which speeds to the remotest corner of the great land not only with the swiftness of lightning but by lightning itself.

Although the States have more than doubled since the days of this first discussion on where the Capital of the

3

United States should be, it is a curious fact that the centre of population has not traveled westward in any proportionate ratio.   According to a table calculated by Dr. Patterson of the United States mint, in 1840 the centre of population was then in Harrison County, Virginia, one hundred and seventy-five miles west of the city of Washington.   At that time the average progress westward since 1790 had been, each ten years, thirty-four miles.   "This average has since increased, but if it be set down at fifty miles, it will require a century to carry this centre five hundred miles west of Washington, or as far as the city of Nashville, Tennessee."   I state this fact for the benefit of crazy capital-movers who are in such haste to set the Capital of the Nation in the centre of the Continent.

I have given but a few of the questions which were discussed in the great debates which preceded the final locating of the Capital on the banks of the Potomac.   They are a portion of its history, and deeply interesting in their bearing on the present and future of the Capital city.

The long strife ended in the amendatory proclamation of President Washington, done at Georgetown the 30th day of March, in the year of our Lord 1791, and of the independence of the United States the fifteenth, which concluded with these words: "I do accordingly direct the Commissioners named under the authority of the said first mentioned act of Congress to proceed forthwith to have the said four lines run, and by proper metes and bounds defined and limited, and thereof to make due report under their hands and seals; and the territory so to be located, defined and limited shall be the whole territory accepted by the said act of Congress as the district for the permanent seat of the government of the United

States." Maryland had ceded of her land ten miles square
for the future Capital. Nothing seemed easier than for
these three august commissioners, backed by the powerful Congress, to go and take it. But it was not so easy
to be done. In addition to the State of Maryland the
land belonged to land-holders, each one of whom was a
lord on his own domain. Some of these held land patents still extant, dating back to 1663, and 1681. These
lords of the manor were not willing to be disturbed even
for the sake of a future Capital, and displayed all the iras-
cibility and tenacity regarding price which characterize
land-holders of the present day. If we may judge from
results and the voluminous correspondence concerning
it, left by George Washington, the three commissioners
who were to act for the government did not "get on"
very well with the pugnacious planters who were ready
to fight for their acres—and that the greater part of the
negotiating for the new city finally fell to the lot of the
great Executive. One of the richest and most famous
of these land-owners was David Burns. He owned an
immense tract of land south of where the president's
house now stands, extending as far as the Patent Office
called in the land patent of 1681 which granted it, "the
Widow's Mite, lyeing on the east side of the Anacostin
River, on the north side of a branch or inlett in the said
river, called Tyber." This "Widow's Mite" contained six
hundred acres or more, and David Burns was in no wise
willing to part with any portion of it. Although it laid
within the territory of Columbia, ceded by the act of
Maryland for the future Capital, no less a personage than
the President of the United States could move one whit
David Burns, and even the President found it to be no

easy matter to bring the Scotchman to terms. More than once in his letters he alludes to him as "the obstinate Mr. Burns," and it is told that upon one occasion when the President was dwelling upon the advantage that the sale of his lands would bring, the planter, testy Davy, exclaimed: "I suppose you think people here are going to take every grist that comes from you as pure grain, *but* what would *you* have *been if you hadn't married the widow Custis.*"

After many interviews and arguments even the patience of Washington finally gave out and he said: "Mr. Burns, I have been authorized to select the location of the National Capital. I have selected your farm as a part of it, and the government will take it at all events. I trust you will, under these circumstances, enter into an amicable arrangement."

Seeing that further resistance was useless, the shrewd Scotchman thought that by a final graceful surrender he might secure more favorable terms, thus, when the President once more asked: "On what terms will you surrender your plantation?" Said humble Davy: "*Any* that your Excellency may choose to name." The deed conveying the land of David Burns to the commissioners in trust, is the first on record in the city of Washington. This sale secured to David Burns and his descendants an immense fortune. The deed provided that the streets of the new city should be so laid out as not to interfere with the cottage of David Burns. That cottage still stands in famous "Mansion Square," and the reader will find its story further on in the chapter devoted to the Old Homes and Haunts of Washington. The other original owners of the soil on which the city of Washington was built were

Notley Young, who owned a fine old brick mansion near the present steamboat landing, and Daniel Carroll, whose spacious abode known as the Duddington House, still stands on New Jersey Avenue, a little south-east of the Capitol. On the 31st of May, Washington wrote to Jefferson from Mount Vernon, announcing the conclusion of his negotiations in this wise—the owners conveyed all their interest to the United States on consideration that when the whole should be surveyed and laid off as a city the original proprietors should retain every other lot. The remaining lots to be sold by the government from time to time and the proceeds to be applied toward the improvement of the place. The land comprised within this agreement contains over seventy-one hundred acres. The city extends from north-west to south-east about four miles and a half, and from east to south-west about two miles and a half. Its circumference is fourteen miles, the aggregate length of the streets is one hundred and ninety-nine miles, and of the avenues sixty-five miles. The avenues, streets and open spaces contain three thousand six hundred and four acres, and the public reservations exclusive of reservations since disposed of for private purposes, five hundred and thirteen acres. The whole area of the squares of the city amounts to one hundred and thirty-one million, six hundred and eighty-four thousand, one hundred and seventy-six square feet, or three thousand and sixteen acres. Fifteen hundred and eight acres were reserved for the use of the United States.

CHAPTER III.

THE WORK BEGUN IN EARNEST.

Washington's Faith in the Future—Mr. Sparks is "inclined to think"—A
Slight Miscalculation—Theoretical Spartans—Clinging to Old World
Glories—Jefferson Acts the Critic—He Communicates Some Ideas—
Models of Antiquity—Babylon Revived—Difficulty in Satisfying a
Frenchman's Soul—The Man who Planned the Capital—Who was
L'Enfant?—His Troubles—His Dismissal—His Personal Appearance,
Old Age, Death and Burial-Place—His Successor—The French Genius
"Proceeded"—The New City of Washington—A Magnificent Plan—All
About the City—The Major not Appreciated—"Getting on Badly"—L'En-
fant Worries Washington—A Record which Can Never Perish—An Over-
paid Quaker—Jefferson Expresses his Sentiments—A Sable Franklin—
The Negro Engineer, Benjamin Bancker—A Chance for a Monument.

THE majority of Congress were opposed to a commercial Capital, yet there are many proofs extant that
to the hour of his death George Washington cherished
the hope that the new city of his love would be not
only the capital of the nation, but a great commercial
metropolis of the world. Mr. Jared Sparks, the histo-
rian, in a private letter says: "I am inclined to think
that Washington's anticipations were more sanguine than
events have justified. He early entertained very large
and just ideas of the vast resources of the West, and of
the commercial intercourse that must spring up between
that region and the Atlantic coast, and he was wont to
regard the central position of the Potomac as affording
the most direct and easy channel of communication.

Steamboats and railroads have since changed the face of the world, and have set at defiance all the calculations founded on the old order of things; and especially have they operated on the destiny of the West and our entire system of internal commerce, in a manner that could not possibly have been foreseen in the life-time of Washington." Throughout the correspondence of Washington are scattered constant allusions to the future magnificence of the Federal City, the name by which he loved to call the city of his heart, allusions which show that his faith in its great destiny never faltered. In a letter to his neighbor, Mrs. Fairfax, then in England, he said: "A century hence, if this country keeps united, it will produce a city, though not as large as London, yet of a magnitude inferior to few others in Europe." At that time, after a growth of centuries, London contained eight hundred thousand inhabitants. Three-fourths of Washington's predicted century have expired, and the city of Washington now numbers one hundred and fifty thousand people.

The founders of the Capital were all very republican in theory, and all very aristocratic in practice. In speech they proposed to build a sort of Spartan capital, fit for a Spartan republic; in fact, they proceeded to build one modeled after the most magnificent cities of Europe. European by descent and education, many of them allied to the oldest and proudest families of the Old World, every idea of culture, of art, and magnificence had come to them as part of their European inheritance, and we see its result in every thing that they did or proposed to do for the new Capital which they so zealously began to build in the woods. The art-connoisseur of the day was

Jefferson. He knew Europe, not only by family tradition but by sight. Next to Washington he took the deepest personal interest in the projected Capital. Of this interest we find continual proof in his letters, also of the fact that his taste had much to do with the plan and architecture of the coming city. In a letter to Major L'Enfant, the first engineer of the Capital, dated Philadelphia, April 10, 1791, he wrote: "In compliance with your request, I have examined my papers and found the plans of Frankfort-on-the-Main, Carlsruhe, Amsterdam, Strasburg, Paris, Orleans, Bordeaux, Lyons, Montpelier, Marseilles, Turin, and Milan, which I send in a roll by post. They are on large and accurate scales, having been procured by me while in those respective cities myself. . . . . Having communicated to the President before he went away, such general ideas on the subject of the town as occurred to me, I have no doubt in explaining himself to you on the subject, he has interwoven with his own ideas such of mine as he approved. . . . . Whenever it is proposed to present plans for the Capital, I should prefer the adoption of some one of the models of antiquity, which have had the approbation of thousands of years; and for the president's house I should prefer the celebrated fronts of modern buildings, which have already received the approbation of good judges. Such are Galerie du Louise, the Gardes Meubles, and two fronts of the Hotel de Salm." On the same day he writes to Washington: "I received last night from Major L'Enfant a request to furnish any plans of towns I could for examination. I accordingly send him by this post, plans of Frankfort-on-the-Main, etc., which I procured while in those towns respectively. They are none of them, however, comparable to the old Babylon revived in Philadelphia and exemplified." But these two fathers of their country, as time proved, "did not know their man." Had they done so, they would have known in advance that a mercurial Frenchman would never attempt to satisfy his soul with acute angles of old Babylon revived through the arid and level lengths of Philadelphia.

The man who planned the Capital of the United States not for the present but for all time, was Peter Charles L'Enfant, born in France in 1755. He was a lieutenant in the French provincial forces, and with others of his countrymen was early drawn to these shores by the magnetism of a new people, and the promise of a new land. He offered his services to the revolutionary army as an engineer, in 1777, and was appointed captain of engineers February 18, 1778. After being wounded at the siege of Savannah, he was promoted to major of engineers, and served near the person of Washington. Probably at that time there was no man in America who possessed so much genius and art-culture in the same directions as Major L'Enfant. In a crude land, where nearly every artisan had to be imported from foreign shores, the chief designer and architect surely would have to be. Thus we may conclude at the beginning, it seemed a lucky circumstance to find an engineer for the new city on the spot.

The first public communication extant concerning the laying out of the city of Washington is from the pen of General Washington, dated March 11, 1791. In a letter dated April 30, 1791, he first called it the Federal City. Four months later, without his knowledge, it received its present name in a letter from the first commissioners, Messrs. Johnson, Stuart, and Carroll, which bears the date of Georgetown, September 9, 1791, to Major L'Enfant, which informs that gentleman that they have agreed that the federal district shall be called The Territory of Columbia, (its present title,) and the federal city the city of Washington, directing him to entitle his map accordingly.

In March, 1791, we find Jefferson addressing Major L'Enfant in these words: "You are desired to proceed to Georgetown, where you will find Mr. Ellicott employed in making a survey and map of the federal territory. The special object of asking your aid is to have the drawings of the particular grounds most likely to be approved for the site of the federal grounds and buildings."

The French genius "proceeded," and behold the result, the city of "magnificent distances," and from the beginning of magnificent intentions,—intentions which almost to the present hour, have called forth only ridicule—because in the slow mills of time their fulfillment has been so long delayed. As Thomas Jefferson wanted the chessboard squares and angles of Philadelphia, L'Enfant used them for the base of the new city, but his genius avenged itself for this outrage on its taste by transversing them with sixteen magnificent avenues, which from that day to this have proved the confusion and the glory of the city. French instinct diamonded the squares of Philadelphia with the broad corsos of Versailles, as Major L'Enfant's map said, "to preserve through the whole a reciprocity of sight at the same time."

A copy of the Gazette of the United States, published

in Philadelphia, January 4, 1792, gives us the original magnificent intentions of the first draughtsman of the new city of Washington.

The following description is annexed to the plan of the city of Washington, in the District of Columbia, as sent to Congress by the President some days ago:

PLAN OF THE CITY INTENDED AS THE PERMANENT SEAT OF THE GOVERNMENT OF THE UNITED STATES, PROJECTED AGREEABLY TO THE DIRECTION OF THE PRESIDENT OF THE UNITED STATES IN PURSUANCE OF AN ACT OF CONGRESS, PASSED ON THE 16TH OF JULY, 1790, "ESTABLISHING A PERMANENT SEAT ON THE BANKS OF THE POTOMACK."

BY PETER CHARLES L'ENFANT.

OBSERVATIONS EXPLANATORY OF THE PLAN.

I. The positions of the different grand edifices, and for the several grand squares or areas of different shapes as they are laid down, were first determined on the most advantageous ground, commanding the most extensive prospects, and the better susceptible of such improvements as the various interests of the several objects may require.

II. Lines or avenues of direct communication have been devised to connect the separate and most distant objects with the principals, and to preserve throughout the whole a reciprocity of sight at the same time. Attention has been paid to the passing of those leading avenues over the most favorable ground for prospect and convenience.

III. North and south lines, intersected by others running due east and west, make the distribution of the city into streets, squares, &c., and those lines have been so combined as to meet at certain points with those diverging avenues so as to form on the spaces "first determined," the different squares or areas which are all proportioned in magnitude to the number of avenues leading to them.

MR. ELLICOTT "DOES BUSINESS."

Every grand transverse avenue, and every principal divergent one, such as the communication from the President's house to the Congress house, &c., are 160 feet in breadth and thus divided :

Ten feet for pavement on each side, is	20 feet
Thirty feet of gravel walk, planted with trees on each side, ...	60 feet
Eighty feet in the middle for carriages, ...	80 feet
	160 feet

The other streets are of the following dimensions, viz. :

Those leading to the public buildings or markets, . .	130
Others, ...	110–90

In order to execute the above plan, Mr. Ellicott drew a true meridian line by celestial observation, which passes through area intended for the Congress house. This line he crossed by another due east and west, and which passes through the same area. The lines were accurately measured, and made the basis on which the whole plan was executed. He ran all the lines by a transit instrument, and determined the acute angles by actual measurement, and left nothing to the uncertainty of the compass.

REFERENCES.

A. The equestrian figure of George Washington, a monument voted in 1783 by the late Continental Congress.

B. An historic column—also intended for a mile or itinerary column, from whose station, (at a mile from the Federal House,) all distances and places through the Continent are to be calculated.

C. A Naval itinerary column proposed to be erected to celebrate the first rise of a navy, and to stand a ready monument to perpetuate its progress and achievements.

D. A church intended for national purposes, such as public prayers, thanksgivings, funeral orations, &c., and assigned to the special use of no particular sect or denomination, but equally open to all. It will likewise be a proper shelter for such monuments as were voted by the late Continental Congress for those heroes who fell in the cause of liberty, and for such others as may hereafter be decreed by the voice of a grateful nation.

E. E. E. E. E. Five grand fountains intended with a constant spout of water.

N. B. There are within the limits of the springs twenty-five good springs of excellent water abundantly supplied in the driest seasons of the year.

F. A grand cascade formed of the waters of the sources of the Tiber.

G. G. Public walk, being a square of 1,200 feet, through which carriages may ascend to the upper square of the Federal House.

H. A grand avenue, 400 feet in breadth and about a mile in length, bordered with gardens ending in a slope from the house on each side; this avenue leads to the monument A, and connects the Congress garden with the

I. President's park and the

K. Well improved field, being a part of the walk from the President's House of about 1,800 feet in breadth and three-fourths of a mile in length. Every lot deep colored red, with green plats, designating some of the situations which command the most agreeable prospects, and which are best calculated for spacious houses and gardens, such as may accommodate foreign ministers, &c.

L. Around this square and along the

M. Avenue from the two bridges to the Federal House, the pavements on each side will pass under an arched way, under whose cover shops will be most conveniently and agreeably situated. This street is 106 feet in breadth, and a mile long.

The fifteen squares colored yellow are proposed to be divided among the several States of the Union, for each of them to im-

prove, or subscribe a sum additional to the value of the land for
that purpose, and the improvements around the squares to be
completed in a limited time. The centre of each square will
admit of statues, columns, obelisks, or any other ornaments,
such as the different States may choose to erect, to perpetuate
not only the memory of such individuals whose councils or military achievements were conspicuous in giving liberty and independence to this country, but those whose usefulness hath
rendered them worthy of imitation, to invite the youth of succeeding generations to tread in the paths of those sages or heroes whom their country have thought proper to celebrate.

The situation of those squares is such that they are most
advantageously seen from each other, and as equally distributed
over the whole city district, and connected by spacious avenues
round the grand federal improvements and as contiguous to
them, and at the same time as equally distant from each other
as circumstances would admit. The settlements round these
squares must soon become connected. The mode of taking
possession of and improving the whole district at first must
leave to posterity a grand idea of the patriotic interest which
promoted it.

Two months after the publication of those magnificent
designs for posterity, Major L'Enfant was dismissed from
his exalted place. He was a Frenchman and a genius.
The patrons of the new Capital were *not* geniuses, and
not Frenchmen, reasons sufficient why they should not
and did not " get on " long in peace together. Without
doubt the Commissioners were provincial, and limited in
their ideas of art and of expenditure; with their colonial
experience they could scarcely be otherwise; while L'Enfant was metropolitan, splendid, and willful, in his ways
as well as in his designs. Hampered, held back, he yet
"builded better than he knew," builded for posterity.
The executor and the designer seldom counterpart each

other. L'Enfant worried Washington, as a letter from the latter, written in the autumn of 1791, plainly shows. He says: "It is much to be regretted that men who possess talents which fit them for peculiar purposes should almost invariably be under the influence of an untoward disposition. . . . . I have thought that for such employment as he is now engaged in for prosecuting public works and carrying them into effect, Major L'Enfant was better qualified than any one who has come within my knowledge in this country, or indeed in any other. I had no doubt at the same time that this was the light in which he considered himself." At least, L'Enfant was so fond of his new "plan" that he would not give it up to the Commissioners to be used as an inducement for buying city lots, even at the command of the President, giving as a reason that if it was open to buyers, speculators would build up his beloved avenues (which he intended, in time, should outrival Versailles) with squatter's huts—just as they afterwards did. Then Duddington House, the abode of Daniel Carroll, was in the way of one of his triumphal avenues, and he ordered it torn down without leave or license, to the rage of its owner and the indignation of the Commissioners. Duddington House was rebuilt by order of the government in another place, and stands to-day a relic of the past amid its old forest trees on Capitol Hill. Nevertheless its first demolition was held as one of the sins of the uncontrollable L'Enfant, who was summarily discharged March 6, 1792. His dismissal was thus announced by Jefferson in a letter to one of the Commissioners: "It having been found impracticable to employ Major L'Enfant about the Federal City in that degree of subordination which was lawful

and proper, he has been notified that his services are at
an end. It is now proper that he should receive the reward of his past services, and the wish that he should
have no just cause of discontent suggests that it should
be liberal. The President thinks of $2,500, or $3,000,
but leaves the determination to you." Jefferson wrote
in the same letter: "The enemies of the enterprise will
take the advantage of the retirement of L'Enfant to
trumpet the whole as an abortion." But L'Enfant lived
and died within sight of the dawning city of his love
which he had himself created—and never wrought it, or
its projectors any harm through all the days of his life.
He was loyal to his adopted government, but to his last
breath clung to every atom of his personal claim upon it,
as pugnaciously as he did to his maps, when commanded to
give them up. He lived without honor, and died without
fame. Time will vindicate one and perpetuate the other
in one of the most magnificent capitals of earth. His
living picture lingers still with more than one old inhab-
itant. One tells of him in an unchangeable "green sur-
tout, walking across the commons and fields, followed by
half-a-dozen hunting dogs." Also, of reporting to him at
Fort Washington in 1814 to do duty, and of first receiving a glass of wine from the old soldier-architect and engineer before he told him what to do. Mr. Corcoran, the
banker, tells how L'Enfant looked in his latter days: "a
rather seedy, stylish old man, with a long blue or green
coat buttoned up to his throat, and a bell-crowned hat;
a little moody and lonely, like one wronged."

He lived for many years on the Digges' farm, the estate
now owned by George Riggs, the banker, situated about
eight miles from Washington. He was buried in the

COLUMBIA SLAVE PEN.   FREEDMAN'S SAVINGS BANK.

SMITHSONIAN INSTITUTE.

MAJOR L'ENFANT'S RESTING PLACE.

family burial-ground, in the Digges' garden. When the Digges family were disinterred, his dust was left nearly alone. There it lies to day, and the perpetually growing splendor of the ruling city which he planned, is his only monument.

He was succeeded by Andrew Ellicott, a practical engineer, born in Buck's County, Pennsylvania. He was called a man of "uncommon talent" and "placid temper." Neither saved him from conflicts, (though of a milder type than L'Enfant's,) with the Commissioners. A Quaker, he yet commanded a battalion of militia in the Revolution, and "was thirty-seven years of age when he rode out with Washington to survey the embryo city." He finished, (with certain modifications,) the work which L'Enfant began. For this he received the stupendous sum of $5.00 per day which, with "expenses," Jefferson thought to be altogether too much. In his letter to the Commissioners dismissing L'Enfant, he says: "Ellicott is to go on to finish laying off the plan on the ground, and surveying and plotting the district. I have remonstrated with him on the excess of five dollars a day and his expenses, and he has proposed striking off the latter."

After Ellicott concluded laying out the Capital, he became Surveyor-General of the United States; laid out the towns of Erie, Warren and Franklin, in Pennsylvania, and built Fort Erie. He defined the boundary dividing the Republic from the Spanish Possessions; became Secretary of the Pennsylvania Land Office, and in 1812 Professor of Mathematics at West Point, where he died August, 1820, aged 66.

Ellicott's most remarkable assistant was Benjamin Bancker, a negro. He was, I believe, the first of his

4

race to distinguish himself in the new Republic. He was
born with a genius for mathematics and the exact sciences, and at an early age was the author of an Almanac,
which attracted the attention and commanded the praise
of Thomas Jefferson. When he came to "run the lines"
of the future Capital, he was sixty years of age. The
caste of color could not have grown to its hight at that
day, for the Commissioners invited him to an official seat
with themselves, an honor which he declined. The picture given us of him is that of a sable Franklin, large,
noble, and venerable, with a dusky face, white hair, a
drab coat of superfine broadcloth, and a Quaker hat.
He was born and buried at Ellicott's Mills, where his
grave is now unmarked. Here is a chance for the rising
race to erect a monument to one of their own sons, who
in the face of ignorance and bondage proved himself
"every inch a man," in intellectual gifts equal to the
best.

CHAPTER IV.

OLD WASHINGTON.

NOTHING in the architecture of the city of Washington calls forth more comment from strangers than the distance between the Capitol and the Executive Departments. John Randolph early called it "the city of magnificent distances," and it is still a chronic and fashionable complaint to decry the time and distance it takes to get any where. In the days of a single stage line on Pennsylvania Avenue, these were somewhat lamentable. But five-minute cars abridge distances, and make them less in reality than even in the city of New York. It is a mile and a half from the northern end of the Navy-yard bridge to the Capitol, a mile and a half from the Capitol to the Executive Mansion, and a mile and a half from the Executive Mansion to the corner of Bridge and High Streets, Georgetown. We are constantly hearing exclamations of what a beautiful city Washington would be with the Capitol for the centre of a square formed by a chain of magnificent public buildings. John Adams wanted the Departments around the

Capitol. George Washington but a short time before his death, gave in a letter the reasons for their present position. In going through his correspondence one finds that there is nothing, scarcely, in the past, present or future of its Capital, for which the Father of his Country has not left on record a wise, far-reaching reason. In this letter, he says: "Where or how the houses for the President, and the public offices may be fixed is to me, as an individual, a matter of moonshine. But the reverse of the President's motive for placing the latter near the Capitol was my motive for fixing them by the' former. The daily intercourse which the secretaries of departments must have with the President would render a distant situation extremely inconvenient to them, and not much less so would one be close to the Capitol; for it was the universal complaint of them all, *that while the Legislature was in session, they could do little or no business, so much were they interrupted by the individual visits of members in office hours, and by calls for paper.* Many of them have disclosed to me that they have been obliged often to go home and deny themselves in order to transact the current business." The denizen of the present time, who knows the Secretaries' dread of the average besieging Congressman, will smile to find that the dread was as potent in the era of George Washington as it is to-day. A more conclusive reason could not be given why Capitol and Departments should be a mile apart. The newspapers of that day were filled with long articles on the laying out of the Capital city. We find in a copy of *The Philadelphia Herald* of January 4, 1795, after a discussion of the Mall—the yet-to-be garden extending from the Capitol to the President's house—

the following far-sighted remarks on the creation of the Capital. It says: "To found a city, for the purpose of making it the depository of the acts of the Union, and the sanctuary of the laws which must one day rule all North America, is a grand and comprehensive idea, which has already become, with propriety, the object of public respect. The city of Washington, considered under such important points of view, could not be calculated on a small scale; its extent, the disposition of its avenues and public squares should all correspond with the magnitude of the objects for which it was intended. And we need only cast our eyes upon the situation and plan of the city to recognize in them the comprehensive genius of the President, to whom the direction of the business has been committed by Congress."

The letters of Washington are full of allusions to the annoyance and difficulty attending the raising of sufficient money to make the Capitol and other public buildings tenantable by the time specified, 1800. He seemed to regard the prompt completion of the Capitol as an event identical with the perpetual establishment of the government at Washington. Virginia had made a donation of $120,000, and Maryland one of $72,000; these were now exhausted. After various efforts to raise money by the forced sales of public lots, and after abortive attempts to borrow money, at home and abroad, on the credit of these lots, amidst general embarrassments, while Congress withheld any aid whatever, the urgency appeared to the President so great as to induce him to make a personal application to the State of Maryland for a loan, which was successful, and the deplorable credit of the government at that time is exhibited in the fact that the

State called upon the credit of the Commissioners as an additional guarantee for the re-payment of the amount, $100,000, to which Washington alludes as follows : "The necessity of the case justified the obtaining it on almost any terms; and the zeal of the Commissioners in making themselves liable for the amount, as it could not be had without, cannot fail of approbation. At the same time I must confess the application has a very singular appearance, and will not, I should suppose, be very grateful to the feelings of Congress."

I have cited but a few of the tribulations through which the Capital of the nation was born. Not only was the growth of the public buildings hindered through lack of money, but also through the "jealousies and bickerings" of those who should have helped to build them. Human nature, in the aggregate, was just as inharmonious and hard to manage then as now. The Commissioners did not always agree. Artisans, imported from foreign lands, made alone an element of discord, one which Washington dreaded and deprecated. He went down with his beloved Capital into the Egypt of its building. He led with a patience and wisdom undreamed of and unappreciated in this generation, the straggling and discordant forces of the Republic from oppression to freedom, from chaos to achievement—he came in sight of the promised land of fruition and prosperity, but he did not enter it, this father and prophet of the people! George Washington died in December, 1799.

The city of Washington was officially occupied in June, 1800.

The only adequate impression of what the Capital was at the time of its first occupancy, we must receive from those who beheld it with living eyes. Fortunately several have left graphic pictures of the appearance which the city presented at that time. President John Adams took possession of the unfinished Executive Mansion in November, 1800. During the month Mrs. Adams wrote to her daughter, Mrs. Smith, as follows: "I arrived here on Sunday last, and without meeting with any accident worth noticing, except losing ourselves when we left Baltimore, and going eight or nine miles on the Frederic road, by which means we were obliged to go the other eight through the woods, where we wandered for two hours without finding guide or path. . . . . But woods are all you see from Baltimore till you reach *the city*, which is only so in name. Here and there is a small cot, without a glass window, interspersed amongst the forests, through which you travel miles without seeing any human being. In the city there are buildings enough, if they were compact and finished, to accommodate Congress and those attached to it; but as they are, and scattered as they are, I see no great comfort for them. . . . . . If the twelve years in which this place has been considered as the future seat of government had been improved as they would have been in New England, very many of the present inconveniences would have been removed. It is a beautiful spot, capable of any improvement, and the more I view it the more I am delighted with it."

Hon. John Cotton Smith, of Connecticut, a distinguished member of Congress, of the Federal school of politics, also gives his picture of Washington in 1800: "Our approach to the city was accompanied with sensations not easily described. One wing of the Capitol only had been erected, which, with the President's house, a mile distant from it, both constructed with white sandstone, were shining objects in dismal contrast with the scene around them. Instead of recognizing the avenues and streets portrayed on the plan of the city, not one was visible, unless we except a road, with two buildings on each side of it, called the New Jersey Avenue. The Pennsylvania, leading, as laid down on paper, from the Capitol to the presidential mansion, was then nearly the whole distance a deep morass, covered with alder bushes which were cut through the width of the intended avenue during the then ensuing winter. Between the President's house and Georgetown a block of houses had been erected, which then bore and may still bear, the name of the *six buildings.* There were also other blocks, consisting of two or three dwelling-houses, in different directions, and now and then an insulated wooden habitation, the intervening spaces, and indeed the surface of the city generally, being covered with shrub-oak bushes on the higher grounds, and on the marshy soil either trees or some sort of shrubbery. Nor was the desolate aspect of the place a little augmented by a number of unfinished edifices at Greenleaf's Point, and on an eminence a short distance from it, commenced by an individual whose name they bore, but the state of whose funds compelled him to abandon them, not only unfinished, but in a ruinous condition. There appeared to be but two really comfortable habitations in all respects, within the bounds of the city, one of which belonged to Dudley Carroll, Esq., and the other to Notley Young, who were the former proprietors of a large proportion of the land appropriated to the city, but who reserved for their own accom-

modation ground sufficient for gardens and other useful
appurtenances. The roads in every direction were muddy
and unimproved. A sidewalk was attempted in one instance by a covering formed of the chips of the stones
which had been hewn for the Capitol. It extended but a
little way and was of little value, for in dry weather the
sharp fragments cut our shoes, and in wet weather covered
them with white mortar, in short, it was a "new settlement." The houses, with one or two exceptions, had been
very recently erected, and the operation greatly hurried
in view of the approaching transfer of the national government. A laudable desire was manifested by what few
citizens and residents there were, to render our condition
as pleasant as circumstances would permit. One of the
blocks of buildings already mentioned was situated on the
east side of what was intended for the Capitol square, and
being chiefly occupied by an extensive and well-kept hotel, accommodated a goodly number of the members.
Our little party took lodgings with a Mr. Peacock, in
one of the houses on New Jersey Avenue, with the addition of Senators Tracy of Connecticut, and Chipman
and Paine of Vermont, and Representatives Thomas of
Maryland, and Dana, Edmond and Griswold of Connecticut. Speaker Sedgwick was allowed a room to himself
—the rest of us in pairs. To my excellent friend Dav-
enport, and myself, was allotted a spacious and decently
furnished apartment with separate beds, on the lower
floor. Our diet was varied, but always substantial,
and we were attended by active and faithful servants.
A large proportion of the Southern members took lodgings at Georgetown, which, though of a superior order,
were three miles distant from the Capitol, and of course

rendered the daily employment of hackney coaches indispensable.

Notwithstanding the unfavorable aspect which Washington presented on our arrival, I can not sufficiently express my admiration of its local position. From the Capitol you have a distinct view of its fine undulating surface, situated at the confluence of the Potomac and its Eastern Branch, the wide expanse of that majestic river to the bend at Mount Vernon, the cities of Alexandria and Georgetown, and the cultivated fields and blue hills of Maryland and Virginia on either side of the river, the whole constituting a prospect of surpassing beauty and grandeur. The city has also the inestimable advantage of delightful water, in many instances flowing from copious springs, and always attainable by digging to a moderate depth, to which may be added the singular fact that such is the due admixture of loam and clay in the soil of a great portion of the city that a house may be built of brick made of the earth dug from the cellar, hence it was not unusual to see the remains of a brick-kiln near the newly-erected dwelling-house or other edifice. In short, when we consider not only these advantages, but what, in a national point of view is of superior importance, the location on a fine navigable river, accessible to the whole maritime frontier of the United States, and yet easily rendered defensible against foreign invasion,—and that by the facilities of inter-population of the Western States, and indeed of the whole nation, with less inconvenience than any other conceivable situation,—we must acknowledge that its selection by Washington as the permanent seat of the federal government, affords a striking exhibition of the discernment, wisdom and forecast which characterized that illustrious man. Under this impression, whenever, during the six years of my connection with Congress, the question of removing the seat of government to some other place was agitated—and the proposition was frequently made—I stood almost alone, as a northern man, in giving my vote in the negative."

Sir Augustus Foster, secretary of legation to the British minister at Washington, during the years 1804-6, has left an amusing account on record both of the appearance of the Capital and the state of its society during the administration of President Jefferson: "The Spanish envoy, De Caso Yrujo, told Sir Augustus it was difficult to procure a decent dinner in the new Capital without sending the distance of sixty miles for its materials. Things had mended somewhat before the arrival of Sir Augustus, but he still found enough to surprise and bewilder him in the desolate vastness and mean accommodations of the unshaped metropolis."

Of private citizens Sir Augustus says: "Very few private gentlemen have their houses in Washington. I only recollect three, Mr. Brent, Mr. Tayloe, and Mr. Carroll." . . . . Most of the members of Congress, it is true, keep to their lodgings, but still there are a sufficient number of them who are sociable, or whose families come to the city for a season, and there is no want of handsome ladies for the balls, especially at Georgetown; indeed, I never saw prettier girls anywhere. As there are but few of them, however, in proportion to the great number of men who frequent the places of amusement in the federal city, it is one of the most marrying places on the whole continent. . . . . Meagre the march of intellect so much vaunted in the present century; the literary education of these ladies is far from being worthy of the age of knowledge, and conversation is apt to flag, though a seat by the ladies is always much coveted. Dancing and music serve to eke out the time, but one got tired of hearing the same song everywhere, even when it was :

"Just like love is yonder rose."

"No matter how this was sung, the words alone were the man-traps ; the belle of the evening was declared to be just like both, and the people looked around as if the listener was expected to become on the instant very tender, and to propose. . . . . Between the young ladies, who generally not only good looking, but good tempered, and if not well informed, capable of becoming so, and the ladies of a certain time of life, there is usually a wide gap in society, young married women being but seldom seen in the world ; as they approach, however, to middle age, they are apt to become romantic, those in particular who live in the country and have read novels fancying all manner of romantic things, and returning to the Capital determined to have an adventure before they again retire ; or on doing some wondrous act which shall make them be talked about in all after time. Others I have known to contract an aversion to water, and as a substitute, cover their faces and bosoms with hair powder, in order to render the skin pure and delicate. This was peculiarly the case with some Virginia damsels, who came to the halls at Washington, and who in consequence were hardly less tolerable than negroes. There were but few cases of this I must confess, though as regards the use of the powder, they were not so uncommon, and at my balls I thought it advisable to put on the tables of the toilette room not only rouge, but hair powder, as well as blue powder, which had some customers. . . . .

"In going to assemblies one had sometimes to drive three or four miles within the city bounds, and very often at the great risk of an overthrow, or of being what is termed 'stalled,' or stuck in the mud. . . . . Cards were a great resource during the evening, and gaming was all the fashion, at brag especially, for the men who frequented society were chiefly from Virginia or the Western States, and were very fond of this the worst gambling of all games, as being one of countenance as well as of cards. Loo was the innocent diversion of the ladies, who when they looed pronounced the word in a very mincing manner. . . . .

"Church service can certainly never be called an amusement; but from the variety of persons who are allowed to preach in the House of Representatives, there was doubtless some alloy of curiosity in the motives which led one to go there. Though the regular Chaplain was a Presbyterian, sometimes a Methodist, a minister of the Church of England, or a Quaker, or sometimes even a woman took the speaker's chair; and I don't think that there was much devotion among the majority. The New Englanders, generally speaking, are very religious; though there are many exceptions, I cannot say so much for the Marylanders, and still less for the Virginians."

Notwithstanding the incongruous and somewhat disgraceful picture which Sir Augustus paints of the Capital City of the new Republic, he goes on to say: "In spite of its inconveniences and desolate aspect, it was I think the most agreeable town to reside in for any length of time," which if true insures our pity for what the remainder of our native land must have been.

CHAPTER V.

THE NOBLEST WARD OF CONGRESS.

A Ward of Congress—Expectations Disappointed—Funds Low and People
Few—Slow Progress of the City—First Idea of a National University—
A Question of Importance Discussed—Generous Proposition of George
Washington—Faith Under Difficulties—Transplanting an Entire Col-
lege—An Old Proposition in a New Shape—What Washington "Society"
Lacks—The Lombardy Poplars Refuse to Grow—Perils of the Way—A
Long Plain of Mud—" The Forlornest City in Christendom"—Egyptian
Dreariness—Incomplete and Desolate State of Affairs—The End of an
Expensive Canal—The Water of Tiber Creek—American " Boys" on the
March—Divided Allegiance of Old—The Stirring of a Nation's Heart—
Ready to March to her Defense — A Personal Interest — Patriotism
Aroused—The First-born City of the Republic—Truly the Capital of
the Nation.

WASHINGTON was incorporated as a city by act of
Congress, passed May 3, 1802. The city, planned
solely as the National Capital, was laid out on a scale so
grand and extensive that scanty municipal funds alone
would never have been sufficient for its proper improvement. From the beginning it was the ward of Congress.
Its magnificent avenues, squares and public buildings,
could receive due decoration from no fund more scanty
than a national appropriation. At first Congress appropriated funds with much spirit and some liberality, but
there were many reasons why its zeal and munificence
waned together. At this day it has not fulfilled the most
sanguine expectations of its founders. In Jefferson's

time its population numbered but five thousand persons, and for forty years its increase of population only averaged about five hundred and fifty per annum. Many stately vessels sail down the Potomac to the Chesapeake and the James and out to the ocean; but the Potomac is far from being the highway of commerce. The wharves of Washington and Georgetown are empty compared with those of New York, or even of Baltimore. For generations there was neither commerce nor manufacture to induce men of capital to remove from large cities of active business to the new city in the wilderness, whose very life depended on the will of a majority of Congress. Washington's idea of the National Capital far outleaped his century. His vision of its future greatness comprehended all that the capital of a great nation should be. He foresaw it, not only as the seat of national commerce, but the seat of national learning. One of the dearest projects of his last days was the founding of a National University at the city of Washington. The following references to this subject in a letter from him to the commissioners of the Federal districts, with an extract from his last will, but faintly express the intense interest which he manifested in the National University, both in his daily life, and familiar correspondence :—

WASHINGTON TO COMMISSIONERS OF FEDERAL DISTRICTS.

" The Federal city, from its centrality and the advantages which in other respects it must have over any other place in the United States, ought to be preferred as a proper site for such a University. And if a plan can be adopted upon a scale as extensive as I have described, and the execution of it should commence under favorable auspices in a reasonable time, with a fair prospect of success, I will grant in perpetuity fifty shares in the navigation of the Potomac River toward the endowment of it."

FROM WASHINGTON'S WILL.

"I give and bequeath in perpetuity the fifty shares which I hold in the Potomac Company (under the aforesaid acts of the legislature of Virginia) toward the endowment of a University to be established within the limits of the District of Columbia, under the auspices of the general government, if that government should incline to extend a fostering hand toward it. And until such Seminary is established and the funds arising from these shares shall be needed for its support, my further will and desire is, that the profits arising therefrom whenever the dividends are made be laid out in purchasing stock in the Bank of Columbia, or some other bank at the discretion of my executors, or by the Treasurer of the United States for the time being, under the direction of Congress, providing that honorable body should patronize the measure; and the dividends proceeding from the purchase of such stock are to be vested in more stock, and so on, till a sum adequate to the accomplishment of the object be obtained, *of which I have not the smallest doubt before many years pass away,* even if no aid and encouragement is given by legislative authority, or from any other source."

The correspondence of Washington and Jefferson abound with consultations concerning this great National University. During his stay in Europe, Jefferson had become personally conversant with its ancient seats of learning, and longed to see somewhat of the splendor of their culture transferred to his own native land. So great was his zeal on this subject, both he and John Adams favored the plan at one time of transferring to this city the entire college of Geneva, professors, students, all. But George

Washington opposed the transplanting of an entire body of foreign scholars to the new Republic, almost as earnestly as he did that of a horde of foreign laborers to build the Capitol, he believing both to be inimical to the growth of republican principles and feelings in a newly created republic.

Three-fourths of a century have passed since Washington, Jefferson and Adams consulted together concerning the National University of the future. Alas! it is still of the future. The dream of its fulfillment was dearer to the father of his country, probably, than to any other mortal. The explicit provision made for it in his will proves this. That bequest went finally, I believe, to a college in Virginia. Columbia College, feeble, small and old, is the nearest approach to the National University of which the National Capital can boast to-day. Strange after the lapse of nearly a century, the other evening the friends of this feeble and stunted college, including the President of the United States, high officials, learned professors, foreign ministers, and gentlemen of the press, assembled in Wormley's comfortable dining-room, and over an "epicurean banquet" discussed what Jefferson and Washington did in their letters—a National University for the National Capital. The desire of Washington although not yet fulfilled, must in time become a reality. The National Capital, already the centre of fashion, and rapidly becoming the seat of National Science as well as of National Politics and Government, is the natural seat of National Learning. The educational element, the high-toned culture which always marks the mental and moral atmosphere surrounding a university is to-day the marked lack of what is termed "society in Washington."

5

The United States Government is doing much for science. There is a greater number of persons actively devoted to scientific pursuits in the National Capital than in any other city of the Union. Washington is already the seat of more purely intellectual activity than any other American city. The scientific library of the Smithsonian Institute is one of the best in the world. New departments of the Government devoted to Science are continually being established on sure and ever-spreading foundations. All these facts point to the final and crowning one—the University of the Nation at the National Capital.

For a time, after the incorporation of the city, its founders and patrons zealously pursued plans for its improvement. But failing funds, a weak municipality, and indifferent Congresses, did their work, and for many years "the city of magnificent distances" had little but those distances of which to boast. Jefferson had Pennsylvania avenue planted with double rows of Lombardy poplars from Executive Mansion to Capitol, in imitation of the walk and drive in Berlin known as *Unter den Linden.* But the tops of the poplars did not flourish, and the roots were troublesome, and in 1832 the hoped for arcade came to naught. In truth Pennsylvania avenue was one long plain of mud, punched with dangerous holes and seamed with deep ravines. The interlacing roots of the poplars made these holes and ravines the more dangerous, till an appropriation, during the administration of Jackson, caused them to be dug up and the entire avenue to be macadamized, notwithstanding a large minority in Congress could find no authority in the Constitution for such an unprecedented provision for the public safety. Every Congress was packed with strict constructionists and economists, who opposed every effort to improve the National Capital. Many, narrow, sectional and provincial, had no comprehension of the plan of a city founded to meet the wants of a great nation, rather than to suit the convenience of a meagre population. A city planned to become the magnificent Capital of a vast people could not fail through its very dimensions to be oppressive to its citizens, if the chief weight of its improvement was laid upon their scanty resources. A National Capital could only be fitly built by the Nation. For many years the Congress of the United States refused to do this to any fit degree, and the result for more than one generation was the most forlorn city in Christendom. At a recent meeting of the friends of Columbia College Attorney General Williams stated that when he first visited Washington, in 1853, the "Egypt" of Indiana could not compare in dreariness and discomfort with the Capital of the Nation.

In 1862 Washington was a third rate Southern city. Even its mansions were without modern improvements or conveniences, while the mass of its buildings were low, small and shabby in the extreme. The avenues, superb in length and breadth, in their proportions afforded a painful contrast to the hovels and sheds which often lined them on either side for miles. Scarcely a public building was finished. No goddess of liberty held tablary guard over the dome of the Capitol. Scaffolds, engines and pulleys everywhere defaced its vast surfaces of gleaming marble. The northern wing of the Treasury building was not even begun. Where it now stands then stood the State departments, crowded, dingy and old. Even the southern wing of the Treasury was not completed as it was begun. Iron spikes and saucers on its western side had been used to conclude the beautiful Greek ornamentation begun with the building. All public offices, magnificent in conception, seemed to be in a state of crude incompleteness. Everything worth looking at seemed unfinished. Everything finished looked as if it should have been destroyed generations before. Even Pennsylvania avenue, the grand thoroughfare of the Capital, was lined with little two and three story shops, which in architectural comeliness have no comparison with their ilk of the Bowery, New York. Not a street car ran in the city. A few straggling omnibuses and helter-skelter hacks were the only public conveyances to bear members of Congress to and fro between the Capitol and their remote lodgings. In spring and autumn the entire west end of the city was one vast slough of impassible mud. One would have to walk many blocks before he found it possible to cross a single street, and that often one of the most fashionable of the city. "The water of Tiber Creek," which in the magnificent intentions of the founders of the city were " to be carried to the top of Congress House, to fall in a cascade of twenty feet in height and fifty in breadth, and thence to run in three falls through the gardens into the grand canal," instead stretched in ignominious stagnation across the city, oozing at last through green scum and slime into the still more ignominious canal, which stood an open sewer and cess-pool, the receptacle of all abominations, the pest-breeder and disgrace of the city. Toward the construction of this canal the city of Washington gave $1,000,000 and Georgetown and Alexandria $250,000 each. Its entire cost was $12,000,000. It was intended to be another artery to bring the commerce of the world to Washington, and yet the Washington end of it had come to this!

Capitol Hill, dreary, desolate and dirty, stretched away into an uninhabited desert, high above the mud of the West End. Arid hill, and sodden plain showed alike the horrid trail of war. Forts bristled above every hill-top. Soldiers were entrenched at every gate-way. Shed hospitals covered acres on acres in every suburb. Churches, art-halls and private mansions were filled with the wounded and dying of the American armies. The endless roll of the army wagon seemed never still. The rattle of the anguish-laden ambulance, the piercing cries of the sufferers whom it carried, made morning, noon and night too dreadful to be borne. The streets were filled with marching troops, with new regiments, their hearts strong and eager, their virgin banners all untarnished as they marched up Pennsylvania avenue, playing "The girl I left behind me," as if they had come to holiday glory— to easy victory. But the streets were filled no less with soldiers foot-sore, sun-burned, and weary, their clothes begrimed, their banners torn, their hearts sick with hope deferred, ready to die with the anguish of long defeat. Every moment had its drum-beat, every hour was alive with the tramp of troops going, coming. How many an American "boy," marching to its defence, beholding for the first time the great dome of the Capitol rising before his eyes, comprehended in one deep gaze, as he never had in his whole life before, all that that Capitol meant to him, and to every free man. Never, till the Capital had cost the life of the beautiful and brave of our land, did it become to the heart of the American citizen of the nineteenth century the object of personal love that

it was to George Washington. To that hour the intense
loyalty to country, the pride in the National Capital which
amounts to a passion in the European, in the American
had been diffused, weakened and broken. In ten thousand instances State allegiance had taken the place of
love of country. Washington was nothing but a place
in which Congress could meet and politicians carry on
their games at high stakes for power and place. New
York was the Capital to the New Yorker, Boston to the
New Englander, New Orleans to the Southerner, Chicago
to the man of the West. There was no one central rally-
ing point of patriots to the universal nation. The unfinished Washington monument stood the monument of the
nation's neglect and shame. What Westminster Abbey
and Hall were to the Englishman, what Notre Dame and
the Tuileries were to the Frenchman, the unfinished
and desecrated Capitol had never been to the average
American. Anarchy threatened it. In an hour the
heart of the nation was centered in the Capital. The
nation was ready to march to its defence. Every public
building, every warehouse was full of troops. Washington city was no longer only a name to the mother waiting and praying in the distant hamlet; *her boy* was
camped on the floor of the Rotunda. No longer a far off
myth to the lonely wife; *her* husband held guard upon
the heights which defended the Capital. No longer a
place good for nothing but political schemes to the village sage; *his boy*, wrapped in his blanket, slept on the
stone steps under the shadow of the great Treasury. The
Capital, it was sacred at last to tens of thousands, whose
beloved languished in the wards of its hospitals or slept
the sleep of the brave in the dust of its cemeteries. Thus

from the holocaust of war, from the ashes of our sires and
sons arose new-born the holy love of country, and veneration for its Capital. The zeal of nationality, the passion
of patriotism awoke above the bodies of our slain. National songs, the inspiration of patriots, soared toward
heaven. National monuments began to rise consecrated
forever to the martyrs of Liberty. Never, till that hour,
did the Federal city—the city of George Washington,
the first-born child of the Union, born to live or to perish with it,—become to the heart of the American people that which it had so long been in the eyes of the
world—truly the CAPITAL OF THE NATION.

CHAPTER VI.

THE WASHINGTON OF THE PRESENT DAY.

AND now! The citizen of the year of our Lord 1873 sees the dawn of that perfect day of which the founders of the Capital so fondly and fruitlessly dreamed. The old provincial Southern city is no more. From its foundations has risen another city, neither Southern nor Northern, but national, cosmopolitan.

Where the "Slough of Despond" spread its waxen mud across the acres of the West End, where pedestrians were "slumped," and horses "stalled," and discomfort and disgust prevailed, we now see broad carriage drives, level as floors, over which grand equipages and pony phaetons glide with a smoothness that is a luxury, and an ease of motion which is rest. Where ravines and holes made the highway dangerous, now the concrete and Nicholson pavements stretch over miles on miles of inviting road. Where streets and avenues crossed and re-crossed their long vistas of shadeless dust, now plat on plat of restful grass "park" the city from end to end. Double rows of young trees line these parks far as the

THE NATIONAL CAPITOL.—WASHINGTON.

It covers more than three and a half acres. Over thirteen million dollars have thus far been expended in its erection.

sight can reach. In these June days they fill the air with
tender bloom. Gazing far on through their green arcades the sight rests at last where poor Major L'Enfant
dreamed and planned that it one day would,—on the
restful river, with its white flecks of sails, upon distant
meadows and the Virginia hills. Old Washington was
full of small Saharas. Where the great avenues intersected acres of white sand were caught up and carried .
through the air by counter winds. It blistered at white
heat beneath your feet, it flickered like a fiery veil before
your eyes, it penetrated your lungs and begrimed your
clothes. Now where streets and avenues cross, emerald
" circles " with central fountains, pervading the air with
cooling spray, with belts of flowers and troops of children,
and restful seats for the old or the weary take the place
of the old Saharas. In every direction tiny parks are
blooming with verdurous life. Concrete walks have
taken the place of their old gravel-stone paths. Seats—
thanks to General Babcock—everywhere invite to sit
down and rest beneath trees which every summer cast a
deeper and more protecting shadow. The green pools
which used to distill malaria beneath your windows are
now all sucked into the great sewers, planted at last in
the foundations of the city. The entire city has been
drained. Every street has been newly graded. The
Tiber, inglorious stream, arched and covered forever
from sight, creeps in darkness to its final gulf in the
river. The canal, drained and filled up, no longer
breeds pestilence. Pennsylvania avenue has outlived its
mud and its poplars, to be all and more than Jefferson
dreamed it would be,—the most magnificent street on
the continent. Its lining palaces are not yet built, but

more than one superb building like that of the Daily
National Republican soars high above the lowly shops of
the past, a forerunner of the architectural splendor of the
buildings of the future.   Cars running every five minutes have taken the place of the solitary stage, plodding
its slow way between Georgetown and the Capital.   Capitol Hill, which had been retrograding for more than
forty years, has taken on the look of a suddenly growing
city   Its dusty ways and empty spaces are beginning to
fill with handsome blocks of metropolitan houses.   Even
the old Capital prison is transformed into a handsome
and fashionable block of private dwellings.   The improvements at the West End are more striking.   Solid
blocks of city houses are rising in every direction, taking
the place of the little, old, isolated house of the past, with
its stiff porch, high steps, and open basement doorway.
Vermont, Massachusetts and Connecticut avenues are already lined with splendid mansions, the permanent winter
homes of Senators and other high official and military
officers.   The French, Spanish, English and other foreign
governments have bought on and near these avenues for
the purpose of building on them handsome houses for
their separate legations.   The grounds of the Executive
Mansion are being enlarged, extending to the Potomac
with a carriage drive encircling, running along the shore
of the river, extending through the Agricultural Smithsonian and Botanical garden grounds, thus fulfilling the
original intent of connecting the White House with the
Capitol by a splendid drive.   The same transformation is
going on in the Capitol grounds.   Blocks of old houses
have been torn down and demolished, to make room for
a park fit to encircle the Capitol, which can never be

complete till it takes in all the rolling slopes which lie between it and the Potomac. No scaffolding and pulleys now deface the snowy surfaces of the Capitol. Unimpeded the dome soars into mid-air, till the goddess of liberty on its top seems caught into the embrace of the clouds. The beautiful Treasury building is completed, and a block further on, the click of ceaseless hammers and the rising buttresses of solid stone tell of the new war and navy departments which are swiftly growing beside the historic walls of the old. Even the Washington monument has been taken into hand by General Babcock, to whom personally the Capital owes so much, and by a fresh appeal to the States he hopes to re-arouse their patriotism and insure its grand completion. Flowers blossom on the ramparts of the old forts, so alert with warlike life ten years ago. The army roads, so deeply grooved then, are grass-grown now. The long shed-hospitals have vanished, and stately dwellings stand on their already forgotten sites. The " boys " who languished in their wards, the boys who marched these streets, who guarded this city, how many of them lie on yonder hill-top under the oaks of Arlington, and amid the roses of the Soldier's Home. Peace, prosperity and luxury have taken the place of war, of knightly days and of heroic men.

The mills of time grind slowly. What a tiny stroke in its cycles is a single century. One hundred years! The year nineteen hundred! Then if the father of his country can look down from any star upon the city of his love he will behold in the new Washington that which even he did not foresee in his earthly life—one of the most magnificent cities of the whole earth.

CHAPTER VII.

WHAT MADE NEW WASHINGTON.

Municipal Changes—Necessity of Reform—Committee of One Hundred Constituted—Mr. M. G. Emery Appointed Mayor—The "Organic Act" Passed—Contest for the Governorship of Columbia District—Mr. Henry D. Cooke Appointed—Board of Public Works Constituted—Great Improvements Made—Opposition—The Board and its Work—Sketch of Alexander R. Shepherd—His Efforts During the War—Patriotic Example.

A SKETCH of the territorial government which now rules the District of Columbia, will account for new Washington and the many beneficent changes which have renovated the city.

As early as the winter of 1868, efforts were made to secure a united government for the entire District, instead of the triple affair then in operation, viz.: municipal corporations for Washington and Georgetown, and the Levy court for the County. Under that *regime* no system of general improvements could be established. The District was under the exclusive jurisdiction of Congress and was obliged to beg and plead with that body for permission to begin and for appropriations to pay for each improvement, as its increasing business and population imperatively demanded. Again, the extension of the right of suffrage and the consequent increase of the number of ignorant voters, made it apparent that something must be done to prevent the control of the cities falling into the power of a class of petty ward politicians of the very worst order, who had sprung up just after the war, and who had already caused considerable uneasiness in the minds of the solid and thinking portion of the community, by the rapid manner in which they had managed to increase the public debt without showing any corresponding public benefits.

It was at first proposed to have the District governed by commissioners to be appointed by the President, and I believe bills to that effect were introduced into Congress by Senator Hamlin, and Mr. Morrill, of Maine, but were defeated. Of course the proposed change was very unpopular, and the Washington Common Council passed a series of resolutions protesting against any interference with the government then existing. The extravagance and venality of the administration of 1868-9, however, awakened the sober and thoughtful minded citizens to the absolute necessity of a radical and vigorous reform, and during the winter of 1869-70 a committee of one hundred was constituted, to whom was given the task of perfecting a bill granting a territorial government to the District, and of the urging of its passage by Congress. This bill failed to pass that session, and there next came a bitter political contest, resulting in the election of Hon. M. G. Emery as Mayor of Washington.

The evils which it was supposed Mr. Emery would correct, did not seem to lessen during his administration, and in the following winter the project of a new government was revived and urged with so much vigor that Congress, on the 21st of January, 1871, passed what is now known as the "Organic Act," establishing and defining the powers of the territorial government of the District of Columbia. Immediately following the passage of this act there appeared four prominent candidates for the governorship of the young territory, viz: Messrs. M. G. Emery, Sayles J. Bowen, Jas. A. Magruder, and Alex. R. Shepherd. Messrs. Emery and Bowen soon subsided, and the contest narrowed to between Messrs. Shepherd and Magruder.

It was unmistakably the popular desire that the appointment should be given to Mr. Shepherd. He had been more prominent than any other individual named in securing the change effected; the nucleus of the Organic Act is said to have been drafted by him, and the energy and sagacity he had shown in his public life pointed him out as peculiarly fit for the position. Besides, he had gained the popular confidence by his unvarying integrity and fearless independence, and by a quality too rarely observed in a public man—positive manliness. Colonel Magruder, the Georgetown candidate, was quite popular in that city, where he had for a number of years been the collector of customs. Though at that time he was not extensively known in Washington, those who were his friends were ardent and untiring in their support. It soon became evident that the appointment of either of these gentlemen would cause extreme dissatisfaction to the supporters of his competitors, and as it was especially desirable that the new government should commence its operations with perfect good feeling pervading all the different parties, a governor was sought who should harmonize all differences, and Henry D. Cooke, of the firm of Jay Cooke & Co., a gentleman of unimpeachable integrity, who had kept aloof from all factions and who, in fact, was one of Mr. Shepherd's warmest supporters, was at length selected.

Then came the appointment of that body of men, against whom so much abuse has been hurled, but to whose energies the existence of the new Washington I have portrayed is wholly attributable, viz: the Board of Public Works. This Board was at first composed of Messrs. A. R. Shepherd, A. B. Mullett, S. P. Brown, and James A. Magruder, with the Governor as president *ex-officio*. Since then Messrs. Mullett and Brown have resigned, and their places have been filled by Messrs. Adolf Cluss, and Henry A. Willard.

I may state also that the first Secretary of the District was N. P. Chipman, and that when he was elected as the delegate to Congress, the position was given to E. L. Stanton, the son of the late Secretary Stanton, by whom it is now filled.

All the gentlemen I have named are men of clear intelligence, excellent business capacity, and positive energy.

The amount of labor performed by the Board of Public Works can scarcely be imagined by one who has not lived right here in the District, and observed the complete and almost magical changes that have taken place. Embarrassed at the very commencement of their career by the slipshod manner in which improvements had been carried on under the old corporations, they soon encountered a violent opposition from many citizens who should have heartily supported their efforts. This opposition was organized and persistent, leaving no artifice untried to hinder and check the efforts of the Board, seeking injunction after injunction in the courts, and finally appealing to Congress and effecting an investigation which lasted for four months, and was as searching and minute as any ever attempted by that body, but which ended not only in the absolute acquittal of the Board of every charge alleged, but in a cordial commendation of their acts by the committee which conducted the inquiry.

I wish to give this Board of Public Works the credit to which they are justly entitled. When I read the slanders that are cast upon them, I want to ask the authors if they would prefer the dingy, straggling, muddy, dusty Washington of two years ago to the bright, compact, clean and beautiful city of to-day?

The "head and front" of this Board, the man who has infused a portion of his own enthusiasm into his fellow members, the man to whose comprehensive mind and untiring energy the success of the Board is almost entirely due, who was made vice-president and executive officer by his colleagues because they recognized his great abilities, and were content to follow where he should lead, is Alexander R. Shepherd of Washington.

He is a native of Washington, was born in 1835, and is consequently now but thirty-eight years old. His father died when he was quite a boy, and at the early age of ten years he began the rough struggle of life. He at first started to learn the carpenter's trade, but finding that unsuitable to his tastes he entered a store, as errand boy. At seventeen he was taken into the plumbing establishment of Mr. J. W. Thompson, as clerk. By industry, fidelity and ability, he at length attained a partnership in that house, and upon Mr. Thompson's retirement, succeeded to the full control of the business, which under his skillful management has so rapidly grown that it now defies competition with any similar establishment south of New York.

When the war of the Rebellion broke out, Mr. Shepherd was mainly instrumental in forming the Union party in Washington, proving loyal amidst the bitter hostility of many of his best friends. As early as the 15th of April, 1861, he enlisted as a private soldier, and for three months shouldered his musket in defense of the National Capital. In the same year he was elected a member of the Common Council, and again in 1862, when he was made president of that body. In 1867 he was appointed a member of the Levy court, and in that capacity first developed his ability and energy as a public man. He was president of the Citizens' Reform Association during the Emery campaign, and was, I believe, the prime mover of Mr. Emery's nomination, and contributed by his efforts largely to that gentleman's success. At that election Mr. Shepherd was chosen to the Board of Aldermen, which position he held when appointed to the Board of Public Works.

In person Mr. Shepherd is a tall, noble looking man, with a large, well-formed head, sharply-defined features, massive under jaw and square chin, indicative of the indomitable perseverance and firmness which are the most prominent traits in his character. Although a self-made man, he has acquired a fund of information which many a collegian might envy. His mind is thoroughly disciplined, his perceptions keen, his decisions rapid, and his language vigorous and terse. In private life he is universally respected and esteemed. His benevolence is unbounded, and beside subscribing liberally to every public appeal, he performs innumerable acts of private charity, which few know save the grateful recipients.

It was believed by the majority of people that Governor Cooke would retain his position only until the fu-

sion of the irritated factions was effected, and that in the
event of his resignation Mr. Shepherd would be appointed his successor. Whether Governor Cooke retires
before the end of his term or not, it is the universal belief that Mr. Shepherd will be the second governor of
the District of Columbia.

He is a representative man, embodying in his history
and character more emphatically, perhaps, than any other
man, the new life of the new city of Washington.

CHAPTER VIII.

BUILDING THE CAPITOL.

GEORGE WASHINGTON believed the building of the Capitol to be identical with the establishment of a permanent seat of government. To the consummation of this crowning building, the deepest anxiety and devotion of his later years were dedicated. Next to determining a final site for the city was the difficulty of deciding on a plan for its Capitol.

Poor human nature had to contend awhile over this as it seems to have to about almost everything else. A Mr. S. Hallet had a plan: Dr. Thornton had one, also. Jefferson wrote "to Dr. Stewart, or to all the gentlemen" Commissioners, January 31, 1793:

"I have, under consideration, Mr. Hallet's plans for the Capitol, which undoubtedly have a great deal of merit. Doctor

Thornton has also given me a view of his. The grandeur, simplicity and beauty of the exterior, the propriety with which the departments are distributed, and economy in the mass of the whole structure, will, I doubt not give it a preference in your eyes as it has done in mine and those of several others whom I have consulted. I have, therefore, thought it better to give the Doctor time to finish his plan, and for this purpose to delay until your meeting a final decision. Some difficulty arises with respect to Mr. Hallet, who, you know, was in some degree led into his plan by ideas which we all expressed to him. This ought not to induce us to prefer it to a better; but while he is liberally rewarded for the time and labor he has expended on it, his feelings should be saved and soothed as much as possible. I leave it to yourselves how best to prepare him for the possibility that the Doctor's plans may be preferred to his."

February 1, 1793, Jefferson writes from Philadelphia to Mr. Carroll—

"DEAR SIR:—Doctor Thornton's plan for a Capitol has been produced and has so captivated the eyes and judgments of all as to leave no doubt you will prefer it when it shall be exhibited to you; as no doubt exists here of its preference over all which have been produced, and among its admirers no one is more decided than him, whose decision is most important. It is simple, noble, beautiful, excellently distributed and moderate in size. A just respect for the right of approbation in the Commissioners will prevent any formal decision in the President, till the plan shall be laid before you and approved by you. In the meantime the interval of *apparent* doubt may be improved for settling the mind of poor Hallet whose merits and distresses interests every one for his tranquillity and pecuniary relief."

These quotations are chiefly interesting in connection with the fact that poor, pushed-to-the-wall Hallet rebounded afterwards, notwithstanding Jefferson's enthusiasm over Thornton's plan, and Washington's declaration that it combined "grandeur, simplicity and convenience." The architects preferred the design of Hallet and in building retained but two or three of the features of Doctor Thornton's plan.

After the burning of the Capitol wings by the British, August, 1814, Mr. B. H. Latrobe, of Maryland, began to rebuild the Capitol on Stephen Hallet's plan. The foundations of the main building were laid March 24, 1818, under the superintendence of Charles Bulfinch, and the original design was completed in 1825. The site of the Capitol was chosen by George Washington, on a hill ninety feet above tide-water, commanding a view of the great plateau below, the circling rivers, and girdling hills—a hill in 1663 named "Room," later Rome, and owned by a gentleman named "Pope."

September 18, 1793, the south-east corner of the Capitol was laid by Washington with imposing ceremonies. A copy of *The Maryland Gazette*, published in Annapolis, September 26, 1793, gives a minute account of the grand Masonic ceremonial, which attended the laying of that august stone. It tells us that "there appeared on the southern bank of the river Potomac one of the finest companies of artillery that hath been lately seen parading to receive the President of the U. S." Also, that the Commissioners delivered to the President, who deposited in the stone a silver plate with the following inscription :

"This south-east corner of the Capitol of the United States of America, in the city of Washington, was laid on the 18th day of September, 1792, in the thirteenth year of American Independence ; in the first year, second term of the Presidency of George Washington, whose virtues in the civil administration of his country have been as conspicuous and beneficial, as his military valor and prudence have been useful, in establishing her liberties, and in the year of Masonry, 5793, by the President of the United States, in concert with the Grand Lodge of Maryland, several lodges under its jurisdiction and Lodge No. 22 from Alexandria, Virginia.

[Signed]   THOMAS JOHNSON, ⎫
                 DAVID STEWART, ⎬ *Commission-*
                 DANIEL CARROLL, ⎭ *ers, etc."*

The *Gazette* continues :—

" The whole company retired to an extensive booth, where an ox of 500 lbs. weight was barbecued, of which the company generally partook with every abundance of other recreation. The festival concluded with fifteen successive volleys from the artillery, whose military discipline and manœuvres merit every commendation."

" Before dark the whole company departed with joyful hopes of the production of their labors."

Fifty-eight years later, near this spot another corner-stone was deposited bearing the following inscription in the writing of Daniel Webster :—

" On the morning of the first day of the seventy-sixth year of the Independence of the United States of America, in the city of Washington, being the fourth day of July, eighteen hundred and fifty-one, this stone designed as the corner-stone of the extension of the Capitol, according to a plan approved by the President in pursuance of an act of Congress was laid by

MILLARD FILMORE,

PRESIDENT OF THE UNITED STATES,

Assisted by the Grand Master of the Masonic Lodges, in the presence of many Members of Congress, of officers of the Executive and Judiciary departments, National, State and Districts, of officers of the Army and Navy, the Corporate authorities of this and neighboring cities, many associations, civil and military and Masonic, officers of the Smithsonian Institution, and National Institute, professors of colleges and teachers of schools of the Districts, with their students and pupils, and a vast concourse of people from places near and remote including a few surviving gentlemen who witnessed the laying of the corner-stone of the Capitol by President Washington, on the 18th day of September, 1793. If, therefore, it shall hereafter be the will of God that this structure shall fall from its base, that its foundation be upturned, and this deposit brought to the eyes of men ; be it then known that on this day the Union of the United States of America stands firm, that their constitution still exists unimpaired, and with all its original usefulness and glory growing every day stronger and stronger in the affections of the great body of the American people, and attracting more and more the admiration of the world. And all here assembled, whether belonging to public life or to private life, with hearts devoutly thankful to Almighty God for the preservation of the liberty and happiness of the country, unite in sincere and fervent prayer, that this deposit, and the walls and arches, the domes and towers, the columns and entablatures, now to be erected over it may endure forever.

" God Save the United States of America.

DANIEL WEBSTER,

Secretary of State of the United States."

In the speech made by Mr. Webster on this occasion he uttered the following words :—

" Fellow citizens, what contemplations are awakened in our minds as we assemble to re-enact a scene like that performed by Washington! Methinks I see his venerable form now before me as presented in the glorious statue by Houdon, now in the Capitol of Virginia. . . . . We perceive that mighty

thoughts mingled with fears as well as with hopes, are struggling with him. He heads a short procession over these then
naked fields ; he crosses yonder stream on a fallen tree ; he as-
cends on the top of this eminence, whose original oaks of the
forest stand as thick around him as if the spot had been devoted
to Druidical worship and here he performs the appointed duty of
the day."

Fifty-eight years stretched between this scene and the
last and already the mutterings of civil revolution stirred
in the air. Could Webster have foreseen that the marble walls of the Capitol whose corner-stone he then laid
would rise amid the thunder of cannon aimed to destroy
it and the great Union of States which it crowned, to
what anguish of eloquence would his words have risen!
    The Capitol fronting the east was set by an astronomi-
cal observation of Andrew Ellicott. Its founders were as
much mistaken in the direction which the future city
would take as they were in the future commerce of the
Potomac. They expected that a metropolis would spring
up on Capitol Hill, spreading on to the Navy Yard and
Potomac. Land-owners made this impossible by the price
they set upon their city lots. The metropolis defied them
—went down into the valley and grew up behind the
Capitol.
    The north wing of the central Capitol was made ready
for the first sitting of Congress in Washington, November
17, 1800. By that time the walls of the south wing had
risen twenty feet and were covered over for the temporary use of the House of Representatives. It sat in this
room named "the oven" from 1802, until 1804. At that
time the transient roof was removed and the wing completed under the superintendence of B. H. Latrobe until

its completion. The House occupied the room of the Library of Congress. The south wing was finished in 1811.

The original Capitol was built of sandstone taken from an island in Acquia Creek, Virginia. The island was purchased by the government in 1791 for $6,000 for the use of the quarry. The interior of both wings was destroyed by fire when the British took the city in 1814, the outer walls remaining uninjured. Latrobe, who had resigned in 1813, was re-appointed after the fire to reconstruct the Capitol. The following December, Congress passed an act leasing a building on the east side of the Capitol, the building afterwards so famous as "Old Capitol Prison," and which was crowded with prisoners during the war of the Rebellion. Congress held its sessions in this building till the rebuilt Capitol was ready for occupation.

By act of Congress, September 30, 1850, provision was made for the grand extension wings of the Capitol, to be built on such a plan as might be approved by the President. The plan of Thomas C. Walter was accepted by President Fillmore, June 10, 1851, and he was appointed architect of the Capitol to carry his plan into execution. Walter was the architect of Girard College, Philadelphia, and to him we owe the magnificent marble wings and iron dome of the Capitol. The dome cost one million one hundred thousand dollars. The wings cost six millions five hundred thousand dollars. The height of the interior of the dome of the Capitol from the floor of the rotunda is 180 feet and 3 inches. The height of the exterior from the floor of the basement story to the top of the crowning statue is 287 feet and 5 inches. The interior diameter is 97 feet. The exterior diameter of the drum is 108 feet. The greatest exterior diameter is

135 feet, 5 inches.   The Capitol is 751 feet, 4 inches long,
31 feet longer than St. Peter's in Rome, and 175 feet longer
than St. Paul's in London.   The height of the interior of
the dome of St. Peter's is 330 feet.   The height of the
interior of the dome of St. Paul's is 215 feet.   The
height of the exterior of St. Peter's to the top of lantern
is 432 feet.   The height of the exterior of the dome of
St. Paul's is 215 feet.

The ground actually covered by the Capitol is 153,112
square feet or 652 square feet more than 3 1-2 acres.   Of
these the old building covered 61,201 square feet and the
new wings with connecting corridors, 91,311 square feet.

The dome of the Capitol is the highest structure in
America.   It is one hundred and eight feet higher than
Washington Monument in Baltimore; sixty-eight feet
higher than Bunker Hill Monument and twenty-three
feet higher than the steeple of Trinity Church, New York.
Mr. Walter was succeeded by Mr. Edward Clarke, the
present architect of the Capitol.   Thus far Mr. Clarke's
work has consisted chiefly in finishing and harmonizing
the work of his varied and sometimes conflicting predecessors.   Under his supervision the dome has been completed, and Thomas Crawford's grand goddess of liberty,
sixteen and one-half feet high, has ascended to its summit
while he has wrought out in the interior the most harmonious room of the Capitol—the Congressional Library.

The greatest work which he still desires to do is to put
the present front on the rear of the Capitol facing the
city, and to draw forth the old freestone fronts and rebuild it with marble, making a grand central portico parallel with the magnificent marble wings of the Senate and
House extension.   To rebuild the central front will cost

two millions of dollars. The face of the Capitol will never be worthy of itself till this is accomplished. The grand outward defect of the Capitol is the slightness and insignificance of the central portico compared with the superlative Corinthian fronts of the wings. Between their outreaching marble steps, beside their majestic monoliths the central columns shrink to feebleness and give the impression that the great dome is sinking down upon them to crush them out of sight. There is something soaring in the proportions of the dome. Its summit seems to spring into the empyrean. Its proud goddess poised in mid-air, caught in their swift embrace, seems to sail with the fleeting clouds. Nevertheless its tremendous base set upon that squatting roof threatens it with perpetual annihilation.

From the very beginning the Capitol has suffered as a National Building from the conflicting and foreign tastes of its decorators. Literally begun in the woods by a nation in its infancy, it not only borrowed its face from the buildings of antiquity, but it was built by men, strangers in thought and spirit to the genius of a new Republic, and the unwrought and unimbodied poetry of its virgin soil. Its earlier decorators, all Italians, overlaid its walls with their florid colors and foreign symbols; within the American Capitol, they have set the Loggia of Raphael, the voluptuous ante-rooms of Pompeii, and the Baths of Titus. The American plants, birds and animals, representing prodigal nature at home, though exquisitely painted are buried in twilight passages, while mythological bar-maids, misnamed goddesses, dance in the most conspicuous and preposterous places. The Capitol has already survived this era of false decorative art.

Congress in 1859 authorized a Commission of distinguished American artists, comprising Messrs. Brown, Lumsden and Kensett, to study the decorations of the Capitol and report upon their abuses. Their suggestions are beginning to be followed, and yet so carelessly, that after the lapse of fourteen years they need reiteration. The Artist Committee recommended an Art Commission, composed of those designated by the united voice of America. Artists as competent to the office who shall be the channels for the distribution of all appropriations to be made by Congress for art purposes, and who shall secure to artists an intelligent and unbiased adjudication upon the designs they may present for the embellishment of the national buildings. When one remembers some of the Congressional Committees who have decided on decorations for the Capitol even within the last ten years, it is enough to make one cry aloud for a Commission designated by artists, whose art-culture shall at least be sufficient to tell a decent picture from a daub, a noble statue from a pretense and a sham.

In conclusion the Commission of Artists said :—

" The erection of a great National Capitol seldom occurs but once in the life of a nation. The opportunity such an event affords is an important one for the expression of patriotic elevation, and the perpetuation, through the arts of painting and sculpture, of that which is high and noble and held in reverence by the people ; and it becomes them as patriots to see to it that no taint of falsity is suffered to be transmitted to the future upon the escutcheon of our national honor in its artistic record. A theme so noble and worthy should interest the heart of the whole country, and whether patriot, statesman or artist, one impulse should govern the whole in dedicating these buildings and grounds to the national honor."

CHAPTER IX.

INSIDE THE CAPITOL.

A Visit to the Capitol—The Lower Hall—Its Cool Tranquillity—Artistic
   Treasures—The President's and Vice-President's Rooms—The Marble
   Room—The Senate Chamber—"Men I have Known "—Hamlin—Foote—
   Foster—Wade—Colfax—Wilson—The Rotunda—Great Historical Paint-
   ings—The Old Hall of Representatives—The New Hall—The Speaker's
   Room—Native Art—"The Star of Empire "—A National Picture.

COME with me. This is your Capitol. It is like
   passing from one world into another, to leave behind the bright June day for the cool, dim halls of the
lower Capitol. No matter how fiercely the sun burns in
the heavens, his fire never penetrates the twilight of this
grand hall, whose eight hundred feet measure the length
of the Capitol from end to end.

Here, in Egyptian Colonnades, rise the mighty shafts
of stone which bear upon their tops the mightier mass
of marble, and which seem strong enough to support the
world. In the summer solstice they cast long, cool
shadows, full of repose and silence. The gas-lights flick-
ering on the walls, send long golden rays through the
dimness to light us on. We have struck below the jar
and tumult of life. The struggles of a nation may be
going on above our heads, yet so vast and visionary are
these vistas opening before us, so deep the calm which
surrounds us, we seem far away from the world that we

have left, in this new world which we have found. Every time I descend into these lower regions I get lost. In wandering on to find our way out, we are sure to make numerous discoveries of unimagined beauty. Here are doors after doors in almost innumerable succession, opening into departments of commerce, agriculture, etc., whose every panel holds exquisite gems of illustrative painting. Birds, flowers, fruits, landscapes, in rarest fresco and color, here reveal themselves to us through the dim light.

It would take months to study and to learn these pictures which artists have taken years to paint. They make a department of art in themselves, yet thousands who think that they know the Capitol well are not aware of their existence. At the East Senate entrance, look at these polished pillars of Tennessee marble, their chocolate surface all flecked with white, surrounding a staircase meet for kings. They are my delight. Look at these foliated capitals, flowering in leaves of acanthus and tobacco. Look up to this ceiling of stained glass, its royal roses opening wide their crimson hearts above you; these too are my delight. I am not one of those who can sneer at the Capitol. Its faults, like the faults of a friend are sacred. I know them, but wish to name them not, save to the one who only can remedy. It bears blots upon its fair face, but these can be washed away. It wears ornaments vulgar and vain, these can be stripped off and thrown out. Below them, beyond them all, abides the Capitol. The surface blemish vexes, the pretentious splendor offends. These are not the Capitol. We look deeper, we look higher, to find beauty, to see sublimity, to see the Capitol, august and imperishable!

The four marble staircases leading to the Senate Cham-

THE MARBLE ROOM.

INSIDE THE CAPITOL.—WASHINGTON.

ber and Hall of Representatives, in themselves alone embody enough of grace and magnificence to save the Capitol from cynical criticism.   We slip through the Senate
corridor, you and I, to the President's and Vice-President's
rooms.   Their furniture is sumptuous, their decoration oppressive.   Gilding, frescoes, arabesques, glitter and glow
above and around.   There is not one quiet hue on which
the tired sight may rest.   Gazing, I feel an indescrib-
able desire to pluck a few of Signor Brumidi's red leg-
ged babies and pug-nosed cupids from their precarious
perches on the lofty ceilings, to commit them to nurses or
to anybody who will smooth out their rumpled little legs
and make them look comfortable.

We are Americans, and need repose ; let us, therefore,
pass to the Marble Room, which alone, of all the rooms
of the Capitol, suggests it—

"The end of all, the poppied sleep."

Its atmosphere is soft, serene, and silent.   Its ceiling is of
white marble, deeply paneled, supported by fluted pillars
of polished Italian marble.   Its walls are of the exquisite
marble of Tennessee—a soft brown, veined with white—
set with mirrors.   One whose æsthetic eyes have studied the finest apartments of the world says that to him·
the most chaste and purely beautiful of all is the Marble
Room of the American Capitol.   Americans though we
are, we have no time to rest, albeit we sorely need it.

It is not for you or me to linger in marble rooms,
maundering of art.   Molly, rocking her baby out on the
Western prairie, wants to know all about the Senate ;
baby is going to be a senator some day.   Moses, on that
little rock-sown farm in New England, has his "chores all

done." He rests in the Yankee paradise of kerosene, butternuts, apples, and cider. Yet to make his satisfaction complete, he must know a little more about the Capitol. Molly and Moses both expect us to see for them what they can not come to see for themselves. So let us peep into the Senate. It can not boast of the ampler proportions of the Hall of Representatives. Its golden walls and emerald doors can not rescue it from insignificance.

The ceiling of this chamber is of cast-iron, paneled with stained glass—each pane bearing the arms of the different States, bound by most ornate mouldings, bronzed and gilded. The gallery, which entirely surrounds the hall, will seat one thousand persons. Over the Vice-President's chair, the section you see separated from the rest by a net-work of wire, is the reporters' gallery. The one opposite, lined with green, is the gallery of the diplomatic corps; next are the seats reserved for the Senators' families. The Senators sit in three semi-circular rows, behind small desks of polished wood, facing the Secretary of the Senate, his assistants, the special reporters of debates, and the Vice-President.

On a dais, raised above all, sits the Vice-President. I have seen six men preside over the Senate. Hamlin, slow, solid, immobile, and good-natured. Foote, silver-haired, silver-toned, the king of parliamentarians. Foster of Connecticut, that most gentle gentleman, who went from the Senate bearing the good will of every Senator whatever his politics. Wade, the most positive power of all, with his high, steep head, shaggy eyebrows, beetling perceptive brow, half roofing the melancholy eyes, the rough-hewn nose, the dogged mouth, and broad immovable chin. Life lines our faces according to its will and gazing on the furrows of this one, one reads the story of the whole battle. Looking, there was no need that its owner should tell what a warfare life had been since the poor farmer-boy, more than half a century ago, turned his face from the Connecticut Valley and striving with the earth beneath his feet dug his way (on the Erie Canal) toward the West to fortune, and to an honorable fame. Then came Schuyler Colfax, who brought into the silent and stately Senate the habits of the bustling noisy house. It was a hard seat for "Schuyler," that Vice-President's chair, and he came at last to vacate it regularly by two o'clock that he might write in the seclusion of the Vice-President's room a few of those ten thousand popular personal letters which made his chief lever of influence with the people and which he always used to write in the Speaker's chair. As President of the Senate he was usually just, always urbane, never impressive. He had not the presence which filled the seat to the sight, nor the dignity which commanded attention, and silence. Under his ruling the Senate changed its character perceptibly from a grave august body to a buzzing and inattentive one. As the President of the Senate seldom listened to a speaker, the Senators as rarely took the trouble to listen to each other. The question discussed might be of the gravest import to the whole nation, the speaker's words, to himself, might be of the most tremendous importance to the national weal, just the same he had to empty them upon vacancy, speaking to nothing in particular, while the Vice-President looked another way, and his colleagues went on scribbling letters, whispering political secrets to each other, munching apples in the aisles or smoking in the open cloak-rooms, with feet aloft.

7

Vice-President Wilson, without an atom of parliamentary experience, has already won the hearts and improved the manners of the Senate by simply giving attention to its debates. No matter how tiresome, he steadfastly looks and listens. The humblest speaker—seeing that he has one pair of eyes fixed upon him, one direct immovable point toward which he may direct his remarks—takes heart, and in spite of himself makes a better speech than would be possible were he beating a vacuum, and speaking to nobody in particular. Even his listening constituency and the next day's *Globe* is not such an incentive to present inspiration as two steadfast eyes and one pair of good listening ears.

We leave the Senate Chamber by the western gallery. Here in the niche at the foot of the staircase, corresponding to Franklin's on the opposite side, stands the noble figure of John Hancock. The stairs are of polished white marble and the painting above them leading to the gentlemen's gallery of the Senate, in its setting of maroon cloth represents the battle of Chapultapec in all the ardor of its fiery action. We saunter on along the breezy corridors through whose open windows we catch delicious glimpses of the garden city, the gliding river and the distant hills, past the Supreme Court room into the great rotunda.

The rotunda is ninety-five feet in diameter, three hundred feet in circumference and over one hundred and eighty feet in height. Its dome contains over eight millions eight hundred thousand pounds of iron, presenting the most finished specimen of iron architecture in the world. The panels of the rotunda are set with paintings of life-size, painted by Vanderlyn, Trumbull and others.

THE SENATE CHAMBER.

INSIDE THE CAPITOL.—WASHINGTON.

The Declaration of Independence; the surrender of Burgoyne; surrender of the British Army, commanded by Lord Cornwallis, at Yorktown, Virginia, October 19, 1781; resignation of General Washington at Annapolis, December 23, 1783, all by Colonel Trumbull; the baptism of Pocahontas by Chapman; landing of Columbus by Vanderlyn; De Soto's discovery of the Mississippi, by Powell. Like most works of genius these paintings have many merits and many defects. Perhaps the favorite of all is the Embarcation of the Pilgrims in the Speedwell at Delft Haven, by Robert W. Weir. Its figures and the fabrics of its costumes are wonderfully painted; so, too, is the face of the hoary Pilgrim who is giving thanks to God for their safe passage across stormy seas to the land of deliverance; but the enchantment of the picture is the face of Rose Standish. If I were a man, I would marry such a face out of all the faces on the earth, for the being which it represents. These eyes, blue as heaven and as true, would never fail you. No matter how low *you* might fall, you could see only in them purity, faith, devotion, tenderness, and unutterable love—and all for you.

The group in bas-relief over the western entrance of the rotunda was executed by Cappelano, a pupil of Canova. It represents the preservation of Captain Smith by Pocahontas. The design was taken from a rude engraving of the event in the first edition of Smith's History of Virginia. The idea is national, but you see the execution is preposterous. Powhatan looks like an Englishman, and Pocahontas has a Greek face and a Grecian head-dress. The alto-relievo over the eastern entrance of the rotunda represents the Landing of the Pilgrims. The pilgrim, his wife and child are stepping from the prow of a boat to receive from the hand of an Indian, kneeling on the rock before them, an ear of corn. Good Indian. He was no relation to the Modoc! Still the little boy evidently has no faith in him for he is tugging at his father's arm as if to hold him back from that ear of corn or the hand that holds it.

Over the south door of the rotunda we have Daniel Boone and two Indians in a forest. Boone has dispatched one Indian and is in close battle with the other. The latter is doing his best to strike Boone with his tomahawk, but Boone averts the blow, by his rifle in one hand, while the other drawn back holds a long knife which he is about to run through his foe. The action is exciting enough for the *New York Ledger*, although rendered tangled and cramped by a too narrow space. It commemorates an occurrence which took place in the year 1773. This, as well as the landing of the Pilgrims, was executed by Causici, another pupil of Canova. Over the northern door of the rotunda we have William Penn standing under an elm, in the act of presenting a treaty to the Indians. Penn is dressed as a Quaker, and looks as benevolent as the crude stone out of which he is made will let him. This panel was executed by a Frenchman named Genelot.

We pass through the noblest room of the Capitol, the old Hall of Representatives and through the open corridor directly into the new Hall of Representatives. It occupies the precise place in the south wing which the Senate Chamber does in the northern wing. Like the Senate room, the light of day comes to it but dimly through the stained glass roof overhead. Like that, also, it is entire, encircled by a corridor opening into smoking apartments, committee rooms, the Speaker's room, etc., which

THE HALL OF REPRESENTATIVES.

INSIDE THE CAPITOL.—WASHINGTON.

monopolize all the out of door air, and every out of door view. The air of the central chamber is pumped into it by a tremendous engine at work in the depths of the Capitol and admitted through ventilators one under each desk. You see these are covered with shining brass plates which by a touch of the foot can be adjusted to admit a current of fresh air, or shut it off, according to the wish of the occupant of the chair above it. In former times these ventilators were uncovered, and then were used to such an extent as spittoons by the honorable gentlemen above them, and filled to such a depth with tobacco quids and the stumps of cigars that the odor from them became unbearable and they had to be covered up.

The Hall of Representatives is 139 feet long, 93 feet wide and 30 feet high with a gallery running entirely around the Hall, holding seats for 1200 persons. Like the Senate, the ceiling is of iron work bronzed, gilded and paneled with glass, each pane decorated with the arms of a State. At the corners of these panels in gilt and bronze are rosettes of the cotton plant in its various stages of bud and blossom. The Speaker's desk, splendid in proportion, is of pure white marble, while crossed above his head are two brilliant silk flags of the United States. One of the panels under the gallery at his left is filled with a painting in fresco, by Brumidi.

The Speaker's room, in the rear of his chair across the inner lobby, is one of the most beautiful rooms in the Capitol. Its ornaments are not as glaring as those of the President's and Vice-President's rooms, while its mirrors, carved book-cases, velvet carpets and chairs, give it a look of home comfort as well as of luxury. It has a bright outlook upon the eastern grounds of the Capitol, and its

walls are hung with portraits of every speaker from the
First Congress to the present one.

We pass through the private corridor looking from the
Speaker's room out into the grand colonnaded vestibule
opening upon the great portico of the south extension.
These twenty-four columns and forty pilasters have blossomed from native soil. Athens, Pompeii, Rome, are left
out at last, and looking up to these flowering capitals
we see corn-leaves, tobacco, and magnolias budding and
blooming from their marble crowns. Every column, every pilaster bears a magnolia, each of a different form, all
from casts of the natural flower. And far below, beneath
the Representatives' Hall, there is a row of monolithic
columns formed of the tobacco and thistle. It is above
the marble staircase opposite, leading to the ladies' gallery, that we see painted on the wall covering the entire
landing, the great painting of Leutze, representing the
"Advance of Civilization;" "Westward the Star of Empire takes its way"—is its motto. At the first glance
it presents a scene of inextricable confusion. It is an
emigrant train caught and tangled in one of the highest
passes of the Rocky Mountains. Far backward spread
the Eastern Plains; far onward stretches the Beulah of
promise, fading at last in the far horizon. The great wagons struggling upward, tumbling downward from mountain precipice into mountain gorge, hold under their shaking covers every type of westward moving human life.
Here is the mother sitting in the wagon-front, her blue
eyes gazing outward, wistfully and far, the baby lying
on her lap; one wants to touch the baby's head, it looks
so alive and tender and shelterless in all that dust and
turmoil of travel. A man on horseback carries his wife,

her head upon his shoulder. Who that has ever seen it will forget her sick look and the mute appeal in the suffering eyes. Here is the bold hunter with his racoon cap, the pioneer boy on horseback, a coffee-pot and cup dangling at his saddle, and oxen—such oxen! it seems as if their friendly noses must touch us; they seem to be feeling out for our hand as we pass up to the gallery. Here is the young man, the old man, and far aloft stands the advance guard fastening on the highest and farthest pinnacle the flag of the United States.

Confusing, disappointing perhaps, at first glance, this painting asserts itself more and more in the soul the oftener and the longer you gaze. Already the swift, smooth wheels of the railway, the shriek of the whistle, and the rush of the engine have made its story history. But it is the history of our past—the story of the heroic West. It is one of a thousand which should line the walls of the Capitol, feeding the hearts of the American people to the latest generation with the memory of our forefathers, showing by what toilsome ways they followed the Star of Empire and made the paths of civilization smooth for their children's feet.

CHAPTER X.

OUTSIDE THE CAPITOL.

The Famous Bronze Doors—The Capitol Grounds—Statue of Washington Criticised—Peculiar Position for " the Father of his Country "—Horace Greenough's Defence of the Statue—Picturesque Scenery Around the Capitol—The City and Suburbs—The Public Reservation—The Smithsonian Institution—The Potomac and the Hights of Arlington.

WE come back to the grand vestibule of the southern wing, to the flowering magnolias, tobacco and corn-leaves of the marble capitals, and pass out to the great portico. This is one of the famous bronze doors designed by Rogers, and cast in Munich. How heavy, slow, and still, its swing! The other opens and closes upon the central door of the north wing, leading to the vestibule of the Senate.

Here, from the portico we look out upon the eastern grounds of the Capitol in the unsullied panoply of a June morning, across the closely shorn grass, the borders of roses and beds of flowers, through the vista of maples with their green arcade of light and shadow, to the august form of George Washington sitting in the centre of the grounds in a lofty cerule chair mounted on a pedestal of granite twelve feet high.

This is the grandest and most criticised work of art about the Capitol. The form being nude to the waist and the right arm outstretched, it is a current vulgar joke that he is reaching out his hand for his clothes which are on exhibition in a case at the Patent Office. It is true that a sense of personal discomfort seems to emanate from the drapery—or lack of it—and the *posé* of this colossal figure. George Washington with his right arm outstretched, his left forever holding up a Roman sword, half naked, yet sitting in a chair, beneath bland summer skies, within a veiling screen of tender leaves is a much more comfortable looking object than when the winds and rains and snows of winter beat upon his unsheltered head and uncovered form. This statue was designed in imitation of the antique statue of Jupiter Tonans. The ancients made their statues of Jupiter naked above and draped below as being visible to the gods but invisible to men. But the average American citizen, being accustomed to seeing the Father of his country decently attired in small clothes, naturally receives a shock at first beholding him in next to no clothes at all. It is impossible for him to reconcile a Jupiter in sandals with the stately George Washington in knee-breeches and buckled shoes. The spirit of the statue, which is ideal, militates against the spirit of the land which is utilitarian if not commonplace.

Nevertheless, in poetry of feeling, in grandeur of conception, in exquisite fineness of detail and in execution, Horatio Greenough's statue of George Washington is transcendently the greatest work in marble yet wrought at the command of the government for the Capitol. It is scarcely human, certainly not American, but it is godlike. The face is a perfect portrait of Washington. The veining of a single hand, the muscles of a single arm are triumphs of art.

Washington's chair is twined with acanthus leaves and

garlands of flowers. The figure of Columbus leans against
the back of the seat to the left, connecting the history of
America with that of Europe; an Indian chief on the right
represents the condition of the country at the time of its
discovery. The back of the seat is ornamented in *basso-relievo* with the rising sun, the crest of the American
arms, under which is this motto : " *Magnus ab integro
sæculorum nascitur ordo.*" On the left is sculptured in
bas-relief the genii of North and South America under
the forms of the infant Hercules strangling the serpent,
and Iphiclus stretched on the ground shrinking in fear
from the contest. The motto is " *Incipe posse puer cui
non risere parentes.*" On the back of the seat is the following motto : " *Simulacrum istud ad magnum Liber-
tatis exemplum. Nec sine ipsa duraturum.*"

One of the greatest works of contemporary art, the
masterpiece of a master, it has been the subject of more
rude and vulgar jests than any other piece of American
sculpture. The painful disparity which so often exists
between the judgment of the multitude and the inspiration of the creator has never been more touchingly illustrated than in the following words of Horatio Greenough,
concerning this monument to his own genius and to the
Father of his country. He says : " It is the birth of my
thoughts, I have sacrificed to it the flower of my days, and
the freshness of my strength ; its every lineament has
been moistened with the sweat of my toil and the tears of
my exile. I would not barter away its association with
my name for the proudest fortune that avarice ever
dreamed of. In giving it up to the nation that has done
me the honor to order it at my hands, I respectfully claim
for it that protection which is the boast of civilization to

afford art, and which a generous enemy has more than once been seen to extend even to the monuments of its own defeat."

Retracing our steps to the rotunda, we turn westward through the main hall of the Congressional Library to the lofty colonnade outside, from whose balcony we look down upon the view which Humbolt declared to be the most beautiful of its type in the whole world. Directly below us, past the western terrace of the Capitol, with its open basin full of gold fishes flashing in the sun, stretch the Capitol grounds. Many varieties of trees already grown to forest hight spread their interlacing roof of cool, green shadow over the malachite sward below. Beds of flowers set in the grass, from the early March crocuses to the November blooming roses, make the grounds fragrant and precious with their presence. Here the dandelion spreads its cloth of gold in early May. Here the chrysanthemums fringe the snow with pallid gold in white December. Now the fountains are lapsing in dreamy tune through the long June hours, and the seats under the trees are filled with visitors. Nurses with children in their arms, old men and women leaning on their staffs, lovers "billing and cooing" through the long twilight and starlight seasons. Beyond spreads the city, every ugly outline hidden and lost in a waving sea of greenery rippling and tossing above it. The great avenues run and radiate in all directions. Pennsylvania Avenue stretches straight on between its border of shade trees to its acropolis one mile distant, the great Treasury gleaming in the sun, and the white chimneys of the Executive Mansion peering above the trees; and still on, till it joins the primitive streets of Georgetown. Massachusetts Avenue, broad, straight,

magnificent, spans the city from end to end unbroken.
Virginia Avenue to the left, goes on to meet Long
Bridge, leading far into the Old Dominion.   Directly in
front stretches the public reservation yet to be made
splendid as the Nation's Boulevards, but already holding
the Congressional gardens and conservatories, the unique
towers, and picturesque grounds of the Smithsonian Institution, the broad flower-banded terraces of the Agricultural Department, and the incomplete Washington
Monument.   Beyond we see the wide Potomac, flecked
all over with snowy sails, far down old Alexandria, dingy
on its farther shore; opposite the Heights of Arlington,
and amid its immemorial oaks; Arlington House with
the stars and stripes floating free from its crowning
summit.

CHAPTER XI.

ART TREASURES OF THE CAPITOL.

A SOLITARY lady has arrived in the old Hall of the
House of Representatives; or, as Senator Anthony
eloquently calls it, " the Pantheon of America." " Considering her age," (as women sweetly say of each other,)
"she looks quite young." What her precise age may
be, I am as unable to tell you as that of any other of
my friends. The daughter of Saturn and Vesta, we may,
at least, conclude that she has lived long enough to look
older than she does. Her name is " Il Penserosa," and,
"to judge by appearances," she seems to have flourished
about twenty-five of our mortal years. Yet Milton sung
of her in his youth, before an unruly wife and three dis-
obedient daughters, (who perversely wished to understand

the alphabet which they read to their blind father,) had made him crabbed and loftily sour towards women—Milton sung of this maid who has but lately arrived in Washington:

> " Come, pensive nun, devout and pure,
> Sober, steadfast, and demure,
> All in a robe of darkest grain
> Flowing with majestic train,
> And sable stole of cypress lawn,
> Over thy decent shoulders drawn ;
> Come, but keep thy wonted state
> With even step and musing gait,
> And looks commercing with the skies,
> Thy rapt soul sitting in thine eyes."

Now, if this maiden can keep on holding her head up, with looks perpetually " commercing with the skies " so that it will be impossible for her to see all the tobacco-juice and apple-cores beneath and round about her, it will conduce greatly to her peace of mind. I am sorry that "the Pantheon of America" is not a cleaner looking place. It's a pity, as we have a Pantheon, that its shabbiness and dirt should flourish to a degree that is absolutely melancholy. I am sure it was in obedience to the law of fitness that the committee of the Congressional Library or some other committee, brought the Goddess of Melancholy in here, to hold her eyes and nose aloft, and to stand supreme queen, regnant of dust and gloom and American " expectoration." " Hail! divinest Melancholy." I am glad, judging by your face, that you are of the lymphatic temperament, and that consequently, all this dirt will afflict you less than it does me. But the more I look at your impassive and soulless countenance the more I fear that, after all, you are but a feeble counterfeit of Milton's goddess or of the divine maiden conceived and born in,

"Woody, Ida's inmost grove."

In speaking of this marble, my heart will not let me forget that it was wrought by a hand self-taught; yet no less, standing where it does, it must be measured—somewhat, at least—by the standards of art. The figure, diminutive even in its femininity, suffers to insignificance by being set almost directly behind the gaunt and elongated form of Miss Ream's "Lincoln;" yet it is in the figure, in its posé and gentle curves, its chaste and graceful drapery, "the stole of cypress lawn, over the decent shoulders drawn" in the firm yet delicate hand which holds it in its place—in these only it is that the artist has caught and fastened in stone the aspect of the "goddess, sage and holy." The face is meaningless. Not a line, not a curve, not an expression indicates a capacity for melancholy, contemplation or anything else emotional or intellectual. No mortal woman ever really meditated for a minute who did not get her hair pushed back further from her eyes than this, but these regulation locks run straight down the little, senseless Greek face in a mathematical angle, indissolubly banded by a little perked up helmet, embossed with seven stars. Why these stars? "Il Penserosa" was not nearly enough related to "that starred Ethiop queen" Cassiope, to have borrowed the helmet to wear even in the old Hall of the old House of Representatives "in the United States of America."

As for the Ream statue of Lincoln, (like many people,) the first glance at it is the most satisfactory that you will

ever have. It will never look as well again. Some declare this very palpable lack to be in the subject—Mr.
Lincoln's own face and form—but many others note it to
be in this representation of them. Mr. Lincoln's living
face was one of the most interesting ever given to man.
There was more than fascination in its rugged homeliness;
there was in it the deeper attraction of suffering and sympathy. It outrayed from every line engraven there by
human pain and love and longing. But no soul can put
into a statue or painting more than it has in itself. In
this statue of Mr. Lincoln we have his rude outward image, unilluminated by one mental or spiritual characteristic. It is mechanical, material, opaque. Mrs. Sarah
Ames, in her bust of Lincoln, which stands just behind
our friend, "Il Penserosa," has transfixed more of the
soul of Lincoln in the brow and eyes of his face than
Miss Ream has in all the weary outline of her many feet
of marble. In the bust the lower part of the face is ideal-
ized into weakness. Without his gauntness and rugged-
ness Lincoln is not Lincoln. But any one who ever saw
and felt the deep, tender, sad outlook of his living humanity must thank Mrs. Ames for having reflected and
transfixed it in the brows and eyes of this marble.

Just outside of its alcove, at the right hand of the door
which enters the New House of Representatives, stand
side by side, the two statues from Rhode Island—one of
General Green, the other of Roger Williams. That of
General Green is spirited and exquisitely fine in detail;
while that of Roger Williams is the one ideal statue in
our Pantheon. Both were executed in Rome—the first
by Henry R. Brown, the second by Franklin Simmons,
of Providence, Rhode Island. No portrait of Roger Wil-

liams being in existence, Mr. Simmons has evolved from
imagination and his inner consciousness a quaint, poetic
figure and a dreamlike face, above whose lifted eyelids
seems to hover a seraphic smile. Then it is refreshing
to turn from the stove-pipe hats, shingled heads and angular garments in which the men of our generation do pen-
ance, to the flowing locks, puckered knee-breeches, with
their dainty tassels, and the ample ruffs in which the
holy apostle of liberty represents his name and time.
He holds a book in his hand, on whose cover is inscribed
the words, "Soul Liberty," and, with open, uplifted glance
and free *posé* seems about to step forward into air, with
lips just ready to open with words of inspiration.

Opposite, on the other side of the Hall, stand together
Connecticut's contribution—the statues of Jonathan Trumbull and Roger Sherman. They are of heroic size and at
first glance are most imposing. When you walk nearer,
and soberly survey them, you see that Roger Sherman
looks solid and stolid, and you see also (at least, I do,)
that old Jonathan Trumbull, with his down-perked head
and narrow-lidded eyes, looks like a meditative rooster—
an immense human chanticleer, who had paused in his
lording career for a minute's meditation. Mind, I don't
say but this may be a grand statue, in its way, I only ob-
serve that it is a very repelling one to me.

Just round the angle of the alcove on a box set on
end, covered with tattered black cambric, stands a bust
of Kosciusko, by H. D. Saunders. Poor Kosciusko! His
nose always needs wiping; and what a pedestal for a
Pantheon! A candle or a soap box, probably, half covered with black tags; then on his nose celestial, the dust
alights and lodges always. It is so provocative—the tip

8

of it; every bumpkin who approaches it taps or pulls it.
Thus, literally, Kosciusko's nose is seldom clean. One
day it was. Some pitying hand had washed the entire
face. If you could have seen the difference between
Kosciusko clean and Kosciusko exiled, dirty and forlorn!
A few steps from this bust stands the statue of Alexander
Hamilton, by Horatio Stone—a noble figure, spirited in
posture and beautiful in countenance. No painted portrait can give so grand an idea of the great Federalist to
posterity. It is eight feet high and represents Hamilton
in the attitude of impassioned speech. It is persuasive
rather than declamatory, for the lifted hands droop, the
face presses slightly forward, the eyes look out from under their royal arches deep and steadfast, while the sunshine pouring down the dome lights up every lineament
with the intensity of life. The execution of the statue is
exquisite, while in *posé* and expression it is the embodiment of majesty and power. Burr—who presided over
the Senate, who with the pride, subtlety and ambition of
Lucifer, planned and executed to live in the future amid
the most exalted names of his time—sleeps dishonored
and accursed; while the great rival that he hated, whose
success he could not bear, whose life he destroyed, comes
back in this majestic semblance to abide in the Capitol.
Thus we behold in this statue not only a "triumph of
art" but also a triumph of that final retributive compensation of justice which sooner or later crushes every
wrong. This image of Hamilton looks forth from an era
which, across the gulf of our later revolution, seems already remote. It recalls Washington the friend, Jefferson the foe, the war of Colonist and Tory, the war of
ideas between Federalist and Republican, the struggles

and successes of a splendid career; yet how far removed
seem all across the graves of the men of our own generation whom patriotism and death have made illustrious and
immortal. Thus nearer and dearer to the hearts of to-
day must be the image of "the noblest Roman of them
all." It is a statue of Baker, also executed by Horatio
Stone, in Rome, in 1863. Hamilton stands forth in heroic
size, while the statue of Baker is under that of life, and
barely suggests the grand proportions of the man. Yet
the dignity and grandeur of his mien are here, as he
stands wrapped in his cloak, his arms folded, his head
thrown back, his noble face lifted as if he saw the
future—*his future*—and awaited it undaunted and with
a joyful heart. At his side is the plumed hat of a soldier,
and on the pedestal on which he stands are graven words
from his last speech in the United States Senate, when
he replied to Breckenridge, "There will be some graves
reeking with blood, watered by the tears of affection.
There will be some privation. There will be some loss
of luxury; there will be somewhat more need of labor
to procure the necessaries of life. When that is said, all
is said. If we have the country, the whole country,
the Union, the constitution, free government—with these
will return all the blessings of a well ordered civilization.
The path of the country will be a course of grandeur and
glory such as our fathers in the olden time foresaw in
the dim visions of years to come—such as would have
been ours to-day, had it not been for the treason for
which the senator too often seeks to apologize."

Thus to the land he loved he gave his life—a life so
rich in every quality that rounds and completes the highest manhood.

At sight of this mute marble, what memories are stirred! Again, in and around Union Square throbs the vast human mass. Banners wave, cannons boom, drums beat, men march. Every pulse of the air thrills with the cry, "To Arms!" Amid all the orators of that hour, whose voice uttered such burning words as Baker—he who left the seat of a senator for the grave of a soldier. Thank God for our dead who yet live. No land has a more priceless legacy. No soil was ever planted with richer blood. No freedom ever bought with a costlier victory. Let me tell you, public men, amid all your lavish expenditures of money wrung from the people, never begrudge the price you pay for the fit statue of a great character. Line the corridors of the Capitol with the images of the noble and the good, that, by suggestion and semblance, they may arouse to a purer purpose the emulation of the living. In these halls where lobbyists congregate, where money-changers stand with shameless faces offering their venal price for truth and honor, buying and selling the integrity of manhood, give to our eyes at least the memories of high example. If men in the rush of affairs and the absorption of their ambitions take no time to study them, thoughtful women will pause and ponder, and then teach the children who are to rule after us to love and remember.

I look on these statues and think of the man who wrought them—think of him as I saw him every day six years ago, a pale, dissatisfied, restless man, whose hands were busy with uncongenial tasks, but whose brain was haunted with noble ideals, to which he was powerless to give form or substance. Opportunity, the ultimate test of all power, came to him and at last Congress voted ten thousand dollars to Horatio Stone to execute the statue of Alexander Hamilton in Rome. And, lo! the intangible vision of the weary man is embodied in imperishable marble—the most majestic statue beneath the dome of the Capitol. A little way before it is a plaster cast, mounted high on a wooden block, of Houdin's bronze figure of Washington, the original of which is in the State Capitol at Richmond, Virginia. Such a peaked-headed, idiotic-looking Washington I never saw elsewhere. If he looked like this, it is perfectly plain why he passed through life without ever once having done anything naughty. But if he did look like this he was a stupid mortal to live with. Most of the marbles of our Pantheon are poorly set. Even the seraphic apostle of "soul liberty" stands on a box covered with cinnamon-colored cambric, and his martial brother does likewise. Abraham Lincoln is ensconced within an unpainted wooden fence, and the great lawgivers of Connecticut stand in their big cloaks upon cotton covered boxes. Mrs. Ames' bust of "Lincoln" is poised on a handsome pedestal of Scotch granite; but, with few exceptions, though not utterly barren of fine marbles, the present aspect of the American Pantheon is chiefly suggestive of crudeness, shabbiness, and—the exorbitant necessity of spittoons. Over the entrance is a clock, having for its dial the wheels of a winged car, resting on a globe. In this car sits a lady called History, with a scroll and pen in hand. Oh! the story she could tell if she could tell the truth. Opposite, twenty-four Corinthian columns of variegated Potomac marble shoot to the roof, and shadow what was once the gallery of the Old Hall of Representatives. In the centre stands a horrid-looking plaster image of Liberty, modeled by Cansici;

and under it the American bird, modeled from life and cut in sandstone by Volaperti. Besides, scattered about are portraits of Henry Clay, a mosaic portrait of Lincoln, by Signor Salviato of Venice, of Charles Carroll of Carrollton, and of Joshua Giddings.

I have meant to pass nothing over that graces or disgraces our American Pantheon, that you, afar, may see it as it is. In itself it is the most majestic room in the Capitol. Set apart to enshrine the sculptured forms of illustrious dead, already its arches and alcoves are fraught with their living memoirs. Here Webster spoke, here Clay presided, here Adams died.

It is modeled from the Roman Pantheon, and its roof, at least, is like it. We have no proof that the Roman Pantheon was set apart for such a purpose as that to which our own is dedicated ; indeed, in the beginning it was supposed to be connected with the Roman baths. To-day it is chiefly sacred to art as the burial-place of Raphael. The French Pantheon, also, was comparatively poor in statues, though boasting of immense compositions in painting, by David and Gros. Herein the great men who have illustrated France appear in the forms of Fenelon, Malesherbes, Mirabeau, Voltaire, Rousseau, Lafayette, and others ; while at their feet, as befits their sex, sit History and Liberty, properly employed making wreaths for the heads of these masculine heroes. From the dome look down Clovis, Charlemagne, St. Louis, Louis XIV., XVI., XVII., Marie Antoinette, Madame Elizabeth, with a central glory to represent Deity. The dome of our own rotunda is a florid imitation of this. We have Franklin, Washington, and troops of goddesses, who look like bar-maids; but from

COMING GLORY OF THE FUTURE.

the focal apex we have omitted God, whose eye is needed for such an assembly.

The magnificent facade which leads to the Houses of Parliament in Westminster Palace is nine hundred feet long, paneled with tracery and decorated with rows of majestic statues of the kings and queens of England, from the conquest to the present time. Let us hope that it will never be defiled from beginning to end, as our own magnificent legislative halls, with tobacco-juice from the mouths of demoralized men. The earth has never had but one absolutely perfect building, in itself the final consummate flower of art—the Parthenon—consecrated first to woman, the Virgin House, sacred to Athena. Beneath its pure and perfect dome there was nothing to divert the gazer's contemplation from the simplicity and majesty of mass and outline. The whole building, without and within, was filled with the most exquisite pieces of sculpture, executed under the guidance of Phidias. The grand central figure was the colossal statue of the Virgin Goddess, wrought by the hand of Phidias himself. The weight of gold which she carried, says Thucydides, was forty talents. Could a wooden fence guard so much gold in our Christian Pantheon to-day? It was a happy thought which dedicated this old hall of the nation to national art, but it far outleaped its century. That which shall truly be the Pantheon of America is not for us. The children of later generations, a far-off procession, may come up hither to worship the diviner forms of the future, the majestic statues of the nation's best—its sons grand in manhood, its daughters divine in womanhood; but, with here and there a rare exception, our eyes who live to-day will see them not.

CHAPTER XII.

WOMEN WITH CLAIMS.

THE room itself means only grace, beauty and silence. The moment had not come for dis-illusion, thus I went forth without a word regarding its human aspect.

To-day, dear friends, we will go in and face that. We sit down in the shadow of this Corinthian pillar, and, looking out see the most noticeable fact is that this lofty apartment is thronged with women. A number are conversing with senators; others are gazing toward the doors which lead into the Senate. Some seem to be waiting with eager eyes and anxious faces; others are leaning back upon the sofas in attitudes of luxurious listlessness. Do you ask why they are here? Are they studying the stately proportions and exquisite *finesse* of the anteroom? Not at all. It is not devotion to the aesthetic arts nor the inspiration of patriotism, which brings these women thither. They are a few, only a very few, of the

THE LADIES' RECEPTION ROOM.

INSIDE THE CAPITOL.—WASHINGTON.

women—with "claims," who, through the sessions of Congress haunt the departments, the White House and the Capitol.

The dejected looking woman on the sofa opposite is a widow, with numerous small children. You may be certain by the unhopeful expression of her face that it is her own claim which, almost unaided and alone, she is trying to "work through" Congress. Her home is far distant. She borrowed money to come here, she borrows money to support her children, money to pay her own board; borrows money to pay the exorbitant fees of the claim-agent, who, constantly fanning the flame of "great expectations," assures her every day that Congress will pay her the thousands which she demands for her losses—will pay her this very session. Meantime the session is almost ended, and the widow's claim, on which hangs such a heavy load of debt and fear, lies hidden and forgotten in the pigeon-hole of the Committee of Claims. While it lies there, gathering dust, she a cheaply clad, care-faced woman, no longer young, and never pretty, has grown to be most burdensome to Senator ———, especially to the chairman of that committee. Irksome, not to be desired, is the importunate presence of this forlorn woman. No less irksome to these functionaries is the sight of her hundred sisters in distress—more or less; poor widows, with small children, with personal claims upon the Government. The chairman dreads the sight of this woman and of her like. He dreads it the more that he is perfectly certain that her case is not reached, and will not be this session. A kind-hearted man, he is unwilling to set the seal of despair on her face by telling her the truth. She finds it out at last, and then remem-

bering all his evasions, in her disappointment and hopeless
poverty, she denounces him as "deceitful and heartless,"
whereas the honorable gentleman was only trying to be
kind.   Meanwhile the Senate is too much interested in
immense claims involving millions, to be paid out of the
National Treasury, too much absorbed in the discussion
of the universal, to be able to come down to the small
particular of a poor widow, with hungry children, whose
only heritage was lost in the war.   In time, whose
cycles may be as long as those of the Circumlocution Office and the Court of Chancery—but *some* time, when
the widow has borrowed and spent more money than the
whole claim is worth, it may be investigated, and full or
partial justice done.   In either case, it will take more
than she receives to pay the many expenses which she
has incurred during her long years of waiting.   Do you
wonder that her face looks doleful while she waits for
Senator ———— to come in to answer her card, sent
into the Senate Chamber.   Here he is and we can hear
what he says, "I am very sorry, Madame; but it has
grown to be too late.   I fear that your case can not be
reached this session."   Poor woman. It would have been
better for you to have staid at home, kept out of debt,
worked with your hands to have supported your children.
That would have been a hard life, but not so hard as the
mortification, suspense, and defeat of this, and the long
years of labor after all.

See that sharp-faced woman, with darting, prying eyes.
She rushes in one door and out of another.   She hurries
back.   She meets a senator, and "button-holes him,"
after the fashion of men, and begins conversing in the
most importunate manner. He makes a retreat.   Lo! in

a moment she attacks another, leading him triumphantly to a sofa, where we witness a *teté-a-teté*, on the feminine side, carried on with marked emphasis and much gesticulation. This woman not only has one claim in Congress, she has many, and not one her own. She is a claim-agent, an office-brokeress. She buys claims, and speculates in them as so much stock. She takes claims on commission, deluding many a poor victim into the belief that "my influence" and " my friends," Senator So-and-So and Secretary P. Policy, will insure it a triumphant passage and a remunerative end, "without *fail.*" It is not strange, through sheer pertinacity and by dint of endless worrying, she often succeeds. She is purely feline in her tactics—ever alert, watchful, wary, cunning, and so she worries her victims and wins. She is one of the world's disappointed, dissatisfied ones; so, more than all else, we will be sorry for her. What God meant to be a fair life has been striven away in one weary struggle for the worldly honor and conventional *prestige* lying just above her reach. And to her the most pleasurable excitement in all the claim profession is the delusion that it affords her of personal power and of association with the great!

Pardon me, good friends, for calling a name. I *must* call it, for it is true. Here comes a very dragon of a woman. I am as afraid of her as if she had horns. I was going to say that she was a man-woman, which is the greatest monstrosity of the genus feminine. But I honor my brethren too much for such a comparison, and so will simply say—in manners, she is a dragon. The men whom she seizes must think so ; they give her her way, because they are afraid of her. Too well they know that, if they do not yield her point—if they do not at least promise her their influence—if they do not assure her that they will do all in their power to carry "*her measure*"—that she will attack them in the street, in the legislative lobbies, in the quiet of their lodgings, everywhere, anywhere, till they do. She is no covert power. She proclaims aloud that she has come to Washington to carry a measure through Congress to establish some man in power. And she does it because her tongue is a scourge and her presence a fear.

Leaning back in a chair, no one near her, you see a fair woman, whose beautiful presence seems at variance with the many anxious and angular and the few coarse women around her. The calmness of assured position, the serene satisfaction of conscious beauty, envelop her and float from her like an atmosphere. We feel it even here. Plumes droop above her forehead, velvet draperies fall about her form. We catch a glimpse of laces, the gleam of jewels. Look long into her face; its splendor of tint and perfection of outline can bear the closest scrutiny. Look long, and then say if a soul saintly as well as serene looks out from under those penciled arches, through the dilating irises of those beguiling eyes. Look, and the unveiled gaze which meets yours will tell you, as plainly as a gaze can tell, that adulation is the life of its life, and seduction the secret of its spell. This beauty would not blanch before the profanest sight; it is the beauty of one who tunes her tongue to honeyed accents, and lifts up her eyelids to lead men down to death. She comes and goes in a showy carriage. She glides through the corridors, haunts the galleries and the ante-rooms of the Capitol—everywhere conspicuous in her beauty. All who behold

her inquire, Who is that beautiful woman?, Nobody
seems quite sure. Doubt and mystery envelop her like
a cloud. "She is a rich and beautiful widow," "She is
unmarried," "She is visiting the city with her husband."
Every gazer has a different answer. There are a few,
deep in the secrets of diplomacy, of legislative venality,
of governmental prostitution, who can tell you she is one
of the most subtle and most dangerous of lobbyists. She
is but one of a class always beautiful and always successful. She plays for large stakes, but she always wins. The
man who says to her, "Secure my appointment, make sure
my promotion, and I will pay you so many thousands,"
usually gets his appointment, and she her thousands. Does
she wait like a suppliant? Not at all. She sits like an
empress waiting to give audience. Will she receive her
subjects in promiscuous assemblage? No; if you wait
long enough you will see her glide over these tessellated
floors, but not alone. Far from the ears of the crowd, in
rooms sumptuous enough for the Sybarites, this woman
will dazzle the sight of a half-demented and wholly bewildered magnate, and then tell him what prize she
wants. With alluring eyes and beguiling voice she
will besiege his will through the outworks of his senses,
and so charm him on to do her bidding. He promises
her his influence; he promises her his power; her favorite shall have the boon he demands, whether it be of
emolument or power.

Thus some of the highest prizes in the Government
are won. Unscrupulous men pay wily women to touch
the subtlest and surest springs of influence, and thus
open a secret way to their public success. No longer
the question is: Shall women participate in politics?

shall they form a controlling element in the Government? But, as there are women who will and do exert this power, shall it remain abject, covert, equivocal, demoralizing, base? Or shall it be brave and pure and open as the sun?

CHAPTER XIII.

THE CONGRESSIONAL LIBRARY.

THE most remarkable fact of the present connected with the Congressional Library, is its Librarian, Mr. Ainsworth R. Spofford.

Mr. Spofford was appointed Assistant Librarian by President Lincoln, December 31, 1864, and upon the resignation of Mr. Stephenson the same month succeeded him as Librarian. Mr. Spofford was formerly connected with the secular press of Cincinnati, Ohio, and was also engaged in the book trade in the same city. But neither fact accounts for his almost unlimited practical knowledge of books of every age and in every language. He is him-

self a vast library in epitome. If you wish to inform
yourself upon any subject under the sun, if you have any
right or privilege to inform Mr. Spofford of that fact, in
five minutes you will have placed before you a list, written down rapidly from memory, of the best works extant
upon the subject named, and in as few moments as it will
take to find them, and draw them forth from their dusty
nests, you will have them all heaped on a table before
you, ready for your search and research, and all the head-
aches they will be sure to give you.

Mr. Spofford has the credit among experts of writing
many Congressional speeches for honorable gentlemen
whose verbs and nominatives by chronic habit disagree,
and whose spelling-books were left very far behind them,
but who nevertheless are under the imperative necessity
of writing learned speeches of which their dear constituents may boast and be proud. By the way, a lady in private life in Washington,—a scholar and caustic writer,—
used to earn all her pin money, before her ship of fortune
came in, by writing, in the solitude of her room, the
learned, witty and sarcastic speeches which were thun-
dered in Congress the next day, by some Congressional Jupiter, who could not have launched such a thunder-bolt to
have saved his soul had it not been first forged and elec-
trified by a woman. The Librarian of Congress is too
much absorbed by his routine labors to have much time
or strength to spare for the writing out of Congressional
speeches. But daily and almost hourly he suggests and
supplies the materials for such speeches. When a member whose erudition is not remarkable, stands up in his
seat, backing every sentence he utters on finance, law
or politics, by great authority, more than one mentally

exclaims, "Spofford!" We know where he has been. Mr. Spofford is a slight gentleman in the prime of life, of nervous temperament with very straight, smooth hair, classic features and a placid countenance. Always a gentleman, his patience and urbanity are inexhaustible, if you have the slightest claim upon his care. If you have not, and he has no intention of being "bothered," his "shoo fly" capabilities are equally effectual. Like most book-people, Mr. Spofford's nervous life far outruns his material forces. He needs more sunshine, air and out-of-door existence, as most Americans do. Therefore I here cast him a crumb of sisterly counsel, born of gratitude and selfishness. Spend more time on the Rock Creek and Piney Branch roads, on the hills and by the sea, Mr. Spofford. Then may you live long, prosper, and grow wiser, for the sake of my books, and everybody's!

The halls of the Library of Congress are among the most chaste, unique and indestructible of all the halls of the Capitol. The Library occupies the entire central portion of the western front of the original Capitol. The west hall extends the entire length of the western front flanked by two other halls, one on the north the other on the south side of the projection.

DIAGRAM OF THE LIBRARY OF CONGRESS.

9

The west hall which a few years since made the whole
Library, is 91 feet 6 inches in length, 34 feet wide and
38 feet high, the other two halls of the same hight are
29 feet 6 inches wide and 95 feet long. The halls are
lighted by windows looking out upon the grounds of
the Capitol and by roof lights of stained glass. The
ceiling is iron and glass, and rests on foliated iron brackets each weighing a ton. The pilasters and panels are of
iron painted a neutral hue tinged with pale green and
burnished with gold leaf. The floors are of tessellated
black and white marble. The iron book-cases on either
side rise story on story, floored with cast-iron plates, protected by railings, and traversed by light galleries. Including the Law Library, these halls contain 26,148 feet,
or nearly five miles of book-shelving, and contain over
210,000 volumes. The iron floors are covered with
kamptulicon floor cloth, a compound of India-rubber and
cork, which possesses the triple advantage of being clean,
light and cheap. The leg of every chair has a pad of
solid India-rubber under it. Nobody is allowed to speak
above a whisper; thus the stolid turning, or the light flut-
ter of leaves make the only sound which stirs the silence.
Alcove after alcove line the halls, but with the exception of two devoted to novels and other light reading,
left open for the ladies of members' families, they are
all securely locked and protected by a net-work of wire,
and thus the chance of pilfering and of flirting are both
shut in behind that securely fastened little padlock.

Before the era of locking up, many books were
"abstracted" from the Library and never returned.
And it is said that the alcoves were used during the sessions of Congress by the belles of the Capitol for recep-

THE CENTRAL ROOM, CONGRESSIONAL LIBRARY,
INSIDE THE CAPITOL.—WASHINGTON.

tion rooms in which they received homage and listened to marriage proposals. The story is told of "a wealthy Southern representative gleaning materials for a speech in an upper section," who was suddenly stopped in his pursuit after knowledge above by the knowledge ascending from below that "a penniless adventurer" was that moment persuading his pretty daughter to elope in the alcove under him. It did not take the parent long to descend into that alcove. The daughter did not elope.

The halls are lined with wide tables and arm-chairs provided for all who wish to make use of the treasures of the Library. Tickets with blanks can be filled with the name of any book desired, over the signature of the applicant, who retains the book while remaining in the Library. On the back of those tickets are printed the following regulations of the Library :

1. Visitors are requested to remove their hats.
2. No loud talking is permitted.
3. No readers under sixteen years of age are permitted.
4. No book can be taken from the Library.
5. Readers are required to present tickets for all books wanted, and to return their books and take back their tickets before leaving the Library.
6. No reader is allowed to enter the alcoves.

No books can be taken out of the Library except on the responsibility of a member of Congress. Till within a very few years, books were allowed to be taken by strangers who presented a written permit to do so from a Congressional official. This courtesy resulted in the destruction and loss of so many valuable works, it had to be abolished and the stringent rules of the present time established and strictly enforced. An act of Congress provided that books can be taken out of the Library only by the President of the United States, Members of the Cabinet, Judges of the United States Supreme Court, Members of the Senate and House of Representatives, Secretary of the Senate, Clerk of the House and members of the Diplomatic Corps. This privilege of course includes the families of these official gentlemen.

Forgetting this fact, the long list of story-books and new novels often " charged" to these State names would be something ridiculous. Dealers in light literature suffer somewhat from this privilege. The copyright law and the Congressional Library together provide society and State with all the surface literature that they want during their sojourn in Washington. For reference the books are most extensively and thoroughly used by all seekers after knowledge. American and foreign authors line the tables in these quiet halls daily, and the results of their research are usually given to the world. Legal, political, and historical works are the ones most constantly called for and searched.

From 1815 to 1864 the Library was catalogued on the system adopted by Mr. Jefferson according to Bacon's Division of Science. This classification adapted to a small library was inadequate to the necessities of thousands of consulting readers. Mr. Spofford, on his advent as Librarian, went to work to simplify the system. The result was a complete catalogue of all the books in the great Library arranged alphabetically under the heads of authors. A proof of the perfection of this arrangement is, that any book hidden in the farthest corner of the most distant alcove is handed to a reader at the tables within five minutes after his application, while in the British Museum he would do well if he got it in the space of half an hour.

Till the reign of Mr. Spofford, newspapers, as valuable documentary history, had almost been ignored by the guardians of the Library. This great defect Mr. Spofford has done much to eradicate and remedy. Files of all the leading New York dailies are now regularly kept. Some unbroken files have been secured, including those of the *New York Evening Post*, from its beginning in 1801, the *London Gazette* from 1665, the French *Moniteur* (Royal, Imperial, and Republican,) from 1789, the *Illustrated London News*, the *Almanac de Gotha* from 1776, and a complete set of every newspaper ever published in the District of Columbia, including over one hundred now no more. Before the last progressive regime, even after Congress had appropriated $75,000 for the replenishing of the Library, the entire national collection did not contain a modern encyclopedia, or a file of a New York daily newspaper, or of any newspaper except the venerable *Washington National Intelligencer*. *De Bow's Review* was the only American magazine taken, "but the *London Court Journal* was regularly received, and bound at the close of each successive year!"

The Congressional Library is the only one in the world utterly fire-proof, without an atom of wood or of any combustible material in its miles of shelving. Before it attained to this indestructible state it suffered much. First from the British. On the evening of August 24, 1814, after the battle of Bladensburg, General Ross led his victorious troops into the Federal City. As they approached the Capitol a shot was fired by a man concealed in a house on Capitol Hill. The shot was aimed at the

British general, but only killed his horse. The enraged Britons immediately set fire to the house which contained the sharp-shooter, who, it is said, was a club-footed gardener-barber Irishman. The unmanageable troops were drawn up in front of the unfinished Capitol, a wooden scaffolding, occupying the place of the Rotunda, joining the two wings. They first fired a volley into the windows and then entered the building to prepare it for destruction. Admiral Cockburn ascended to the Speaker's chair, and derisively exclaimed:

"Shall this harbor of Yankee Democracy be burned? All for it say 'Aye!'"

It was carried unanimously, and the torch of the Englishman applied to the hard-earned treasures of the young Republic. The Library of Congress, used as lighting paper, was entirely destroyed. With it, two pictures of national value were burned; portraits of Louis XVI. and Marie Antoinette, which, richly framed, had been sent to the United States Government in Philadelphia, by the unfortunate French King.

While the Capitol was burning, clouds and columns of fire and smoke were ascending from the President's house and all the other public buildings of the young city. The conflagration below was dulled by the conflagration above; one of the most dreadful storms of thunder and lightning ever known in Washington, met and lighted on the British invaders, dimming and quenching their malicious fires.

In 1851 the magnificent new library-room of the Central Capitol, which now held 55,000 volumes and many works of art, was discovered to be on fire. The destruction was immense. Thirty-five thousand volumes were destroyed.

Among the valuable pictures burned at the same time were Stuart's paintings of the first five Presidents; an original portrait of Columbus; a second portrait of Columbus; an original portrait of Peyton Randolph; a portrait of Boliver; a portrait of Baron Steuben; one of Baron de Kalb; one of Cortez, and one of Judge Hanson, of Maryland, presented by his family. Between eleven and twelve hundred bronze medals of the Vattemare. Exchange, some of them more than two centuries old, were destroyed; also, an Apollo in bronze, by Mills; a very superior bronze likeness of Washington; a bust of General Taylor, by an Italian artist; and a bust of Lafayette, by David.

The divisions of Natural History, Geography, and Travels, English and European History, Poetry, Fiction, and the Mechanic Arts and Fine Arts were all burned. The whole of the Law Library escaped the fire.

It indicates the intellectual vitality of the nation that an appropriation of $10,000 was immediately made for the restoration of the Library, and by the close of the year $75,000 more for the same purpose.

Like most beginnings, that of the Congressional Library was humble in the extreme. The first provision for this great National collection was made at Philadelphia by an act of the Sixth Congress, April 24, 1800, appropriating $5,000 for a suitable apartment and the purchase of books for the use of both Houses of Congress. The first books received were forwarded to the new seat of Government in the trunks in which they had been imported. President Jefferson, from its inception, an ardent friend of the Library, called upon the Secretary of the Senate, Samuel Allyne Otis, to make a statement on the first day of the session, December 7, 1801, respecting the books, the act of Congress having provided that the Secretary of the Senate, with the Clerk of House of Representatives, should be the purchasers of the books. The Congressional provision for the Library in 1806 was $450.00.

In a report made by Doctor Samuel Latham Mitchell from New York to the House, January 20, 1806, he says:

" Every week of the session causes additional regret that the volumes of literature and science within the reach of the National Legislature are not more rich and ample. The want of geographical illustration is truly distressing, and the deficiency of historical and political works is scarcely less severely felt."

President Madison always exercised a fostering care over the Library and an act approved by him, December 6, 1811, appropriates, for five additional years, the sum of one thousand dollars annually for its use.

The whole number of books accumulated in fourteen years, from 1800 to 1814, amounted only to about three thousand volumes. The growth of the Library may be traced in the relative sums appropriated to its benefit by successive Congresses. In 1818, $2,000 were appropriated for the purchase of books. From 1820 to 1823, $6,000 were voted to buy books.

In 1824, $5,000 were appropriated for the purchase of books under the Joint Committee; also $1,546 for the purchase of furniture for the new Library in the centre building of the Capitol.

The yearly appropriation for the increase of the Library, for many successive years after the accession of General Jackson, was $5,000; these were exclusive of the appropriations made for the Law Department of the Library. In 1832 an additional appropriation of $3,000 was made for Library furniture and repairs. In 1850 the annual appropriation of $1,000 to purchase books for the Law Library was increased to $2,000. Within a year of the burning of the Library in 1851, $85,000 had been voted by Congress for the restoration of the Library and the purchase of books.

The west hall of the New Library was completed and occupied July 1, 1853. It was designed by Thomas A. Walter, the architect of the Capitol. The appropriation for miscellaneous books alone in the years 1865 and 1866 amounted to $16,000. In 1866, $1,500 were set apart for procuring files of leading American newspapers, and the sum of $4,000 was voted June 25, 1864, to purchase a complete file of selections from European periodicals from 1861 to 1864 relating to the Rebellion in the United States. July 23, 1866, the amount of $10,000 was voted by Congress for furniture for the two wings of the extension. The present magnificent halls of the Library of Congress were built at an expense of $280,500. The main hall cost $93,500, and the other two halls $187,000. The last two have been built under the superintendence of Mr. Edward Clark. Beautiful and ample as these three halls are in themselves, they are already too small to hold the rapidly accumulating treasures of the Library.

The next appropriation will take the Congressional Library out of the Capitol altogether into a magnificent building, built expressly for and devoted exclusively to the uses of the Grand Library of the Nation.

CHAPTER XIV.

A VISIT TO THE NEW LAW LIBRARY.

How a Library was Offered to Congress—Mr. King's Proposal—An Eye to Theology—The Smithsonian Library Transferred—The Good Deeds of Peter Force—National Documents—"American Archives"—Congress Makes a Wise Purchase—Eliot's Indian Bible—Literary Treasures—The Lawyers Want a Library for Themselves—Their "Little Bill" Fails to Pass—They are Finally Successful—The Finest Law Library in the World—First Edition of Blackstone—Report of the Trial of Cagliostro, Rohan and La Motte—Marie Antoinette's Diamond Necklace—A Long Life-Service—The Law Library Building—An Architect Buried Beneath his own Design—"Underdone Pie-crust"—"Justice" Among the Books—Reminiscence of Daniel Webster and the Girard Will.

A LITTLE more than a month after the burning of the Library by the British in 1814, a letter was read in the Senate, from Thomas Jefferson at Monticello, tendering to Congress the purchase of his library of nine thousand volumes.

The collection of this library had been the delight of Mr. Jefferson's life, and, long before, he had written of it as "the best chosen collection of its size probably in America." Pecuniary embarrassments had already begun to cloud his closing years, and the double hope of relieving these, and of adding to the treasures of his beloved Republic, impelled him to this personal sacrifice. In his letter to the Committee he said:

"I should be willing indeed to retain a few of the books to amuse the time I have yet to pass, which might be valued with the rest, but not included in the sum of valuation until they should be restored at my death, which I would cheerfully provide for."

The sum of $23,950 in Treasury notes, of the issue ordered by the law of March 4, 1814, was paid him. The actual number of volumes thus acquired was 6,700. Although a Mr. King, of Massachusetts, more burdened with zeal than knowledge, made a motion which called out a loud and long debate, that all books of an atheistical, irreligious, and immoral tendency should be extirpated from the Library and sent back to Mr. Jefferson, the department of Theology in his library was found to be large, sound, and valuable.

In 1866 the custody of the Library of the Smithsonian Institution, with the agreement of the Regents, was transferred to the Library of Congress. It brought forty thousand additional volumes to the Congressional Library.

When you come to Washington, you will see in the gallery of the Smithsonian Institution the bust of a noble man standing on a simple plaster column, bearing the name PETER FORCE. He, during his life, did more than any one American to rescue from oblivion the early documentary history of the United States. He came from his native city, New York, to Washington, as a printer, in 1815. In 1820 he began the publication of the *National Calendar*, an annual volume of national statistics, and also published the *National Journal*, the Administration organ during the Presidency of John Quincy Adams. In 1833 the Government entered into a contract with Mr. Force to prepare and publish a " Documentary History of the American Colonies." Nine volumes subsequently appeared under the title of the " American Archives." In preparing this work, Mr. Force gathered a collection of books, manuscripts, and papers relating to American History, unequalled by any private collection in the world. At the request of the Joint Library Committee of the Thirty-ninth Congress, Mr. Spofford, the Librarian, entered into a thorough examination of the Force Library. After spending from two to three hours per day on it for two months, he presented to Congress an exhaustive classified report of its treasures, which resulted in the purchase of the entire Force Library by the Joint Library Committee for the sum of one hundred thousand dollars, the sum offered by the New York Historical Society for the same collection. It occupies the South Hall of the Congressional Library.

Before this purchase, the largest and most complete collection of books relating to America was tucked away on the shelves of the British Museum. Among the treasures of the Force Library is a perfect copy of Eliot's Indian Bible, the last copy of which sold brought $1,000 ; forty-one different works of Cotton and Increase Mather, printed at Boston and Cambridge, from 1671 to 1735 ; complete files of the leading journals of Massachusetts, New York, Pennsylvania, Virginia, and other States, from 1735 to 1800, with 245 bound volumes of American newspapers printed prior to 1800; and these make but a small proportion of its priceless historical wealth.

February 18, 1816, a bill was introduced in the Senate to establish a Law Library at the Seat of Government, for the use of the Supreme Court of the United States. It passed that body, but never went into effect, from the non-action of the House of Representatives on the bill. July 14, 1832, [Andrew Jackson, President,] a bill was approved, entitled, " An Act to increase and improve the Law Department of the Library of Congress," which, in its four sections, contained the following provisions :

" For the present year a sum not exceeding five thousand dollars, and a farther annual sum of one thousand dollars for the period of five years, to be expended in the purchase of law books."

The number of law books owned by the Library at that time was 2,011; 639 of these belonged to the Jefferson collection. From this beginning, within forty years has grown the finest law library in the world. It contains every volume of English, Irish and Scotch reports, besides the American; an immense collection of case law, a complete collection of the Statutes of all civilized countries since 1649, filling one hundred quarto volumes. It includes the first edition of Blackstone's Commentaries, an original edition of the report of the trial of Cagliostro, Rohan and La Motte, for the theft of Marie Antoinette's diamond necklace—that luckless bauble which fanned to such fury the fatal flames of the Revolution. When Andrew Jackson became President, in 1829, he appointed John S. Meehan, a printer of Washington, the first editor and publisher of the *Columbia Star* and *United States Telegraph*, Librarian of Congress. He continued in that office till the accession of Mr. Lincoln—a period of thirty-two years. His son, Mr. C. H. W. Meehan, relinquished his boy pageship under his father, in 1832, to be transferred to the new Law Library. The lapse of forty years finds this gentleman still the special custodian of the Law Library. In 1835 he was entrusted with the choice of all books purchased for the Library, which trust he con-

tinues to hold. He adds another to the many faithful
and learned lives whose entire span is measured by devoted service to the State, under the shadow of the Capitol. In December, 1860, the Law Library was removed
into the basement room of the Capitol, just vacated by
the Supreme Court. This room is unique and beautiful.
Its vestibule is supported by pillars in clusters of stalks of
maize, with capitals of bursting ears of corn, the design
of Mr. Latrobe. The chamber itself is of semi-circular
form seventy-five feet in length. The arches of the ceiling rest upon immense Doric columns. The spandrels of
the arches are filled in with solid masonry—blocks of
sandstone, strong enough to support the whole Capitol.
Their tragic strength springs from the fact that the arch
above fell once, burying and killing beneath it its designer, Mr. Lenthal. The plan of his arch in proportion
to its height was pronounced unsafe by all who examined
the drawing, except himself. To prove his own faith
in his theory he tore away the scaffolding before the
ceiling was dry. It fell, and he was taken out hours
after, dead and mangled, from its fallen ruins. It will
never fall again. The tremendous masonry which now
supports a very light burden makes it impossible. The
Doric columns diverge from the centre to the circumference like the radii of a circle. From this centre
diverge the alcoves lined with books in the regulation
binding, likened by Dickens to "underdone pie-crust."
On the western wall near the ceiling is a group in plaster, representing Justice holding the scales, and Fame
crowned with the rising sun, pointing to the Constitution
of the United States, the work of Franzoni, the sculptor of
the History-winged clock, in the old Hall of Representa-

tives. In this room, Daniel Webster made his great speech in the Dartmouth College case, and Horace Binney his argument in the case of the Girard Will. The Librarian's semi-circular mahogany desk, with its faded green brocade draperies, once stood in the old Senate Chamber and re-echoed to the gavel of every Vice President who reigned in the Senate from 1825 to 1860.

CHAPTER XV.

THE HEAVEN OF LEGAL AMBITION—THE SUPREME COURT ROOM.

Memories of Clay, Webster and Calhoun—Legal Giants of the Past—Stately Serenity of the Modern Court—"Wise Judgment and Wine-Dinners"—The Supreme Court in Session—Soporific Influences—A Glimpse of the Veritable "Bench"—The Ladies' Gallery—The Chief Justices of the Past—Taney Left Out in the Cold—His Apotheosis—Chief Justice Chase—Black Robed Dignitaries—An Undignified Procession—The "Crier" in Court—Antique Proclamation—The Consultation Room—Every Man in his Proper Place—Gowns of Office—Reminiscence of Judge McClean—"Uncle Henry and his Charge"—Fifty Years in Office.

ONE of the few rooms in the Capitol wherein harmony and beauty meet and mingle, is the Old Senate Chamber, now the Supreme Court Room of the United States.

Here Clay, and Webster, and Calhoun,—those giants of the past, whom octogenarians still deplore with all their remembered and forgotten peers,—once held high conclave. Defiance and defeat, battle and triumph, argument and oratory, wisdom and folly once held here their court. It is now the chamber of peace. Tangled questions concerning life, liberty and the pursuit of personal happiness are still argued within these walls, but never in tones which would drown the sound of a dropping pin. Every thought is weighed, every word measured that is uttered here. The judges who sit in silence to listen and decide, have outlived the tumult of youth and the summer of manhood's fiercer battles. They have earned fruition; they have won their gowns—which, while life lasts, can never be worn by others. Theirs is the mellow afternoon of wise judgment and wine-dinners.

In the Court room itself we seem to have reached an atmosphere where it is always afternoon. The door swings to and fro noiselessly, at the pull of the usher's string. The spectators move over a velvet carpet, which sends back no echo, to their velvet cushioned seats ranged against the outer-walls. A single lawyer arguing some constitutional question, drones on within the railed inclosure of the Court; or a single judge in measured tones mumbles over the pages of his learned decision in some case long drawn out. Unless you are deeply interested in it you will not stay long. The atmosphere is too soporific, you soon weary of absolute silence and decorum, and depart. The chamber itself is semi-circular, with snow white walls and windows crimson-curtained. It has a domed ceiling studded with stuccoed mouldings and sky-lights. The technical "bench" is a row of leather backed arm-chairs ranged in a row on a low dais. Over the central chair of the Chief Justice a gilt eagle looks down from a golden rod. Over this eagle, and parallel with the bench below, runs a shallow gallery, from which many fine ladies of successive administrations have looked down on the gods below. At intervals around the white walls are set brackets on which are perched the first four Chief Justices—John Jay, John Rutledge, Oliver Ellsworth and John Marshall. There have been but six Chief Justices of the Supreme Court since its beginning. Chief Justice Taney's bust for years was left out in the cold on a pedestal within a recess of one of the windows of the Senate wing. It was voted in the Senate that it should there wait a certain number of expiatory years until in the fulness of time it should be sufficiently absolved to enter the historic heaven of its brethren.

One more is yet to be added—the grand head and face of Chief Justice Chase. The May flowers have scarcely faded since he held high court here alone. As ever his was the place of honor. A crown of white rose-buds shed incense upon his head—placed there by the beautiful daughter who crowned him in death, as in life, the first of men. Crosses, anchors and columns of stainless blossoms were heaped high above his head. Here in the silence of death, for one day and night, the great Chief Justice held Supreme Court alone.

During the session of the Supreme Court, the hour of meeting is 11 A. M. Precisely at that hour a procession of black-robed dignitaries, kicking up their long gowns very high with their heavy boots, may be seen wending their way from the robing-room to the Supreme Court room. They are preceded by the Marshal, who, entering by a side-door, leads directly to the Judges' stand, and, pausing before the desk, exclaims:

" The Honorable the Chief Justice and Associate Justices of the Supreme Court of the United States."

With these words all present rise, and stand to receive the Justices filing in. Each Justice passes to his chair. The Judges bow to the lawyers; the lawyers bow to the Judges; then all sit down. The Crier then opens the Court with these words:

" O, yea! O, yea! O, yea! All persons having business

with the honorable the Supreme Court of the United States are admonished to draw near and give their attendance, as the Court is now sitting. God save the United States and this honorable Court."

At the close of this antique little speech, the Chief Justice motions to the lawyer whose case is to be argued, and that gentleman rises, advances to the front, and begins his argument.

The chairs of the Judges are all placed in the order of their date of appointment. On either side of the Chief Justice sit the senior Judges, while the last appointed sit at the farther ends of each row. In the robing-room, their robes, and coats and hats, hang in the same order. In the consultation-room, where the Judges meet on Saturday to consult together over important cases presented, their chairs around the table are arranged in the same order, the Chief Justice presiding at the head. Both the robing and consultation-rooms command beautiful views from their windows of the city, the Potomac, and the hills of Virginia. In the former, the Judges exchange their civic dress for the high robes of office. These are made of black silk or satin, and are almost identical with the silk robe of an Episcopal clergyman. The gown worn by Judge McLlean still hangs upon its hook as when he hung it there for the last time—years and years ago. The consultation-room is across the hall from the Law Library, whose books are in constant demand by the lawyers and Judges of the Supreme Court. This room is in charge of " Uncle Henry," a colored man, who has held this office for fifty years, and, at the age of eighty, still fulfils his duties with all the alacrity and twice the devotion of a much younger man.

CHAPTER XVI.

THE "MECCA OF THE AMERICAN."

The Caaba of Liberty—The Centre of a Nation's Hopes—Stirring Reminis-
cences of the Capitol—History Written in Stone—Patriotic Expression
of Charles Sumner—Ruskin's Views of Ornament—Building "for all
Time"—"This our Fathers Did for Us"—The Parthenon and the Capitol
Compared—The Interest of Humanity—A Secret Charm for a Thought-
ful Mind—An Idea of Equality—The Destiny of the Stars and Stripes—
A Mother's Ambition—Recollections of the War—The Dying Soldier—
"The Republic will not Perish."

THE Capitol of his country should be the Mecca of
the American. It is *his* Capitol, and his country's,
through such extreme cost, that he should make pilgrim-
ages hither to behold with his own eyes the Caaba of
Liberty. This august building should gather and concentrate within its walls the holy love of country.

In our vast land the passion of nationality has become
too much diffused. It has been broken into the narrower
love bestowed upon a single State. It has been bruised
by faction. It has been broken by anarchy. But within
the walls of the Capitol, every State in the Union holds
its memories, and garners its hopes. Every hall and
corridor, every arch and alcove, every painting and
marble is eloquent with the history of its past, and the
prophecy of its future. The torch of revolution flamed
in sight, yet never reached this beloved Capitol. Its
unscathed walls are the trophies of victorious war; its

dome is the crown of triumphant freemen; its unfilled niches and perpetually growing ˉsplendor foretell the grandeur of its final consummation. Remembering this, with what serious thought and care should this great national work progress:

> "The hand that rounded Peter's dome,
> And groined the aisles of ancient Rome,
> Wrought with a sad sincerity."

Let no poor artist, no insincere spirit, assume to decorate a building in whose walls and ornaments a great nation will embody and perpetuate its most precious history. The brain that designs, the hand that executes for the CAPITOL, works not for to-day, but for all time. It was with a profound consciousness, not only of what this building is, but of all that it must yet be to the American people, that Charles Sumner, that profound lover of beauty, said, with so much feeling: "Surely this edifice, so beautiful and interesting, should not be opened to the rude experiment of untried talent. It ought not to receive, in the way of ornamentation, anything which is not a work of art." In every future work added to the Capitol, let the significant words of Ruskin, the great art critic, be remembered:

"There should not be a single ornament put upon a great civic building, without an intellectual intention. Every human action gains in honor, in grace, in all true magnificence, by its regard to things to come. There is no action nor art whose majesty we may not measure by this test. Therefore, when we build a public building, let us think that we build it for ever. Let us remember that a time is to come when men will say: 'See, this our fathers did for us.'"

Phidias created the Parthenon. Beneath his eyes it slowly blossomed, the consummated flower of Hellenic art. It has never been granted to another one man to create a perfect building which should be at once the marvel and the model of all time. Many architects have wrought upon the American Capitol, and there are discrepancies in its proportions wherein we trace the conflict of their opposing idiosyncrasies. We see places where their contending tastes met and did not mingle, where the harmony and sublimity which each sought was lost. We see frescoed fancies and gilded traceries which tell no story ; we see paintings which mean nothing but glare. But a human interest attaches itself to every form of noble building. Its very defects the more endear it to us, for, above all else, these are human. We love our Capitol, not that it is perfect, but because, being faulty, it still is great, and worthy of our reverence. Its wondrous possibilities, its inadequate fulfilment, its very incompleteness, but make it nearer kin to ourselves. Like the friend tantalizingly and delightfully faulty, its many shaded humanity is full of varied charm. It has all the secret ways of a profound nature. We fancy that we know it altogether, that we could never be lost in its labyrinths ; yet we are constantly finding passages that we dreamed not of, and confronting shut and silent doors which we may not enter. But the deeper we penetrate into its recesses, the more positively we are pervaded by its nobleness, and the more conscious we become of its magnitude and its magnificence.

No matter how we condemn certain proportions of the Capitol, it grows upon the soul and imagination more and more, as does every great object in art or nature.

Beside, the Capitol is vastly more than an object of mere personal attachment to be measured by a narrow individual standard. To every American citizen it is the majestic symbol of the majesty of his land. You may be lowly and poor. You may not own the cottage which shelters you, nor the scanty acres which you till. Your power may not cross your own door-step; yet these historic statues and paintings, these marble corridors, these soaring walls, this mighty dome, are yours. The highest man in the nation owns nothing here which does not belong equally to you. The Goddess of Liberty, gazing down from her shield, bestows no right upon the lofty which she does not extend equally to the lowliest of her sons.

The temple of Pallas Athena, the stones of Venice, the mighty mementos of a mightier Mexico do not tell to any human gazer one-half so grand a story as the Capitol of America will yet proclaim to the pilgrim of later ages. In far-off time I see it stand forth the conqueror of the forgetfulness and the indifference of men. A solemn teacher, with stern, watchful, yet silent sympathy, it will impart to a proud people the profound lesson of their past. A loving mother, it will hold before her living children the sacred faces of her dead for the emulation, the reverence, the love, of all who came after. In its halls will stand the sculptured forms of famed men, and of women great in goodness, great in devotion, great in true motherhood. Through sight and sympathy, through the inspiration of grand example, the living woman as she lays her moulding hand upon the budding heart and tender brain of the boy-man, will rise to the true dignity of the wife and mother of the Republic.

With psychical sight we see what the Capitol will one day be, to later generations; by our own heart-throbs, we know what it is to ourselves. Strength and depth are in its foundations, power and sublimity in its dome, and these are ours. Its mighty masses of gleaming marble, all veined with azure; its Corinthian capitals, flowering at the top like a palm in nature ; its tutelary statue of freedom, are joys to our eyes forever. Serene Mother of our liberties, she watches always and never wearies. When the whole land lay in shadow, when the blood of her sons ran in rivers, when her heart was pierced nigh unto death, in moveless calm she held her steadfast shield ; and gazing into her eyes, through the dimness of tears, we read the promise of peace. No matter where darkness fell, she bore the sunlight upon her crest. The dying statesman asked to be lifted up that his eyes might behold her last. The soldier, who gave his all, to perish in her name, watched for the sight of her from afar, and beheld her first with the shout of joy. When the slow river bore him back wounded from battle, he strained his eyes to catch a glimpse of Freedom on the dome, and looking up, was content, to know that he was dying for her sake.

Factions will fight and fall. Political parties will struggle and destroy each other. The passions of men are but the waves which beat and break on her feet. Above, beyond them all Freedom lives for evermore. Because she lives, Truth and Justice must survive, and the Republic will not perish.

CHAPTER XVII.

THE CAPITOL—MORNING SIGHTS AND SCENES.

WE rarely have spring in this latitude. Full panoplied, summer springs from under the mail of long lingering winter. We had a fine yesterday. From my window this morning lo! the miracle! my dear long-timed friend, the maple across the street, amazes me once more, though I declared to it last year I never would be amazed again. It beckons me, its myriad little wands all aquiver with the tenderest green, and says: "There now, you can't help it! Again I am a beauty and a wonder!" No long waiting and watching for slow budding blossoms here. Some night when we are all asleep there is a silent burst of bloom; and we wake to find the trees that we left here, when we shut our blinds on them the night before, all tremulous with new life, and the whole city set in glowing emerald.

I invite you to the western front of the Capitol, to stand with me in the balcony of the Congressional Library, to survey the city lying at our feet within the amphitheatre of hills soaring beyond, the river running its shining thread between. I am quite ready to believe what Charles Sumner said when pleading against the mooted depot site on its Central Avenue, that this city is more beautiful than ancient Rome. In itself it is absolutely beautiful, and that is enough; and it grows more and more so as the sea of greenery, which now waves and tosses about its housetops, rises each year higher and higher. The Capitol in early spring and summer is in no wise the Capitol of the winter. Every door swings wide; from the doors in the under-ground corridors to the wondrous doors, designed in Rome and cast in Munich, which open into the rotunda. What long, cool, green vistas run out from every angle. You stand beneath the dome; but your eyes find rest in the far shadow of the Virginia hills.

And so many people seem to have come under the great dome to rest. You wonder where they could all have appeared from. They are not at all the people who crowd and hurry through the corridors in winter—the claimants, the lobbyists, the pleasure-seekers from great cities who come to spend the "season" in Washington. Nearly all are people from the country, the greater proportion brides and grooms, to whom the only "season" on earth is spring—the marriage season. Pretty pairs! They seem to be gazing out upon life through its portal with the same mingling of delight and wonder with which they gaze through the great doors of the Capitol upon the unknown world beyond. Early summer always brings a great influx of bridal pairs to Washington. Whence they all come no mortal can tell; but they do come, and can never be mistaken. Their clothes are as new as the spring's, and they look charmingly vernal. The groom often seems half to deprecate your sudden glance, as if, like David Copperfield, he was afraid you thought him " very young." And yet he invites you to glance again, by his conscious air of proud possession, which says : " Behold! I may be young—very. But I have gotten me a wife ; she is the loveliest creature upon earth." The affections of the lovely creature seem to be divided between her new lord and her new clothes. She loves him, she is proud of him ; but this new suit, who but she can tell its cost. What longing, what privation, what patient toil has gone into its mouse or fawn-like folds; for this little bride, who regretfully drags her demi-train through the dust of the rotunda in summer, is seldom a rich man's daughter. You see them everywhere repeated, these two neophytes—in the hotel-parlor, in the street-cars, in the Congressional galleries.

When Jonathan read to Jane, in distant Mudville, the record of Congressional proceedings in Washington, in the *Weekly Tribune*, both imagined themselves deeply interested in the affairs of their country; but here, on the spot, how small seem Tariff, Amnesty, Civil Rights, and Ku-Klux bills beside the ridiculous bliss of these two egotists. They do not even pretend to listen. But they have some photograph cards, and seek out their prototypes below. On the whole, Jane is disappointed. She was not prepared for so many bald heads, or for so much of bad manners. After all, not one of these men, in her mind, can compare with the small law-giver, the newly-found Lycurgus by her side. Before she became calm enough to reach this judicial decision, she visited the ladies' dressing-room and shook out her damaged plumes.

"Is Washington *always* so dusty?" she asked, with a sigh, looking down on her pretty mouse-colored dress, with its piping decidedly grimed.

"Nearly always," I answered.

"Then how *can* people live here?" she exclaimed.

When she goes home, she will tell that the dome of the Capitol is very high; that Conkling looks thus, and Sumner so. But what she will tell oftenest and longest—perhaps to her children's children—will be that it was in Washington she ruined her wedding dress.

"I was married yesterday, and see how I look!" said Jane, ruefully.

"You look very pretty," I said. "It will all shake off." Wherewith Jane proceeded to shake, to wash her face, and brush her curls over her fingers. I helped her re-drape her lace shawl, and was repaid a moment later by her graceful *posé* in the front seat of the Senate Gallery, her hand in Jonathan's. It was refreshing, in the face of such a conglomeration of doubtful wisdom, to see two happy idiots, if they did not know it. The city is full of Janes and Jonathans.

The Capitol grounds are lovely as the gardens of the blessed, these hours.

The armies of violets which swarmed its green slopes a month ago are gone, and the dandelions have gone up higher, and are now sailing all around us through the deep, still air. There is a ripple in the grass that invites the early mower. The fountains toss their spray into the very hearts of the old trees that bend above them, and on the easy seats beneath their shadow, sit black and white, old and young, taking rest.

These grounds, perfect in themselves, utter but one reproach to the men legislating within yonder walls, and that, because they are not larger and meet in proportion to the august Capitol which they encircle. We pass through them out into Pennsylvania avenue—this great and yet to be fulfilled expectation. Broadway cannot compare with it in magnificent proportions. It is as wide as two Broadways, and at this hour of the afternoon its turn-outs are metropolitan. Nevertheless, judged by its trees and houses, it has a rural, second-rate look. Though here and there a lonesome building shoots up above its fellows, its average shops are shabby and small, and do not compare favorably with those of Third avenue in New York. The idealistic Statesmen of Washington and Jefferson's time modelled it to repeat the *Unter der Lindens* of Berlin. As a result, the ample rows of Lombardy poplars are defunct, and the Gradgrind politicians of to-day have voted to dump down a railroad " depot " in its very centre, because Mr. Thomas Scott wants it, and because they have free railroad-passes, and a few other little perquisites in their pockets. This, of course, is very shocking to say ; but then it is much more shocking to be true. Excepting Mr. Sumner, Mr. Morrill, Mr. Thurman and a few others, who really care for the future of Washington and who love this Capital, the remainder would, for a sufficient price, sell out the entire city, Capitol and all, to monopolies and corporations. But this broad thoroughfare, stretching straight for a mile be-

tween Treasury and Capitol, with its double drive, smooth
as a floor, its borders of bloom, its gay promenades and
flashing turn-outs has a certain splendor of its own, of
which no monopoly can wholly rob it.

Here is the Grant carriage, with its plain brown linings,
and in it Mrs. Grant and her father. A light buggy flies
past, drawn by superb horses, driven by a single occupant.
He is the President—small, slight, erect, smoking a cigar.
The courtly equipages of the Peruvian, Argentine,
Turkish and English Ministers, with liveried outriders
and beautiful women occupants, with the no less elegant
establishments of American Senators, Members and citizens, swell the gay cavalcade on this truly splendid
Corso.

Standing on the curb-stone, gazing on it with an expression which would have made Dickens wild till he
had reproduced it, stands Beau Hickman, long a character
of Washington. He is an old man, long and lean, with a
face corrugated like a wizened apple and a complexion
like parchment or an Egyptian mummy. His aspect is a
strange compound of gentility and meanness. His stove-
pipe hat, which evidently has survived many a batter-
ing, is carefully brushed; his standing collar is very stiff
and very high. His vest is greyish white, his coat is dingy
and shiny. His faded pantaloons have been darned, and
need darning again. His toes are peering through his
shoes, and they are down at the heels; yet he carries a
foppish cane and wears his hat in a rakish manner. Beau
Hickman was born a Virginia gentleman, insomuch as
he still manages to live without labor, it being the pride
of his heart that he never did anything useful in his life.
He ekes out a wretched existence by filching small sums

from friends and strangers for telling stories and relating experiences, for which he invariably demands a drink or a supper. One of the most miserable objects I ever beheld is Beau Hickman hungry, hobbling through the Senate restaurant, gazing at one table and then at another, at the comfortable people sitting by them, filling their stomachs, not one alas! asking him to partake.

Here with a sweep and swing, with head thrown back, and arms at rest, comes a man as supremely indifferent to all this show as the other is abjectly enthralled by it. This man, slowly swinging down the Avenue, is a "cosmos" in himself. Locks profuse and white, eyes big and blue, cheeks ruddy, throat bare, wide collar turned back, slouched felt hat punched in, a perfect lion apparently in muscle and vitality—this is Walt Whitman. Every sunshiny day he "loafs" and invites his soul on the Avenue, and there are other poets who do likewise. Here sometimes may be seen John James Piatt, now Librarian of the House of Representatives, with his blonde hair and brown-eyed wife, who is quite as much a poet as he is; and John Burrough the Thoreau of the Treasury Department, gentle as one of his own birds; and William O'Connor whose poetical fires burn undimmed within the same dim old walls; and, clad in mourning, Harriet Prescott Spofford, sweet poet and sweeter woman. Here of old were seen the gigantic forms of Charles Sumner and of Chief Justice Chase. When the Supreme Court is in session, at a certain hour, a company of immense gentlemen doff their long black silk gowns, and slowly and ponderously wend their way along the Avenue, in mild, dignified pursuit of exercise and dinner. Here, before the sun grows too hot, may be seen the moustached, ges-

ticulating, voluble young *attachés* of the foreign embas-
sies with the pretty girls of the West End, who they like
to flirt with but rarely marry—which is fortunate for the
girls.

I cannot divorce myself long enough from this divine
day to write about men. There is not a man on the face
of the earth that would not be tiresome if one had to think
of him, to the exclusion of this weather. To think that
there are any to be written about when I want to sit in the
sun and do nothing, stirs up a perfect rumpus between
desire and duty. I am not so fond of my duty that I
always spell it with a big " D," or in every emergency put
it foremost. I would like to put it out of sight some
times. Wouldn't you? But then I cannot. " It's too
many for me," as poor Tulliver said of his enemy. It
won't go out of sight, much less stay there. Something
clever might have come to me about tedious men if I had
not reached Lafayette Square this morning. There is that
in this new bloom so tender, so unsullied, which makes
politicians seem paltry, and all their outcry a mockery and
an impertinence. To be sure, these green arcades in their
outer bound touch another world. Beyond, and above
them, floats the flag on the Arlington House. Below, the
windows of Charles Sumner's home hint of art and beauty
within. The abodes of famous men and of beautiful
women encircle all the square. On one side the white
cornices of the Executive Mansion peer above the trees.

Almost within call are men and women whose names
suggest histories and prophecies, all the tangled phenomena of individual life. Yet how easy to forget them
all on these seats, which Gen. Babcock has made so restful—thank him. The long summer wave in the May

grass; the low, swaying boughs, with their deep, mysterious murmur, that seems instinct with human pleading; the tender plaint of infant leaves; the music of birds; the depth of sky; the balm, the bloom, the virginity, the peace, the consciousness of life, new yet illimitable, are all here, just as perfectly as they are yonder in God's solitude, untouched of man. If you need help to love a tree read the diary of Maurice de Guerin. No one else, not even Thoreau, (whose nature lacked in depth and breadth of tenderness perhaps in the deepest spiritual insight,) ever came so near or drew forth with such deep feeling the very soul of inanimate Nature. He felt the soul of the tree, heard it in the moaning of its voice as it stood with its roots bound in the earth and its arms outstretched with a never-ceasing sigh towards infinity. But why do I speak of him? He lived and died and never saw Washington.

11

CHAPTER XVIII.

FAIR WASHINGTON—A RAMBLE IN EARLY SPRING.

Washington Weather—Sky Scenery—Professor Tyndall Expresses an Opinion—A Picture of Beauty—"A City of Enchantment"—"My Own Washington"—Prejudiced Views—Birds of Rock Creek—The Parsonage—A Scene of Tranquil Beauty—A Washington May—Charms of the Season—Mowers at Work—The Public Parks—Frolics of the Little Ones—Strawberry Festivals—"Flower Gathering."

THE climate of Washington has a villainous reputation, and at certain times and seasons it deserves it. Yet it tantalizes us with days which prelude Paradise. Under their azure arch, through their beguiling air, with reluctant steps we enter winter—the oozy, clammy, coughing winter, which waits us just the other side of the gate of January. But they linger long—the preluding days. They seem reluctant to yield us to our impending foes—society and wet weather.

These are the days of days, swathed in masses of lights and color unfathomable. It is one of the wonders of Washington too rarely noted—its sky-scenery. So few people take the trouble to look at the sky save to see if "it looks like rain." All that New York can afford to give to tired mortals is a scanty slice of light through which to let a glimpse of glory down upon its palaces and catacombs of humanity. But across these banding hills, this broad amphitheatre of space, mass and sweep on, in the

empyrean, wave on wave of polarized light, with a deli-
cacy of tint, a depth of hue, an immensity of volume,
which no words can portray. This vast sea of color (in
its deeps of orange, purple and gold, which now trans-
figure the twilight sky, till the Virginia hills look like
open gates to the city of gold) Professor Tyndall, in one
of his lectures on light, in this city, said that he had never
seen approached on the other side of the Atlantic, save
by the intense refractions of light on the Alpine glaciers.

In the autumnal days, and in the advancing spring,
through the blue spaces steals a tremulous, ever hover-
ing purple, like opaline doves' necks' lustre, penetrating
all the atmosphere like the purple haze above the hills
of Rome, till the yellow walls of Arlington House, and
the snowy masses of the Capitol seem actually to shim-
mer through waves of amethystine mist. Under such a
light, some morning, spring suddenly spreads forth its
whole panoply, with a vividness of green, a prodigality
of foliage never seen in a more northern latitude. One
wide wilderness of unbroken bloom sends up its fragrance through waves of purple yellow and azure light,
and then, till the day when, without warning, summer
suddenly transmutes all into molten brass, Washington
in light and color, in bloom and fragrance, is a city of
enchantment.

Thus I have a Washington of my own, dear friends. I
never find it till some March day, when in walking down
the Capitol grounds I discover that the shining runlets
on either side of the Avenue have broken loose and are
racing free through their sluices of stone, and that all
the crocuses in the broad beds under the trees are pushing their little yellow noses out of the ground. To be

sure, they almost always draw them back again to get them out of the snow which falls after; nevertheless on that day I find my Washington. Then it is, that just as the grey lenten veil has covered and extinguished the gay season of the "German," we come unaware upon another Washington, which I vainly essay to portray for you. My season is not fashionable. No portrayer of costumes is "liberally paid" by "the most enterprising of publishers" to describe the transcendent suit which decks this season of mine. *My* Washington has no chronicler. The scribes are all so busy abusing the Capitol, depicting its follies and its crimes, that, though they have eyes, they see not, and ears, they hear not, the sights and sounds of this other Washington—fair Washington, outlying, above and beyond all.

If I could only paint for you the fathomless purples in which the hills enfold themselves, the wide glimmering rosy spaces, reaching on and on; or tell you of the nations of birds in the Rock Creek woods, which have made there a supreme haunt for naturalists; of its nations of flowers, which beckon and nod from the Rock Creek and Piney Branch roads; the anemones, the arbutus, the honeysuckle, the laurel, the violets, the innocents, covering wide acres with color and perfume; of the shy Rock Creek parsonage, built of brick brought from England more than a century ago, above whose trees the Capitol gleams, yet within whose porch you seem shut in peace away from this loud world, with the bees droning in the still warm air, and humming-birds drinking from the lilac cups; with the gentle Christian hearts which abide beneath its roof and minister beneath the shadow of its venerable church; if I could paint all these as they are, you would care for my Washington, but as I cannot, I fear that you never will.

A Washington May is the June of the north, with a pomp of color, an exuberance of foliage, an allurement of atmosphere which a northern June has not.

It is May now. All the ugly outlines and shabby old houses are softened and covered with beneficent foliage. Already the mowers are at work in the Capitol grounds and in the little public parks, and the sweetness of the slain grass pervades the atmosphere. The children are everywhere pretty things. Washington is full of them, tumbling amid the flowers and in the dirt. It is May, yet June, impatient, has reached across her sister, dropping her roses everywhere. Washington is one vast garden of roses. It is the hour of strawberry festivals and of

FLOWER GATHERING.

Miles away from the dusty town,
   Out in the beautiful June-time weather,
The wind of the south is rippling down,
   And over the purple hills of heather.

Dim, in the distance, the city walls
   Rise, like the walls of a dreary prison ;
On the healing sward where the sunshine falls,
   We stand 'mid the flowery folk arisen.

We watch their innocent eyelids ope,
   And below we hear the river flowing ;
While wilting sweet on the upland slope
   Lies the grass of the early mowing.

On through the bees and butterflies,
   The grass and the flowers, the hours are walking ;
And we seem to catch their low replies
   To the flowing waters forever talking.

We listen and question the fathomless space,
   In the deeps of its emerald silence lying,
While we watch the leaves turning face to face,
   And their lovers—the winds—wooing and sighing.

And still, like a dream, fades the dusty town,
   And dumb on our ear dies its distant murmur;
But the speech, in the stilly air steals down,
   And the fainting heart grows calmer and firmer.

Hearts that ache with a wounding smart,
   Wander out from the heedless city;
The human yearning on Nature's heart
   Is a thing that God in his love must pity.

Sorrow and sin are in the mart,
   And greed and gain killing tender feeling;
Here we draw close to the god Pan's heart,
   And feel on *our* hearts his touch of healing.

Often we ask, is there room to grow
   'Neath the bands of the earth, so hard and binding?
The wisdom of life we are fain to know;
   Does it ever pay for the pain of finding?

So, far away from the dissonant town,
   Out in the marvellous June-time weather,
We climb the hills to their blossoming crown,
   And rest and gather our flowers together.

Lo! we gather our flowers to-day,
   We are like thee, O restless river—
We loiter for play on our endless way—
   While life, our life, rolls on forever.

CHAPTER XIX.

THE WHITE HOUSE, *i. e.* THE PRESIDENT'S HOUSE.

Haunted Houses—Shadows of the Past—Touching Memories—The Little
Angels Born There—Building of the Presidential Mansion—A State of
Perpetual Dampness—Dingy Aspect of a Monarch's Palace—Outside the
White House—A Peep Inside the Mansion—The Emperor of Japan Su-
persedes the Punch-Bowl—The Unfinished "Banqueting Hall"—Glories
of a *Levée*—Magnificent Hospitalities—A Comfortable Dining-Room—
Interesting Labors of Martha Patterson—A Lady of Taste—An Amer-
ican "Baronial Hall"—The Furniture of Another Generation—A Valu-
able Steward—A Professor of Gastronomy—Paying the Professor and
Providing the Dinner—Feeding the Celebrities—Mrs. Lincoln's Unpopu-
lar Innovations—Fifteen Hundred Dollars for a Dinner—How Prince Ar-
thur, of England, was Entertained—Domestic Economy—"Not Enough
Silver"—A Tasty Soup—The Recipe for an Aristocratic Stew—Having a
"Nice Time"—Mrs. Franklin Pierce Horrified—"Going a Fishing on
Sundays"—Hatred of Flummery—An Admirer of Pork and Beans and
Slap-jacks—A Presidential Reception—Ready for the Festival—"Such a
Bore!"—Splendor, Weariness, and Indigestion—Paying the Penalty—
In the Conservatory—Domestic Arrangements—The Library—Statue of
Jefferson—Pleasant Views—Reminiscence of Abraham Lincoln.

> "All houses wherein men have lived and died
> Are haunted houses. Through the open doors
> The harmless phantoms on their errands glide,
> With feet that make no sound upon the floors."

> "There are more guests at table, than the hosts
> Invited; the illuminated hall
> Is thronged with quiet, inoffensive ghosts,
> As silent as the pictures on the wall."

THESE lines were never truer of any human habitation than of the White House at Washington.

The Nation's House! The procession of families which
the people have sent to inhabit it, in moving on to make

place for others, have left memories behind which haunt these great rooms and fill staircase, alcove, and pictorial space with historic recollections. Here human life has been lived, enjoyed, suffered and resigned, just as it is lived every day in any house wherein human beings are born, wherein they live and die. Within its walls children have first opened their eyes upon this tantalizing life, and here children have died, leaving father and mother deso- late amid all the pomp of place and state. In this room the hero Taylor laid his earthly burdens and honors down; here, by this eastern window, stood a girl-bride crowned with beautiful youth and marriage flowers. In this east room the supreme martyr of freedom, white, still and cold, received the nation who wept at his feet; in this dim cham- ber a woman-saint read her Bible and communed with God, while pardon crokers crept into secret door-ways, and passion and treason ran riot in the great rooms which she never entered.

The first child born in the White House was the grand- son of Jefferson—James Madison Randolph; and the last child who died here was " Willie " Lincoln. Here, also, President Harrison, President Taylor, and Mrs. Tyler passed through death unto life.

The corner stone of the President's house was laid October 13, 1792. We have seen how anxious Jefferson was that it should be modelled after some famous modern palace of Europe. The one, at last selected, was the country house of the Duke of Leinster. It was designed by James Hoban, and open, though not ready for occu- pancy, in the summer of 1800. The house is built of porous Virginia freestone, which accounts for the fact of its perpetual dampness, and the more expensive fact

THE RED ROOM.

INSIDE THE WHITE HOUSE.—WASHINGTON.

that no amount of money and white-lead can make it a dry and desirable abode. And yet it is always pleasant and restful to the sight when the eyes fall upon its Ionic columns, peering pure and softened through the sea of greenery which sways and dips around it. One front alone of Buckingham Palace, cost more than the entire White House. Yet, to behold it, the palace is a black and ugly pile, and in simplicity and purity of outline bears no comparison with the Nation's White House. This is 170 feet broad and 86 feet deep. Its north front has a lofty portico with four Ionic columns and a projecting screen of three columns. Between these columns pass the carriages which form a perpetual line moving on and round forever through the gay season. The house is three high stories, with the rusticated basement which reaches below the Ionic ordonnance.

The portico opens upon a spacious hall forty by fifty feet. It is divided by a row of Ionic columns, through which we pass to the reception-room opposite. This is the Red Room. Its light is dim and rosy. Its form is elliptical, and its bow window in the rear looks out on the park and away to the Potomac, as do the windows of all the corner parlors. In this room the President receives foreign ministers and the officers of the republic. The space over the marble mantel is entirely occupied with a life size painting of President Grant and his family. We pass through the Red Room into the Blue Room. All is cool azure here. The chairs, the sofas, the carpet, the paper on the wall, all are tinged with the celestial hue, flushed here and there with a tint of rose. In the Blue Room the President's wife holds her morning receptions. Here, with the daylight excluded, soft rays falling from the chandelier above, flowers in mounds and vases everywhere pouring out fragrance, surrounded by a group of ladies, chosen and invited to "assist," decked in jewels and costly raiment. One day of each week of the season, from three to five P. M., the President's wife receives her critic—the public.

The Blue Room opens into the Green Room, the most cosy and home-like of all the public parlors. It is vividly emerald, softly malachite, all touched and gleaming with gold. A large mirror covers the space above the mantel. Beside vases in the centre of the marble mantel-piece stands an exquisite clock of ebony and malachite; tall vases filled with fresh flowers rise from the carpet. On the centre table used to stand the immense punch-bowl, presented to the White House by the Emperor of Japan. It is now supplanted by a statue in bronze. The furniture is of rose-wood, cushioned with brocatelle of green and gold, while the same in heavy hangings are looped back from the lace curtains on the windows.

From the Green Room we enter the famous East Room, extending the entire eastern side of the house. It is eighty-six feet long, forty feet wide, and twenty-eight feet high. Three immense chandeliers hang from the ceiling. It has already taken on the mellowness, not of age but of use, and in aspect bears no kin to the unfinished "Banqueting Hall" in which Mrs. Adams dried the family linen, and Mrs. Monroe's little daughters played. Now, on a *levée* night, the East Room presents a sight never to be forgotten. The enormous chandeliers seem to pour the splendor of noon upon the glittering and moving host below. Satins, velvets, diamonds, plumes and laces rise and fall, and sway beside the gleaming gold lace of American officers, and the jewelled decorations of Foreign ministers.

Eight mirrors repeat the glory of the sights. Eight Presidents, from their golden frames on the wall, seem to gaze out of the past upon the feverish splendor of a new generation. The most exquisite carpet ever on the East Room was a velvet one, chosen by Mrs. Lincoln. Its ground was of pale sea green, and in effect looked as if ocean, in gleaming and transparent waves, were tossing roses at your feet.

Coming back to the Red Room, we pass into a narrow corridor, at the opposite end from which, on either side, open the family and state dining-room. The state dining-room is a staid and stately apartment, touched equally with new grace and old time grandeur. Martha Patterson, the daughter of President Johnson, redeemed it from wreck, and instead of ruin, adorned it with the harmony of her own artistic nature. The neutral-tinted walls and carpet, the green satin damask hangings on the windows, and covering of the quaint furniture, are all her choice. An antique clock and grim candlesticks, from the Madison reign, stand stiffly on the marble mantels. With the exception of a pair of modern sideboards, the furniture of this "baronial hall," solid and sombre, has descended from the eras of Washington and Jefferson.

The state dining-room, and its state dinners, are controlled entirely by "Steward Melah, the silver-voiced Italian," who was graduated from the Everett House, the Astor House, and the St. Charles, New Orleans, to the higher estate of superintending "goodies" for the palates of Diplomatists, Princes, and Members of Congress in the White House at Washington. The government pays Professor Melah for his services, but the President pays for the dinners, and he is expected to continue giving them till every foreign dignitary and home functionary, from the highest Diplomat to the most obscure Member of Congress, is invited. Mrs. Lincoln's presuming to abolish the time-honored but costly state-dinner of the White House, increased her personal unpopularity to an intense degree.

The average state-dinner costs about seven hundred dollars, the special state dinner may cost fifteen hundred dollars. The one given to Prince Arthur, of England, cost that sum, without including the wines and other beverages. The dinner proper consisted of twenty-nine courses. The President puts a sum of money into the hands of the steward, and his expenditure is supposed to be in proportion to the official rank and grandeur of the invited guests. It is said that Professor Melah wrings his hands in distress when he is about to set the State table for a supreme occasion, and exclaims to the lady of the White House, who may be looking on : " Why Madam, there is not silver enough in the White House to set a respectable free-lunch table."

At a state dinner the table is always profusely decorated with flowers, and the " first course " is invariably a soup of French vegetables, which Miss Grundy says has " never been equalled by any other soup, foreign or domestic." "It is said to be a little smoother than peacock's brains, but not quite so exquisitely flavored as a dish of nightingales' tongues ; and Professor Melah is the only man in the nation who holds in his hands the receipt for this aristocratic stew." No general conversation prevails at the state dinner. If the lady and gentleman elected to go in together happen to be agreeable to each other, they have a " nice time." If not, they have a stiff and tiresome one. Exquisite *finesse* is needed to fitly pair these mentally incongruous diners. Mike Walsh once horrified the shrinking and saintly Mrs. Franklin Pierce at a state-dinner by the story of his going " a fishing on Sunday; " while Hon. Mr. Mudsill, of Mudtown, has been known to regale dainty Madame Mimosa, of Mignonnette Manor, between the courses, with his hatred of flummeries and French dishes, and his devotion to pork and beans and slapjacks.

The President and his wife receive the guests in the Red Room at seven o'clock. Mrs. President is always attired in full evening dress, with laces and jewels, and her lady guests likewise, while each gentleman rejoices in a swallow-tail, white or tinted gloves, and white necktie. The President leads the way to the state-table with the wife of the senator the oldest in office, while Mrs. President brings up the rear of the small procession with the senatorial husband of the President's lady companion. Six wine glasses and a *bouquet* of flowers garnish each plate. From twelve to thirty courses are served, and the middle of the feast is marked by the serving of frozen punch. After hours of sitting, serving and eating, the procession returns to the Red Room in the order that it left it. Then, after a few moments of conversation, it disperses,—its honored individuals more than once heard to say in private, " Such a bore.". Yet what an ado they would make if not invited to discover for them-selves the tiresome splendor and fit of indigestion attendant upon a state-dinner.

Leaving the state dining-room behind, we pass through the western wing into the conservatory, one of the largest in the country. It is a favorite resort for lady and gen-

tlemen promenaders on reception days, lined, as it is, on
either side with the bloom and fragrance of rare exotics.
A large aquarium stands at one end, and a short passage
and flights of steps lead down to a greenhouse and
grapery filled with flowers and luscious fruit. Three
other greenhouses flourish in the gardens west of the
mansion.

The White House contains thirty-one rooms. Excepting the family dining-room, every one on the first floor is
devoted to state purposes. The basement contains eleven
rooms, used as kitchens, pantries and butler's rooms. These
are open, spacious, comfortable and cheerful to the sight.
On the second floor, the six rooms of the north front are
used as chambers by the Presidential family. The south
front has seven rooms—the ante-chamber, audience room,
cabinet room, private office of the president, and the ladies'
parlors. The ladies' or private parlor is furnished with
ebony, covered with blue satin, with hangings of blue
satin and lace. The daughter of the house has a blue
boudoir lined with mirrors—its pale blue carpet strewn
with rose-buds. The state bedroom of this floor is a
grand apartment, furnished with rose-wood and crimson
satin ; its walls hang with purple and gold. The bedstead
is high, massive, carved and canopied, its damask curtains
hanging from a gilded hoop near the ceiling. Before the
bed lie cushions for the feet ; against the walls stand two
stately wardrobes, with full length mirrors lining their
doors, while arm-chairs and couches, deeply cushioned, are
scattered over the velvet carpet. Its articles of furniture
are stained with purple devices—national, historical scenes,
and have for their arms the American Eagle. The ceiling
is profusely frescoed, and hung with a central chandelier,

THE CONSERVATORY.

INSIDE THE WHITE HOUSE.—WASHINGTON.

while in the winter a coal fire, under the marble mantle, suffuses the sumptuous room with a genial glow. One of the curiosities of the chamber is a cigar-case, inlaid with pearls and mosaics of wood from China, presented to President Grant by Captain Ammon, of the United States Navy.

The Secretaries' room, on this floor, is a large airy apartment, with mahogany furniture, set there in Martin Van Buren's time, with green curtains, twenty-five years old, on the windows. The President's business and reception-room is a large apartment, looking out on the southern grounds, and carpeted with crimson and white. A large black walnut table, surrounded with chairs, stands in the centre of the room. It is furnished with black walnut desks and sofas. On the mantel stands a clock which tells the time of day and the day of the month, and which is a thermometer and barometer besides. The walls are high, and frescoed on a yellow ground tint. Tapestry and lace curtains are looped back from the windows, which look down upon the lovely southern grounds, and to the river, gleaming at intervals through the foliage beyond.

The stateliest room on this floor is the library, used in Mrs. John Adams' time as a reception-room, furnished then in crimson. It was almost bookless till Mr. Filmore's administration, when it was fitted up as a library, and many books were added during the administration of President Buchanan. It is now lined with heavy mahogany book-cases, finished with solid oak, covered with maroon. It is sometimes used by the President as an official reception-room, and sometimes as an evening lounging-place for the Presidential family and their guests.

On the north lawn of the President's house, which in

Jefferson's time was a barren, stony, unfenced waste, under the green arcade made by glorious trees, now stands a bronze statue of Jefferson. It was presented to the government by Captain Levy, of the United States' army, who in 1840 owned Monticello.

From the great portico, we look beyond this statue, across Pennsylvania avenue, to an equestrian image of Jackson, rearing frantically and preposterously in the centre of Lafayette square. Lovely Lafayette square, laid out by Downing—perfect in blending tint and outline, flower of mimic parks! Beyond its trees we catch a glimpse of its encircling historic houses, and of the brown ivy-hung walls of St. John's venerable church, its tiny and old time tower showing so picturesquely against the evening sky.

The avenue of lofty trees on the west side of the President's house—beneath whose shade, in the dimness of the night, Lincoln used to take his solitary walk, and carry his heavy heart to the War Department—were planted by John Quincy Adams. No swelling tree-crowned knolls, no grassy glades could be more restful to the sight than the southern grounds of the President's house. From its height it looks down upon this rolling park, reaching now to the Potomac, bounded by its gleaming waters, on which so many white sails drift, and doze, and dream in the languid summer weather.

CHAPTER XX.

LADIES OF THE WHITE HOUSE.

A Morning Dream—Wives and Daughters of the Presidents—Memories of
Martha Washington—An Average Matron of the 18th Century—Educa-
tional Disadvantages—Comparisons—A Well-Regulated Lady—A Useful
Wife—Warm Words of Abigail Adams—Advantages of Having a Dis-
tinguished Husband—A Modern Lucretia—Washington's Inauguration
Suit—An Awkward Position for a Lady—A Primitive *Levée*—Festivities
in Franklin Square !—Decorous Ideas of the Father of His Country—
The Government on Its Travels—Transporting the Household Gods—
Keeping Early Hours—Primitive Customs—A Dignified *Congé*—Much-
Shaken Hands—Remembrances of a Past Age—An English Manufacturer
" Struck with Awe "—Very Questionable Humility—The Room in which
Washington Died—Days of Widowhood—A Wife's Congratulations—A
True Woman—Domestic Affairs at the White House—An Unfinished
Mansion—Interesting Details—A Woman's Influence—A Monument
Wanted—Devotion of a Husband—The " Single Life "—Theodocia Burr
and Katherine Chase—" *Levées* " Summarily Abolished—Disappointed
Belles—An Extraordinary Reception—Blacked His Own Boots—A Dig-
nified Foreigner Shocked—Governmental Enquiries—Womanly Indig-
nation—The Poet Pardoned—" The Sweetest Creature in Virginia "—
A Daughter's Affection.

SITTING in the lovely Blue Room this June morning,
the breezes from the Potomac floating through the
closed blinds and lace curtains, drifting over the mounds
of flowers which, rising high above the great vases, fill
all the air with fragrance, I evoke from the past a company of fair and stately women who have dwelt under
this roof, or influenced the life and happiness of men who
have ruled the nation.

12

First, Martha Washington. To be sure, she never reigned in the Blue Room; but who can recall the wives of the Presidents and not see the very first, the serenely beautiful old lady whose face is so familiar to us all.

In herself, Martha Washington was in no wise a remarkable woman. Personally, she was a fair representative of the average American matron of the eighteenth century. I say American, for whatever may be her right to boast of superior educational advantages to-day, in the time of Martha Washington and Abigail Adams, New England ignored utterly the education of her women. They were shut out even from the Boston High-School, because they had flocked to it in such numbers in pursuit of knowledge. While her brother went to Harvard, the girl of Massachusetts, if taught at all, was self-taught. Massachusetts had no right to boast over Virginia in that day. The daughters of the cavalier probably were oftener taught to dance and to play the spinnet than the daughters of the Puritans; but neither could spell, nor many more than barely read. But had Martha Washington enjoyed the highest mental privileges, she would never have been known to the world as an intellectual woman, or as a woman who, by any impulse of her unassisted nature, would ever have risen above the commonplace. She could spin, but she could not spell. She could bask in the warmth of the bountiful home whose heavy cares were all carried by her illustrious husband. She could pack the family coach with delicacies, and go through storm and mud once a year to his camp, when the perils of his country had made him its deliverer; but it is doubtful if any impulse of her soul would ever have roused her to the majestic eloquence of Abigail Adams, who, when she read the English King's proclamation to his rebellious colonies, with her little children about her in the depth of the night, wrote to her absent husband: " This intelligence will make a plain path for you, though a dangerous one. I could not join to-day in the petition of our worthy pastor for a reconciliation between our no longer parent state, but tyrant state, and these colonies. Let us separate ; they are unworthy to be our brethren. Let us renounce them, and instead of supplications as formerly for their prosperity and happiness ; let us beseech the Almighty to blast their counsels and bring to naught all their devices."

Abigail Adams comes down to posterity, independently of all relations to others, as one of the grandest women of her time. Martha Washington's only claim to veneration is because she was the wife of Washington. As his wife, her homely virtues and moral rectitude show to unclouded advantage. Personally, her most marked characteristics were her strong natural sense of propriety and fitness and high moral qualities. In these, if she never added lustre to it, she always honored the name of Washington. We see the former characteristic in the fact, that during the Revolution she never wore foreign or costly attire. While all the outer affairs of the estate, to their minutest detail, were superintended by General Washington, in addition to the mighty burdens of state which he bore, Mrs. Washington superintended her handmaidens and spinning-wheels. Looms were constantly plying in her house, and General Washington wore, at his first inauguration, a full suit of fine cloth woven in his own house. At a ball given in New Jersey, in honor of herself, Martha Washington appeared in "simple russet gown," with a white handkerchief about her neck. To the state *levées* of New York and Philadelphia she carried the same stately simplicity. A lady of the olden time, a daughter of Virginia, her ideas of court forms and etiquette had all been received from the mother country. Hers was the difficult task to harmonize aristocratic exclusiveness with republican plainness. She was never to forget that she was the wife of the President of a Republic,—and also never to forget that she was to command the respect of the old monarchies who were ready to despise everything poor and crude in the efforts of the new government to maintain itself in poverty, difficulty and inexperience. Thus the social *levées* of the first President of the United States, at No. 3, Franklin square, New York, were held under the most rigorous and exclusive rules. They were only open to persons of privileged rank and degree, and they could not enter unless attired in full dress. The receptions of Mrs. Washington merely reproduced, on a smaller plan, the customs and ceremonies of foreign courts.

The first President and his wife never forgot their personal dignity, and never forgot that they represented a republic which was already an object of interested scrutiny to the whole civilized world. President Washington wrote to his friend Mrs. Macaulay: "Mrs. Washington's ideas coincide with my own as to simplicity of dress and everything which can tend to support propriety of character without partaking of the follies of luxury and ostentation."

In the second year of Washington's administration, the government was removed to Philadelphia, there to remain for the next ten years. The household furniture of the Washingtons was moved thither by slow and weary processes of land and water, the President, in addition to his public cares, superintending personally the preparation and embarkation of every article himself. Mrs. Washington was sick at the time, but the following year, the house of Robert Morris having been taken by the corporation, as the President's house, Mrs. Washington again opened her drawing-rooms from seven to ten P. M. Sensible woman! No haggard and faded beauties dancing all night, faded and old before their time, owed their wasted lives and powers to *her*. In Philadelphia and New York, when the clock's hand pointed to ten, she arose with affable dignity, and, bowing to all, retired, leaving her guests to do likewise. With this action, it was unnecessary to repeat the announcement which she made at the first *levée* held by her in New York, viz.: "General Washington retires at ten o'clock, and I usually precede him. Good-night."

At these *levées* Mrs. Washington sat. The guests were grouped in a circle, round which the President passed, speaking politely to each one, but *never shaking hands*. It was reserved to a later generation to shake that poor member till it has to be poulticed after official greetings. It was the habit of Mrs. Washington to return the calls of those who were privileged to pay her visits. A Philadelphia lady who, as a child, remembered her, wrote: "It was Mrs. Washington's custom to return visits on the third day. In calling on my mother she would send a footman over, who would knock loudly and announce Mrs. Washington, who would then come over with Mr. Lear. Her manners were very easy, pleasant and unceremonious, with the characteristics of other Virginia ladies."

An English manufacturer, who breakfasted with the President's family in 1794, says:

"I was struck with awe and veneration when I recollected that I was now in the presence of the great Washington, the noble and wise benefactor of the world. . . . . Mrs. Washington herself, made tea and coffee for us. On the table were two small plates of sliced tongue and dry toast, bread and butter; but no broiled fish, as is the custom here. She struck me as being somewhat older than the President, though I understand both were born the same year. She was extremely simple in her dress, and wore a very plain cap, with her gray hair turned up under it."

It is as the wife of Washington, through sentiments called out by the greatness of his character and the love which she bore him, that the moral capacity of Martha Washington's nature ever approaches greatness. In her reply to Congress, who asked that the body of George Washington might be placed beneath a monument in the capitol which his patriotism had done so much to rear, her words rise to the patriotic grandeur of Abigail Adams, they could not rise higher. She says:

" Taught by that great example, which I have so long had before me, never to oppose my private wishes to the public will, I must consent to the request made by Congress, which you have had the goodness to transmit to me, and in doing this, I need not, I cannot say what a sacrifice of individual feeling I make to a sense of public duty."

But it is in the little room at Mount Vernon, in which she died, that Martha Washington, as a woman, comes nearest to us. Here one can realize how utterly done with earth, its pangs and glory, was the soul who shut herself within its narrow walls, there to take on immortality. The rooms of Washington below, a thrifty mechanic of the present day would think too small and shabby for him. Here he died. And when the great soul went forth to the unknown, as a human presence to inhabit it never more, the wife also went forth, and never again crossed its threshold. Here, in this little room, scarcely more than a closet, surrounded only by the simplest necessaries of existence, Martha Washington lived out the lonely days of her desolate widowhood—and here she died.

Abigail Adams was the first wife of a President who ever presided at the White House—the President's house, as it was so fitly called in those days. Only in this latter time of degenerate English has it swelled into the " Executive Mansion."

In February, 1797, John Adams was elected President of the United States, to succeed President Washington. From her country home in Massachusetts, Mrs. Adams sent to her husband the following recognition of his exaltation to be chief ruler of the United States:

" You have this day to declare yourself head of a nation. ' And now, O Lord, my God, thou hast made thy servant ruler over the people, give unto him an understanding heart, that he may know how to go out and to come in before this great people ; that he may discern between good and bad. For who is able to judge this, thy so great a people ? ' were the words of a royal sovereign, and not less applicable to him who is invested with the chief magistracy of a nation, though he wear not a crown nor the robes of royalty. My thoughts and meditations are with you, though personally absent ; and my petitions to heaven are, that the things which make for your peace may not be hidden from your eyes. My feelings are not those of pride or ostentation upon the occasion. They are solemnized by a sense of the obligations, the important trusts, and numerous duties connected with it. That you may be enabled to discharge them with honor to yourself, with justice and impartiality to your country, and with satisfaction to this great people, shall be the daily prayer of yours—"

In such exaltation of spirit, and with such grandeur of speech, did the wife of the second President receive the fact of her husband's elevation. As devout as Deborah, her utterance is equally marked by its comprehensiveness of view, its devotion and self-forgetfulness. No visions of personal finery, of fashionable entertainments and show, gleam through the grand utterances of this majestic woman. And yet no pictures of the White House, no sketches of the social life of her time begin to be as graphic, frequent and " telling," as those of Abigail Adams. Nothing has been more quoted than her sketch of the White House as she found it.

" The house is upon a grand and superb scale, requiring about thirty servants to attend and keep the apartments in proper order, and perform the ordinary business of the house and stables—an establishment very well proportioned to the President's salary. The lighting the apartments from the kitchen to parlors and chambers, is a tax indeed, and the fires we are obliged to keep to secure us from daily agues is another very cheering comfort. To assist us in this castle, and render less attendance necessary, bells are wholly wanting, not one single one being hung through the whole house, and promises are all you can obtain. This is so great an inconvenience that I know not what to do or how to do. The ladies from Georgetown and in the city have many of them visited me. Yesterday I returned fifteen visits. But such a place as Georgetown appears! Why, our Milton is beautiful. But no comparisons ; if they put me up bells, and let me have wood enough to keep fires, I design *to be pleased*. But surrounded with forests, can you believe that wood is not to be had, because people cannot be found to cut and cart it. . . . . We have indeed come into a new country.

"The house is made habitable, but there is not a single apartment finished, and all within side, except the plastering, has been done since B. came. . . . . If the twelve years in which this place has been considered as the future seat of government, had been improved as they would have been in New England, very many of the present inconveniences would have been removed. It is a beautiful spot, capable of any improvement, and the more I view it the more I am delighted with it.

. . . .

"The ladies are impatient for a drawing-room : I have no looking-glasses but dwarfs, for this house; and a twentieth part lamps enough to light it. My tea-china is more than half missing. . . . . You can scarcely believe that here in this wilderness city I should find my time so occupied as it is. My visitors, some of them, came three or four miles. The return of one of them is the work of one day. . . . . We have not the *least fence, yard, or other conveniences without*, and the great unfinished audience-room—(the East room) I make a drying-room of to hang my clothes in. Six chambers are made comfortable ; two lower rooms, one for a common parlor and one for a ball-room."

Abigail Adams is an illustrious example of the grandeur of human character. She proved in herself how potent an individual may be, and that individual a woman, in spite of caste, of sex, or the restrictions of human law or condition. She never went to school in her life, yet her thoughtful utterances will live where the labored utterances of her scholarly husband are forgotten. She was less than a year the mistress of the President's house, yet she has lived ever since in memory a grand model to all who succeed her. The daughter of a country clergyman, the wife of a patriotic and ambitious man, whether she gathered her children about her or sent them forth across stormy seas, while she left herself desolate ; whether she

stood the wife of the Republican Minister before the
haughty Charlotte in the stateliest and proudest court of
Europe; whether she presided in the President's house in
the new Capital or in the wilderness, or wrote to statesmen and grandchildren in her own lowly house in Quincy,
in prosperity or sorrow, in youth and in age, in life and
in death, always she was the regnant woman, devout,
wise, patriotic, proud, humble and loving.

Her pictures of the social life of her time are among
the most acute, lively and graphic on record. While in
her letters to her son, to her husband, to Jefferson and
other statesmen, we find some of the grandest utterances
of the Revolutionary period. Cut off by her sex from
active participation in the struggles and triumphs of the
men of her time, not one of them would have died more
gladly or grandly than she, for liberty; denied the power
of manhood, she made the most of the privileges of
womanhood. She instilled into the souls of her children
great ideas; she inspired her husband by the hourly sight
of a grand example; she gave, through them, her life-
long service to the State, and she gave to her country
and to posterity her spotless and heroic memory. Tardy
Massachusetts! You build monuments to your sons, and
ignore the fame of your illustrious daughters. When in
the Pantheon of the States you shall place the sculptured
forms of two of your patriots, honor your ancient fame
by giving to posterity the majestic lineaments of the great
woman of the Revolution—Abigail Adams.

In her portrait, Stuart gives us Minerva in a lace cap.
Dainty and delicate, it softens without veiling her august
features. The exquisite lace ruff about the throat, the
lace shawl upon the shoulders, all indicate the finest of

feminine tastes, while the broad brow, wide eyes, keenly cut nose, firm chin and slightly imperious mouth, proclaim the proud and powerful intellect, and the high head the commanding moral nature of the woman.

The wife of Jefferson died in her youth. His love for her was the passion of his life. In his love, and in his existence, she was never supplanted. Ever after, he lived in his children, his grand-children, his books and the affairs of State.

Jefferson had two daughters, the only two of his children who survived to mature life. One of these, Maria, who in childhood went to Paris in the care of Mrs. Adams, and who was remarkable for her beauty and the loveliness of her nature, died in early womanhood. She was indifferent to her own beauty, and almost resented the admiration which it called forth, exclaiming, "You praise me for *that* because you can not praise me for better things." She set an extraordinary value upon talent, believing that the possession of it alone could make her the worthy companion of her father. She was most tenderly beloved by him, and, at the time of her early death, he wrote to his friend, Governor Page: "Others may lose of their abundance; but I, of my want, have lost even the half of that I had. My evening prospects now hang on the slender thread of a single life." This "single" life was that of Martha Jefferson Randolph. She lived to be not only the domestic comforter, but the intellectual companion of her father. She was one of that type of daughters, of which, in our own country, Theodocia Burr and Katherine Chase have been such illustrious examples. These women, equally beautiful, intellectual, and charming, identified

themselves not only with the private interests, but
with the public life and political ambitions of their
fathers.

Had Martha Jefferson been less womanly and domestic,
she might have made herself famous as a *belle*, a wit, or a
scholar. Married at seventeen, the mother of twelve
children, seven of whom were daughters, the fine quality
of her intellect, and the nobility of her soul were all
merged into a life spent in their guidance, and in devotion and service to her husband and father. The mother
of five children at the time of her father's inauguration as
President of the United States, separated from Washington
by a long and fatiguing journey, which could only be
performed by coach and horse-travel, Mrs. Randolph never
made but two visits to the President's house, during his
two terms of office. Her son, James Madison Randolph
was born in the " White House."

Jefferson began his Presidency with a certain ostentation
of democracy. One of the first declarations of his administration was, " *Levées* are done away." Remembering
what importance was attached to these assemblies by
Washington and Adams, and what grand court occasions
they were made, we can imagine the disapprobation with
which this mandate was received by the " *belles* of society."
A party of these gathered in force, and, all gaily attired,
proceeded to the President's house. On his return from a
horseback ride he was informed that a large number of
ladies were in the " *Levée* room " waiting for him. Covered with dust, spurs on, and whip in hand, he proceeded
to the drawing-room. Shade of Washington! He told
them he was glad to see them, and asked them to remain.
These *belles* and beauties received his polite salutations

with how much delight we may fancy. They never came again.

A Virginian accustomed to the service of slaves, as the President of the United States, Jefferson blacked his own boots. A foreign functionary, a stickler for etiquette, paid him a visit of ceremony one morning, and found him engaged in this pleasing employment. Jefferson apologized, saying, that being a plain man, he did not like to trouble his servants. The foreign grandee departed, declaring that no government could long survive, whose head was his own shoe-black. Jefferson gave great offense to the English Minister, Mr. Merry, because he took Mrs. Madison, to whom he happened to be talking, into dinner instead of Mrs. Merry. Mr. Merry made it an official offense which was reported to his government. Mr. Madison wrote to Mr. Monroe, who was then Minister to England, that he might be ready to answer the call of the British government for explanations. Mr. Monroe wrote back that he was glad of it, for the wife of a British under-secretary had recently been given precedence to Mrs. Monroe, in being escorted to the dinner table. Nevertheless, Mrs. Merry's nose never came down from the air, and she never again crossed the threshold of the President's house.

The same year Jefferson aroused the ire of Thomas Moore, then twenty-four years of age, and without fame, save in his own country. The President, from his altitude of six feet two-and-a-half inches, looked down on the curled and perfumed little poet, and spoke a word and passed on. This was an indignity that London's and Dublin's darling never pardoned, and he went back to lampoon, not only America, but the President. One of his attacks came into the hands of Martha Randolph, who, deeply indignant, placed it before her father in his library. He broke into an amused laugh. Years afterwards, when Moore's Irish melodies appeared, Jefferson, looking them over, exclaimed: "Why, this is the little man who satirized me so! Why, he is a poet after all. And from that moment Moore had a place beside Burns' in Jefferson's library.

John Randolph, her father's political foe, said of Martha Jefferson: "She is the sweetest creature in Virginia," and we all know that John Randolph believed that nothing "sweet" or even endurable existed outside of Virginia. In adversity and sorrow, in poverty and trial, in age as in youth, the steadfast sweetness of character, and elevation of nature, which made Martha Jefferson remarkable in prosperity, shone forth with transcendent lustre when all external accessories had fled. The daughter of a man called a free-thinker, she all her life was sweetly, simply, devoutly religious. In her letters to her daughter, "Septimia," she draws us nearer to her tender soul in its heavenly love and charity. This daughter, to his latest breath, was to Jefferson, the soul of his soul. After his retirement she not only entertained his guests, and ministered to his personal comforts, but shared intellectually all his thoughts and studies. Six months before her death, Sully painted her portrait. Her daughter says:

"I accompanied her to Mr. Sully's studio, and, as she took her seat before him, she said playfully: 'Mr. Sully, I shall never forgive you if you paint me with wrinkles.'

"I quickly interrupted, 'Paint her just as she is, Mr. Sully, the picture is for me.'

"He said, 'I shall paint you, Mrs. Randolph, as I remember you twenty years ago.'

" The picture does represent her younger—but failed to restore the expression of health and cheerful, ever-joyous vivacity which her countenance then habitually wore. My mother's face owed its greatest charm to its expressiveness, beaming, as it ever was, with kindness, good humor, gayety and wit. She was tall and very graceful ; her complexion naturally fair, her hair of a dark chestnut color, very long and very abundant. Her manners were uncommonly attractive from their vivacity, amiability and high breeding, and her conversation was charming."

CHAPTER XXI.

WIVES OF THE PRESIDENTS.

PRESIDENT JEFFERSON showed his personal appreciation as well as his official recognition of Mrs. Madison, both in his letters to his daughters and in the fact that Mrs. Madison, when the wife of the Secretary of State, presided at Jefferson's table during the absence of his own family. But it was as the wife of the fourth

President of the United States that she inaugurated the
golden reign of the President's house.

She was the only woman of absolute social genius, who
ever presided in this house. Thus the beneficence and
brilliancy of her reign was never approached before her
time, and has never been equalled since.

It is a rare combination of gifts and graces which produces the pre-eminent social queen, in any era or in any
sphere. Mrs. Madison seemed to possess them all. During
the administration of her husband she was openly declared
to be "the most popular person in the United States;"
and now, after the lapse of generations, after hosts of
women, bright, beautiful and admired, have lived, reigned,
died, and are forgotten, "Dolly Madison" seems to abide
to-day in Washington, a living and beloved presence.
The house in which her old age was spent, and from which
she passed to heaven, is every day pointed out to the
stranger as her abode. Her face abides with us as the
face of a friend, while her words and deeds are constantly
recalled as authority, unquestioned and benign.

When she began her reign in Washington, steamboats
were the wonder of the world; railroads undreamed of;
turnpike roads scarcely begun; the stagecoach slow, inconvenient, and cumbersome. The daughter of one senator, who wished to enjoy the delights of the new capital,
came five hundred miles on horseback by her father's side.
The wife of a member rode fifteen hundred miles on horseback, passed through several Indian settlements, and spent
nights without seeing a house in which she could lodge.
Under such difficulties did lovely women come to Washington, and out of such material were blended the society
of that conspicuous era.

13

When Mrs. Madison entered the President's house, the strife between the democratic and republican parties was at its highest.   Washington, above all party, had yet declared himself the advocate of the unity and force of the central power.   Jefferson had been the President of the opposition, who wished the supremacy of the masses to overrule that of the higher classes.   On these contending factions Mrs. Madison shed equally the balm of her benign nature. Not because she was without opinions, but because she was without malignity or rancor of spirit.   Born and reared a " Friend," she brought the troubled elements of political society together in the bonds of peace.   She possessed, in pre-eminent degree, the power of intuitive adaptation to individuals, however diversified in character, and the exquisite tact in dealing with them, which always characterizes the true social queen.   She loved human beings and delighted in their fellowship.   She never forgot an old friend, and never neglected the opportunity of making a new one.   She banished from her drawing-room the stately forms and ceremonials which had made the receptions of Mrs. Washington and Mrs. Adams very elegant and rather dreadful affairs.   She was very hospitable, and a table bountifully loaded was her delight and pride. The abundance and size of her dishes were objects of ridicule to a Foreign Minister, even when she entertained as the wife of the Secretary of State, he declaring that her entertainments were more like "a harvest home supper than the entertainment of a Cabinet Minister."

Mrs. Madison never forgot the name of any person to whom she had been introduced, nor any incident connected with any person whom she knew.   Able to summon these at an instant's notice, she instinctively made

each individual, who entered her presence, feel that he or
she was an object of especial interest. Nor was this mere
society-manners. Genial and warm-hearted, it was her
happiness to make everybody feel as much at ease as possible. This gentle kindness, the unknown and lowly shared
equally with the highest in worldly station. At one of
her receptions her attention was called to a rustic youth
whose back was set against the wall. Here he stood as if
nailed to it, till he ventured to stretch forth his hand and
take a proffered cup of coffee. Mrs. Madison, according
to her wont, wishing to relieve his embarrassment, and
put him at his ease, walked up and spoke to him. The
youth, astonished and overpowered, dropped the saucer,
and unconsciously thrust the cup into his breeches pocket.
"The crowd is so great, no one can avoid being jostled,"
said the gentle woman. "The servant will bring you
another cup of coffee. Pray, how did you leave your
excellent mother? I had once the honor of knowing her,
but I have not seen her for some years." Thus she talked,
till she made him feel that she was his friend, as well as his
mother's. In time, he found it possible to dislodge the
coffee cup from his pocket, and to converse with the Juno-
like lady in a crimson turban, as if she were an old acquaintance.

Like Amelia Opie, and other beautiful "Friends," who
have shone amid "the world's people," Mrs. Madison delighted in deep warm colors, the very opposite of the silver grays of a demure Quakeress. At the inauguration
ball, when Jefferson, the outgoing President, came to receive Madison, his successor, Mrs. Madison wore a robe of
buff-colored velvet, a Paris turban with a bird of paradise
plume, with pearls on her neck and arms. A chronicler

of the event says that she "looked and moved a queen."
Jefferson was all life and animation, while the new President looked care-worn and pale. "Can you wonder at
it?" said Jefferson. "My shoulders have just been freed
from a heavy burden—his just laden with it."

When a manager brought Mrs. Madison the first number in the dance, she said, smiling: "I never dance; what
shall I do with it?"

"Give it to the lady next to you," was the answer.

"No, that would look like partiality."

"Then I will," said the manager, and presented it to
her sister.

This lady, who filled every hour of prosperity with the
rare sunshine of her nature, in the hour of trial was not
found wanting, and in the face of danger rose to the dignity of heroism. Her gallant stay in the White House,
while her husband had gone to hold a council of war, and
in spite of every entreaty to leave it, is a proud fact of our
history. In vain friends brought a carriage to the door.
She refused to enter it. The following well-known letter
to her sister, proves how bravely, womanly was this hero-
ine of the President's house.

TUESDAY, August 23, 1814.

DEAR SISTER :—My husband left me yesterday to join
General Winder. He enquired anxiously whether I had the
courage or firmness to remain in the President's house until his
return, on the morrow, or succeeding day, and on my assurance
that I had no fear but for him and the success of our army, he
left me, beseeching me to take care of myself and of the Cabinet papers, public and private.

I have since received two dispatches from him, written with
a pencil ; the last is alarming, because he desires that I should

be ready at a moment's warning, to enter my carriage and leave
the city; that the enemy seemed stronger than had been reported, and that it might happen that they would reach the city
with intention to destroy it. . . . I am accordingly ready; I
have pressed as many Cabinet papers into trunks as to fill one
carriage; our private property must be sacrificed, as it is impossible to procure wagons for its transportation. I am determined
not to go myself, until I see Mr. Madison safe, and he can accompany me—as I hear of much hostility toward him. . . . .
Disaffection stalks around us. My friends and acquaintances
are all gone, even Colonel C. with his hundred men, who were
stationed as a guard in this enclosure. . . . . French John (a
faithful domestic) with his usual activity and resolution offers
to spike the cannon at the gate, and lay a train of powder which
would blow up the British, should they enter the house. To
the last proposition, I positively object, without being able,
however, to make him understand why all advantages in war
may not be taken.

Wednesday morning, twelve o'clock.—Since sunrise, I have
been turning my spy-glass in every direction and watching with
unwearied anxiety, hoping to discover the approach of my dear
husband and his friends; but, alas, I can descry only groups of
military wandering in all directions, as if there was a lack of
arms, or of spirits, to fight for their own firesides.

Three o'clock.—Will you believe it, my sister? we have had
a battle, or a skirmish, near Bladensburg, and I am still here
within sound of the cannon! Mr. Madison comes not; may
God protect him! Two messengers, covered with dust, came
to bid me fly; but I wait for him. . . . . At this late hour
a wagon has been procured; I have filled it with the plate and
most valuable portable articles belonging to the house; whether
it will reach its destination, the Bank of Maryland, or fall into
the hands of British soldiery, events must determine. Our kind
friend, Mr. Carroll, has come to hasten my departure, and is in
a very bad humor with me because I insist on waiting until the
large picture of General Washington is secured; and it requires

to be unscrewed from the wall. This process was found too tedious for these perilous moments; I have ordered the frame to be broken and the canvas taken out; it is done, and the precious portrait placed in the hands of two gentlemen of New York for safe-keeping. And now, dear sister, I must leave this house or the retreating army will make me a prisoner in it, by filling up the road I am directed to take. When I shall again write to you, or where I shall be to-morrow, I cannot tell!

On their return, the President and Mrs. Madison occupied a private house on Pennsylvania avenue till the White House was repaired. After it was rebuilt and the treaty of peace signed, the *levées* given in the East Room, in the winter of 1816, are said to have been the most resplendent ever witnessed in Washington. At these, congregated the Justices of the Supreme Court in their gowns, the Diplomatic Corps in glittering regalia, the Peace Commissioners and the officers of the late war in full dress, and the queen of the occasion in gorgeous robes and turban and bird of paradise plumes.

At one of these Presidential banquets Mrs. Madison offered Mr. Clay a pinch of snuff from her beautiful box, taking one herself. She then put her hand in her pocket, took out a bandanna handkerchief, applied it to her nose and said: "Mr. Clay, this is for rough work," and this, touching the few remaining grains of snuff with a fine lace handkerchief, "is my polisher." This anecdote is an emphatic comment on the change of customs, even in the most polished society. If Mrs. Grant, to-day, were to perpetrate such an act at one of her *levées*, the fact that it stands recorded against the graceful, gracious and glorious Dolly Madison would not save her from the taunt of being "underbred" and suggestive of the land of "snuff dippers."

Another story of Mrs. Madison illustrates the real kindness of her heart. Two plain old ladies from the West, halting in Washington for a single night, yet most anxious to behold the President's famous and popular wife before their departure, meeting an old gentleman on the street, timidly asked him to show them the way to the President's house. Happening to be an acquaintance of Mrs. Madison, he conducted them to the White House. The President's family were at breakfast, but Mrs. Madison good-naturedly came out to them wearing a dark gray dress with a white apron, and a linen handkerchief pinned around her neck. Not overcome by her plumage, and set at ease by her welcome, when they rose to depart one said : " P'rhaps you would n't mind if I jest kissed you, to tell my gals about."

Mrs. Madison, not to be outdone, kissed each of her guests, who planted their spectacles on their noses with delight, and then departed.

Poverty compelled Martha Jefferson to part with Monticello after her father's death, and the same cruel foe forced Mrs. Madison to sell Montpelier in her widowhood.

A special message of President Jackson to Congress, concerning the contents of a letter from Mrs. Madison, offering to the government her husband's manuscript record of the debates in Congress of the convention during the years 1782–1787, caused Congress to purchase it of her, as a national work, for the sum of thirty thousand dollars. In a subsequent act Congress gave to Mrs. Madison the honorary privilege of copyright in foreign countries. The degree of veneration in which she was held may be judged by the fact that Congress conferred upon Mrs. Madison the franking privilege and unanimously voted her a seat upon the Senate floor whenever she honored it with her presence ; two privileges never conferred upon any other American woman.

The last twelve years of her life were spent in Washington, in a house still standing on Lafayette square. Here, on New Year's day and Fourth of July, she held public receptions, the dignitaries of the nation, after paying their respects at the White House, passing directly to the abode of the venerable widow of the fourth President of the United States—a woman who had honored her high station by her high qualities more than it could possibly honor her.

She died at her home, Lafayette square, Washington, July, 1849, holding her mental faculties unimpaired to the last. In her later days, while suffering from great debility, she took extreme delight in having old letters read to her, whose associations were so remote that they were unknown to all about, but yet which brought back to her her own beloved past. She delighted, also, in listening to the reading of the Bible—and it was while hearing a portion of the gospel of St. John that she passed in peace into her last sleep.

Mrs. Madison was not the last President's wife whom the dangers of war exalted to heroism. Yet, with a few exceptions, she has been followed by a line of ladies of average gifts and graces, whose domestic virtues and negative characters are seen but dimly through the reflected glory of their President husbands' administrations. The faint outline which we catch of Mrs. Monroe is that of a serene and aristocratic woman, too well bred ever to be visibly moved by anything—at least in public. She was Elizabeth Kortright, of New York—an ex-British officer's daughter, a *belle* who was ridiculed by her gay friends for having refused more brilliant adorers to accept a plain member of Congress.

During Mr. Monroe's ministry to Paris, she was called " *la belle Americaine*," and entertained the most stately society of the old *régime* with great elegance. The only individual act which has survived her career, as the wife of the American minister to France, is her visit to Madame Lafayette in prison. The indignities heaped on this grand and truly great woman, were hard to be borne by an American, to whom the very name of Lafayette was endeared. The carriage of the American minister appeared at the jail. Mrs. Monroe was at last conducted to the cell of the emaciated prisoner. The Marchioness, beholding the stranger sister woman, sank at her feet, too weak to utter her joy. That very afternoon she was to have been beheaded. Instead of the messenger commanding her to prepare for the guillotine, she beheld a woman and a friend ! From the first moment of its existence the American Republic had *prestige* in France. The visit of the American ambassadress changed the minds of the blood-thirsty tyrants. Madame Lafayette was liberated the next morning,—she gladly accepted her own freedom, that she might go and share the dungeon of her husband.

The same quiet splendor of spirit and bearing reigned through Mrs. Monroe in the unfinished " White House." Mrs. Madison maintained the courtly forms copied from foreign courts—but the richness of her temperament and the warmth of her heart pervaded all the atmosphere around her with a genial glow. Mrs. Monroe mingled very little in the society of Washington, and secluded herself from the public gaze, except when the duties of her position compelled her to appear. Her love was for silence, obscurity, peace, not for bustle, confusion, or glare. Yet, even in her courtly reign, " the dear people " were many and strong enough to arise and push on to their rights in the " people's house."

James Fennimore Cooper has left on record a letter describing a state dinner and *levée*, during Mr. Monroe's time, and any one who has survived a latter-day jam at the President's house, will say it was precisely what a Presidential reception was in the stately Monroe day. Says Mr. Cooper:

The evening at the White House, or drawing-room, as it is sometimes pleasantly called, is in fact, a collection of all classes of people who choose to go to the trouble and expense of appearing in dresses suited to an evening party. I am not sure that even dress is very much regarded, for I certainly saw a good many there in boots. . . . . Squeezing through a crowd, we achieved a passage to a part of the room where Mrs. Monroe was standing, surrounded by a bevy of female friends. After making our bow here, we sought the President. The latter had posted himself at the top of the room, where he remained most of the evening, shaking hands with all who approached. Near him stood the Secretaries and a great number of the most distinguished men of the nation. Besides these, one meets here a great variety of people in other conditions of life. I have known a cartman to leave his horse in the street, and go into the reception room, to shake hands with the President. He offended the good taste of all present, because it was not thought decent that a laborer should come in a dirty dress on such an occasion ; but while he made a mistake in this particular, he proved how well he understood the difference between government and society.

It is very doubtful, however, if a cartman would have

found it possible to have paid his respects to the government in the person of Washington, in such a plight. Such a visitor in the Blue Room, to-day, would make a sensation. In spite of the "cartman," we read that at Mrs. Monroe's drawing-rooms "elegance of dress was absolutely required." On one occasion, Mr. Monroe refused admission to a near relative, who happened not to have a suit of small-clothes and silk hose, in which to present himself at a public reception. He was driven to the necessity of borrowing.

When the Monroes entered the White House, it had been partly rebuilt from its burning in 1814, but it could boast of few comforts, and no elegance. The ruins of the former building lay in heaps about the mansion; the grounds were not fenced, and the street before it in such a condition that it was an hourly sight to see several four-horse wagons "stalled" before the house. In the early part of the administration, the East Room was the play-room of Mrs. Monroe's daughters. It was during her reign here that the stately furniture, which now stands in the East Room, was bought by the government in Paris. Each article was surmounted by the royal crown of Louis XVIII. This was removed, and the American Eagle took its place. These chairs and sofas have more than once been "made over, good as new," but the original eagles remain, more brightly burnished than ever. May they gleam forever, and let no "modern furniture," with surface gilding and thin veneering, take the place of this historic furniture, in the Nation's house, fraught, as it is, with so many memories of the illustrious dead.

CHAPTER XXII.

A CHAPTER OF GOSSIP.

Quaint Habiliments—Portrait of a President's Wife—A Travelling Lady—
Life in Russia—A Model American Minister—A Long and Lonely Jour-
ney—When Napoleon Returned from Elba—The Court of St. James—
" Mrs. Adams' Ball "—Mr. John Ogg's Little " Poem "—Verses which
Our Fathers Endured—Peculiar Waists—Costume of an Ancient *Belle*—
Fearful and Wonderful Attire of a *Beau*—" A Suit of Steel "—" Smiling
for the Presidency"—Attending Two Balls the Same Evening—An As-
cendant Star—A Man who Hid his Feelings—The Candidate at a Cattle
Show—" She Often Combed Your Head "—" I Suppose She Combs
Yours Now "—Giving " Tone " to the Whole Country—A Circle of
" Rare " Women—A " Perpetual Honor to Womanhood "— Charles's
Opinion of His Mother—How a Lady " Amused" Her Declining Days—
Lafayette's Visit to Washington—His Farewell to America—" A Species
of Irregular Diary "—" For the Benefit of My Grandfather "—Mrs. An-
drew Jackson—A Woman's Influence—Politics and Piety Disagree—
Why the General Didn't Join the Church—A Head " Full of Politics "—
Swearing Some—The President Becomes a Good Boy—Domestic Ten-
dencies—His Greatest Loss—Sad News from the Hermitage.

THE portrait which Leslie gives us of Louisa Catharine
Johnson, the wife of John Quincy Adams, reminds
us in outline and costume of the Empress Josephine and
the Court of the first Napoleon.

She wears the scanty robe of the period, its sparse outline revealing the slender elegance of the figure, the low
waist and short sleeves trimmed with lace and edged with
pearls. One long glove is drawn nearly to the elbow, the
other is held in the hand, which droops carelessly over the
back of the chair. There is a necklace round the throat.

From over one shoulder, and thrown over her lap, is a mantle of exquisite lace. The close bands of the hair, edged with a few deft curls, and fastened high at the back with a coronet comb, reveals the classic outline of the small head; the face is oval, the features delicate and vivacious; the eyes, looking far on, are beautiful in their clear, spiritual gaze. This is the portrait of a President's wife, whose early advantages of society and culture far transcended those of almost any other woman of her time.

The daughter of Joshua Johnson, of Maryland, she was born, educated and married in London. As a bride she went to the court of Berlin, to which her husband was appointed American Minister on the accession of his father to the Presidency. In 1801 she went to Boston, to dwell with her husband's people, but very soon came to Washington as the wife of a senator. On the accession of Madison, leaving her two elder children with their grandparents, she took a third, not two years of age, and embarked with her husband for Russia, whither he went as United States Minister.

Nothing could be more graphic than the diary which she kept on this voyage. It consumed three months. Summer merged into winter before the little wave-and-wind-beaten bark touched that then inhospitable shore. The first American Minister to Russia, Mr. Adams lived in St. Petersburg for six years, " poor, studious, ambitious and secluded." Happily for him, his wife possessed mental and spiritual resources, which lifted her above all dependence on surface or conventional attention from the world, and made her in every respect the meet companion of a scholar and patriot.

In the wake of furious war, through storm and snowdrifts, through a country ravaged by passion and strife, she traveled alone, with her only child, from St. Petersburg to Paris, whither she went to meet her husband. Here she witnessed the storm of delight which greeted Napoleon on his return from Elba. Mr. Adams was appointed Minister to the Court of St. James, and after a separation of six years Mrs. Adams was re-united to her children.

In 1817 Mr. Monroe, on his accession to the Presidency, immediately appointed John Quincy Adams Secretary of State, when Mrs. Adams returned with him to Washington. For eight years she was the elegant successor of Mrs. Madison, who filled the same position with so much distinction. No one was excluded from her house on account of political hostility—all sectional bitterness and party strife were banished from her drawing-rooms.

As the wife of the Secretary of State, Mrs. Adams gave a famous ball, whose fame still lives in Washington. "Mrs. Adams's Ball" lives in history as well as in the memories of a few still living. It was given January 8th, 1824, in commemoration of General Jackson's victory at New Orleans. It was announced in advance by the newspapers, and on the morning before its occurrence its splendor was anticipated and celebrated by the following lines written by Mr. John Agg, who has passed into oblivion, although his early poems in his native England were said to have been taken for Byron's, and although he was one of the first of newspaper correspondents and the first short-hand reporter ever in Washington.

The ladies referred to in the following lines were among the most celebrated beauties of their day, many of whose descendants still live in Washington.

MRS. ADAMS'S BALL.

[From the Washington *Republican*, Jan. 8th, 1824.]

Wend you with the world to-night?
Brown and fair, and wise and witty,
Eyes that float in seas of light,
Laughing mouths and dimples pretty,
Belles and matrons, maids and madams,
All are gone to Mrs. Adams's.
There the mist of the future, the gloom of the past,
All melt into light at the warm glance of pleasure ;
And the only regret is, lest melting too fast,
Mammas should move off in the midst of a measure.

Wend you with the world to-night?
Sixty grey, and giddy twenty,
Flirts that court, and prudes that slight,
Stale coquettes and spinsters plenty.
Mrs. Sullivan is there
With all the charms that nature lent her ;
Gay M'Kim, with city air,
And charming Gales, and Vandeventer ;
Forsyth, with her group of graces ;
Both the Crowninshields in blue ;
The Peirces, with their heavenly faces,
And eyes like suns, that dazzle through ;
Belles and matrons, maids and madams,
All are gone to Mrs. Adams's.

Wend you with the world to-night?
East and West, and South and North,
Form a constellation bright,
And pour a blended brilliance forth.
See the tide of fashion flowing,
'Tis the noon of beauty's reign ;
Webster, Hamiltons are going,
Eastern Lloyd and Southern Hayne ;
Western Thomas, gaily smiling ;
Borland, nature's *protégé ;*

Young De Wolfe, all hearts beguiling;
Morgan, Benton, Brown and Lee;
Belles and matrons, maids and madams,
All are gone to Mrs. Adams's.

Wend you with the world to-night?
Where blue eyes are brightly glancing,
While to measures of delight
Fairy feet are deftly dancing;
Where the young Euphrosyne
Reigns, the sovereign of the scene,
Chasing gloom and courting glee
With the merry tambourine.
Many a form of fairy birth,
Many a Hebe yet unwon;
Wirt, a gem of purest worth,
Lively, laughing Pleasanton,
Vails and Taylor will be there;
Gay Monroe, so *débonnaire*,
Helen, pleasure's harbinger,
Ramsay, Cottringers, and Kerr;
Belles and matrons, maids and madams,
All are gone to Mrs. Adams's.

Wend you with the world to-night?
Juno in her court presides,
Mirth and melody invite,
Fashion points and pleasure guides!
Haste away then, seize the hour,
Shun the thorn and pluck the flower.
Youth, in all its spring-time blooming,
Age, the guise of youth assuming,
Wit, through all its circle gleaming,
Glittering wealth, and beauty beaming;
Belles and matrons, maids and madams,
All are gone to Mrs. Adams's.

The picture of this celebrated entertainment is still

extant, and shows the *belles* in the full dress of the period, when the dress waists ended just under the arms, and its depth, front and back, was not over three or four inches. The skirts, narrow and plain, were terminated by a flounce just resting on the floor. The gloves reached to the elbow, and were of such fine kid that they were often imported in the shell of an English walnut. Slippers and silk stockings of the color of the dress were worn, crossed and tied with gay ribbons over the instep. The hair was combed high, fastened with a tortoise-shell comb—the married ladies wearing ostrich feathers and turbans. While the *belles* were thus attired, their *beaux* were decked in blue coats, and gilt buttons, with white or buff waistcoats, white neck-ties and high " chokers," silk stockings and pumps.

In this picture Daniel Webster, Clay and Calhoun are conspicuous in this dress. General Jackson, wearing bowed pumps, with Mrs. Adams on his arm, make the central figures of the assembly. Mrs. Adams wore " a suit of steel." The dress was composed of steel llama; her ornaments for head, throat and arms, were all of cut steel, producing a dazzling effect. General Jackson's entire devotion to her, during the evening, was the subject of comment. After the manner of to-day, it was declared that he was " smiling for the Presidency." He was the lion of the evening. All the houses of the first ward were illuminated in his honor. Bonfires made the streets light as day, and the " sovereign people " shouted his name and fame. The same evening, he attended a ball given by the famous dancing-master, Carusi, and finished the festivities, celebrating his glory by the side of the reigning lady, the wife of the Secretary of State.

14

That night fixed his presidential star in the ascendency. A few days later the name of Calhoun was withdrawn as the nominee of his party, and that of Jackson put in its place. The house, a double one, in which this famous ball was given, still stands unaltered, on F street, opposite the Ebbitt House. A portion of it was long occupied as lodgings by Hon. Charles Sumner.

Through fiery opposition, John Quincy Adams was elected President. From the time she became mistress of the President's house, failing health inclined Mrs. Adams to seek seclusion, but she still continued to preside at public receptions. Her vivacity and pleasing manners did much to warm the chill caused by Mr. Adams' apathy or apparent coldness. Those who knew him, declared that he had the warmest heart and the deepest sympathies, but he had an unfortunate way of hiding them. It is told that when he was candidate for the Presidency, his friends persuaded him to go to a cattle show. Among the persons who ventured to address him, was a respectable farmer who impulsively exclaimed : " Mr. Adams, I am very glad to see you. My wife, when she was a gal, lived in your father's family ; you were then a little boy, and she has often combed your head."

" Well," said Mr. Adams, in a harsh voice, " I suppose she combs yours now ? "

The poor farmer slunk back extinguished. If he gave John Quincy his vote, he was more magnanimous than the average citizen of to-day would be to so rude a candidate.

A writer of her time speaks of Mrs. Adams' " enchanting, elegant and intellectual *régime*," declaring that it should give tone to the whole country. Her fine culture, intellectual tastes, and charming social qualities, combined to attract about her a circle of rare and distinguished women. Among these were Mrs. Richard Rush, Mrs. Van Rensselaer, the wife of the Patroon, and Mrs. Edward Livingston. Notwithstanding the opposition of her husband's politics, Mrs. Livingston was Mrs. Adams' most intimate friend; a lady whom any land might be proud to claim, and whose memory lives a perpetual honor to womanhood.

Mrs. Adams' son, Charles Francis Adams, writing of his mother in 1839, says:

" The attractions of great European capitals, and the dissipations consequent upon high official stations at home, though continued through that part of her life when habits become the most fixed, have done nothing to change the natural elegance of her manners, nor the simplicity of her tastes. . . . . To the world, Mrs. Adams presents a fine example of the possibility of retiring from the circles of fashion, and the external fascinations of life, in time still to retain a taste for the more quiet, though less showy attractions of the domestic hearth.

A strong literary taste, which has caused her to read much, and a capacity for composition in prose and verse, have been resources for her leisure moments; not with a view to that exhibition which renders such accomplishments too often fatal to the more delicate shades of feminine character, but for her own gratification, and that of a few relatives and friends.

The late President Adams used to draw much amusement, in his latest years at Quincy, from the accurate delineation of Washington manners and character, which was regularly transmitted, for a considerable period, in letters from her pen. And if, as time advances, she becomes gradually less able to devote her sense of sight to reading and writing, her practice of the more homely virtues of manual industry, so highly commended in the final chapter of the book of Solomon, still amuses the declining days of her varied career.''

Mrs. Adams was the "lady of the White House" when, in 1825, Lafayette visited the United States, and, at the invitation of the President, spent the last weeks of his stay at the "Executive Mansion," from which, on the seventh of September, he bade his pathetic farewell to the land of his adoption.

Notwithstanding the rare qualities of mind and heart which she brought to it, and the popularity which she attained in it, her son writes :

"Her residence in the President's house I have always considered as the period she enjoyed the least during the public career of my father. All this appears more or less in her letters, and especially in a species of irregular diary which she kept for some time at Washington, for the benefit of my grandfather, John Adams, then living at Quincy, and of her brother, who was residing in New Orleans."

Mrs. Adams died May 14, 1852, and was buried beside her husband, in the family burying ground at Quincy, Massachusetts.

In mental attainments, there was an absolute contrast between Mrs. Adams and Rachel Donaldson, the next President's wife.

Mrs. Andrew Jackson never entered the President's house in visible form, for she had passed from earth before her husband became the Chief Magistrate of the Nation. Yet it is doubtful if the wife of any other President ever exerted so powerful and positive an influence over an administration in life as did she in death.

Born and reared on the frontiers of civilization, her educational advantages had been most scanty, and she

never mastered more than the simplest rudiments of knowledge. Yet, looking on her pictured face, it is easy to
fathom and define the power which, through life and beyond the grave, held the master will of the husband who
loved her in sweet abeyance. It was a power purely
womanly—the affectional force of a woman of exalted
moral nature and deep affections. It was impossible that
such a woman should use arts to win love, and equally
impossible that she should not be loved. Men would love
her instinctively, through the best and highest in their
natures.

With the wound of her loss fresh and bleeding, President Jackson entered upon his high office. Thus in death
Rachel Jackson became the tutelary saint of the President's house. Wherever he went, he wore her miniature.
No matter what had been the duties or pleasures of the
day, when the man came back to himself, and to his lonely
room, her Bible and her picture took the place of the
beloved face and tender presence which had been the one
charm and love of his heroic life.

No other President's wife looks down upon posterity
with so winsome and innocent a gaze as Rachel Jackson.
A cap of soft lace surmounts the dark curls which cluster
about her forehead, falling veil-like over her shoulders.
The full lace ruffle around her neck is not fastened with
even a brooch, and, save the long pendants in her ears,
she wears no ornaments. Her throat is massive, her lips
full and sweet in expression, her brow broad and rounded,
her eye-brows arching above a pair of large, liquid, gazelle-
like eyes, whose soft, feminine outlook is sure to win and
to disarm the beholder. This remarkable loveliness of
spirit and person was the source of fatal sorrow to Rachel

Jackson. It won her reverence, amounting almost to adoration, but it made her also the victim of jealousy, envy and malice. These made the shadow always flung athwart the sunshine of love which made her life.

She was a woman of deep personal piety, and longed for nothing so much as the time when her husband would be done with political honors, as he had assured her that then, and not till then, could he " be a Christian." The following anecdote, told by the late Judge Bryan of Washington, illustrates the piety of her character and the profound personal influence she held over the moral nature of her husband :

The father of Judge Bryan, an intimate friend of Mrs. Jackson, was on a visit to the Hermitage. Mrs. Jackson talked to him of religion, gave him a hymn to read that was sung at a late funeral, and said the General was disposed to be religious, and she believed would join the church but for the coming presidential election ; that his head was now full of politics. While they were conversing, the General came in with a newspaper in his hand, to which he referred as denouncing his mother as a camp follower. " This is too bad ! " he exclaimed, rising into a passion and swearing terribly as our " army in Flanders." When nearly out of breath, his wife approached him and, looking him in his face, simply said : *Mr.* Jackson. He was subdued in an instant, and did not utter another oath.

In the same presidential contest this gentle being did not herself escape calumny. When her husband was elected President of the United States, she said : " For Mr. Jackson's sake, I am glad ; for my own, I never wished it." To an intimate friend she said in all sincerity : " I assure you I would rather be a door-keeper in the house

of my God than to dwell in that palace in Washington."
Dearer to her heart was the Hermitage, with the little
chapel built by her husband for her own especial use, than
all the prospective pomp of the President's house.

She was a mother to every servant on the estate, and
anxious to make every one comfortable during her absence in Washington. She made numerous journeys to
Nashville, to purchase, for all left behind, their winter supplies. Worn out, after a day's shopping, she went to the
parlor of the Nashville Inn to rest. While she waited
there for the family coach which was to convey her back
to the Hermitage, she heard her own name spoken in the
adjoining room. She was compelled to hear, while she sat
there, pale and smitten, the false and cruel calumnies
against herself which had so recklessly been used during
the campaign to defeat her husband, and which he had
zealously excluded from her sight in the newspapers.
Here the arrow came back from the misfortune of her
youth, when she married a man intellectually and morally
her inferior, from whom she was afterwards divorced, and
it entered her gentle heart too deep to be withdrawn.
She was seized almost immediately with spasmodic disease
of the heart. Everything possible was done for her relief without avail. A few nights afterwards she exclaimed :
"I am fainting," was lifted to her bed, and in a few moments had breathed her last sigh.

The grief of her husband amounted to agony. It
seemed for a time that his frame must break under such
grief, but he lived to worship and serve her memory for
many years. December 23, 1828, a great ball and banquet was to have been given in Nashville, in honor of
General Jackson's victory at New Orleans. The whole,

city was gay with preparations, when the word came from the Hermitage: "The President's wife is dead!"

From that hour her husband seemed to live to avenge her wrongs and to honor her memory. Probably into no other administration of the government, from its first to the present, has personal feeling had so much to do with official appointments as in the offices emptied and filled by Andrew Jackson. It had only to enter his suspicion that a man had failed to espouse the cause of the beloved Rachel, and his unlucky official head immediately came off. It was told him that Mr. Watterson, the Librarian of Congress, had told, or listened to something to the detriment of Mrs. Jackson, and Mr. Watterson was immediately deposed. Thus she was avenged at times, probably in acts of personal injustice, but in her own pure tones she spoke through him in all the higher acts of his administration. Thus it was in spirit that Rachel Jackson lived and reigned at the White House.

The "lovely Emily" Donelson, wife of Andrew Jackson Donelson, Mrs. Jackson's nephew and adopted son, with Mrs. Andrew Jackson, Jr., the wife of another adopted son, shared together the social honors of the White House during the administration of President Jackson. The delicate question of precedence between them was thus settled by him. He said to Mrs. Jackson: "You, my dear, are mistress of the Hermitage, and Emily is hostess of the White House."

This Emily was of remarkable beauty, strongly resembling Mary, Queen of Scots. Her manners were of singular fascination, and she dressed with exquisite taste. The dress she wore at the first inauguration is still preserved. It is an amber-colored satin, brocaded with *bou-*

quets of rose-leaves and violets, trimmed with white lace and pearls. It was a present from General Jackson, and even at that day, before"Jenkins"supposed birth, it was described in every paper of the Union. General Jackson always called her "my daughter." She was the child of Mrs. Jackson's brother, and married to her cousin. She was quick at repartee, and possessed the rare gift of being able to listen gracefully. A foreign minister once said: "Madame, you dance with the grace of a Parisian. I can hardly realize that you were educated in Tennessee."

"Count, you forget," was the spirited reply, "that grace is a cosmopolite, and, like a wild flower, is found oftener in the woods than in the streets of a city."

Her four children were all born in the White House. But in the midst of its honors, in the flower of her youth, "the lovely Emily" went out from its portals to die. She sought the softer airs of "Tulip Grove," her home in Tennessee, where she died of consumption, December, 1836. A lady gives the following picture of an evening scene at the White House, in the early part of Jackson's administration:

"The large parlor was scantily furnished; there was light from the chandelier, and a blazing fire in the grate; four or five ladies sewing around it; Mrs. Donelson, Mrs. Andrew Jackson, Jr, Mrs. Edward Livingston. Five or six children were playing about, regardless of documents or work-baskets. At the farther end of the room sat the President, in his arm-chair, wearing a long loose coat, and smoking a long reed pipe, with bowl of red clay—combining the dignity of the patriarch, monarch, and Indian chief. Just behind, was Edward Livingston, the Secretary of State, reading a dispatch from the French Minister for Foreign Affairs. The ladies glance admiringly, now and then, at the President, who listens, waving his pipe toward the children, when they become too boisterous."

CHAPTER XXIII.

SCENES AT THE WHITE HOUSE—MEN AND WOMEN OF NOTE.

THREE of the first four Presidents of the United States married widows. Jefferson, Jackson, Martin Van Buren, and Tyler, were all widowers while occupying the White House. Neither Washington, Jefferson, Madison, or Monroe, left sons to succeed them. The wife of Martin Van Buren died in her youth, long before he had grown to high political honors. She had been dead seventeen

years when, as the eighth President of the United States,
he entered the White House.   During his administration,
its social honors were dispensed by his daughter-in-law,
Mrs. Abram Van Buren, born Angelica Singleton, of South
Carolina, who entered upon her duties and pleasures as a
bride.   She was of illustrious lineage, possessed finely
cultivated powers, and "is said to have borne the fatigue
of a three hours' *levée* with a patience and pleasantry
inexhaustible."   Doubtless she shared some of the help
which bore Mr. Monroe triumphantly through a similar
scene.

"Are you not completely worn out?" inquired a friend.

"O, no," replied the President.   "A little flattery will
support a man through great fatigue."

Anna Symmes, the wife of President Harrison, a lady
of strong intelligence and deep piety, never came to the
White House.   Her delicate health forbade it, when her
husband made his presidential journey to Washington.
In a little more than a month he was borne back to her,
redeemed by death.   She survived, almost to the age of
ninety, to bid sons and grandsons Godspeed when they
went forth to fight for their country—as she had bidden
her gallant husband the same, when he left her amid
her flock of little ones, in the days of her youth, for the
same cause.   From time to time sons and grandsons came
from the field of battle to receive her blessing anew.   She
said to one: "Go, my son.   Your country needs your
services.   I do not.   I feel that my prayers in your behalf will be heard, and that you will return in safety."
And the grandson did come back to receive her final blessing, after many hard-fought battles.   Her only surviving

son writes: "That I am a firm believer in the religion of Christ, is not a virtue of mine. I imbibed it at my mother's breast, and can no more divest myself of it, than of my nature."

Mrs. Letitia Christian Tyler, wife of the tenth President of the United States, was another sensitive, saintly soul, whose children rise up to-day, and call her blessed. She died in the White House, September 10, 1842. Her daughter-in-law, Mrs. Robert Tyler, writing of the event, says:

"Nothing can exceed the loneliness of this large and gloomy mansion, hung with black, its walls echoing only sighs and groans. My poor husband suffered dreadfully when he was told his mother's eyes were constantly turned to the door, watching for him. He had left Washington to bring me and the children, at her request. She had every thing about her to awaken love. She was beautiful to the eye, even in her illness; her complexion was clear as an infant's, her figure perfect, and her hands and feet were the most delicate I ever saw. She was refined and gentle in every thing that she said and did; and, above all, a pure and spotless Christian. She was my *beau ideal* of a perfect gentlewoman.

"The devotion of father and sons to her was most affecting. I don't think I ever saw her enter a room that all three did not spring up to lead her to a chair, to arrange her footstool, and caress and pet her."

Mrs. Robert Tyler presided at the White House till June, 1844, when President Tyler was married to Julia Gardiner, of Gardiner's Island, New York, a youthful beauty and *belle*. After many vicissitudes Mrs. Tyler entered the Catholic church, and now resides in Georgetown. Like

Mrs. Madison, she has returned to the scenes of her early triumphs, and during the sessions of Congress may often be seen in the diplomatic gallery of the senate chamber, a stately black-eyed matron dressed in deep mourning.

Mrs. Polk, intellectually, was one of the most marked women who ever presided in the White House. A lady of the old school, educated in a strict Moravian Institute, her attainments were more than ordinary, her understanding stronger than that of average women; but she obeyed St. Paul, and held her gifts in silence. She never astonished or offended her visitors by revealing to them the depth or breadth of her intelligence; nevertheless she used that intelligence as a power — the power behind the throne. Never a politician, in a day when politics, by precedent and custom, were forbidden grounds to women, she no less was thoroughly conversant with all public affairs, and made it a part of her duty to inform herself thoroughly on all subjects which concerned her country, or her husband.

She was her husband's private secretary, and, probably, was the only lady of the White House who ever filled that office. She took charge of his papers, he trusting entirely to her memory and method for their safe keeping. If he wanted a document, long before labeled and "pigeonholed," he said: "Sarah knows where it is;" and it was "Sarah's" ever ready hand that laid it before his eyes. At the age of twenty she came to Washington as the wife of Mr. Polk, then a Member of Congress from Tennessee. Many years of her youth and prime were spent at the Capital, and, as she had no children, she had more than ordinary opportunity to devote herself exclusively to the service of her husband. She was the wife of the Speaker of the House before she was the wife of the President of the United States, and in every position seems to have commanded superlative respect and admiration on her own behalf, aside from the honor always paid to the person holding high station. Many poems in the public prints were addressed to her—one, while she was the wife of a Member of Congress, by Judge Story. When her husband became the President, Mrs. Polk was deemed the supreme ornament of the White House, and the public journals of the land broke forth into gratulation that the domestic life of the Nation's house was to be represented by one who honored American womanhood. Mrs. Polk was tall, slender, and stately, with much dignity of bearing, and a manner said to resemble that of Mrs. Madison. The stateliness of her presence was conspicuous, and so impressed an English lady, that she declared that "not one of the three queens whom she had seen, could compare with the truly feminine, yet distinguished presence of Mrs. Polk."

Mrs. Polk was considered a very handsome woman. Her hair and eyes were very black, and she had the complexion of a Spanish donna. Without being technically "literary," she was fond of study, and of intellectual pursuits, and possessed a decided talent for conversation. In her youth, she became a member of the Presbyterian church, and through a long life her character has been eminently a Christian one. Always devout, her piety in later years is said to have merged into austerity; but even in the prime of her beauty and power, she never gave her smile or presence to the dissipation, the insidiously corrupting influence of what is termed "gay life in Washington," whose baleful exponent to-day is the all-night

"German" so destructive to freshness of beauty and purity of soul.

Mrs. Polk still lives at "Polk Place," Nashville, Tennessee, a stately and noble home, like the Hermitage in this respect, that the mortal remains of its master, amid verdure and flowers, beneath the shadow of its trees, await the final call. The inscription on the monument, to the memory of President Polk, is in Mrs. Polk's own words; and here, in this home, consecrated by his death, the venerable widow of the eleventh President of the United States peacefully awaits the summons which will recall her to the Soul whose life and name it has been her chief earthly glory to embellish and to represent.

Mrs. Taylor, the wife of General Taylor, the twelfth President of the United States, was one of those unknown heroines of whom fame keeps no record. Her life, in its self-abnegation and wifely devotion, under every stress of privation and danger on the Indian's trail, amid fever-breeding swamps, and on the edge of the battle-field, was more heroic than that ever dreamed of by Martha Washington—or continuously lived by any Presidential lady of the Revolution—yet time will never give her a chronicler.

When General Taylor received the official announcement that he was elected President of the United States, among other things he said: "For more than a quarter of a century my house has been the tent, and my home the battle-field." This utterance was simply true, and through all these years, this precarious house and home were shared by his devoted wife. He was one of the hardest worked of fighting officers. Intervals of official repose at West Point and Washington never came to this young "Indian fighter." His life was literally spent in the savage wilderness, but whether in the swamps of Florida, on the plains of Mexico, or on the desolate border of the frontier, the young wife persistently followed, loved and served him. Thus all her children were born, and kept with her till old enough to live without her care; then, for their own sakes, she gave them up, and sent them back to "the settlements," for the education indispensable to their future lives—but, whatever the cost, she stayed with her husband.

The devotion to duty, and the cheerfulness under privation of this tender woman,—the wife of their chief,—penetrated the whole of his pioneer army. It made every man more contented and uncomplaining, when he thought of her. Her entire married life had been spent thus; but when her husband, as Colonel Taylor, took command against the treacherous Seminoles, in the Florida war, when the newspapers heralded the new-made discovery, that the wife of Colonel Taylor had established herself at Tampa Bay, it was considered unpardonably reckless, that she should thus risk her life, when the odds of success seemed all against her husband. Nothing could move her from her post. As ever, she superintended the cooking of his food; she ministered to the sick and wounded; she upheld the *morale* of the little army by the steadfastness of her own self-possession and hope, through all the long and terrible struggle. Time passed, and the brave Colonel of the Border became the conquering hero from Mexico, bearing triumphantly back to peace the victories of Palo Alto, Monterey, and Buena Vista, inscribed upon his banners. The obscure "Indian fighter" was at once the hero and idol of the Nation. The long day of battle and glory was ended at last, the wife thought,—and now she, the General, their children, in a four-roomed home, were to be kept together at last, in peace unbroken.

It is not difficult to imagine what a home so hardly earned, so nobly won, was to such a woman. Nor is it hard to realize that when that home was almost immediately invaded by a nomination of its chief to the Presidency of the Nation, the woman's heart at last rebelled. The wife thought no new honor could add to the lustre of her husband's renown. She declared that the life-long habits of her husband would make him miserable under the restraints of metropolitan life, and the duties of a civil position. From the first, she deplored the nomination of General Taylor to the Presidency as a misfortune, and sorrowfully said : " It is a plot to deprive me of his society, and to shorten his life by unnecessary care and responsibility."

When, at last, she came to the White House, as its mistress, she eschewed the great reception-rooms and received her visitors in private apartments. She tried, as far as possible, to establish her daily life on the routine of the small cottage at Baton Rouge, and she essayed personally to minister to her husband's comforts, as of old, till her simple habits were ridiculed and made a cause of reproach by the " opposition."

The .reigning lady of the White House, at this time, was General and Mrs. Taylor's youngest daughter, Elizabeth, or, as she was familiarly and admiringly called, " Betty Bliss." She entered the White House at the age of twenty-two, a bride, having married Major Bliss, who served faithfully under her father as Adjutant-general. Perhaps no other President was ever inaugurated with

15

such overwhelming enthusiasm as General Taylor—and the reception given his youngest child, who greatly resembled him, and who, at that time, was the youngest lady who had ever presided at the White House, was almost as overpowering. The vision that remains of her loveliness, shows us a bright and beaming creature, dressed simply in white, with flowers in her hair. She possessed beauty, good sense and quiet humor. As a hostess she was at ease, and received with affable grace ; but an inclination for retirement marked her as well as her mother. Formal receptions and official dinners were not to their taste. Nevertheless, these are a part of the inevitable penalty paid by all who have received the Nation's highest honor. Society, in its way, exacts as much of the ladies of the White House, as party politics do of the men who administer state affairs in it. A lack of entertainment caused part of the universal discontent, already voiced against the hero President, whose heroic ways were naturally not the ways of policy or diplomacy.

The second winter of President Taylor's term, the ladies of his family seemed to have assumed more prominently and publicly the social duties of their high position. A reception at the President's house, March 4, 1850, was of remarkable brilliancy. Clay, Calhoun, Webster, Benton and Cass, with many beautiful and cultured women, then added their splendor to society in Washington. The auguries of a brilliant year were not fulfilled. Amid the anguish of his family, President Taylor died at the White House, July 9, 1850. When it was known that he must die, Mrs. Taylor became insensible, and the agonized cries of his family reached the surrounding streets.

Dreadful to the eyes of the bereaved wife were the pomp and show with which her hero was buried.

After he became President, General Taylor said, that "his wife had prayed every night for months that Henry Clay might be elected President in his place." She survived her husband two years, and to her last hour never mentioned the White House in Washington, except in its relation to the death of her husband.

She was succeeded by a woman of superior intellect, who in a different sphere had proved herself an equally devoted wife. Mrs. Abigail Filmore, the daughter of a Baptist clergyman, grew up in Western New York, when it was a frontier and a wilderness. Yearning for intellectual culture, with all the drawbacks of poverty and scanty opportunity, she obtained sufficient knowledge to become a school-teacher. It was while following this avocation that she first met her future husband, the thirteenth President of the United States, then a clothier's apprentice, a youth of less than twenty years, himself, during the winter months, a teacher of the village school. They were married in 1826, and began life in a small house built by her husband's hands. In this little house the wife added to her duties of maid-of-all-work, house-keeper, hostess and wife, the avocation of teacher. She bore full half of the burden of life, and the husband, with the weight of care lifted from him by willing and loving hands, rose rapidly in the profession of law, and in less than two years was chosen a member of the State Legislature. Thus, side by side, they worked and struggled from poverty to eminence.

Strong in intellect and will, her delights were all feminine. Her tasks accomplished, she lived in books and

music, flowers and children.   At her death, her husband
said : " For twenty-seven years, my entire married life, I
was always greeted with a happy smile."   She entered the
White House a matron of commanding person and beautiful countenance.   She was five feet six inches in height,
with a complexion extremely fair and pure, blue, smiling
eyes, and a wealth of light-brown curling hair.   A personal friend of Mrs. Filmore, writing from Buffalo, says :

" When Mr. Filmore entered the White House, he found it
entirely destitute of books.   Mrs. Filmore was in the habit of
spending her leisure moments in reading, I might almost say, in
studying.   She was accustomed to be surrounded with books of
reference, maps, and all the other requirements of a well furnished library, and she found it difficult to content herself in a
house devoid of such attractions.   To meet this want, Mr. Filmore asked of Congress, and received an appropriation, and selected a library, devoting to that purpose a large and pleasant
room in the second story of the White House.   Here Mrs. Filmore surrounded herself with her little home comforts ; here
her daughter had her own piano, harp, and guitar, and here Mrs.
Filmore received the informal visits of the friends she loved,
and, for her, the real pleasure and enjoyments of the White
House were in this room."

Mrs. Filmore was proud of her husband's success in
life, and desirous that no reasonable expectation of the
public should be disappointed.   She never absented herself from the public receptions, dinners, or *levées*, when it
was possible to be present; but her delicate health frequently rendered them very painful.   She sometimes kept
her bed all day, to favor that weak ankle, that she might
be able to endure the fatigue of the two hours she would
be obliged to stand for the Friday evening *levées*.

Mrs. Filmore was destined never to see again her old home in Buffalo, with mortal eyes. She contracted a cold on the day of Mr. Pierce's inauguration, which resulted in pneumonia, of which she died, at Willard's Hotel, Washington, 1853. What she is in the memory of her husband, may be judged by the fact—that he has carefully preserved every line that she ever wrote him, and has been heard to say that he could never destroy even the little notes that she sent him on business, to his office.

The child of this truly wedded pair, Mary Abigail Filmore, was the rarest and most exquisite President's daughter that ever shed sunshine in the White House. She survived her mother but a year, dying of cholera, at the age of twenty-two, yet her memory is a benison to all young American women, especially to those surrounded by the allurements of society and high station. She was not only the mistress of many accomplishments, but possessed a thoroughly practical education. She was taught at home, at Mrs. Sedgwick's school, in Lenox, Massachusetts, and was graduated from the State Normal School of New York, as a teacher, and taught in the higher departments of one of the public schools in Buffalo. She was a French, German, and Spanish scholar; was a proficient in music; and an amateur sculptor. She was the rarest type of woman, in whom were blended, in perfect proportion, masculine judgment and feminine tenderness. In her were combined intellectual force, vivacity of temperament, genuine sensibility, and deep tenderness of heart. She saw clearly through the forms and shows of life, her views of its duties were grave and serious; yet, in her intercourse with others, she overflowed with bright wit, humor and kindliness. Her character was revealed in her

face, for her soul shone through it. Words cannot tell
what such a nature and such an intelligence would be,
presiding over the social life of the Nation's House. She
used her opportunities, as the President's daughter, to
minister to others. She clung to all her old friends, without any regard to their position in life; her time and talents were devoted to their happiness. She was constantly
thinking of some little surprise, some gift, some journey,
some pleasure, by which she could contribute to the happiness of others. After the death of her mother, she
went to the desolate home of her father and brother, and,
emulating the example of that mother, relieved her father
of all household care; her domestic and social qualities
equalled her intellectual power. She gathered all her
early friends about her; she consecrated herself to the
happiness of her father and brother; she filled her home
with sunshine. With scarcely an hour's warning, the
final summons came. "Blessing she was, God made her
so," and in her passed away one of the rarest of young
American women.

CHAPTER XXIV.

THE WHITE HOUSE DURING THE WAR.

MRS. FRANKLIN PIERCE entered the White House under the shadow of ill-health and sore bereavement, having seen her last surviving child killed before her eyes on a railroad train, after the election of her husband to the Presidency of the United States.

Mrs. Pierce was remarkable for fragility of constitution, exquisite sensitiveness of organism, and deep spirituality of nature. She instinctively shrank from observation, and nothing could be more painful to her in average life than the public gaze. She found her joy in the quiet sphere of domestic life, and herein, through her wise counsels, pure tastes, and devoted life, she exerted a powerful influence. One who knew her writes:

"Mrs. Pierce's life, as far as she could make it so, was one of retirement. She rarely participated in gay amusements, and never enjoyed what is called fashionable society. Her natural endowments were of a high order. She inherited a judgment singularly clear, and a taste almost unerring. The cast of her beauty was so dream-like; her temper was so little mingled with the common characteristics of woman; it had so little of caprice, so little of vanity, so utter an absence of all jealousy and all anger; it was so made up of tenderness and devotion, and yet so imaginative and fairy-like in its fondness, that it was difficult to bear only the sentiments of earth for one who had so little of life's clay."

It was but natural that such a being should be the life-long object of a husband's adoring devotion. Nor is it strange that the husband of such a wife, reflecting in his outer life the urbanity, gentleness, and courtesy which marked his home intercourse, in addition to his own personal gifts, should have been, what Franklin Pierce was declared to be, the most popular man, personally, who ever was President of the United States. Notwithstanding her ill health, her shrinking temperament, and personal bereavement, Mrs. Pierce forced herself to meet the public demands of her exalted station, and punctually presided at receptions and state dinners, at any cost to herself. No woman, by inherent nature, could have been less adapted to the full blaze of official life than she, yet she met its demands with honor, and departed from the White House revered by all who had ever caught a glimpse of her exquisite nature. She died December, 1863, in Andover, Massachusetts, and now rests, with her husband and children, in the cemetery at Concord, New Hampshire.

During the administration of Mr. Buchanan, the White House seemed to revive the social magnificence of old days. Harriet Lane brought again into its drawing-rooms the splendor of courts, and more than repeated the elegance and brilliancy of fashion, which marked the administration of Mr. John Quincy Adams.

Harriet Lane, the adopted daughter of James Buchanan, and " lady of the White House " during his administration, was one of those golden blondes which Oliver Wendell Holmes so delights to portray. " Her head and features were cast in noble mould, and her form which, at rest, had something of the massive majesty of a marble pillar, in motion was instinct alike with power and grace." Grace, light and majesty seemed to make her atmosphere. Every motion was instinct with life, health and intelligence. Her superb *physique* gave the impression of intense, harmonious vitality. Her eyes, of deep violet, shed a constant, steady light, yet they could flash with rebuke, kindle with humor, or soften in tenderness. Her mouth was her most peculiarly beautiful feature, capable of expressing infinite humor or absolute sweetness, while her classic head was crowned with masses of golden hair, always worn with perfect simplicity.

As a child she was a fun-loving, warm-hearted romp.

When eleven years of age she was tall as a woman, nevertheless Mr. Buchanan, one day looking from his window, saw Harriet with flushed check and hat awry, trundling through the leading street of Lancaster a wheelbarrow, full of wood. He rushed out to learn the cause of such an unseemly sight, when she answered in confusion, "that she was on her way to old black Aunt Tabitha with a load of wood, because it was so cold." A few years later this young domestic outlaw, having been graduated with high honor from the Georgetown convent, was shining at the Court of St. James, at which her uncle was American Minister. Queen Victoria, upon whom her surpassing brightness and loveliness seemed to make a deep impression, decided that she should rank not as niece or daughter, but as the wife of the United States Minister. Thus the youthful American girl became one of the "leading ladies" of the diplomatic corps of St. James.

On the continent and in Paris she was everywhere greeted as a girl-queen, and in England her popularity was immense. On the day when Mr. Buchanan and Mr. Tennyson received the degree of Doctor of Civil Laws at the University of Oxford, her appearance was greeted by loud cheers from the students, who arose *en masse* to receive her. From this dazzling career abroad, she came back to her native land, to preside over the President's House. She became the supreme lady of the gayest administration which has marked the government of the United States. Societies, ships of war, neck-ties were named after her. Men, gifted and great, from foreign lands and in her own, sought her hand in marriage. Such cumulated pleasures and honors probably were never heaped upon any other one young woman of the United States.

At White House receptions, and on all state occasions, the sight of this golden beauty, standing beside the grand and gray old man, made a unique and delightful contrast, which thousands flocked to see. Her duties were more onerous than had fallen to the share of any lady of the White House for many years; the long diplomatic service of Mr. Buchanan abroad involving him in many obligations to entertain distinguished strangers privately, aside from his hospitalities as President of the United States. During his administration the Prince of Wales was entertained at the White House, who presented his portrait to Mr. Buchanan and a set of valuable engravings to Miss Lane, as "a slight mark of his grateful recollection of the hospitable reception and agreeable visit at the White House."

During the last troubled months of Mr. Buchanan's administration, he always spoke with warmth and gratitude of Miss Lane's patriotism and good sense. Neither he nor her country ever suffered from any conversational lapse of hers, which, in a day so rife with passion and injustice, is saying much. In 1863, Miss Lane was confirmed in the Episcopal church at Oxford, Philadelphia, of which her uncle, Rev. Edward L. Buchanan, was the rector.

In 1866, Miss Lane was married, at Wheatland, to Mr. Henry Elliott Johnston of Baltimore, a gentleman who had held her affections for many years. The congenial pair now abide in their luxurious home in Baltimore, and in private life, as wife and mother, she is as beautiful and more beloved than when, as Miss Lane, she was the proud lady of the President's House.

It was the misfortune of Mrs. Lincoln to be the only

woman personally assailed who ever presided in the White House. She entered it when sectional bitterness was at its height, and when the need of her country for the holiest and highest ministry of women was deeper than it had been in any era of its existence, even that of the Revolution. In that troubled hour, the White House needed a woman to preside over it of lofty soul, of consecrated purpose, of the broadest and profoundest sympathies, and of self-forgetting piety.

The life of the Nation was threatened. The horror of war was imminent. The capital was menaced, as it had never been before, by the treason of its own children. Wives, mothers and daughters, in ten thousand homes, were looking into the faces of husbands, sons and fathers, with trembling and with tears, and yet with sacrificial patriotism. They knew, they felt that the best-beloved were to be slain on their country's battle-fields. With what supreme devotion and consecration would Abigail Adams, or a thousand women of her heroic type, have approached the Nation's House as the wife of its President in such an hour. It was the hour for self-forgetting— the hour of sacrifice. Personal vanity and elation, excusable in a more peaceful time, seemed unpardonable in this. Yet, in reviewing the character of the Presidents' wives, we shall see that there was never one who entered the White House with such a feeling of self-satisfaction, which amounted to personal exultation, as did Mary Lincoln. To her it was the fulfillment of a life-long ambition, and with the first low muttering of war distinctly heard, on every side, she made her journey to Washington a triumphal passage.

A single month, and the President's call for troops to

protect the capital had penetrated the remotest hamlet of the land. All the manly life-blood of the Nation surged toward its defence. All the heart of its womanhood went up to God, crying for its safety. In the distant farm-house women waited, breathless, the latest story of battle. In the crowded cities they gathered by thousands, crying, only, "Let me work for my brother : he dies for me ! "

With the record of the march and the fight, and of the unseemly defeat, the newspapers teemed with gossip concerning the new lady of the White House. While her sister-women scraped lint, sewed bandages, and put on nurses' caps, and gave their all to country and to death, the wife of its President spent her time in rolling to and fro between Washington and New York, intent on extravagant purchases for herself and the White House. Mrs. Lincoln seemed to have nothing to do but to " shop," and the reports of her lavish bargains, in the newspapers, were vulgar and sensational in the extreme. The wives and daughters of other Presidents had managed to dress as elegant women, without the process of so doing becoming prominent or public. But not a new dress or jewel was bought by Mrs. Lincoln that did not find its way into the newspapers.

Months passed, and the capital had become one vast hospital. The reluctant river every hour laid at the feet of the city its priceless freight of lacerated men. The wharves were lined with the dying and dead. One ceaseless procession of ambulances moved to and fro. Our streets resounded with the shrieks of the sufferers which they bore. Churches, halls and houses were turned into hospitals. Every railroad-train that entered the city bore fresh troops to the Nation's rescue, and fresh mourners seeking their dead, who had died in its defence. Through all, Mrs. Lincoln "shopped."

At the White House, a lonely man, sorrowful at heart, and weighed down by mighty burdens, bearing the Nation's fate upon his shoulders, lived and toiled and suffered alone. His wife, during all the summer, was at the hotels of fashionable watering-places. Conduct comparatively blameless in happier times, became culpable under such exigencies and in such shadow. Jarred, from the beginning, by Mrs. Lincoln's life, the Nation, under its heavy stress of sorrow, seemed goaded at last to exasperation. Letters of rebuke, of expostulation, of anathema even, addressed to her, personally, came in to her from every direction. Not a day that did not bring her many such communications, denouncing her mode of life, her conduct, and calling upon her to fulfil the obligations, and meet the opportunities of her high station.

To no other woman of America had ever been vouchsafed so full an opportunity for personal benevolence and philanthropy to her own countrymen. To no other American woman had ever come an equal chance to set a lofty example of self-abnegation to all her countrywomen. But just as if there were no national peril, no monstrous national debt, no rivers of blood flowing, she seemed chiefly intent upon pleasure, personal flattery and adulation; upon extravagant dress and ceaseless self-gratification.

Vain, seeking admiration, the men who fed her weakness for their own political ends were sure of her favor. Thus, while daily disgracing the State by her own example, she still sought to meddle in its affairs. Woe to Mr. Lincoln if he did not appoint her favorites. Prodigal

THE CABINET ROOM.

INSIDE THE WHITE HOUSE.—WASHINGTON.

in personal expenditure, she brought shame upon the President's House, by petty economies, which had never disgraced it before. Had the milk of its dairy been sent to the hospitals, she would have received golden praise. But the whole city felt scandalized to have it haggled over and peddled from the back door of the White House. State dinners could have been dispensed with, without a word of blame, had their cost been consecrated to the soldiers' service ; but when it was made apparent that they were omitted from personal penuriousness and a desire to devote their cost to personal gratification, the public censure knew no bounds.

From the moment Mrs. Lincoln began to receive recriminating letters, she considered herself an injured individual, the honored object of envy, jealousy and spite, and a martyr to her high position. No doubt some of them were unjust, and many more unkind ; but it never dawned upon her consciousness that any part of the provocation was on her side, and after a few tastes of their bitter draughts she ceased to open them. Even death did not spare her. Willie Lincoln, the loveliest child of the White House, was smitten and died, to the unutterable grief of his father and the wild anguish of his mother. She mourned according to her nature. Her loss did not draw her nearer in sympathy to the nation of mothers that moment weeping because their sons were not. It did not lead her in time to minister to such, whom death had robbed and life had left without alleviation. She shut herself in with her grief, and demanded of God why he had afflicted *her!* Nobody suffered as she suffered. The Nation's House wore a pall, at last, not for its tens of thousands of brave sons slain, but for the President's child. The Guests' Room, in which he died, Mrs. Lincoln never entered again ; nor the Green Room, wherein, decked with flowers, his fair young body awaited burial.

In the same way, Mrs. Lincoln bewept her husband. And there is no doubt but that, in that black hour, she suffered great injustice. She loved her husband with the intensity of a nature, deep and strong, within a narrow channel. The shock of his untimely and awful taking-off, might have excused a woman of loftier nature than hers for any accompanying paralysis.

It was not strange that Mrs. Lincoln was not able to leave the White House for five weeks after her husband's death. It would have been stranger, had she been able to have left it sooner. It was her misfortune, that she had so armed public sympathy against her, by years of indifference to the sorrows of others, that when her own hour of supreme anguish came, there were few to comfort her, and many to assail. She had made many unpopular innovations upon the old, serene and stately *régime* of the President's house. Never a reign of concord, in her best day, in her hour of affliction it degenerated into absolute anarchy. I believe the long-time steward had been dethroned, that Mrs. Lincoln might manage according to her own will. At-any-rate, while she was shut in with her woe, the White House was left without a responsible protector. The rabble ranged through it at will. Silver and dining-ware were carried off, and have never been recovered. It was plundered, not only of ornaments, but of heavy articles of furniture. Costly sofas and chairs were cut and injured. Exquisite lace curtains were torn into rags, and carried off in pieces.

While all this was going on below, Mrs. Lincoln, shut up in her apartments, refused to see any one but servants, while day after day, immense boxes, containing her personal effects, were leaving the White House for her newly-chosen abode in the West. The size and number of these boxes, with the fact of the pillaged aspect of the White House, led to the accusation, which so roused public feeling against her, that she was robbing the Nation's House, and carrying the national property with her into retirement. This accusation, which clings to her to this day, was probably unjust. Her personal effects, in all likelihood, amounted to as much as that of nearly all other Presidents' wives together, and the vandals who roamed at large through the length and breadth of the White House, were quite sufficient to account for all its missing treasures.

The public also did Mrs. Lincoln injustice, in considering her an ignorant, illiterate woman. She was well-born, gently reared, and her education above the average standard given to girls in her youth. She is a fair mistress of the French language, and in English can write a more graceful letter than one educated woman in fifty. She has quick perceptions, and an almost unrivalled power of mimicry. The only amusement of her desolate days, while shut in from the world in Chicago, when she refused to see her dearest friends and took comfort in the thought that she had been chosen as the object of pre-eminent affliction, was to repeat in tone, gesture and expression, the words, actions and looks of men and women who, in the splendor of her life in Washington, had happened to offend her. Her lack was not a lack of keen faculties, or of fair culture, but a constitutional

16

inability to rise to the action of high motive in a time
when every true soul in the nation seemed to be impelled to unselfish deeds for its rescue. She was incapable
of lofty, impersonal impulse. She was self-centred, and
never in any experience rose above herself. According
to circumstance, her own ambitions, her own pleasures,
her own sufferings, made the sensation which absorbed
and consumed every other. As a President's wife she
could not rise above the level of her nature, and it was
her misfortune that she never even approached the bound
of her opportunity.

CHAPTER XXV.

THE WHITE HOUSE NOW—ITS PRESENT OCCUPANTS.

After the War—The Home of President Johnson—Shut Up in the Mountains—Two Years of Exile—A Contrast—Suffering for their Country—
Secretly Burying the Dead—A Wife of Seventeen Years—Midnight
Studies—Broken Down—A Party of Grandchildren—" My Dears, I am
an Invalid "—" God's Best Gift to Man "—The Woman Who Taught the
President—A " Lady of Benign Countenance "—Doing the Honors at
the White House—" We are Plain People "—The East Room Filled
with Vermin—Traces of the Soldiers—A State of Dirt and Ruin—Mrs.
Patterson's Calico Dress—In the Dairy—A Nineteenth Century Wonder
—How the Old Carpets were Patched—The Greenbacks are Forthcoming
—How $30,000 were Spent—Buying the Furniture—Working in Hot
Weather—" Wrestling with Rags and Ruins "—" Renovated from Top to
Bottom "—What the Ladies Wore, and What They Didn't—The Mem-
ory of Elegant Attire—Impressing the Public Mind—How Unperverted
Minds are Affected—" Bare-necked Dowagers—" A Large Crowd of
Bare Busts "—Elderly Ladies with Raven Locks—The Opinion of a
Woman of Fashion—Very Good Dinners—Obsequious to the Will of
" the People "—Doors Open to the Mob—Sketching a Banquet—Senti-
mental Reflections on the Dining Room—The Portraits of the Presidents
—The Impeachment Trial—Peace in the Family—The Grant Dynasty—
Looking Home-like—Mrs. Grant at Home—What Might Be Done, if—
What Won't Work a Reformation—A Pity for Miss Nellie Grant—How
She Suddenly " Came Out "—" A Full Fledged Woman of Fashion "—
A " Shoal of Pretty Girls "—How a Certain Young Lady was Spoilt—
Brushing Away " the Dew of Innocence "—Need of a Centripetal Soul
—Society in the Season—Rare Women with no Tastes—The Wives of
the Presidents Summed Up.

M RS. LINCOLN was succeeded in the White House
by three women, who entered its portals through
the fiery baptism of suffering for their country's sake.

While President Johnson was performing his duties as Senator in Washington, his family were shut up in the mountains of East Tennessee, where the ravages of war were most dreadful. For more than two years he was unable to set eyes on either wife or child. While many of the mushroom aristocracy, who afterwards looked upon them so superciliously, were coining their ill-gotten dollars out of the blood of their country, these brave, loyal women were being " hunted from point to point, driven to seek refuge in the wilderness, forced to subsist on coarse and insufficient food, and more than once called to bury with secret and stolen sepulture those whom they loved, murdered because they would not join in deeds of odious treason to union and liberty."

President Johnson's youngest daughter entered the White House a widow, recently bereaved of her husband, who fell a soldier in the Union cause. His wife, who at seventeen was his teacher, when " in the silent watches of the night the youthful couple studied together," when their weary tasks were done, came to the White House broken in health and spirits, through the suffering and bereavements through which she had passed. She was never seen but on one public occasion at the White House, that of a children's party, given to her grandchildren. At that time she was seated in one of the republican court-chairs of satin and ebony. She did not rise when the children or guests were presented, but simply said, "My dears, I am an invalid," and her sad, pale face and sunken eyes proved the expression. She is an invalid now; but an observer would say, contemplating her, "A noble woman, God's best gift to man." It was that woman who taught the President, after she became his wife; and in all their early years she was his assistant counsellor and guide.

Liable to be arrested for the slightest offense; ofttimes insulted by the rabble, Mrs. Johnson performed the perilous journey from Greenville to Nashville. Few who were not actual participators in the civil war can form an estimate of the trials of this noble woman. Invalid, as she was, she yet endured exposure and anxiety, and passed through the extended lines of hostile armies, never uttering a hasty word, or, by her looks, betraying in the least degree her harrowed feelings. She is remembered by friend and foe as a lady of benign countenance and sweet and winning manners.

During her husband's administration, the heavy duties and dubious honors of the White House were performed by her oldest daughter, Martha Patterson, the wife of Senator Patterson of Tennessee. That lady's utterance, soon after entering the White House, was a key to her character, yet scarcely a promise of her own distinguished management of the President's house. She said: "We are plain people from the mountains of Tennessee, called here for a short time by a national calamity. I trust too much will not be expected of us." The career of Mrs. Lincoln had chilled the people to expect little from the feminine administrator of the White House; but from Martha Patterson they received much, and that of the most unobtrusive and noble service.

The family of the new President arrived in June. Here was a new field entirely for the diffident woman who was compelled to do the honors, in lieu of her mother—a confirmed invalid. The house looked anything but inviting. Soldiers had wandered unchallenged through the entire *suites* of parlors. The East Room, dirty and soiled, was filled with vermin. Guards had slept upon the sofas and carpets till they were ruined, and the immense crowds who, during the preceding years of war, filled the President's house continually had worn out the already ancient furniture. No sign of neatness or comfort greeted their appearance, but evidences of neglect and decay everywhere met their eyes. To put aside all ceremony and work incessantly, was the portion of Mrs. Patterson from the beginning. It was her practice to rise very early, don a calico dress and spotless apron, and then descend to skim the milk and attend to the dairy before breakfast. Remembering this fact, of a President's daughter, in the President's house, in the nineteenth century, for a brief moment, let us cease to bemoan the homely virtues of our grandmothers as forever dead and buried.

At the first reception of President Johnson, held January 1, 1866, the White House had not been renovated. Dingy and destitute of ornament Martha Patterson had by dint of covering its old carpets with pure linen, and hiding its wounds with fresh flowers, and letting her beautiful children loose in its rooms, given it an aspect of purity, beauty and cheer, to which it had long been a stranger.

In the spring, Congress appropriated thirty thousand dollars to the renovation of the White House. After consulting various firms, Mrs. Patterson found that it would take the whole amount to furnish simply the parlors. Feeling a personal responsibility to the government for the expenditure of the money, unlike her predecessor, she determined not to surpass it. She made herself its

THE BLUE ROOM.
INSIDE THE WHITE HOUSE.—WASHINGTON.

agent, and superintended the purchases for the dismantled house herself. Instead of seeking pleasure by the sea, or ease in her own mountain home, the hot summer waxed and waned only to leave the brave woman where it found her, wrestling with rags and ruins that were to be reset, repolished, " made over as good as new." For herself? No, for her country; and all this in addition to caring for husband, children and invalid mother.

The result of this ceaseless industry and self-denial was, the President's house in perfect order and thoroughly renovated from top to bottom. When it was opened for the winter season, the change was apparent and marvelous, even to the dullest eyes, but very few knew that the fresh, bright face of the historic house was all due to the energy, industry, taste and tact of one woman, the President's daughter. The warm comfort of the dining room, the exquisite tints of the Blue Room, the restful neutral hues meeting and blending in carpets and furniture in many rooms of the White House still remain harmonious witnesses of the pure taste of Martha Patterson. The dress of the ladies of the White House was equally remarkable. The public had grown to expect loud display in the costume of its occupants. But all who went to see the " plain people from Tennessee " overloaded with new ornaments, were disappointed. Instead, they saw beside the President a young, golden-haired woman, dressed in full mourning, — the sad badge still worn for the gallant husband slain by war, — and a slender woman with a single white flower in her dark hair. Instead of the bare bosom and arms, the pronounced hues and glittering jewels which had so long obtained in that place, they saw soft laces about the throat ending the high corsage ; a robe of soft tints and a shawl of lace veiling the slender figure. It was like a picture in half tints, soothing to the sight; yet the dark hair, broad brow and large eyes were full of silent force and reserved power. Little was expected, even in dress, of these " plain people from Tennessee," yet the chaste elegance of their attire was never surpassed by any ladies of the White House, and its memory remains an example which it is a pity that ladies of society are so slow to imitate.

The impression made upon the public mind by the tone and spirit of their attire is significant as gathered from the utterance of contemporaneous newspapers. It betrays how dress of an opposite character always affects unperverted minds. A journal of the day says : " Mrs. Patterson, who stood at the right of the President, wore a black Lyons velvet, a shawl of white thread lace falling over her dress. The simple, unaffected grace of this lady, and her entire freedom from pretension, either in garb or manner, attracted highly favorable comment. Mrs. Patterson is quite a young lady, and when some of the barenecked would-be juvenile dowagers were presented to her, the contrast was entirely in favor of the President's daughter."

" Mrs. Stover assisted the President, and won golden opinions from sensible people for her faultless taste, and high-necked costume in a large crowd of bare busts. Elderly ladies, whose truthful wrinkles, despite their raven locks, betrayed their years, stood about her in low bodices, exposing to view shoulders long ago bereft of beauty and symmetry. Mothers, whose daughters walked beside them, in similar attire, gathered about her in their flashing diamonds and expensive apparel, but no peer of hers eclipsed her rich simplicity. Alone she stood, so tastefully arrayed that the poor who came were not abashed by her presence, nor the rich offended by her rarer *toilette*. The perfect harmony of her appearance pleased the eyes of all."

The spirit of these comments redeems them from the faintest touch of Jenkinsism. In this connection, it is easy to understand the comment of a woman of fashion, on Mrs. Stover. She said: "She has very fine points, which would make any woman a *belle*, if she knew how to make the most of them."

The state dinners given by President Johnson, were never surpassed in any administration. They were conducted on a generous, almost princely scale, and reflected lasting honor upon his daughter, to whom was committed the entire care and arrangement of every social entertainment. Simple and democratic in her own personal tastes, Mrs. Patterson had a high sense of what was due to the position, and to the people, from the family of the President of a great Nation. This sense of duty and justice led her to spare no pains in her management of official entertainments, and the same high qualities made her keep the White House parlors and conservatories open and ready for the crowds of people who daily visited them, at any cost to her own taste or comfort.

The following sketch of the last state dinner given by President Johnson, written by a personal friend, is so vivid and life-like, bringing the historic house so near, in the closing hours of an administration, I am constrained to give it to you:

"Late in the afternoon, I was sitting in the cheerful room occupied by the invalid mother, when Mrs. Patterson came for me to go and see the table. The last state dinner was to be given this night, and the preparation for the occasion had been commensurate with those of former occasions.

"I looked at the invalid, whose feet had never crossed the apartment to which we were going, and by whom the elegant entertainments, over which her daughters presided, were totally unenjoyed. Through the hall, and down the stairway, I followed my hostess, and stood beside her in the grand old room.

"It was a beautiful, and altogether a rare scene, which I viewed in the quiet light of that closing winter day. The table was arranged for forty persons, each guest's name being upon the plate designated on the invitation list. In the centre stood three magnificent *ormolu* ornaments, filled with fadeless French flowers, while, beside each plate, was a *bouquet* of odorous greenhouse exotics. It was not the color or design of the Sèvres China, of green and gold, the fragile glass, nor yet the massive plate, which attracted my admiration, but the harmony of the whole, which satisfied and refreshed. From the heavy curtains, depending from the lofty windows, to the smallest ornament in the room, all was ornate and consistent. I could not but contrast this vision of grandeur with the delicate, child-like form of the woman who watched me with a quiet smile, as I enjoyed this evidence of her taste, and appreciation of the beautiful. All day she had watched over the movements of those engaged in the arrangement of this room, and yet so unobtrusive had been her presence, and so systematically had she planned, that no confusion occurred in the complicated domestic machinery. For the pleasure it would give her children, hereafter, she had an artist photograph the interior of the apartment, and he was just leaving with his trophy, as we entered. All was ready and complete, and when we passed from the room, there was still time for rest before the hour named in the cards of invitation.

. . . . . . "It was almost twilight, as we entered the East Room, and its sombreness and wondrous size struck me forcibly. The hour for strangers and visitors had passed, and we felt at liberty to wander, in our old-fashioned way, up and down its great length."

" It was softly raining, we discovered, as we peered through the window, and a light fringe of mist hung over the trees in the grounds. The feeling of balmy comfort one feels in watching it rain, from the window of a cozy room, was intensified by the associations of this historic place, and the sadness of time was lost in the outreachings of eternity. Its spectral appearance, as we turned from the window and looked down its shadowy outlines, the quickly succeeding thoughts of the many who had crowded into its now deserted space, and the remembrance of some who would no more come, were fast crowding out the practical, and leaving in its place mental excitement, and spiritualized nervous influences. Mrs. Patterson was the first to note the flight of time, and, as we turned, to leave with the past the hour it claimed, her grave face lighted up with a genuinely happy expression, as she said : 'I am glad this is the last entertainment ; it suits me better to be quiet, and in my own home. Mother is not able to enjoy these things. Belle is too young, and I am indifferent to them—so it is well it is almost over.'

" As she ceased speaking, the curtains over the main entrance parted, and the President peered in, ' to see,' he said, ' if Martha had shown me the portraits of the Presidents.' Joining him in his promenade, we passed before them, as they were hanging in the main hall, he dwelling on the life and character of each, we listening to his descriptions, and personal recollections.

" At the dinner, afterwards, not the display of beautiful *toilettes*, nor the faces of lovely women, could draw from my mind the memory of that afternoon. More than ever, I was convinced that the best of our natures is entirely out of the reach of ordinary events, and the finest fibres are rarely, if ever, made to thrill in sympathy with outward influences. Grave statesmen, and white-haired dignitaries chatted merrily with fair young ladies, or sedate matrons ; but turn where I would, the burden of my thoughts were the remarks of Mrs. Patterson, whose unselfish devotion to her father, deserves a more fitting memorial than this insignificant mention. With her opposite

him, and by her proximity, relieving him of much of the necessity of entertaining, he enjoyed and bestowed pleasure, and won
for these social entertainments a national reputation.

"During the impeachment trial of her father, unflinchingly
Mrs. Patterson bent every energy to entertain, as usual, as became her position, wearing always a patient, suffering look.
Through the long weeks of the trial, she listened to every request, saw every caller, and served every petitioner, (and only
those who have filled this position, know how arduous is this
duty,) hiding from all eyes the anxious weight of care oppress-
ing herself. That she was sick after the acquittal, astonished
nobody who had seen her struggling to keep up before."

But no matter what the accusations against Andrew
Johnson, they died into silence without touching his family. If corruption crossed the outer portals of the White
House, the whole land knew that they never penetrated
into the pure recesses of the President's home. Whatever
Andrew Johnson was or was not, no partisan foe was
bitter or false enough to throw a shadow of reproach
against the noble characters of his wife and daughters.
There was no insinuation, no charge against them. There
was no furniture or ornaments gone; nor could any one
say that they had received costly presents : — no expensive plate, no houses, horses, or carriages. No family
ever left Washington more respected by the powerful,
more bewept by the poor. From the Nation's House,
which they had redeemed and honored, they went back
empty-handed to their own dismantled home, followed by
the esteem and affection of all who knew them. The
White House holds the record of their spotless fame.
Generations will pass before, from its grand old rooms, will
fade out the healing and saving touches of one President's
daughter.

The life of the White House under the administration of President Grant is a purely domestic one. It is the remark of all who have known its past, that the White House never looked so home-like as at the present time. It took on this aspect under the reign of Martha Patterson. But since then, pictures and ornaments have been added, one by one, till all its old-time stiffness seems to have merged into a look of grand comfort. Its roof may leak occasionally, and it certainly was built before the day of " modern conveniences," and may be altogether inadequate to be the President's house of a great Nation ; nevertheless, that Nation has no occasion to be ashamed of its order or adornment to-day.

As in the Johnson administration, the house is brightened by ever-blooming flowers, and the presence of happy children. Mr. Dent, the venerable father of Mrs. Grant, also makes a marked feature of its social life, and is the object not only of the ceaseless devotion of his family, but of the respect of all their visitors.

Mrs. Grant is now, as she always has been, devoted to her family. Her chief enjoyment is in it, in its cares and pleasures ; the latter, however, in her present life, largely preponderating. Born without the natural gifts or graces which could have made her a leader of other minds, even in the surface realm of society, she is, nevertheless, very fond of social entertainments, and enters into them with a good nature, and visible enjoyment, which at times goes far to take the place of higher and more positive characteristics. If to the affectionate domestic life of the White House could be added a finer culture and higher intellectual quality as the highest social centre of the land, giving exclusive tone to the official society, it might do more than words could tell to redeem from frivolity and vicious dissipation the fashionable life of the capital. Mere good nature, good clothes, and unutterable commonplace are not forces sufficient to, in themselves, work out this reformation.

On the whole it is a sad sight to see a President's daughter, an only daughter, at an age when any thoughtful mother would shield her from the allurements of pleasure, and shut her away in safety to study and grow to harmonious and beautiful womanhood, suddenly launched into the wild tide of frivolous pleasure. Thus, while the daughters of Senators and Cabinet ministers, far from Washington, under faithful teachers, were learning truly how to live, and acquiring the discipline and accomplishments which would fit them to adorn their high estate, Ellen Grant, a gentle girl of seventeen, with mind and manners unfed and unformed, suddenly " came out " a full-fledged young woman of fashion, spoken of almost exclusively as the driver of a phaeton, and the leader of the all-night " German."

As a result, Washington is crowded with a shoal of pretty girls, bright and lovely as God had made them ; by a false life, late hours, voluptuous dances, made already hard, old, *blasé*, often before their feet have touched the first verge of womanhood. I think of one, but one, amid hundreds, the daughter of a high officer, graceful, tasteful, the queen of dancers, and of all night revels, but empty of mind, hard of heart, brazen of manners ! Who looking on her face can fail to see that the dew of innocence is brushed from it forever.

The prevailing lack of fashionable society in Washington, to-day, is high motive, purity of feeling, a more varied and brighter intelligence. These all exist, and in no meagre proportion, but as scattered elements, they wait the supreme social queen, the centripetal soul which shall draw them into one potent and prevailing power that shall lift the whole social life of the capital to a higher plane of æsthetic attire, culture, and amusement. Fortunately, Mrs. Grant has been surrounded by numerous ladies in official life of superior mental endowment and culture, and true social grace. This is especially true of a portion of " the ladies of the Cabinet," of the Senators' wives from several States, and of no small number among the wives of Representatives. Many ladies, whose husbands are in Congress, bring the most exquisite tastes in art, music and literature, and the loveliest of womanhood to grace the life of Washington. For what is termed its " society " in the " season," the pity is these rare women have no taste, it is to them a burden, or an offence, and they have never yet combined in organized force (which alone is power) to uplift and redeem it.

Nevertheless, Washington is rapidly becoming an intellectual as well as social centre. The large and varied interests which concentrate in a national capital tend more and more to draw the highest intellectual as well as social forces into its life. These need but assimilation, fusion, unity and purpose to develop into the most superb manifestation of civilization. In looking back upon the wives of the Presidents, we discover, with but two or three exceptions, they were women of remarkable powers and exalted character.

CHAPTER XXVI.

MRS. GRANT'S RECEPTION—GLIMPSES OF LIFE.

IT is Tuesday—Mrs. Grant's day—and all the gay world
is going to the White House, besides a portion of that
world which is not gay.

Mrs. Grant's morning receptions are very popular, and
deservedly so. This is not because the lady is in any

sense a conversationalist, or has a fine tact in receiving, but rather, I think, because she is thoroughly good-natured, and for the time, at least, makes other people feel the same.   At any rate, there was never so little formality or so much genuine sociability in the day-receptions at the White House as at the present time.   General Babcock pronounces your name without startling you out of your boots by shouting it, as on such occasions is usually done.   He passes it to the President, the President to Mrs. Grant, Mrs. Grant to ladies receiving with her.   After exchanging salutations with each, you pass on to make room for others, and to find your own personal friends dispersed through the great rooms.   They are in each of them ; loitering in the Blue Room, where the receiving is going on ; chatting in the Green Room ; promenading in the East Room.   You may go through the long corridor into the state dining-room, into the conservatories, full of flowers and fragrance, and back, if you choose, to your starting-point, where the President and Mrs. Grant are still receiving.

This is one of the pleasantest facts of these morning receptions—the informal coming down of the President to receive with Mrs. Grant.   I have never been accused of over enthusiasm for him, but find myself ready to forgive in him the traits which I cannot like, when I see him, with his daughter, beside Mrs. Grant.   *Then*, it is so perfectly evident that, whatever the President may or may not be, "Mr. Grant" has a very true and likeable side, with which nobody is so well acquainted as Mrs. Grant.

Here is the East Room, that you have read about so long.   It never looked so well before.   There are flaws in the harmony of its decorations which we might pick
17

at ; but we won't, as we are not here to-day to find fault.
Besides, it is too pleasant to see that the nation's parlor,
erst so forlorn, has absolutely taken on a look of home
comfort. In proportions it is a noble room, long and
lofty. It has seven windows — three in front, facing
Pennsylvania avenue and Lafayette square ; three looking out upon the presidential grounds and the Potomac ;
and a stately bay window overlooking the Treasury. It
has four white marble mantel-pieces, two on each side.
It has eight mirrors, filling the spaces over the mantels
and between the windows. Richly wrought lace curtains
have taken the place of the tatters left there a few years
ago, when the curtains of the White House windows
were scattered over the country in tags, taken home by
relic-hunters. Over these hang draperies of crimson
brocatelle, surmounted by gilt cornices, bearing the arms
of the United States. The walls and ceilings are frescoed,
and from the latter depend three immense chandeliers of
cut glass, which, when lighted, blaze like mimic suns.
On the walls hang the oil portraits, in heavy gilt frames,
of eight Presidents of the United States. Opposite the
door, as you enter, is the portrait of Filmore. On the
other side of the mantel, that of Lincoln. Next beyond
the bay window, that of Washington ; all of life size.
Beyond the further mantel is that of Franklin Pierce.
Above the door opposite, one of John Adams. Above
the next door, of Martin Van Buren ; the next, of Polk ;
the last above the entrance door, of John Tyler.

The carpet on the East Room, last year, was presented
to the United States by the Sultan of Turkey. It seemed
like one immense rug, covering the entire floor, and filled
the room with an atmosphere of comfort, grand, soft, and

THE GREAT EAST ROOM.

THE GREEN ROOM.

INSIDE THE WHITE HOUSE.—WASHINGTON.

warm. The chairs and sofas are of carved wood, crimson
cushioned. A handsome bronze clock ticks above one ,
of the mantels, the others are adorned with handsome
bronzes. The air is summer warm. On the whole, isn't
the people's parlor a pleasant place? I never enter it,
but comes back to me that tearful April morning when,
in the centre of this floor, under the white catafalque, lay ·
the body of Abraham Lincoln, dead. The crowd pressing
in then, how different from this one! Rugged soldiers
bent down and kissed his face and wept, women scattered
flowers upon his breast, with their tears. Rich and poor,
old and young, black and white, all crowded round his
coffin, and wept for him,—one, *only one*, if the most august, of the martyrs of liberty.

Think what tales the room could tell, since the day when
Abigail Adams dried her clothes from the weekly wash,
in it, if it but had a tongue. Stand here, and see the
stately procession move by. Believe in your own day,
my dears. You need not go back to Sir Philip Sidney,
to find a perfect gentleman, nor to David and Jonathan,
to find faith and love between man and man, passing the
love of woman, nor to the days of chivalry, to find true
knights who would die for you. Here are men bearing,
under all this glitter of gold and lace, bodies battered and
maimed in their country's cause. There, is a man, pouring foolish nothings into the ear of a foolish girl, who
would die for the truth.

We are far from being a thorough-bred people. The
census of spittoons is a horror in our land. We talk too
loud, and too long; we gesticulate too much; we can not
keep quiet. We need, at least, more capacity for repose,
more unselfish consideration for the sensibilities of others,

more of the golden rule, before we can flower into the perfection of fine breeding. Yet, no less here, are men at once strong and gentle, brave and tender, gallant and yet true. Here are all and more than Shakespeare's women: Juliet, searching for her Romeo; Miranda, looking through her starry eyes for a "thing divine" even in the Red Room; tender Imogen; fair Titania; Portia, with hair of golden brown; and Desdemona, imprudent, fond, yet truth itself. Here is not only the beauty and the *belle*, but the sibyl, whose divining eyes beyond volition, strike below every sham and every falsehood.

Yet here, too, falls the shadow of human nature. There stand two ladies, whose supreme enjoyment here is "quizzing." Among their thousand "dear friends" here, not one is too sacred to be ridiculed. One of these ladies, at least, would feel as if she had forfeited "her soul's salvation," if she were to go to the theatre, or to give countenance to a dance; but it does not occur to her, that she puts that precarious organ in the slightest peril, when she stands in a public assembly, and ridicules her friends.

These ladies are merely yielding to a vice which has grown with their years, strengthened with their strength, the vice that thrives amid Christian graces, the vice paramount of the Christian church. The most unkind people whom I have ever known, have been distinguished for an ostentatious sort of piety. The most uncharitable conclusions, the most pitiless judgments, the most merciless ridicule, that I have ever listened to, of poor human beings, I have heard from people high in the church, not from people of the so-called "world." This, not because the normal human nature in either differs, but because the people of the world have a thousand outlets and activities which draw them away from microscopic inspection of the flaws in their neighbors; while ascetic pietists, denied legitimate amusements, shut out from innocent recreation, avenge their defrauded souls by feeding them on small vices. I offer no defence for a life of folly; there is nothing I should dread more, save a life of sin. Yet, if I were to make a choice, I would choose foolishness rather than meanness.

This lady, flashing by in many hues, represents what one sees continually in Washington—a new woman. Not new to the city merely, but new to position and honor. These are but slight external accidents to a nature that has ripened from within, drawing culture, refinement, and dignity out of the daily opportunities of retired life. But, when the public position is *all* that gives the honor, how easy to tell it! There is all the difference in the quality of the put-on, puckering manner, and the simple dignity of real ladyhood, that there is between the quality of a persimmon and a pomegranate. All she has is new. She, herself, is new. Her bearing and her honors do not blend. There is no soft and fine shading of thought, of manner, of accent, of attire. The sun of prosperity may strike down to a rarer vein, and draw it outward, to tone down this boastful commonplace; but we must bear the glare, the smell of varnish, and the crackle of veneering, during the process.

When I was a very good little girl, I was allowed to read Mrs. Sherwood's Lady of the Manor, on Sunday. I read, and thought that heaven on earth must be shut up in a manor house. When I grew to be a somewhat bigger girl, sailing down the Hudson, a manor house, rich in historic recollections, was pointed out to me. And here, in my summer-time, comes the lady of this manor house, drops her gentle courtesy, and gives me her hand, making more than real the enchanted story of childhood. The lady of the manor in crude Washington revives the stately graces of old days.

How quaint and rare they are! How I look and long for it; how glad I am when I find it,—that indefinable, yet ever-felt presence of fine womanliness, a thing as precious as the highest manliness,—each the rarest efflorescence of human nature. I confess to a clinging adoration for it, whether felt in the lady of the manor or in the sad-eyed woman who cleans my gloves. The womanliness that is not ashamed nor dissatisfied with womanhood, nor yet vain of it; the womanliness that gives us the gracious, blending dignity and sweetness of wisdom and humility, of self-respect and reticence, of spirituality and tenderness—that ineffable charm of femininity, which is the counterpart and crown of manhood, in very distinction equal with it, each together maintaining in equilibrium the brain and soul of the human race.

Even while I write word comes: The lady of the manor is dead. The quaint hood, the stately grace, the winning smile we shall see no more. All have gone into the darkness of death. And who was the lady of the manor, who for three winters in Washington has been the observed and admired of all who met her in the circles of society? She was Cora Livingston Barton, the reigning *belle* of Jackson's administration. She was the daughter of Edward Livingston, who served his country as Member of Congress and Senator from Louisiana, as Secretary of State during Jackson's administration, and as United States Minister to France. Her father was as distinguished for goodness as he was for noble intellect and exalted public service, and her mother was one of the most remarkable women who ever graced the National Capital. She was a social queen of the rarest endowments. She was the chosen friend and dear counsellor of two persons as opposite in nature and temperament as General Jackson and Mrs. John Quincy Adams. She was a very queen of entertainers, as the wife of the Secretary of State, entertaining foreigners and Americans and political foes, with an ease, elegance and fascination of manner, which annihilated alike all prejudice and animosity. She was a classical scholar, familiar with the best ancient and modern thoughts. The chosen counsellor of her husband in the gravest affairs of State,—a self-abnegating mother,—a devout Methodist, she having chosen that communion as her own on account of the simplicity and fervor of its mode of worship.

Of this rare woman, our "lady of the manor" was the only child. "Upon her she lavished extraordinary maternal devotion, hardly ever suffering her to be out of her sight. Her daughter had hardly reached girlhood when her beautiful mother assumed the simplest matronly attire. Ever afterwards she seemed rather displeased than flattered when allusions were made to her own still remarkable appearance."

Cora Livingston was worthy to be the child of such a mother. She was the most famous *belle* of the Jackson administration. She married Thomas Barton, who went as Secretary of Legation with her father, the Minister to France, and who remained as *Chargé d' Affaires* when Edward Livingston returned.

In the course of time, mother and daughter, both

widows, spent their winters in New York and their sum-
mers at Montgomery Place, that grand old manor on the
Hudson, of which we catch glimpses through its immemorial trees, as we sail by on the river. Here, beautiful
and saintly, that mother died, October, 1860, at the age of
seventy-eight.

Warned by physicians to seek a softer climate, after the
lapse of generations, in the winter of 1871 the daughter
returned to Washington, the scene of her childish home
and early triumphs. She did not belong to things gone
by. With her two stately and beautiful nieces she became at once the centre of a rare group of friends, of
the attention and reverence of the first men in the State,
and an object of admiring comment wherever she appeared.
She appeared at many morning receptions. I see her
now as I saw her the first time stepping from her carriage
into the great portico of the White House, across its corridor to the Blue Room, with the light, springing step of a
girl; and yet, the soft clinging black dress, the quaint
hood of black silk, with its inside snowy *ruche*, all told
that she made not the slightest pretence to youth. And
now, in these summer days, comes the word: "While
packing some books in a trunk to go to Montgomery
Place, she bent down, burst a blood vessel in the head,
and without warning died."

They have all been morning receptions to which I have
asked you,—the "morning" ending at 5 P. M. I cannot invite you to go to the "German," which begins at
11 P. M. and ends at daybreak. I have too deep a care
for your physical and spiritual health to ask you to do
any such thing. When you read of the gay doings and
bright assemblies here, perhaps you think it hard some-

times that you must stay away in a quiet place to work
or study. You feel almost defrauded because you are
shut out from the splendor and mirth and flattery of
fashion. You long for the pomp and glory of the world,
and sigh that so little of either falls on your life-path.
Thus I shall seem cruel to you when I say that you had
better be shut up for the next five years, even in a convent,
silently growing toward a noble life in the world afterward, than to be caught and carried on by its follies now,
before you have learned how to live.

Are you young? Then you should be more beautiful
at twenty-five, at thirty, at thirty-five, than you are now.
Not with the budding bloom of first youth, that is as
evanescent as it is exquisite. What a pity that it is
beauty's only dower to so many American women. They
waste it, lose it, then wilt and wither. I want you so to
feed the sources of life to-day that you may grow, not
wither; that you may bloom, not fade, into the perfect
flower of womanhood.

Terpsichore is a sad sight to me; not because Terpsichore dances, for dancing in itself may be as innocent as
a bird's flying; not because she loves beautiful attire, for
exquisite dress is a feminine fine art, as meet for a woman
as the flower's tint, or the bird's plumage. I sigh at the
sight of my pretty Terpsichore, because the first bloom
of her exquisite youth is being exhaled and lost forever
in a feverish, false atmosphere of being. Something of
delicate sensibility, something of unconscious innocence,
something of freshness of feeling, of purity of soul is
wasted with the fresh young bloom of her cheeks in the
midnight revel, lengthened into morning; wasted in the
heated dance, in the indigestible feast, in the wild, un-

healthy excitement through which she whirls night after
night. Terpsichore, in her tattered tarletan dress, creep-
ing to bed in the gray morning, after having danced all
night, is a sad sight to see to any one who can see her as
she is. Terpsichore's mother would be a sadder sight
still, if she were not a vexatious one. She brought back
from Europe the notion, which so many of our countrywomen think it fine to bring, that "full dress" is necessarily next to no dress. She tells you, in a supreme tone,
that admits no denial, that you would not be admitted
into the drawing-room of a court in Europe unless in full
dress, viz., semi-nakedness. She would be nothing, if not
European in style. Thus, night after night, this mother
of grown-up daughters and sons appears in crowded assemblies in attire that would befit in outline a child of eight
years of age. If we venture to meet her *ipse dixit* on
European style, with the assurance of the Princess Hele-
na, Ghika, Dora D'Istria, one of the most learned and
beautiful women of this world, that the conventional
society dress of Europe is more immodest than any she
saw while traveling over the mountains and valleys of
the East, she will tell you that Princess Ghika "is not an
authority on dress in Paris," which is doubtless true.

Thus, in republican Washington, in glaring drawing-
rooms, we are treated to a study of female anatomy,
which is appalling. Don't jump to the conclusion that I
want every lady to go to a party in a stuff dress, drawn
up to her ears; nor that I am so prudish as to think no
dress can be modestly, as well as immodestly low. No
matter how it be cut, the *way* in which a dress is worn is
more impressive than the dress itself. I have seen a
young girl's shoulders rise from her muslin frock as

unconsciously and as innocently as the lilies in the garden;
and I have come upon a wife and mother, in a public assembly, so dressed for promiscuous gaze that I have in-
voluntarily shut my eyes with shame.

I never saw Lydia Thompson; but from what I have
heard of her, have come to the conclusion that her attire
is just as modest as that of many ladies whom I meet at
fashionable parties. They cast up their eyes in horror at
the name of poor Lydia Thompson. *They* go to see Lydia
Thompson! No, indeed! How could their eyes endure
the sight of that dreadful woman? No less they themselves offer gratis, to a promiscuous company, every evening, a sight, morally, quite as dreadful. The men, who
pay their money to Lydia Thompson and her *troupe*,
know that their dress and their burlesque, however questionable, make at once their business and their livelihood.
They cannot make the same excuse for their wives, their
sisters, and their sweethearts, if they see them scarcely
less modestly attired in some fashionable ball-room. Remember this; if you ever find yourself in such a place,
the best men in that room, at heart, are not delighted
with such displays. Being men, they will look at whatever is presented to their gaze; more, many will compliment and flatter the very woman, whose vanity at heart
they pity or despise; but it will always be with the
mental reservation: "*My wife* should never dress like
that!" "I don't want to see my sister dancing round
dances for hours in the arms of a man whom even I cannot think of without horror; and if —— dances with him
again, I'll not go to another 'German;'" said a young
man to his mother, this very winter.

This is perpetually the fact; and it is the danger and

the shame of the round dances. Young girls guarded, from babyhood, from all contact with vice, from all knowledge of men as they exist, in their own world of clubs and dissipation, suddenly " come out " to whirl, night after night, and week after week, in the arms of men whose . lightest touch is profanation. It would be long before it would dawn upon the girl to dream of the evil in that man's heart ; far longer to learn the evil of his life ; yet no less, to her, innocent and young, in the very association and contact there is unconscious pollution. There is a sacredness in the very thought of the body which God created to be the human home of an immortal soul. Its very beauty should be the seal of its holiness. Every where in Scripture its sacredness is recognized and enforced. Therein we are told that our bodies are the temples of God. We are commanded to make them meet temples for the indwelling of the Holy Spirit ; and our very dress, in its harmony and purity, should consecrate, not desecrate, the beautiful home of the soul.

CHAPTER XXVII.

INAUGURATION DAY AT WASHINGTON.

I DON'T like Inauguration day, but I hope you do, or will, when I have told you what a gala day it is to many—to all who stay at home, and catch the splendor which it sheds, through lines of printer's ink.

Surely, there is something inspiriting and uplifting in the sight of massed humanity, in throbbing drums and soaring music, in waving pennons and flashing lances, all laden with heroic memories, all bristling with intelligence and the conscious power of human freedom; but, in our climate, and at the inauguration season of the year, enthusiasm and patriotism demand a fearful price in nerve, muscle, and human endurance. If you doubt it, think of the West Point Cadets—those young sons of war, inured to martial training—who sank to the pavements in the ranks, at the last inauguration of President Grant, overcome, and insensible with the bitter cold which chilled and benumbed even the warm currents of their strong young hearts. Think of the babies who shuddered and cried in their mothers' arms, who *would* see the sight, if baby died!

No less the second inaugural procession of President Grant transcended, in civic and military splendor, any sight seen in Washington since the great review when the boys in blue, fresh from the victory of bloody battle-fields, broke their backs and skinned their noses, in the June sun of 1865, for the sake of shouting thousands who came hither to behold them. Oh what a sight was that! when the bronzed and haggard, and aged-in-youth faces of the boys before us, made our hearts weep afresh at the thought of the upturned faces of the boys left behind—some in the cruel wilderness, some in half dug graves on solitary hill-sides, and lonely plains—all left behind forever, for freedom's sake. Who that knew old Washington can forget it? This is another Washington. But here they come! Safe from cold and wind, thanks to—I look up. From this window, on Fifteenth street, you can see Pennsylvania avenue past the Treasury building, (whose marble steps are boarded in from the advancing people,) to the Executive Mansion, glittering white through the leafless trees just beyond. Opposite is Lafayette square, the prettiest little park of its size in the United States. Above, you see the towering mansard of Corcoran's building, "Devoted to Art," and just this side, the lofty brown front of the Freedman's Savings Bank. The avenue opens before you—a broad, straight vista, with garlands of flags, of every nation and hue, flung across from roof to roof. Above glitters an absolutely cloudless sky, dazzlingly blue, and pitilessly cold. The very tree-boughs swing like crystals glittering and freezing in the sun. The air seems full of rushing fiends, or rushing locomotives running into each other with hideous shrieks, whichever you please (on the whole, I prefer locomotives, being fresher). Your imagination need not be Dantean to make you feel that there is a dreadful battle going on in the air, above you and about you. The imps come down and seize an old man's hat, and fly off with a woman's veil, and blow a little boy into a cellar. The bigger air-warriors, intent on bigger spoil, sweep down banners, swoop off with awnings, concentrate their forces into swirling cyclones in the middle of the streets, and bang away at plate-glass windows till they prance in their sockets.

Before such unfriendly and tricksy foes, through the biting air, comes the great procession. First, a battalion of mounted police; then West Point, with its band and drum-major. Not a sprite of the air has caught the baton of its drum-major. Not a sting of zero, has stiffened that fantastic arm as he lifts and swings the symbol of his foolishness. He is as inimitable in the bleak and dusty street as when I saw him last, on the velvet sward of West Point, that delicious evening in October. Something utterly ridiculous to look at, is refreshing, and anything more faultlessly ridiculous than the drum-major of West Point I never saw.

I believe it is fashionable to find fault with West Point;

but I wouldn't give much for anybody who could see these boys and not admire them. They have their faults (their caste and their army exclusiveness sometimes reaches an absurd pitch) but look at them! What faces, what muscle, what manhood! Their movement is the perfect poetry of motion; a hundred men stepping as one. What marching, and at what odds! They are so pitilessly dressed! Thousands of men come behind, warmly muffled; but the West Point Cadets have on their new uniforms, single jackets. More than one will receive through it the seeds of death this morning. What wonder, that two while standing in line sank insensible with the cold, not an hour ago. But, dear me! to think that more than one of them should be taken for a "nigger!" The colored Cadet is whiter than a dozen of his class-mates, and has straight hair.

In the distance rises, wave on wave, a glittering sea of helmets; bayonets flash, plumes wave, bands play; all tell one story—the love of military pomp and parade, the pride and patriotism which brings these soldiers back to celebrate the second inauguration of their chief; and at what cost of suffering to many of them. What cold and hunger, and delay on the way, and now! what nerve and will it takes to march in a wind like this!

After West Point comes Annapolis. Pretty "Middies," young and slender, in their suits of dark blue! As a body, they are younger than the West Pointers, and slighter. Nor can any comparison be drawn between their marching, for the Middies drag their howitzers. They look true sons of their class; and for intelligence, chivalric manners, and gentle manhood, the true officer of the American navy is unsurpassed.

The Midshipmen are followed by the famous United States Marine Corps, then the Old Guard of New York with Dodworth's band, the Washington Light Infantry, the Corcoran Zouaves, the Washington Grenadiers, the St. Louis National Guard. The Philadelphia City Troop, in navy-blue jackets, tight knee-breeches, white braid trimming, high boots, bearskin helmets with silver mountings —the oldest regiment in the United States, two years older than the government, organized in 1774, and furnished men to every war of this country since. It was in the battles of Trenton and Princeton, in the Revolutionary War, and has in its armory a letter from General Washington thanking the regiment for its services.

Now, the President's mounted guard, in dark blue, yellow-trimmed uniform, regulation-hat and black feathers. Now, the President in open barouche, drawn by four horses, with the Senate Committee, Senators Cragin, Logan and Bayard. The President looks decidedly cooler than usual, and less indifferent; at least he has just lifted his hat to the shouting crowd in the street, which requires an impulse of self-denial this morning.

Now come the Boston National Lancers. They have left their milk-white steeds there, and to their chagrin, no doubt, are mounted on sorry Virginian roans instead,— old road and car horses, who act dazed and daft under their light unwonted burdens. The Lancers are the oldest cavalry regiment of Massachusetts, organized in 1836, under Governor Edward Everett. This dashing looking squadron, which has the reputation of being one of the most perfect military organizations of the United States, is dressed in scarlet cloth coats, faced with a light blue and trimmed with gold lace, sky-blue pants with yellow

18

stripes on sides, Polish dragoon cap, gold trimmings, flowing white feathers and *aiguillette*, cavalry boots with patent leather tops, white belts and shoulder straps; red epaulettes, with blue trimmings for the privates, and gold for the officers, and armed with cavalry sabre and lance, on which is appended a small red flag.

The Albany Burgess Corps, another famous regiment, led by Capt. Henry B. Beecher, son of the Rev. Henry Ward Beecher, make a splendid appearance. They are uniformed in scarlet coats, trimmed with white, light blue pants, buff stripe, and bearskin shakoes, with gold clasp —similar to the celebrated English Coldstream Guards.

But we shall not reach the capitol till next week, unless we leave the rest of this splendid procession,—the " orphans of soldiers and sailors," the burnished and flower-garlanded fire-engines, the brave firemen, black and white, and the civic societies. The strangers who rushed on to inauguration, swarm the galleries till they overflow as they did on *Credit Mobilier* days. Generals Sherman, and Sheridan and Admiral Porter; the first tall and red; the second, little, round, red and bullet-headed; the third, tall, straight and black, are all being intently gazed at.

The Diplomatic Corps enter the chamber by the main entrance, led by Blacque Bey, the dean of the Corps, a tall, dark, gray-haired, handsome man, wearing scarlet fez and full Turkish court regalia; next, the English Minister, Sir Edward Thornton, a white-haired, ruddy-faced, black-eyed, shrewd-looking gentleman; next, the Peruvian Minister, Colonel Freerye, followed by the Italian and French Ministers, with all the representatives of foreign governments, in order of seniority—over fifty ministers, secretaries and *attachés* in full uniform, excepting

Mr. Mori, Minister from Japan, in citizen's dress. Just now Mr. Sumner appears, for the first time in months. He looks pale, and shows the traces of the acute suffering through which he has passed. His appearance creates a buzz on floor and in gallery, and many senators go over to him and exchange friendly greetings. Now the Supreme Court appear, in their robes of office, kicking them high up behind, as usual, and take their seats in front of the Vice-President's desk. At fifteen minutes to twelve o'clock, Vice-President elect Wilson, escorted by Senators Cragin, Logan, and Bayard, comes down the centre aisle and takes his seat at the right of Vice-President Colfax.

At three minutes before twelve, the President appears, leaning on the arm of Senator Cragin, followed by Logan and Bayard, and takes the seat assigned him, in front of the Secretary's table. A deep hush falls on the throng, as if something awful were about to happen. It's a sort of Judgment-Day atmosphere, yet nothing more terrific follows than the pleasant voice of Vice-President Colfax, beginning the words of his valedictory. (My! I forgot to say that the dying Congress has come to life again, and is comfortably, and perforce quietly seated between the Senate and Diplomatic Corps.) Now comes the new Vice-President's little speech. Then the oaths of office, the swearing in of new senators, the proclamation of the President convening an extra session of the Senate, to begin this minute, when all start for the back door—no, it's the front door of the Capitol, the Supreme Court leading, kicking up their gowns worse than usual.

On the eastern portico, what do we see? Below, a vast mass of human beings, line on line of soldiers—cavalry, artillery and infantry; a line of battle flags at the base of the steps—shot-riddled, battle-torn, all shuddering or numb in the freezing air. Before us, a little gentleman sits down in a big chair—Washington's inaugural chair, we are told. (Oh! no, we're not at all sentimental.)

A big gentleman, the Chief Justice, who has most unaccountably fringed out in a long grey beard and a muffling moustache, holds forth with solemnity a big Bible. The little gentleman kisses it—kisses these words from the eleventh chapter of Isaiah:

"'And the spirit of the Lord shall rest upon him, the spirit of wisdom and understanding, the spirit of counsel and might, the spirit of knowledge and of the fear of the Lord.

"'And shall make him of quick understanding in the fear of the Lord; and he shall not judge after the sight of his eyes, neither reprove after the hearing of his ears.'

Then he rises, and, with manuscript in his hands, begins to "battle with the breeze," and to read his inaugural, which nobody hears. Behind him sits his wife and daughter, the ladies of the Cabinet, the Diplomatic Corps. What a compound of the ornamental and comfortable? Yet nobody is comfortable—not here. We can catch no word through the outbearing wind, yet know that for the second time Ulysses S. Grant has sworn to the oath of office, according to the constitution, and for four more years is made President of the United States. It seems but yesterday we saw a loftier head, a sadder face, bowed above that book, within one little month of its eternity; when, amid the booming of cannon and the huzzas of the people, Abraham Lincoln for the second time was pronounced the people's President, and by the same lips which now utter the same words for another, a happier, a more fortunate man.

Now the carnival of salute; the Middies fire their howitzers, thirty-seven guns; the Second Artillery fire twenty-one salvos; the Firemen ring the bells of their engines; ten thousand men warm their hands with hat swinging, and make their throats sore with shouting. Amid all, the multitude and the procession surge back towards the Executive Mansion. Between the latter and Lafayette square, the review, the return march, the military pageant culminates. The President, with lady friends, enters the pavilion built for the purpose, and the troops march by, encircling two solid squares; the West Point Cadets appear below Corcoran's building, marching downward, as the magnificent New York Regiment—a thousand men—just arrived after an all night's freezing delay, have reached Fifteenth street, marching up. The entire body of soldiery march and mass, till as far as the eyes can reach through the glittering sunshine, one only sees gleaming helmets, flashing bayonets, glancing sabers, the Cadets on double quick, the Middies firing their howitzers, officers displaying fine horses and uniforms, drum-majors tossing their batons, bands playing, and cannon thundering.

Amid all·these the four horses dashing before the Presidential barouche, bear the President to the Executive door, which now mercifully shuts them from our sight.

CHAPTER XXVIII.

THE NEW PRESIDENT—THE INAUGURATION BALL.

UNTOLD time, and trouble, and sixty thousand dollars were expended on the last inauguration ball building, and yet there was something the matter with the inaugural ball. There is always something the matter with every inauguration ball.

When I wish to think of a spot especially suggestive of torments, I think of an inauguration ball. There was the one before the last, held in the Treasury Building. The air throughout the entire building was perforated with a fine dust ground till you felt that you were taking in with every breath a myriad homœopathic doses of desiccated grindstone. The agonies of that ball can never be written. There are mortals dead in their grave because of it. There are mortals who still curse, and swear, and sigh at the thought of it. There are diamonds, and pearls, and precious garments that are not to their owners because of it. The scenes in those cloak and hat rooms can never be forgotten by any who witnessed them. The colored messengers, called from their posts in the Treasury to do duty in these rooms, received hats and wraps with perfect facility, and tucked them in loop-holes as it happened. But to give them back, each to its owner, that was impossible. Not half of them could read numbers, and those who could soon grew bewildered, overpowered, ill-tempered and impertinent under the hosts that advanced upon them for cloaks and hats.

Picture it! Six or more thousand people clamoring for their clothes! In the end they were all tumbled out "promiscuous" on the floor. Then came the siege! Few seized their own, but many snatched other people's garments—anything, something, to protect them from the pitiless morning, whose wind came down like the bite of death. Delicate women, too sensitive to take the property of others, crouched in corners, and wept on window ledges; and there the daylight found them. Carriages, also, had fled out of the scourging blast, and the men and women who emerged from the marble halls, with very little to wear, found that they must "foot it" to their habitations. One gentleman walked to Capitol Hill, nearly two miles, in dancing pumps and bare-headed; another performed the same exploit, wrapped in a lady's sontag.

Poor Horace Greeley, after expending his wrath on the stairs and cursing Washington anew as a place that should be immediately blotted out of the universe, strode to his hotel hatless. The next day and the next week were consumed by people searching for their lost clothes, and General Chipman says that he still receives letters demanding articles lost at that inauguration ball.

Well, our latest brought discomfort, and discomfiture of another sort. Neither money, time nor labor were stinted in this leviathan, that still lifts up its broken and propped up back in Judiciary square. The building was 350 feet long. The ball-room 300 by 100 feet. All this was temporary, built of light boards, lined with lighter muslin. You might as well have attempted to have warmed Pennsylvania avenue as such a place on such a night. Twenty-four hours before the ball the wind-devils went at it. If a host from the pit had received full power to move and dismember it, it could scarcely look more forlorn than it did one Monday morning. They had sat on its spine in one place till it curved in, punched it up in another till it was hunchbacked. They had inflated its sides till they swelled out like an inflated balloon, while the air was black with the tar-rags, seaming its roof, which flying imps were carrying up to high heaven.

No less the official report said of the inside: "The mighty American Eagle spreads his wings above the President's platform. He has suspended, from his pinions, streamers one hundred feet in length, caught up on either side by coats of arms. The circumference of this vast design is one hundred and eighty feet. The President's reception platform is sixty feet long, and thirty feet wide. Twelve pilasters support alternate gold-figured, red and blue stands, on which are pots of blooming flowers. The platform and steps are richly carpeted. In the rear of the balcony, are immense festoons of flags, banners, shields, radiating from a huge illuminated star of gas-lights."

What were all those white and rosy walls of cambric, to the all-pervading polar wave that froze sailors' fingers, and struck West Point Cadets to the pavements, in congestive chills, at noonday? Why, they were nothing but an immense sieve, to strain that same polar wave through on to the persons of delicate (?) women, who, without money, and without price, for the sake of dubious admiration and commend, in promiscuous assemblies, outvie Lydia Thompson in paucity of attire.

But the ball. My intention was to say, that the President was so near frozen in the day-time, he was not sufficiently thawed out to appear under that spreading eagle, until half-past eleven o'clock, when the north wind swooped in from behind, and he congealed again immediately. The President's platform was at the north end, and all the muslin splendors of the presidential dressing and waiting-room could not, and did not, warm that polar wave. The thousands of canary-birds perched aloft, who were expected to burst into simultaneous song at the sight of him, and to trill innumerable preludes in honor of Miss Nelly, instead, poor wretches, had, one and all, gone to bed, with their toes tucked in their feathers, and their bills buried in their breasts, in dumb effort to keep them from freezing. Not a canary-bird sang. No, they were as paralyzed with cold as the bipeds below.

On the presidential platform, the President and Mrs. Grant sat, the central figures. A little in the rear, sat Mrs. Fish—stately, lovely, and serene as ever; and just behind her, the Secretary of State. Next, were Mrs. Boutwell and Miss Boutwell, and the Secretary of the

Treasury; then came, dream-like, Mrs. Creswell, hand-some Mrs. Williams, and motherly Mrs. Delano. Ellen Grant stood beside her mother, and Edith Fish hovered beside her's—both winsome and unaffected girls, though the girlish grace of the latter shows, already, the fine intellectual quality of her mother. The Governor of the District, with his wife and daughter, and numerous other officials, filled the platform.

Back of the Cabinet stood the Foreign Ministers, bereft of their court attire, but glittering with decorations. Tall Lady Thornton bent like a reed in the blast; and Madame Flores, the beautiful young wife of the Minister from Equador, glowed in her warm rich beauty, even at zero. Alas! that all those wondrous tints of blue and gold, of royal purple and emerald, of lavender and rose, all the gleam of those diamonds, all the show of necks and arms, which was to have made the glory of this "court circle," alas! that they were all held in eclipse, by layers on layers of wrappings, till, at a little distance, the whole platform seemed to be filled with a crowd of animated mummies, set upright, whose motions were as spasmodic and jerky as those of Mrs. Jarley's wax works. It was very sensible—the only refuge from certain death—that all those necks and arms, diamonds, pearls, velvets and satins, should hide away under ermine capes, cloaks and shawls; but, lumped in aggregate, they did not make a pretty picture (the wraps, I mean). Indeed, the polar wave submerged the presidential platform, and made anything but a picturesque success. And how unlucky, when for the first time in the history of inauguration balls, there was a "cubby" for every hat and wrap, that every man and woman should be obliged to keep them on.

But why a "presidential platform," and why a private presidential "supper room" at an inauguration ball? Both are vulgarly pretentious. Both are preposterous, in the representatives of a republican people, in a national assembly. I am not a universal leveller. I respect the inevitable distinctions begotten of personal taste and condition. I make this remark to add a little force to my protest against meretricious, and fictitious pretence and shams. The President, as an individual, is not under the slightest obligation to invite anybody that he does not want, to his private dinner table. But when the President, *as* the President, comes into the presence of a promiscuous assembly of the people, through whose gift he holds all the honor he possesses,—a citizen uplifted by citizens to the chief magistracy of their government, how false to republican fact is the feeling that perches him up, and hedges him about, with a mock heroic exclusiveness, as if he were a king, or demi-god, instead of a stolid tanner, who fought his way to place and power, conferred on him by a nation of stavers and fighters like himself.

CHAPTER XXIX.

THE UNITED STATES TREASURY—ITS HISTORY.

AFTER the Declaration of Independence, the first thing that the Continental Congress did was to organize a Treasury Department for the new government of the colonies.

Michael Hilligas and George Clymer were appointed Joint-Treasurers of the United Colonies. They were to reside in Philadelphia, and to receive each a salary of five hundred dollars the first year, and to give bonds in the sum of one hundred thousand dollars. The second year their salary was raised to eight hundred dollars each. In a short time George Clymer was sent to Congress as a delegate from Pennsylvania, and Michael Hilligas re-

UNITED STATES TREASURY.—WASHINGTON.

mained Treasurer for the Colonies to the close of the Revolution.

In six months after the resignation of Mr. Clymer, a committee of five persons was appointed to assist him to superintend the small Treasury. Three months after, an office was created in which to keep the Treasury accounts. That office was an itinerant, like Congress, following it to whatever place it assembled. Acts were passed for the establishment of a National Mint. Alas! the poor Continentals had no precious ore to coin, and never struck off a dollar or cent. An Auditor General's office was organized, and John Gibson appointed, with an annual salary of one thousand and sixty-six dollars and sixty-seven cents.

The office of Comptroller of the Treasury was created November 3, 1778, and Jonathan Trumbull, Jr., appointed, with a salary of four thousand dollars. Money was painfully scarce. That made it the more imperative that this poor little empty Treasury should have some supreme responsible head who, by the adroit magic of financial genius, should create a way to fill it, and by some way provide cash for the unprovided-for emergencies which were perpetually imminent. Thus in September, 1781, Congress repealed the act appointing five Commissioners, and in their stead appointed a single supreme "Superintendent of Finance."

The first high functionary of the Treasury was Robert Morris, of Philadelphia. He had already distinguished himself for his remarkable financial talents as a merchant, and for his devoted patriotism. Besides, he was the intimate friend and confidential adviser of Washington. He was the man for the place and the hour. He kept the credit of the struggling Colonies afloat in their direst moment. He gave from his private fortune without stint, and added thereto the contributions of the infant nation. When even Washington was ready to give up in despair, because he had no money to pay his troops, and the troops were ready to surrender and disband from sheer misery and suffering, Robert Morris applied to "the purser of our allies, the French," and saved the perishing army and the struggling republic. He proved then, what has been proved so conspicuously since during a still greater struggle, that he who preserves the credit of his country in the hour of its peril is as truly a patriot as he who dies for her sake on the battle-field.

Notwithstanding his benefactions, at the close of the Revolution, the jealousy among foremost men was so great, it was found to be impossible to give to one man the precedence and power in so responsible a place. The claims of the three contending sections were acknowledged by the appointment of three Commissioners: one from the Eastern, one from the Middle, and one from the Southern districts, in the persons of Samuel Osgood, Walter Livingston and Arthur Lee. Robert Morris became a member of the Convention which framed the Constitution of the United States, and concluded his public services to his country as United States Senator.

At the end of three years, the administration of the three Commissioners of Finance had proved so inharmonious and unsuccessful that the country was nearly bankrupt, and the Union of States ready to break into ruins, for lack of money to pay its expenses and hold it together.

The Constitution of the United States went into effect

March 4, 1789, and Congress went into its first session in the City of New York. Two subjects moved it to its depths at once—the impending bankruptcy of the country, and the location of the National Capital. The prevention of the first depended upon the establishment of the latter. The Nation was impoverished by a long and harassing war, and depressed by an enormous debt which that war had caused. The Nation possessed no statistics indicating the resources of the country, and there was no department organized through which fiscal operations could be carried on.

The strife between the Northern and Southern States, concerning the location of the Capital, made harmonious financial legislation impossible during the opening session of the first Congress. But the committee appointed to organize a system for the collection of the revenue, were equal to its accomplishment. After four months' deliberation, July 31, 1789, the first important act connected with the Treasury Department was passed, entitled "An act to regulate the collection of the duties imposed by law on the tonnage of ships or vessels, and on goods, wares and merchandise." September 2, 1789, the fundamental act establishing the Treasury Department was enrolled as a whole, and passed.

The new Department consisted of a Secretary of the Treasury, a Comptroller, an Auditor, a Treasurer, a Registrar, and an assistant to the Secretary of the Treasury. It was decided that the settlement of all public accounts should be in the Treasury Department, making the Secretary of the Treasury the head of the Fiscal Department of the Government, placing him, however, under the authority and requirements of either House of Congress.

He superintends the collection and disbursement of the revenue of the United States, from every source derived, except that of the Post Office. He receives the returns of the revenue in general, and reports to Congress all plans of finance, and the final results of his own official action, and that of his subordinates.

The first popular candidate for the position of chief of the Treasury Department was Oliver Wolcott, a son of a signer of the Declaration of Independence, and his own services to his country, both under the Colonial Government and the Union, were acknowledged to have been important. Meanwhile. Washington, who was more anxious to find out how he was to get money to pay the public debt, than to find a man to pay it, invited his intimate and tried friend, Robert Morris, to give him the benefit of his advice. In one of their interviews, the great chief groaned out: "What is to be done with this heavy national debt?" "There is but one man," said the astute financier, "who can help you, and that man is Alexander Hamilton. I am glad that you have given me the opportunity to disclose the extent of the obligation I am under to him."

In ten days after the establishment of the Treasury Department, Alexander Hamilton was appointed its chief. He was still in the flower of his youth, but had already proved himself, not only in practical action, but in the rarest gifts of pure intellect, to be the most versatile and remarkable man of his time. Of good birth, yet, at twelve years of age, dependent upon his own exertions for support, he bore, at that tender age, the entire responsibility of a large shipping house. He seemed endowed with the quality of intellect which amounts to inspiration—unerring in perception, sure of success. The boy-manager of the shipping house earned his bread in the day time, and in the night wrote articles on commercial matters, equally remarkable for their comprehensiveness and practical knowledge. A native of St. Croix, West Indies, at fourteen he came to the United States; at eighteen, entered Kings, now Columbia College, where he at once attracted attention by his brilliant essays on political subjects. At the beginning of the Revolution, he raised and took command of a company of artillery. The same transcendent intuition which made him supreme as a financier, made him remarkable as a soldier. In Washington's first interview with him, he made him his *aide-de-camp*, and through the entire Revolutionary war, he was called "the right arm" of the Commander-in-chief.

At the close of the war he returned to New York, and stepped at once to the very front of his profession. A more remarkable and interesting group of men probably never discussed and decided the fate of a nation, than Washington, Morris, and Hamilton. Morris, wise, experienced, analytic; Washington, grave, thoughtful, far-seeing, slow to invent, but ready to comprehend, and quick to follow the counsel which his judgment approved; Hamilton, young, impetuous, impassioned, prophetic, yet practical; in comprehension and gifts of creation, the supreme of the three. Never was a nation more blessed than this, in the united quality of the men who decided its financial destiny.

The first official act of Hamilton, as Secretary of the Treasury, was to recommend that the domestic and foreign war debt be paid, dollar for dollar. When the paper containing this recommendation was read before Con-

19

gress, it thought that the new Secretary of the Treasury had gone mad. How was a nation of less than four millions of people to voluntarily assume a debt of seventy-five millions of dollars! Hamilton thought that this aggregated debt, created for the support of the national cause, should be assumed by the individual States; the outstanding Continental money to be funded at the rate of one dollar in specie for each hundred in paper, and the whole united to make the national resources available for the security of the public creditors.

The long strife in Congress over this great fundamental financial question is a matter of history. There appeared to be no national resources to meet such a demand. There was not money enough in the Treasury to pay current expenses, to say nothing of paying a debt of tens of millions. Probably no body of legislators in the world ever represented wisdom, statesmanship, pertinacity of opinion so tried in the fiery crucible of war, poverty and suffering, as did this first Congress; yet it was left to the untried minister of finance of thirty-three to save the national credit against mighty odds, and to foresee and to foretell the future resources of a vast, consolidated people. This inspiration of enthusiasm and faith, combined with practical administrative force, and a broad financial policy, averted the horrors of national bankruptcy, preserved the credit of the government, and gave to the sufferings of Valley Forge and the surrender at Yorktown their final fruition.

The young financier, bearing his burden alone, seemed to hold in himself the guarantee of future triumph. He gave to the most despairing a security of success when they remembered that, at the age of nineteen, this same young prophet and patriot was the "right hand" of Washington.

The long struggle ended in the adoption of Hamilton's great financial scheme of funding the domestic debt.

When the government was removed to Philadelphia, the Treasury was established in a plain building in Arch street, two doors east from Sixth. Here Morris, Hamilton and Washington were united in the closest bonds of personal friendship. Then followed, in rapid succession, those great state-papers on finance from Hamilton, whose embodiment into laws fixed the duties on all foreign productions, and taxed with just distinction the home luxuries and necessities of life. From these were evolved in gradual development the entire system of the Treasury Department of the United States. Time has proved how perfect were the plans which sprang without precedent from the brain of Alexander Hamilton.

First, from his suggestions came the act which established the routine by which customs were to be collected. Then came the acts for the levying of taxes and the accumulation of the revenue. Then the imposition on ships and our commercial marine, foreign and domestic. Next, a bank was established for the depository of collected funds, and their distribution throughout the country. Then was needed the crown of the grand financial structure—a legalized institution for the coinage of gold and silver. To accomplish this great design, Hamilton recommended for the adoption of Congress the establishment of a mint for the purposes of national coinage, and the act was passed April 2, 1792, fixing the establishment at the then seat of government, Philadelphia, from whence, through later legislation, it has never been transferred.

While consuming himself for his country, Hamilton was harassed by the abuse of personal and political enemies, and suffering for the adequate means to support his family. While building up the financial system which was to redeem his country, the state of his own finances may be judged by the following letter from him to a personal friend, dated September 30, 1791:

"DEAR SIR:—If you can conveniently let me have twenty dollars for a few days, send it by bearer.   A. H."

The amount of personal toil he performed for the government was enormous. Talleyrand, who was at this time a refugee in Philadelphia, after his return to France, spoke with admiring enthusiasm of the young American patriot. In speaking of his experience in America, he once said:

"I have seen in that country one of the wonders of the world—a man, who has made the future of the Nation, laboring all night to support his family."

Nobody believes that any servant of his country should be compelled to this, to-day, yet had not long-sufficed selfishness made them insensible to it, the over-greedy legislator of to-day might learn from the example of Alexander Hamilton a salutary lesson.

After six years of personal service in the Treasury, amid personal and political opposition, greater than has ever assailed any one statesman; after seeing his financial system a part of the governmental policy of his country, Hamilton resigned his office, and resumed the practice of law in the city of New York.

Established in that day of small things, in human judgment it seems impossible that the brain of one man could

have devised a monetary system that would anticipate all
the varied, conflicting and unexpected demands of a
country as large and swiftly developed as ours.   Yet,
with slight modifications, the system of Hamilton has
met all exigencies, saved the national credit, and assured
the national prosperity through the deepest trials.   It
paid the national debt of the Revolution, and of 1812,
and in the War of the Rebellion, when the governmental
expenses of a single day were more than the national income for a whole year in Hamilton's time, the foresight
and genius of this man of thirty-three had suggested ways
for the vast accumulation and disbursement.   Personally,
Hamilton was under middle size, slight, well-proportioned,
erect and graceful.   His complexion was white and pink,
his features mobile, his expression vivacious, his voice
musical, his manner cordial, his entire appearance attractive and refined.

Alexander Hamilton was succeeded by Oliver Wolcott,
Jr., as Secretary of the Treasury.   The great act of Mr.
Wolcott's administration was the revision and completion
of the laws relative to the collection of the revenue.   He
carried out, through his administration, the great fundamental principles of national finance established by Hamilton, and was re-appointed by John Adams.

When, in 1800, the Treasury Department performed its
six days' journey from Philadelphia to Washington, it went
into a plain, three-story building, facing Fifteenth street,
erected for the Treasury.   It was near the unfinished
White House, and, like all the first Federal buildings, plain
and small.   It was so small, when first taken possession of,
that it did not even afford sufficient room for the clerical
force, then fifty in number.   Its cramped space made it

necessary to deposit all the official records brought from Philadelphia in a house known as Sears' store, and the records, which would now be invaluable, were all consumed.

The first official act of the Treasury Department of national interest, dated at the national capital, directed that the Secretary should make an annual report to Congress of the state of the finances of the nation, containing estimates of the public revenue and expenditure, as well as plans for improving and increasing the revenues. Hamilton had done this voluntarily, and his example, of a Cabinet officer making communications with Congress, was now made imperative by the action of law. May 10, 1800, Samuel Dexter, another signer of the Declaration of Independence, was appointed Secretary of the Treasury in place of Oliver Wolcott. On the election of Jefferson, the foe of the Hamiltonian financial policy, the Washingtonian era of the Federal Government ended, and Mr. Dexter found himself out of harmony with the Government. After the lapse of a year, President Jefferson set the precedent of removal, and, January 26, 1802, appointed Albert Gallatin, Secretary of the Treasury.

Albert Gallatin was born in Geneva, Switzerland, in 1761. After receiving a liberal education, he came to this country at the age of eighteen. He became a tutor in Harvard College, but removing to Philadelphia, then the national capital, rose so high in public esteem that in 1790, at the age of thirty, he was elected to Congress, and afterwards to the Senate. In this body, his reports on matters of finance attracted universal attention, and, as a result, he was made Secretary of the Treasury of the United States. President Jefferson, on handing him his commission, said: "Mr. Gallatin, your most important duty will be to examine the accounts, and all the records of your department, in order to discover the blunders and frauds of Hamilton, and to ascertain what changes will be required in the system. This is a most important duty, and will require all your industry and acuteness. To do it thoroughly, you may employ whatever extra service you require."

Gallatin was an ardent partisan of the President, and declares, himself, that he undertook his task of exposing Hamilton, and bringing his lofty head low, with great zest and thoroughness. But his hunt for "blunders" and venality merged soon into a labor of love. Upon his just and comprehensive mind, Hamilton's perfect system, day by day, revealed itself. By the time he had mastered its details, and measured its completeness, he was filled with admiration. "In the honest enthusiasm of a truly great mind he went to Mr. Jefferson and said: 'Mr. President, I have, as you directed, made a thorough examination of the books, accounts and correspondence of my department, from its commencement. I have found,' said the conscientious Secretary, 'the most perfect system ever formed. Any change under it would injure it.' Hamilton made no blunders, committed no frauds; he did nothing wrong."

Albert Gallatin marked his administration by a series of reports regarding the best method of canceling the na-. tional debt, the proper policy of disposing of the public lands, and the legality and necessity of establishing a national bank. Thus, contrary to his original intention, he associated himself with Morris and Hamilton as one of the three founders of the financial policy of the nation.

By the year 1804, the business of the Treasury had so increased, that an effort was made toward the erection of a building, to become the especial depository of the records. An idea may be given of the demands of the infant government and its notions of economy, in the facts that this vaunted fire-proof public building is much smaller than an unpretentious private dwelling of the present time, and that it cost less than the sum of twelve thousand dollars.

Mr. Madison, on his accession to the Presidency, retained Mr. Gallatin at the head of the Treasury.

On March 1, 1809, an act of Congress directed that all warrants drawn on the Treasury by the Secretaries of the different executive departments, should designate the appropriation to which they were charged.

June 18, 1812, war was declared, and Congress was convened in special session, to consider the necessities of the Treasury. Out of the legislation which followed, came our present internal revenue laws. Mr. Gallatin, after having held his office longer than any of his predecessors, resigned, and went on a foreign mission. A period of extreme money depression succeeded his resignation. August 24, 1814, the British troops entered Washington, and, with the Capitol and other public buildings, burned the Treasury. The business of the Treasury, for a considerable time afterwards, was carried on in what was known as "the Seven Buildings," in the western part of the city.

George N. Campbell, of Tennessee, Mr. Gallatin's successor, attempted to negotiate a loan of twenty-five millions of dollars, but failed, and resigned his office. The national credit was at its lowest ebb.

When the need of a great man is absolute, Providence usually has one ready for the emergency. He appeared at this crisis, in the person of Alexander J. Dallas, of Pennsylvania. On entering upon his office, as head of the Treasury, he replied to the request of Congress, that he should suggest ways for the restoration of the public credit, in one of the most powerful documents extant in the archives of the Treasury. Mr. Dallas so inspired the faith of the capitalists of the country, that the national credit was at once restored. "The Treasury notes, issued on the universal opinion that they would be a drug in the market, rose to a premium."

Mr. Monroe made W. H. Crawford, of Georgia, Secretary of the Treasury. Under him, the routine of the Department was improved by the appointment of a second Comptroller and four additional Auditors. Charges of malfeasance were brought against him toward the close of his term of office. They were examined by a committee consisting of John Randolph, Edward Livingston, and Daniel Webster, who pronounced the charges false. President John Quincy Adams recalled Richard Rush, of Pennsylvania, then Minister to England, and made him Secretary of the Treasury.

Under Andrew Jackson's Presidency, the conservative management of the Treasury Department changed into "the anti-bank period." His administration was marked by five different Secretaries, and a prevailing state of excitement. The first Secretary of the Treasury, under Jackson, was Samuel D. Ingham, of Pennsylvania, whose trust ended in a violent breaking up of the Cabinet. He was succeeded by William J. Doane, of Pennsylvania, who refused to remove the national deposits from the United

States Bank, and was dethroned by Roger B. Taney, of Maryland. The Senate refused to confirm his appointment, and Levi Woodbury, of New Hampshire, was installed in the office, holding it to the end of Jackson's administration.

April 1, 1833, the Treasury Building was for the third time destroyed by fire, and a large amount of valuable public documents destroyed. Afterwards, the business of the Department was carried on in a row of brick buildings opposite Willard's Hotel. At this time the "Agent of the Treasury," was changed to Solicitor of the Treasury, and a sixth Auditor was created. Jackson's administration closed with an "apparent plethora of money among the people, and the glorious consummation of paying off the national debt."

Mr. Woodbury continued at the head of the Treasury, under President Van Buren. It was his fate to be its director " in the times of unparalleled plenty, speculation and extravagance, and two years afterwards, to witness a pecuniary revulsion that had no precedent in financial history." In 1837, financial ruin dismayed the Nation. Congress was convened by special proclamation, to devise ways and means to relieve the people. Specie payments were suspended, and all business involved in apparent ruin. Binding laws were passed, divorcing the Government from all banking institutions, and a new policy was created for the control of our national finances.

Under Presidents Harrison and Tyler there were five Secretaries of the Treasury: Thomas Ewing, of Ohio; Walter Howard, of Pennsylvania; John C. Spencer, of New York, and George M. Beble, of Kentucky. President Polk made Robert J. Walker the head of the Treasury. He was known as "the apostle of free trade." His administration was marked by the introduction of the present warehousing system, based upon English precedent; by his reciprocity system between Canada and the United States abolishing all customs and imports, and the establishment of an "Interior Department" upon the old overgrown Land Office, with a Cabinet officer to administer its affairs, under the title of Secretary of the Interior.

The Secretary of the Treasury, under President Taylor, was William M. Meredith, of Pennsylvania; who was succeeded, under President Fillmore, by Thomas Corwin, of Ohio. Secretary Corwin established the present lighthouse department and wrote the instructions regarding light-vessels, beacons and buoys. This beneficent legislation gave over six hundred lights to protect the hitherto neglected mariner on his way.

The Chief of the Treasury under President Pierce, was James Guthrie, of Kentucky. He is remembered as a strict and efficient officer, carrying out in minutiæ, the duties and laws of the department. He discovered outstanding balances against the Treasury, which, if collected, would more than pay the national debt. Of this sum he collected hundreds of millions into the Treasury, and raised the standard of efficiency in the Treasury service by demanding monthly, instead of quarterly reports, from all its *employés*.

Three Secretaries of the Treasury served under James Buchanan—Howell Cobb, of Georgia; Philip F. Thomas, of Maryland; and John A. Dix, of New York. A monetary crisis, almost as severe as that of 1837, marked this administration. The throes of Secession shook the Union to its foundation, and the Secretaries of the Treasury, like all other public servants, were occupied with the "signs of the times," the swiftly advancing portents of revolution, more than with the mere financial duties of the public Treasury.

Abraham Lincoln began his troubled administration by the appointment of Salmon P. Chase, of Ohio, as Secretary of the Treasury. Never was man asked to help steer the ship of state through more overwhelming breakers. With the dissolution of the Union imminent, the national debt had increased to three times the amount it was at the close of the previous administration. The number of clerks which, in 1861, was three hundred and eighty-three, in 1864 was two thousand. Such a demand was without precedent, and arose from the immense labor of examining accounts, and of preparing and supervising the national currency and securities.

The first important measure of Mr. Chase's administration was the "Internal Revenue Act," which, in four years, increased the income of the Government from forty-one millions to three hundred and nine millions. Next came the great "National Currency Act," which, though severely criticised, and probably not free from defects, nevertheless established a paper currency of equal value in every part of the Union, and was, at least, in keeping with the principles of our Government, and freer from chances of corruption and abuse than any other system yet adopted. It met the awful demand of the hour, and offered the guarantee of redemption, rather than of loss and ruin.

In a single month, the tax upon the income of the Treasury became stupendous. In one day, it paid out for quartermasters' stores alone, forty-six millions of dollars—

more than were needed to support the entire National Government during the first year of Washington's administration. In four years, the public debt, from ninety millions, had grown to be two thousand six hundred millions—yet under this mighty demand, with two millions of its sons withdrawn from productive labor, the exports of the country were double what they had ever been before, and the credit of the Government of the United States day by day increased.

When Mr. Chase was appointed Chief Justice by Mr. Lincoln, his high seat in the Treasury was taken by Hon. William Pitt Fessenden, whose brief career as Secretary of the Treasury was marked by a single State paper of great ability. He was succeeded by Hugh McCulloch, of Indiana, who dispensed the duties of his office creditably till the close of Johnson's administration.

President Grant, upon his accession to the Presidency, chose George S. Boutwell, of Massachusetts, to be Secretary of the Treasury. Mr. Boutwell had already served as Commissioner of Internal Revenue, and now on him devolved the huge task of reducing the high impost and revenue tax created by the war debt, and borne as a mighty burden by the people. He had to lighten the load on the people's shoulders, and yet keep the national tax high enough to meet the interest, and reduce the amount of the national debt—in fine, he was expected to relieve the Nation, and to pay the national debt at the same time. A more conflicting demand never rested on a Financial Minister. How ably he met it, the "monthly statement" of the perpetual ebb of the war debt, with the constant legislation to reduce all revenue taxation to the luxuries of life, were ample proof.

Before the election of Mr. Boutwell, as United States Senator from Massachusetts, to succeed Vice President Henry Wilson, the President appointed Judge Richardson, Acting Assistant Secretary, to be Secretary of the Treasury. Judge Richardson stepped from comparative obscurity, and an opposite sphere of labor, to his present high official position. There are many who challenge his claim to it, and his fitness for it. Time may prove one, and disprove the other. As Secretary of the Treasury, his official record is yet to be made—until his administration has been marked by an act of national importance, it is too early to pronounce a verdict.

In the statistics of the Treasury Department, we read the marvellous financial history of our country. In them we trace the material progress of the Nation from its beginning. In the accounts current business of the country, we learn that in the years 1793, '94, '95, '96, the Nation imported productions valued at one hundred and seventy-four millions of dollars. In the years 1866, '67, '68, '69, the United States exported values to the amount of nineteen hundred millions. The value between these sums marks the growth of population, territory, and material resources in the space of seventy years—surely, a narrow span in the life of a nation!

CHAPTER XXX.

INSIDE THE TREASURY—THE HISTORY OF A DOLLAR.

A Washington Tradition—"Old Hickory" Erects his Cane—"Put the Building Right Here"—Treasury Corner-Stone Laid—Robert Mills' Discolored Colonnade—Where "Privileged Mortals" Work—A Very Costly Building—Rapid Extension of Business—Splendid Situation of the Building—The Workers Within—The Government Takes a Holiday—The Business of Three Thousand People—The Mysteries of the Treasury—Inside the Rooms—Mary Harris's Revenge—The "Drones" in the Hive—Making Love in Office Hours—Flirtations in Public—A Vast Refuge for the Unfortunate—Two Classes of *Employés*—A List of Miserable Sinners—A Pitiful Ancient Dame—A *Protégé* of President Lincoln—Women's Work in the Treasury—The Bureau of Printing and Engraving—A very Hot Precinct—Rendering a Strict Account—Not a Cent Missing—The "Chief's" Report—Dealing in Big Figures—The Story of a Paper Dollar—In the Upper Floor—The Busy Workers—Night Work—Where the Paper is Made—The "Localized Blue Fibre"—*The* Obstacle to the Counterfeiter—The Automatic Register—Keeping Watch—The Counters and Examiners—Supplying the Bank Note Companies—"The American" and "The National"—An Armed Escort—No Incomplete Notes Possible—Varieties of Printing—The Contract with Adams' Express—Printing the Notes and Currency—Internal Revenue Stamps—Thirty Young Ladies Count the Money—Manufacturing the Plates—The Engraving Division—"The Finest Engravers in the Country"—The Likeness of Somebody—Transferring a Portrait—"Men of Many Minds"—The Division of Labor—Delicate Operations—A Pressure of Five or Six Tons—The Plate Complete—"Re-entering" a Plate—An "Impression"—How Old Plates are Used up—A Close Inspection—Defying Imitation—The Geometric Lathe—Tracing "Lines of Beauty" for More than Forty Years.

IT is one of the traditions of Washington that Andrew Jackson decided the exact site of the present Treasury Building.

After the third destruction by fire, in 1833, of the early Treasury Buildings, a great strife came up concerning the location of the new Treasury. Worn out with the claims of "rival factions," it is said that President Jackson walked out a few rods from the White House one morning, and thrusting his cane into the ground, exclaimed : " Put the building right here ! " This ended all disputes, and the end of the " old hero's " cane marked the north-east corner of the present site of the Treasury of the United States.

Though nearly approached by the Patent Office, the Treasury Building, in architectural splendor, ranks next to the Capitol. Its corner-stone was laid in 1834 by Levi Woodbury, then Secretary of the Treasury. The original building was designed by Robert C. Mills, whose long and discolored colonnade on Fifteenth street is still visible. It was built of the freestone brought from near Acquia Creek, Virginia, which has touched with premature dinginess too many of the Federal buildings of the Capital. But in the Treasury its long line of smut is lost in the marble splendor of the extensions. The extension of the building was authorized in 1835, and built from the designs of Thomas W. Walter. It embodies the most perfect Grecian architecture, adapted to modern uses. It surrounds a hollow square, on which its inner offices look out on green grass and cooling fountain through the summer heats. Instead of cooped-up cells, the lower stories of the Treasury are filled with airy apartments, in which privileged mortals serve their country and earn their bread and butter. The new Treasury is built of gleaming granite brought from Dix Island, on the coast of Maine.

The walls of the extension are composed of pilasters, resting on a base which rises some twelve feet above the ground on the southern or lower side. Between the pilasters are *antœ* or belt-courses, nobly moulded; the facings of the doors and windows bear mouldings in harmony. The southern, western and northern fronts present magnificent porticoes. Its lofty pillars are of the Ionic order, and the entire building is at last surmounted by a massive balustrade. The south wing was completed and occupied in 1860. The west wing was completed in 1863—the north in 1867—the whole at a cost of $6,750,000. The exterior is four hundred and sixty-four feet by two hundred and sixty-four feet.

The Treasury was begun and consummated on a truly magnificent scale, and with the expectation that it would meet every demand of its own branch of the public service for at least a century. Like every one of the public buildings, it is already too small to accommodate the over-crowded bureaus of its own departments, several of which, for want of room in the Treasury Building, already occupy other houses in different parts of the city; and yet there is not space left for those who remain. Before the year 1900, another Treasury Building as magnificent as the one now our pride, will be indispensable to the ever-increasing demand of the departments of the financial service.

The Treasury borrowed its face from the Parthenon; and, as it turns it toward the Potomac this May morning, it is one of the fairest sites in Washington. From the southern portico we look across sloping tree-shaded meadows. Beyond, we see the shimmering river, with its girdle of green, and above, "the flush and frontage of the hills." When flowers, and trees and soft lights shall have

20

taken the place of all this glare—how beautiful it will be to the eyes of generations to come. But even now the bright grass, flower-parterres and lapsing fountains are pleasant to behold, while the southern front of the Treasury is an object upon which the eyes must always rest with a sense of satisfaction.

The Capitol lords it over the east, but the Treasury reigns over the west end. To be sure, it stands upon the poorest make-believe of an Acropolis, but coming along Pennsylvania avenue we look up to its noble façade and fair Ionic columns gleaming before us, as a compensation for the poverty of beauty in the streets which we travel. The western windows overlook the grounds of the presidential mansion, now gay with flowers and dazzling with sunshine, their trees decked in the vivid foliage of a southern June-time.

How many pairs of weary human eyes look up from their tasks within these walls, and, without knowing it, thank God for this fair outlook. The breeze-blown grass, the fragrant winds, the lavish light of these open windows— to dusty lips and tired eyes which take them in—are God's own benedictions. Hundreds of such look up from their desks. Past the great fountain, tossing its diamonds below, past the sunny knolls and mimic mounds of newly-cut grass, above the bloom-burdened trees and all the tender verdure of early spring and summer, they see the windows of the presidential reception-room, whose doors, through all the winter months, are besieged by an army of office and favor seekers, but which are shut and silent and deserted now, while " the Government" drives among the hills or loiters by the sea.

But I began to talk about the Treasury, and no matter

how I wander for ever so many pages, I must come back
to it again.

It is easier to comprehend the outside than the inside
of it. One might as well try to snatch up a city and
portray it in a sitting, as even to outline the Treasury
of the United States in a single chapter.

It holds a metropolis within its walls. It affords daily
employment to over three thousand persons, and thousands more daily throng its halls. Just a glimpse into
this vast human hive makes us long for a Dickens to
embody the romance and reveal the mysteries of the
Treasury. The story of the Circumlocution Office and
the Court of Chancery pale before the revelations and undreamed of human experiences which it holds. Before you,
behind you, and on either side stretch out the great marble
paved halls. Out of these open numberless rooms, whose
shut doors stare blankly, or whose half-open blinds wink
and blink at each other through the gleaming cross lights.

Over these doors you read significant inscriptions, such
as First Comptroller's Office, First Auditor's Office, etc.
You ascend the great stairs and find other halls, such as
those below, and like them lined on each side by doors.
Over these you read, "Loan Branch," "Redemption
Branch," "Office of the Register," "Office of Secretary
of the Treasury," etc. Many of the open doors reveal to
you large airy apartments filled with busy men and women.
Many more show you narrow, one-windowed apartments,
each containing a desk, or desks, with its scribe, or scribes.

Here we see men who have grown gray, weak-limbed
and wizened in those rooms beside those desks. They have
grown to be as automatic as their pens, and as narrow as
their rooms. Here also are thousands of men in their

prime and in their youth representing every phase of character. In this hall, just by this door, Mary Harris watched for the man who had robbed and ruined her—and just here she shot him. Poor thing! With her blighted face she is a maniac, now in the Asylum across the river. These halls are as thronged as Broadway, and their denizens are as cosmopolitan. People of all nations and costumes come and go along their vast vistas.

There are drones in this hive. These are office hours, yet here and there may be seen a young man and maiden whose in-door costume marks them as *employés* of the Treasury, loitering in the shadow of pillar or alcove, lingering by stair or doorway, saying very pleasant things to each other, doubtless, after the manner of young maidens and men. Flirting or making love in the flare of the public must always be a desecration of the heart's best sanctities. Beside, Sassafras and Sacharissa, you ought to be at work. It is precisely such as you who have brought discredit even upon the faithful and unfortunate, and sometimes rebuke upon the whole Treasury Department. For, as a rule, the Treasury, like all the other departments of Washington, is a vast refuge for the unfortunate and the unsuccessful. The only exceptions are found in two classes, viz.: those who use departmental life as the ladder by which to climb to a higher round of life and service, and those who seek it without half fulfilling its duties, because too inefficient to fill any other place in the world well. Unpractical authors, sore-throated, pulpitless clergymen, briefless lawyers, broken down merchants, poor widows, orphaned daughters, and occasionally an adventurer, masculine and feminine, of doubtful or bad degree, —all are found within the Treasury.

I remember an aged woman, with bent back and long, wasted fingers, sitting behind the door in the Redemption Bureau. Her dim eyes peered through her spectacles and her poor fingers trembled, as she tried to count the dirty, ragged currency. "Alas! sad eyes," I thought, "by this time rest from toil should have come to you." "It is pitiful," I said, to the kind gentleman who reigned over the division, "that one so old should have to come through rain and snow to fulfil a daily task. Is she not too old to do her duty well!"

"No," was the answer, "she does it very well. But if not, she would never be removed. She is a *protégé* of President Lincoln."

But any one who fancies that even woman's work in the Treasury Department is a sinecure, should climb to the Bureau of Printing and Engraving. You may climb, but you cannot enter unless you hold a written "sesame" from the Secretary of the Treasury; so sacred and guarded is this very hot precinct in which Uncle Samuel creates his "Almighty Dollar." The business of this Bureau is to engrave, print, and perfect for delivery to the United States Treasurer, all United States notes, Treasury checks, gold notes, drafts, fractional currency notes, all bonds and revenue stamps issued by the Government of the United States.

At the close of each day, every fraction which has passed through the division for the last twelve hours must be accounted for. If a cent is missing, all the workers of the Bureau are detained until the missing fraction is certainly found and safely deposited in the vault of the Treasury. The vast monetary responsibility resting on the Chief of this Bureau may be judged from a statement made, in his own report, for the fiscal year ending June 30, 1872.

ʳ "There has been finished and delivered to the proper officers of the Government by this Bureau, during the fiscal years ending June 30, 1870, 1871, 1872, in notes, bonds and securities, $2,050,141, and 331,273,955 stamps, and not a note, nor a sheet, nor a portion of a sheet or note has been lost to the Government."

But I hold the "open sesame;" so come with me and begin the story of a paper dollar. Walking through the long, cool corridors and the airy saloons of the lower Treasury, who would dream that afar up, close under its clinging roof, ceaseless fires burn, engines play, eager shuttles fly, and patient hands ply through all the nights and days to make the people's dollar! Here in these low, close rooms, these crowded halls, whose roofs press down so low that even a child, in many places, could not stand erect beneath it, patient men and women,—weary, gray, and old, —and youth, with its first tints yet unbleached by the burning atmosphere in which it toils,—all are at work making the paper dollar.

Sometimes in the dark night, down the granite colonnades, athwart the great trees dimly waving in mid-air, across the lapsing fountains, stream long gleams of light shooting from the tiny loop-hole windows high up under the Treasury roof. They dart from the Printing Bureau of the Nation. While the Nation sleeps, its servants, through the long, still hours, go on making the people's money!

First, the paper! It is all manufactured at "Glen Mills," near Philadelphia, by the Messrs. Wilcox, who own the mills, and are the patentees of the "localized blue fibre," made of jute, which runs through the right-hand end of the fractional currency and United States notes, and on the back of the bonds, etc. This fiber is *the* obstacle to the counterfeiter, and can only be overcome by oiling or soiling the spurious paper, so that its absence cannot be discovered. The paper is chemically prepared, and the application of an acid will change the tint to one color, and an alkali, to another. Thus any attempt to alter the filling-in or denomination of the stamped check, is defeated.

A Government superintendent resides at Glen's Falls, who, with a corps of assistants, receives the paper from the contractors, counts, examines, holds it carefully guarded night and day, until delivered to the Treasury of the United States. To each paper-making machine is attached an automatic register, by which the mill-owners account to the Government for every square inch and sheet recorded by this register, the register being locked, and the key held securely in the pocket of a Government officer, who watches the work. During its manufacture and storage at the mills, this paper is guarded, by day and night, by a regularly organized "watch." The Government Superintendent has a corps of counters and examiners under his direction, who examine and count the paper, as received from the makers, before it is packed away for shipment. The account is sent to the Department, and paid each day by the Secretary.

The paper is supplied the Bank Note Companies only upon requisition from the Bureau at Washington. Mr. Bemis, the Superintendent, makes a report to the Printing Bureau, also to the Secretary of the Treasury, of all the paper delivered to him. The first journey made by this governmental infant, is to the Bank Note Companies

—two of them, one in New York, the other in Philadelphia—the American and the National—that there may
not be any dangerous monopoly of priceless charms. It
is borne to the depot by an armed escort, and conveyed
on the cars by Adams' Express. The New York Company, printing tints, must turn over to the Company printing backs, notes equivalent to the paper, and the second
Company must similarly account to the Government for
every incomplete note received—thus neither can possess
itself wholly of this beloved child. One Company prints
the tints of one denomination, and the back of the other,
no Company executing on the same note both printings.

The national bank notes, hitherto engraved and printed
entirely in New York, coming only to the Government
Printing Bureau for numbering and sealing, hereafter will
be exclusively engraved and printed in the Treasury.
The jute-fibred paper will also be used in their making, as
it is in the United States notes. The face of the Treasury notes is printed in black and green, the back in green.
The National Bank Note face dares to be printed in black,
and its back in black and green.

This tinted and outlined paper is conveyed to the Treasury by Adams' Express, who have the contract for carrying all the Government moneys and securities.

When it reaches the Treasury, the work yet to be
done by the Printing and Engraving Bureau, before the
paper is complete as Government money, is to print the
face upon the United States notes, and hereafter, on the
National Bank notes, to plate-seal, to number, trim, and
cut them into single notes; to trim, surface-seal, and cut
into single notes the ten, fifteen, and twenty-five, fractional currency notes; to print the face of, trim, surface-

seal, and separate the fifty cent notes; trim, surface-seal, and number the "funded loan bonds;" to trim, number, and surface-seal, the national bank notes; and to print the faces upon all the tints for internal revenue-stamps, already printed in New York. Besides all this work, the following are entirely engraved and printed in the Bureau of the Treasury: All strip-tobacco and snuff-stamps, stub and sheet snuff-stamps, domestic and customs cigar-stamps, compound liquor-stamps, crew lists ships' registers, brewers' permits, all the new special tax-paid stamps, (sixteen in number,) all miscellaneous bonds, gold notes, checks, drafts, etc.

When this precious paper, with its black and green lines and tints, fresh from the Bank Note Companies, arrives at the Treasury, it is placed into the hands of thirty young ladies for counting, one lady counting it twice, then passing it to another, for verification.

The next act in the process of making a dollar, is the manufacture of the plates used in printing. They are made in the engraving division of the Bureau, under the supervision of Mr. Casilear, a gentleman distinguished in his profession, who presides over a corps of the finest en · gravers in the country. Their work upon the plate of the United States note, is the engraving of its different parts. First, the face which it is to bear. This is always noticeably a perfect likeness of the person whom it represents. A daguerreotype or photograph is used. On the metallic plate of the daguerreotype the features are drawn lightly, the artist following accurately the lines of the portrait. If a photograph is used, gelatine is laid over it, and the picture is traced. From this outline on the plate, an impression is printed. This impression, by a

chemical process, is transferred to a steel plate covered
with wax. The outlines are then traced on steel, the
wax removed, and the face, in outline, is then on the
steel. The shading is then completed.

So many phases of consummate skill are necessary to
the completion of a single dollar note, that "many men
of many minds" are required to perfect a single plate.
One has a genius for landscape, another for portraits, another for animal figures. The portrait is given to one,
the lettering to another, the ornamental work to a third,
and on and on. These fragments of the perfect picture
to be, are executed upon separate bits of soft steel.
When the lines on them are completed, these different
bits of soft steel are put into an iron box, case-hardened
and annealed in a crucible of intense heat, then suddenly cooled by dipping them in oil, which utterly hardens the soft steel. Rolls of soft steel are then prepared.
By the application of a powerful press, the various pictures and lines, that the artists have engraved, are taken
up by the soft steel rollers from the hard steel plate.
The intaglio work appears on the roll, just as it afterwards appears on the note.

Now, the note-face is in fragments on the surface of
the separate rolls. Next, the rolls are hardened, and
placed in a transfer press over a flat plate of soft steel.
Upon this plate, the operator of the press, by applying
the lever, can, if necessary, impose a pressure equal to
five or six tons. This pressure transfers the fragmentary
picture to the plate. Then its counterpart picture is set
in exact juxtaposition. The operator uses his steady
hand, and skilled eyes, to set like a mosaic, each fragment
of the complete design. Then moving the roller softly,

to and fro, to equalize the pressure on every part of the picture, he continues to do so till the plate is hardened. He then passes a soft roll over it, and the entire note-face is taken up.   In turn, this roll is hardened, and the note-face transferred from it to a soft steel plate.   This final plate, hardened and polished, is the plate from which the note is at last printed.

After this plate has been used for thirty thousand impressions, its fading lines are restored by "re-entering" the plate with a roll.   It is then used for thirty thousand impressions more.   When finally "used up," these plates are destroyed in the presence of a mixed committee of Treasury officers and members of Congress.

Look closely at the United States notes, the fractional currency bonds, and the most valuable revenue stamps, and you will see many lines involved and intricate, running to and fro in the most marvellous manner.   These lines defy imitation.   They are the best tantalizer and detective of the most accurate counterfeiter.   The most absolute imitation, made by hand, can be instantly perceived under a glass.   These involuting lines are the work of the geometric lathe, an instrument whose complicated wheels can be set to work out any combination of curved lines which the human mind can possibly conceive.   The counterfeiter, with the same lathe, would be powerless to produce the same complications—"he would grow gray in endless and useless experiments, and even with a record of the combination, he could not so exactly re-produce it, that an expert could not detect the imposition."

· The geometric lathe of the Treasury of the United States, is worked by Mr. Tichenor, who has been a skilled artist in such machinery for more than thirty years.

There are no more interesting objects in the Treasury, than the line of clear-eyed men who sit bent over their tasks, their subtle lines tracing the exquisite vignettes which have made the engravings of the United States Treasury so famous. Here is one who has been tracing these lines of beauty for more than forty years: his hair is white, but his keen, strong sight—drawing harmony, poetry, nature, and life, out of barest outline—remains undimmed.

CHAPTER XXXI.

THE WORKERS IN THE TREASURY—HOW THE MONEY IS MADE.

O MY ! that dollar ! I left far back, flying through the fair hands (more or less) of thirty lovely " counters," to find it here, sopped in the tubs of the " wetters."

Long trough-like tubs run down the middle of an attic-room, at whose sides the roof slopes so low, a child could not stand under it. Even at its apex, a slender girl beside her tub can scarcely stand upright. At either side of the long troughs are rowed maids and matrons, some fair and young, some old and worn, all bearing unmistakably the mark of the servant of necessity. So near and hot to the brain is the scorching roof, each woman wears upon her head a covering of brown paper, for protection. Who will say these lowly servants of the Government do not earn the scanty pittance of their daily dollar?

In the " wetting division " is received, counted, and " wet down," all the paper that is to be plate printed. Here, in different stages of progression, we see blank sheets wetted for first printing, and sheets in preparation for second, third, and even fourth printing. The counters of this division put every twenty sheets in the hands of the wetters, who place them between cloths and submerge them in the liquid of the tubs before them. Every one thousand sheets, thus wetted, are placed between wooden boards, under the pressure of two hundred and fifty pounds. In these cerements they remain for three or four hours, when they are taken out, the top sheets made to change places with the middle ones, that uniform dampness may be secured. The sheets are then laid again between the weights, to remain till the next morning, when they are taken out, piled up under damp cloths to wait the call of the plate-printers. All this systematic saturation is indispensable to the securing of a fine print impression.

A distinct account is kept with each printer, which must be " all right " before he goes home. For example, a plate-printer calls at the wetting division for a thousand

MEEDER & CHUBB N.Y.

MAKING MONEY.—THE ROOM IN THE TREASURY BUILDING WHERE THE GREENBACKS ARE PRINTED

sheets. These are given him, and charged at once on the books of the division. As fast as he prints his work, he sends it to the office of his printing division, and is credited with all the work that he has accomplished. At the close of the day, if he has any sheets left unprinted, he returns them to the wetting division, and is credited with them as sheets returned. His work performed and work returned must then be ascertained, and his account strictly balanced, before he can leave the Treasury.

The wetting division is superintended by Mr. J. H. Lamb, who, with Mr. Ward Morgan, the head of the face-printing division, Mr. Edgar of the examining division, and Mr. Evans, the United States Sealer, have all been chosen to preside over their distinct divisions on account of their practical experience in plate-printing, gained by personal toil at the press itself.

Now we come to the Face-printing Room of the troublesome little dollar. One hundred and thirty-five presses are flying in this room and another; the latter printing the seals and tints of cigar-stamps, gold-notes, etc., in hues as varied as the leaves in autumn. Standing in this door, looking down this long apartment, we see seventy-five presses flying at once. The air is quick with dangerous motion. Great shuttle-like fans flap above our heads. At every angle, presses, eager and accurate, seem ready to strike you, as well as the dollar, with unerring skill and execution. Beside each one stands a man, with face begrimed. Beside each man stands a woman, the helpmate of his toil. Between each flames a fiery little brazier, holding the gleaming plate to keen heat. The face printer runs his roller, wet with ink over the face of the absorbing plate. A cloth in his hand comes swiftly after, leaving only the fine lines of the plate traced with ink. The ready woman lays the moist paper on the warm ink-lined plate. The printer touches the wheel, turns it, the sheet flies up. Lo! at last, the beautiful new dollar! The girl takes it instantly, lays it, face down, on top of its new-born brethren. Already the roller is passing again over the polished plate, and her hands are outstretched to lay another sheet upon the waiting plate. In less than a minute another dollar is made.

An automatic register is connected with each press; thus every sheet, note, or stamp printed, is recorded, and serves as a check on the counter and printer. The register is locked, and the key kept with the keeper of the registers, appointed by the Secretary.

After leaving the press and being heaped a few moments by its side, the next thing that happens to our damp little dollar, is to be dried. The moist sheets, spread upon racks, are carried to the drying room until the next morning. The drying process leaves the sheets with a rough, wrinkled surface. The little dollar comes forth from its first bed, looking wizened and old, and is immediately sent to the "pressing division" to be rejuvenated. Here every thousand sheets, for six minutes, are subjected to a slow, steady pressure of two hundred and forty tons, from which every sheet issues smooth, soft, polished, and precious to the touch, as every soul will say who has been the first possessor of a virgin dollar.

The pressing division is superintended by Mr. Rallon, the "Nestor" of the Bureau. Mr. Edgar, superintendent of the examining division, assisted by thirty young ladies, takes care of the face-printed work. Mr. Evans, the

United States Sealer, examines all the seal and tint prints. All mutilated, are carried to the counting division before being sent to the Secretary for destruction. Each printer is allowed a small percentage for unavoidable mutilation. If at the end of the month his number of mutilated exceeds this allowance, he is obliged to pay for the excess. Each printer works by "the piece," and pays the woman who helps him—the price being regulated by the Bureau—one dollar per day.

After coming forth from the hydraulic presses, softly polished, every exquisite line and figure embossed in keen relief, the United States note sheets pass to the surface-sealing division. The process of seal-printing is the same as the first, and each sheet has to go through the same process the second time. Under the superintendence of Mr. Gray, six "Gordon" and six "Campbell" presses print the beautiful pink surface-seals. Here the small currencies, the national bank notes, the new special tax-paid stamps, receive the internal revenue seal. The "funded loan bond" alone is stamped with the aristocratic green seal.

Having been sealed, the dollar must now be numbered, and for that purpose passes into the numbering division, where it receives the last touch of printing from machines attended solely by women and girls. This machine works on the same principle as the famous paging machine. The numbers are set on the surface of a small wheel, and with every stroke of the stamp the next consecutive number flies up into its place ; with the same stroke, a small roller, taking the red ink from the plate and feeding it to the type. These machines are regulated to change the numbers for a whole series. Two red num-

21

bers on each bill are put on by these machines. Intense care is necessary in this work, to prevent mistakes, and each bill is critically examined to ascertain its correctness. If mistakes are discovered at once, they can be rectified ; but the red ink soon hardens and becomes indelible. If the mistake is discovered too late to correct it, it is charged to the lady who made it. This has been found to be the only way to secure adequate care on the part of the numberers.

The last line of printing is received in the red number set at top and bottom; all that remains for the dollar, before starting on its journey into the wide, wide world, is to be divided from its brethren, that it may start alone. Thus the United States note sheet is carried into the separating and trimming room. This used to be done by scissors, and gave to women, I believe, their first work in the Treasury. This room is one of the largest and busiest in the Bureau, and second only to the printing-room in interest. The wheels, straps and pulleys reaching to the ceiling, with which its air is perforated, give it, at first glance, a complicated atmosphere, till the eyes rest upon the many ladies sitting serenely at work below.

This work being all clean, and some of it dainty in its character, the result is visible in the tasteful attire of the workers, whose snowy aprons and delicate ribbons are in direct contrast to the worn and soiled raiment of the weary sisterhood of the tubs, and the inky presses of the wetting and printing divisions. Part of the woman's work of this room is to needle the sheets, which must be done so accurately, that when hundreds together are laid in the cutting machine, the glittering blade will strike through a single line, not wavering a hair's width

through two hundred sheets. The room is thronged with those little guillotines, whose gleaming blades are in constant execution. Each Treasury note sheet which passes under them is cut into four notes at once, each sliding down, correctly sorted, into its own little box waiting below. Excepting the fractional currency cutters, all these exquisite machines are worked by ladies, who manipulate them with unerring accuracy.

In this Bureau but one more thing remains for our dollar, that it should be laid " in its little bed," before it goes down to the Treasurer. This is speedily done, and its bed is a very dainty affair,—a pretty box, made in an adjoining room by pretty hands; and pretty hands lay our dollar away; indeed dollar on dollar, so many in a box, which shuts them in—fair, tempting, tantalizing—out of sight, to await the call of the Treasurer and the mandate of Uncle Samuel.

There are fourteen divisions in the Printing and Engraving Bureau. Yet it is its unyielding rule that not a sheet of paper can pass from the hands of one superintendent to his operatives without a verified count and a written receipt, which is made a permanent record in a book kept for the purpose. At the close of each day's labor, the operatives in every room report to its superintendent, before they leave the building, how much paper they have received, how much finished, returning the balance. The superintendent of each room makes a report, on a printed form, at the end of each day, showing the amount of paper received, delivered up to the morning, through the day, the amount delivered that day, the amount on hand. This report is delivered to the Chief of the Bureau of Engraving and Printing, and a duplicate sent to the

Secretary. From these reports the Secretary compiles his report of the work of the entire Bureau, which must correspond with the report made by the Chief of the Bureau.

When any given issue of notes or bonds is completed, the Secretary of the Treasury holds a report, which is a complete history of the issue through all its stages of growth, from beginning to end. The test of the utter thoroughness of this system, is that every note printed in this department from its beginning, if returned to superintendents, could be traced, through every stage, back to blank paper; the books showing the date of its arrival, and by whom it was printed, sealed, numbered, separated, and delivered to the Treasurer of the United States.

The system of checks used by the Bureau of Printing and Engraving is so perfect that it is almost impossible for the Government to lose a fraction from it. The paper is registered at the mills—every sheet accounted for. Every sheet manufactured is accounted for every day. To perfect a fraudulent issue, there would have to be a universal collusion between all the superintendents of all the divisions and all the operatives, and between the superintendents and operatives. Several high officers of the Printing Bureau are appointed by the Secretary, independent of the Chief of the Bureau of Printing and Engraving, which is another security against danger. These are but a part of the safeguards within which the United States Treasury holds its dollars.

Mr. McCartee, the present Chief of the Bureau of Printing and Engraving of the United States Treasury, is so utterly the master of the momentous machinery which he "runs," that you cannot ask him a question concerning the labor in detail of his eleven hundred *employés*, that he cannot answer more perfectly than the person doing the work.

Beside his own practical knowledge of the business committed to his charge in minutiæ, he employs only men trained from their youth up in the art of plate engraving, to perform the skilled labor, or to superintend the divisions of this most important Governmental Bureau. The responsibilities and mental anxieties of its chief are so inexorable, that he must be at his post by a little past seven in the morning, and remain till five P. M. He must return about seven P. M., and remain until ten at night. Often the wheels and presses, and patient hands of this department, go from day to day to be able to meet the enormous demand of the country upon its resources. No added comment is necessary to prove how honorable is its lowliest toil, or how indispensable to its chief are the highest mental and moral qualities.

CHAPTER XXXII.

THE LAST DAYS OF A DOLLAR.

The Division of Issues—Ready for the World—Starting Right—Forty Busy
Maids and Matrons—Counting Out the Money—Human Machines—A
Lady Counting for a Dozen Years—Fifty Thousand Notes in a Day—
Counting Four Thousand Notes in Twenty Minutes—Travelling on Be-
half of Uncle Sam—In Need of a Looking-Over—" Detailed " for the
Work—What has Passed Through *Some* Fingers—Big Figures—Packing
Away the Dollars—The Cash Division—The Marble Cash-Room—The
Great Iron Vault—Where Uncle Sam Keeps His Money—Some Nice
Little Packages—Taking it Coolly—One Hundred Millions of Dollars in
Hand—Some Little White Bags—The Gold Taken from the Banks of
Richmond—Anxious to Get Their Money Back—A Little Difficulty—Not
yet " Charged "—A Distinction without a Difference—Charming Variety—
A Nice Little Hoard—Five Hundred Millions Stored Away—The Secret
of the Locks—The Hydraulic Elevator—Sending the Money off—How
the Money is Transported—Begrimed, Demoralized, and Despoiled—
Where is our Pretty Dollar?—The Redemption Division—Counting Muti-
lated Currency—Women at Work—Sorting Old Greenbacks—Three
Hundred Counterfeit Dollars Daily—Detecting Bad Notes—" Short,"
" Over," and " Counterfeit "—Difficulty of Counterfeiting Fresh Notes
—Vast Amounts Sent for Redemption—Thirty-one Million Dollars in
One Year—The Assistant Treasurer at New York—The Cancelling
Room—The Counter's Report—The Bundle in a Box—Awkward Respon-
sibility—" Punching " Old Dollars—They are Chopped in Two—Paying
for Mistakes—The Funeral of the Dollar—The Burning, Fiery Furnace
—" The Burning Committee "—What They Burn Every Other Day—
The End of the Dollar.

FOLLOWING our dollar, we come this soft summer
morning to the Division of Issues. It is in the Treasurer's Bureau, and here, crisp, new and ready for its ad-
ventures, our dollar has arrived. The fate that may

await it out in the world, the wildest fancy cannot foretell ; but before it starts on its long pilgrimage, it must
be again manipulated by fair fingers, to see that it starts
"all right."

We enter a long, light, airy room; and here at a table
sit forty or more maids and matrons, counting the new
notes. Pretty maidens! Pretty dollars! Our dollar
among the rest. Crinkling, fluttering, flying, the dollars!
Serene, silent, swift, the maidens! That anything can
be counted so rapidly and yet so accurately, defies belief.
It is the marvel of this counting, that it is as infallible as
it is flying. The fingers of forty women play the part
of perfected machinery, the numbered notes passing
through them with the celerity and regularity of automatic action.

This perfection of mathematical movement is acquired
only by long practice and by one order of intellect.
There are persons who can never acquire this unerring
accuracy of mind and motion combined. There is a lady
sitting here who has been in this division since it was
organized, in 1862, who can, upon demand, count fifty
thousand notes in one day. As the department hours of
work are from nine to three o'clock, and half an hour is
taken at noon for lunch, these fifty thousand notes must
all be counted in the space of five and a half hours.
This is at a rate of nine thousand and ninety notes each
hour, one hundred and fifty each minute and two and a
half each second. The same lady will count four thousand legal tender notes in twenty minutes. These lady
counters, with a number of their sister peers from the
Redemption Division, perform numerous journeys for
Uncle Samuel whenever the Treasury Offices in other

cities need a "looking over." At such times they are "detailed" to go and count the Government funds there.

Through the fingers of these ladies has passed every note—legal tender or fractional—which has been issued by the United States since the beginning of the war of the rebellion. Every note, ever touched or seen, with all the gold-notes and the millions of imperfect bonds and notes never put in circulation—every one has passed through these same deft fingers. The total value of this vast amount, up to July, 1872, was about two thousand nine hundred million dollars, more than two hundred and twenty-three millions of which was in postal and fractional currency.

As soon as the new money is counted, it is again put away—the legal tenders in strong paper wrappers, the fractional currency in paper boxes. All are sealed, put on a hand-cart, and rolled off to the vaults of the cash division, whither we still, you and I, pursue our little dollar.

Passing through the cashier's office and the superb Marble Cash-room (to which we will soon return), at the opposite end we reach one almost exclusively occupied by the iron vault of the United States Treasury. The double iron doors swing slowly back, and we stand in the money vault of the nation. It looks light and airy as a china-closet. The sealed packages, lining the shelves to the ceiling, are full of money. I hold a small package in my hand of crisp, stamped paper, tied with common twine, and "take it coolly" when the keeper of these coffers tells me that the string ties in one hundred millions of dollars. It doesn't seem much!

On the shelf of a cosy closet are piled some little

white bags which have done a deal of travelling. They hold the gold captured from Jefferson Davis's fleeing trains, taken from the banks of Richmond. You know the banks of Richmond have been very anxious to get their money back, and have sent numerous messengers after it. A small obstacle, in the shape of a fact, separates them from the object of their desire. This gold was rifled from the mint in New Orleans, and before it came to the banks of Richmond belonged to the Treasury of the United States.

In this vault is packed away all the money not needed for circulation. A large portion of the money which lines these shelves has never been charged to the Treasurer on the books of the department, therefore, technically, is not yet money, although all ready for use. Every kind of note which the ingenuity of Uncle Sam and his servants ever devised, is here packed and guarded. The compartments of the safe not affording sufficient space, the floor is piled—and as carelessly, apparently, as if with potato or apple bags; but not in fact. The value of every bag and package is known, and not one cent could be taken without being swiftly discovered and pursued. Piles on piles of little bags and packages! this is all, and yet they hold five hundred millions of dollars. Little bags and packages these are, all, and yet for them men toil, struggle, sin—sell their bodies and their souls!

On each of the doors of this iron vault are two burglar-proof locks, of the most complicated construction, each on a combination different from the rest. But two or three persons know these combinations, and no person knows the combination to the locks on both doors.

Thus it is impossible that they should be fraudulently opened, save by collusion between two persons who know the combination. This is but one of the safeguards which the Government sets about its treasures.

A few paces from the door of this vault is the elevator communicating with the room of the agent of Adams' Express Company, on the basement floor below. The motive power of this elevator is Potomac-water, from the water-mains. Two iron pistons, about eight inches in diameter, attached to the elevator platform, one on each side, move smoothly up and down in perpendicular iron cylinders. A turn of the handle admits the water into the cylinder beneath the pistons, which are forced up by the pressure, and with them the elevator. A reverse movement of the handle allows the water to escape from the cylinders, and the elevator descends. Its movements are noiseless, and it is managed with remarkable ease. Up and down, this servant, swift and silent, bears the moneys of the people. It is just descending, piled high with packages, some directed to banks, railroad and manufacturing companies. Others are addressed to assistant treasurers and depositors of the United States. Much is going to replace the old money already sent back to the Treasury for destruction. All will be carried away, as it was brought in its neophite state, by Adams' Express Company, which is bound by contract to transact all the vast money transportation business of the Government. This contract confers mutual advantage, both on the Company and the Government. To the latter, because it obtains transportation at a much lower rate than it could otherwise do, paying but twenty-five cents for each thousand dollars transported; while, at even this per cent., the Company can grow rich on the monopoly of the vast money transportation business of the Government of the United States.

Alas! for our dollar that went forth from the paternal door—as many another child has done—unsullied, only to return at a later day from its contact with the world, begrimed, demoralized, despoiled. Where is our pretty dollar, fresh and pure? Every delicate line defaced, tattered, filthy, worn out—this wretched little rag, surely, cannot be it! And yet it is. This is what the world's hard hand has made our dollar.

We have reached the Redemption Division of the Treasurer's Bureau, and stand in one of the rooms devoted to the counting of mutilated currency and the detection of counterfeits. This difficult and responsible labor of the public service is performed solely by women.

In the long rooms on either side of the marble hall, on the north ground floor of the Treasury Building, may be seen one hundred and fifty women, whose deft and delicate fingers are ceaselessly busy detecting counterfeits, identifying, restoring, counting and registering worn-out currency which has come home to be "redeemed." Each lady sits at a table by herself, that the money committed to her may not become mixed with that to be counted by any other person.

The fractional currency sent to the Treasury for redemption is usually assorted by denominations only. The work of assorting by issues remains to be done by the counters of the Treasury. As there are four distinct issues of most of the denominations, each of which must be assorted by itself, this labor alone is a vast one to the counters. Looking on their tables we see them heaped with little piles of currency, each made of a denomination or issue different from the rest. Thus every new issue increases the labor of currency-redemption. With clear eyes and patient hand, the lady bending over this table takes up slowly every bill and scrutinizes it, first, to see if it be genuine. Over three hundred dollars in counterfeit notes are found in the fractional currency, daily. This fact alone is sufficient to make the counting of the Redemption Division far less rapid than that of the Division of Issues.

The first thing that a lady at a redemption table does with her money packages is, to compare their number with the inventory which accompanies them. If there is none, she makes one. If there is a discrepancy between the packages and the number claimed, she refers to a clerk, that there may be no mistake. She then proceeds to the examination of a single package. After she has placed all the rest in a box, so that no strap or stray scrip from another bundle may mix with the first; when she has scrutinized and counted every note in the package, she puts the strap on again, marking it with her initials, the date, the amount, the "shorts," "overs," and "counterfeits." Thus she continues till every package has been counted. She then proceeds to assort the notes into packages, each containing one hundred notes, each of the same denomination and issue, which she binds with a " brand new " printed strap again, marked with her initials and date. All the notes over even hundreds she places by themselves. These in turn are given to distinct counters, whose sole business it is to make even hundreds out of these odd numbers.

The first counter then enters in a book, having a blank form for the purpose, printed in duplicate on one side of each leaf, a statement of the result of her count, containing the net amount found due to the owner, the aggregate of the "shorts," the "overs," the "counterfeits" discovered and the amount claimed. One of these duplicates is retained in the book as her voucher; the other is attached to the letter which accompanied the money; all together are handed to the clerk, who draws the check which is to be sent in return; or, if new currency is to be sent from the cash division, the clerk writes the order on which it is to be forwarded.

This is the story of but one package of mutilated money of the tens of thousands that are received at the Treasury every day. The Government has provided the most munificent facilities for the redemption of its currency and the maintenance of its credit in circulation. To what an extent the nation avails itself of these facilities no one can realize who has never visited the Treasury. Regular transportation, at the expense of the Government, is provided by express for the redemption of all currency. Everything demanded of its holders is, that they should send it in proper amounts; then its transportation is paid, and new currency sent back in its stead. This liberality in the Government is partly accounted for in the fact that fresh notes are a prevention of counterfeits. A fresh, new note cannot be counterfeited. Its exquisite tints and lines cannot be reproduced by any false hand. Only after its beauty has been obscured is the attempt made. Thus it is said that counterfeiters "soil and rumple their spurious notes, to give them the appearance of having been in circulation a long time." Thus many banks never sort over or pay out any fractional currency which they receive, but put it into packages and send it to the Treasury at the close of each day's business, so that nothing but clean notes are ever paid over their counters. By doing this they are saved the immense labor of re-assorting old notes, and afford their applicants the happiness of always receiving new ones.

Only the room in which the express messengers deliver their remittances can give any idea of the vast amounts sent daily to the Treasury for redemption. Here we find counters, tables, and the floor piled high with damaged money from every State in the Union. Two and three hundred packages are often received by express in a single day. The greater part of these contain postage and fractional currency. The Assistant Treasurer of New York forwards a remittance of fractional currency every ten or twelve days, never less than one hundred thousand dollars, and the amounts sent from other treasury officers are proportionately large. Over thirty-one million dollars in fractional currency were received and counted during the last fiscal year—about one hundred thousand dollars for each working day. Every note in this large sum has to be counted, studied, assorted with all others of the same denomination and issue; strapped, labelled, reported, delivered—all done by women.

The last room to which the counter carries our dollar is the cancelling room. She has just reported to the chief of the Redemption Division the result of her count, in the following duplicate report on the broad paper strap which binds her bundle of soiled notes:

AMOUNT, $5,000 00

From Fiftieth National Bank, New York City.

Received July 9, 1873, by MARY JONES.

Legal, - - - $4,000.00	Counterfeit, - $20.00
Full Currency, - 900.00	Discount, - - 5.00
Odds, - - - 40.00	Rejected, - - - 5.00
Discounted, - - - 20.00	Short by Inventory, 15.00——
$4,960.00	Short by Strap, - $45.00
	Over by Strap, - - 5.00
	Net Short, - - $40.00

The $4,960 is immediately sent to the bank in any denomination of new notes requested, or if no such request has been made, it is sent in exactly the denominations received. And now our lady-counter proceeds to attend the cancelling of the notes which she has counted, and which the Treasury has already redeemed. A messenger carries her precious bundle in a box, but she must keep messenger, box, and bundle in sight; for, from the moment that she receives it, till she places it in the last cash-account clerk's hands, she is personally responsible for its contents. If, by any possibility, it could be spirited away, she would be obliged to pay for every ragged dollar out of her little stipend.

This is a bustling sight. Messengers, each with a counter, are rushing in and out with their boxes full of strapped and labelled currency. Round a large table crowd many fair women, while every instant "thud! thud!" strike the precious packages. Each in turn is taken up by the canceller and set between the teeth of Uncle Sam's cancelling machine. This is fashioned out of two heavy horizontal steel bars, five feet in length, working on pivots. To the shorter end of each is attached a punch, while the other is connected by a lever with a crank, in the sub-basement below, which is propelled by a turbine water-wheel furnished with Potomac-water from one of the pipes of the building. Under its grinding "punch" our poor little dollar goes, and with it a hundred dollars beside. With a savage accuracy it stabs two holes through every one. This is done for the purpose of absolute cancellation. Then each bundle is returned to its box, the messenger picks it up, the counter follows, and both hasten to the cash-account clerk of the division, whose business it is to see if all the money received and delivered to the counters, has been returned and accounted for. Not until she sees her box of cancelled notes safe in the hands of this clerk, does the counter's personal responsibility end.

Near the punches in the cancelling room is a ferocious-looking knife, set in an axle, which is consecrated to the purpose of cutting the cancelled bundles in two, through the middle of each note. These are made into packages of one hundred thousand dollars of fractional currency, and larger sums of legal tender notes; and are sent back to this office to be cut asunder by this knife. The duplicate paper and strap which our fair counter bound about this bundle, is so printed as to show, upon each half, the denomination, issue and amount of the notes enclosed. The counter's initials and the date of counting are also recorded at each end, as well as a number or letter to identify the bundle. These sundered notes are now sent, one-half to counters in the Secretary's office, the other half to counters in the Registrar's office, where every little wretched rag is re-counted. This is done as a check

on the Treasurer's counters, and to secure absolute accuracy. If these second counters discover a "short" or a "counterfeit" passed over by the first fair fingers, the full amount is taken out of the wages of the counter whose initials the tell-tale package bears.

The Treasury mills grind slowly; but in the slow fullness of time the separate "counts" of three offices—the Treasurer's, the Register's, the Secretary's—are finally reconciled. The integrity of the Government, throughout the whole existence of its minutest fraction, has been maintained and demonstrated. In the process there is not much left of our poor little dollar, and nothing left for us but to go to its funeral. Like most of us, it has had rather a hard time in this world of ours. Where has it not lived—from a palace to "a pig's stomach;" and what has it not endured—from the scarlet rash to the small-pox—and to think that nothing remains for it now but to be burned! Only through purgatorial flame can it be fully and finally "redeemed."

About a quarter of a mile from the Treasury Department, in what is called "White Lot," stands the furnace which is to consume our dollar. The furnace, and the building in which it stands, was built expressly for this purpose for the sum of ten thousand dollars. The furnace is ten feet high, seven in diameter, circular and open at the top. With it is connected an air-blower, which is attached to an engine, the steam for which comes from a boiler some twenty rods distant. On the ground about lie piles of cinders—the metallic ashes of extinct dollars, compounded of pins, sulphur, printer's ink and dirt.

To this furnace, filled with shavings in advance, every other day comes "The Burning Committee," bearing the

22

boxes of doomed dollars, sealed finally in the Register's and Secretary's Bureaus. This Committee is formed of a person from each of these Bureaus, with a fourth not connected with the Departments. In their presence the final seals are broken—the complicated locks of the furnace opened. Then the packages are thrown into the flames, each "lot" being called and checked by the Committee, the amount averaging about one million five hundred thousand dollars every other day. At the same hour about one hundred thousand dollars in national bank notes are burned at another and smaller furnace. Beside cancelled money, internal revenue and postage stamps, checks and defective new money are all consumed in this furnace.

Here the three official delegates, with a few spectators, stand to witness the sight. Worn out, used up, gone by —all pass into the furnace, our dollar with the rest. The furnace is locked, by official hands, with nine distinct locks. A match is set to the shavings; the smoke of the sacrifice begins to ascend—the Committee depart. The fire and the money are left alone together for the next twenty-four hours. To-morrow a smutty aerolite, smothered in ashes, will be the significant "finis" of the story of our dollar. It has had its day!

CHAPTER XXXIII.

THE GREAT CASH-ROOM—THE WATCH-DOG OF THE TREASURY.

NOBODY need ever carry a smutty bit of money in Washington. Lay down the worst looking fraction you ever saw, upon the marble counter of the Cash-Room, and a virgin piece, without blemish, will be given you in its stead. Do you wish ten unsoiled " ones " for that ragged " ten " of yours? Take it to the Cash-Room, and the desire of your heart will be granted in a moment.

To do this you turn out of Pennsylvania avenue towards

the north front of the Treasury. On either side, spread away broad beds of flowers. In April, their hyacinths sent great drifts of fragrance, blocks away; in May, it was one great garden of roses, and now it has burst into a passion of bloom, a very carnival of color—the burning scarlet of the geraniums mocking the dazzling azure of the sky. On either side run these lavish hues. Before you, cooling the marble court beneath your feet, the great fountain tosses its spray. Toward you stretches the long restful shadow of the northern portico, inviting you to enter in.

If your visit means "money," as it may, you pass directly through the portico to the Cash-Room, into which it opens. No other room in the world as magnificent is devoted to such a purpose. It is seventy-two feet long, thirty-two feet wide, and twenty-seven feet six inches high. Exclusive of the upper cornice, the walls are built entirely of marble. Seven varieties meet and merge into each other, to make the harmony of its blended hues. From the main floor it rises through two stories of the building. Thus it has upper and lower windows, between which a narrow bronze gallery runs, encircling the entire room. The base of the stylobate of the first story is black Vermont marble, the mouldings are Bardiglio Italian, the styles dove Vermont marble, the panels Sienna Italian, and the dies Tennessee. Above the stylobate, the styles are of Sienna marble. With these are contrasted the pale primrose tints of the Corinthian pilasters and a cornice of white-veined Italian marble. Opposite the windows, and in corresponding positions at the ends of the rooms, are panels of the dark-veined Bardiglio Italian marble, the exact size of the windows.

The stylobate and the styles and pilasters of the second story show the same tints and variety of marbles which mark the first. But the panels are of Sarran Golum marble, from the Pyrenees. The latter is one of the rarest of marbles; at a distance, of a blood-red hue. Upon nearer inspection, it reveals undreamed-of beauties in veining and tint.

The pilasters of the second story are not like those of the first story, pure—but complex. They support a cornice, not of wrought marble, as all the remainder of the room would promise, but of plaster of Paris, fantastically wrought and profusely gilded. This cornice is another blot of that meretricious ornamentation which in so many noble spaces disfigures the Capitol.

Extending the length of the room is a costly counter, of various marbles, surmounted by a balustrade of mahogany and plate-glass. Within this are busy the clerks of the Cash-Room, and over this marble counter you, as one of its many proprietors, may receive, for the asking, ten " ones " for one " ten "—new money for old.

From this superb room of the people we pass to that of the Treasurer,—" the watch-dog of the Treasury,"— the man who holds and guards the untold millions of the nation. It is a plain room, very. No thought of luxury, it is easy to see, has touched an article of its furniture, from his well-worn chair to the broken-nosed pitcher which holds the General's ink; that ink, thick as mud and black as Egyptian night, out of which he constructs these marvellous hieroglyphics, which, on our legal-tender notes, has become one of the most baffling studies of the nation.

" The General! " That's his name, from the roof to

the cellar of the vast Treasury; crooked, crotchety, great-hearted; nobody swears so loud, or is so generous, or just, as "the General." Every afflicted soul, from the women, poor and old, who stand by the printing-presses under the scorching roof, to Mary Walker, whose devotion to "her principles," in the form of a pair of hideous little pantaloons, causes her justly to shed tubs of tears,— all are sure of a hearing, and of redress, if possible, from "the General." His face is as astonishing as his signature. It is a Lincolnian face in this, that its best expression can never be transferred to a picture. In life it is rugged, ugly at first glance, genial at the second. The eyes twinkle with humor and kindness; the wide mouth shuts tight with wilfulness and determination; the whole expression and presence of the man indicate energy, honesty, and power.

General Spinner is an object of personal curiosity to all sight-seers who visit Washington. Dick and Dolly having puzzled their eyes for an hour, studying some fresh legal tender note, to discover by what process of evolution and convolution the remarkable signature which it bears is fashioned, when they came to the Capital, proceeded to the Treasury to see, not only the man who makes it, but how he makes it. Bluff, and even snappish at first approach, after a little wilful snarling, our General subsides into the most amiable of mastiffs. He is an exception to the official class, in his hate of exclusiveness and his never-failing accessibility. Indeed, he would have far less to irritate him, if he made himself more unapproachable and remote. As it is, all sorts of tormenting people, finding it perfectly easy to "get at him," do not neglect the privilege, and altogether keep him pretty thoroughly "wrought up" with their never-ending and perpetually conflicting woes. Dicky and Dolly, fresh from their farm, who ask for no "place" in any "division" whatever, who have no alert grievance grumbling for redress, who wish for nothing but, "Please, sir, *will* you just show us *how* you make it—that queer name?" are sure to be gratified in the very jolliest fashion. The General stabs the old pen with three points down into the pudding-like ink which sticks to the bottom of the broken-nosed pitcher, and proceeds to pile it up in ridiculous little heaps at cross angles on a bit of paper. The result of his "piling," which Dick and Dolly watch with breathless interest, is his signature, which our happy friends bear off in triumph to show to the "folks at home." "Yes, sir, the autograph of the Treasurer of the United States! and we saw him make it, we did! A queer lookin' man, but good as pie, I can tell you; has a feelin' for folks, as if he wasn't no better than them, if he does take care of all the money of the United States Treasury, which, I tell you, is a heap!"

The taking care of this money is a mighty responsibility, which General Spinner realizes to the utmost. From his small room in the Treasury, a door opens into a still smaller one. In this little room, beneath the mighty roof of the Treasury, the keeper of its millions sleeps. Before he essays to do this, twice every night the guardian of the people's treasure goes himself to the money vault, and, with his own hand upon their handles, assures himself beyond doubt that the nation's money safes are inviolably locked.

In order that he may do this every night before he attempts to sleep, and that he may never be beyond call in case of accident or wrong doing, the Treasurer of the United States absolutely lives, by day and by night, in the Treasury. It is told of him that, " Once, before he began sleeping in the Treasury, he was awakened in the night by a strong impression that something was wrong at the Department. He lay for a long time, tossing uneasily upon his bed, and trying to close his eyes and convince himself that it was a mere freak of an over-taxed brain ; but it would not be driven away. At last, about two o'clock in the morning, in order to assure himself that his impression was at fault, he arose, hastily dressed, and set out for the Treasury. On his way he met a watchman from the Department, hastening to arouse him, with the information that the door of one of the vaults had just been found standing wide open. A careless clerk, whose duty it was to close and lock the door, had failed to perform his duty that night, and the watchman, on going his rounds, had discovered the neglect."

Since that night the Treasurer has slept in the Treasury, and been night-inspector of its doors and locks himself.

It is not difficult to appreciate his personal anxiety and consciousness of vast responsibility, when we remember that he is the hourly keeper of at least eight hundred million dollars which belong to the nation. There are very few officers of the Government who are called to bring to bear upon their daily duties the ceaseless vigilance, the sacrifice of personal ease and comfort in the service of the State, which characterizes the honest, tireless, invincible " watch-dog of the Treasury."

The room of the Secretary of the Treasury, in the Treasury building, has its outlook on the eastern side and grounds of the Executive Mansion. A wonderful fountain throws its million jets into the air at the foot of the great portico below, and another tosses its spray amid the green knolls opposite the President's windows. These grounds, swelling everywhere into gentle hills, covered with mossy turf, filled with winding walks, and brightened with *parterres* of flowers in summer months, are enchanting in their beauty.

Thus, you see, the Secretary's windows quite turn their backs on the noisy avenue. Their outlook is most serene. So is the aspect and atmosphere of the room. It is a nun of a room, folded in soft grays, with here and there a touch of blue and gold. The velvet carpet is gray; the furniture, oiled black walnut, upholstered with blue cloth, each chair and sofa bearing "U. S." in a medallion on its back, while the carved window-cornices each hold in their centres the gilded scales of justice above the key of the Treasury. A full-length mirror is placed between these windows. On one side of the room is a book-case, in which the works of Webster, Calhoun, Washington, and Jefferson, are conspicuous. The walls are frescoed in neutral tints, and the only pictures on them are chromo portraits of Lincoln and Grant.

In the centre of this room, at a cloth-covered table, sits the Secretary of the Treasury and his assistants, besides, usually, a third dejected mortal, on the "anxious seat" of expectancy for an office.

The Secretary's office is charged with the general supervision of the fiscal transactions of the Government, and of the execution of the laws concerning the commerce and navigation of the United States. He superintends the survey of the coast, the light-house establishment, the marine hospitals of the United States, and the construction of certain public buildings for custom-houses and other purposes.

The First Comptroller's office prescribes the mode of keeping and rendering accounts for the civil and diplomatic service, as well as the public lands, and revises and certifies the balances arising thereon.

The Second Comptroller's office prescribes the mode of keeping and rendering the accounts of the army, navy, and Indian departments of the public service, and revises and certifies the balances arising thereon.

The office of Commissioner of Customs prescribes the mode of keeping and rendering the accounts of the customs revenue and disbursements, and for the building and repairing custom-houses, etc., and revises and certifies the balances arising thereon.

The First Auditor's office receives and adjusts the accounts of the customs revenue and disbursements, appropriations and expenditures on account of the civil list and under private acts of Congress, and reports the balances to the Commissioner of the Customs and the First Comptroller, respectively, for their decision thereon.

The Second Auditor's office receives and adjusts all accounts relating to the pay, clothing and recruiting of the army, as well as armories, arsenals, and ordnance, and all accounts relating to the Indian Bureau, and reports the balances to the Second Comptroller for his decision thereon.

The Third Auditor's office adjusts all accounts for subsistence of the army, fortifications, military academy, military roads, and the quarter-master's department, as well as for pensions, claims arising from military services previous to 1816, and for horses and other property lost in the military service, under various acts of Congress, and reports the balances to the Second Comptroller for his decision thereon.

The Fourth Auditor's office adjusts all accounts for the service of the Navy Department, and reports the balances to the Second Comptroller for his decision thereon.

The Fifth Auditor's office adjusts all accounts for diplomatic and similar services, performed under the direction of the State Department, and reports the balances to the First Comptroller for his decision thereon.

The Sixth Auditor's office adjusts all accounts arising from the service of the Post-office Department. His decisions are final, unless an appeal be taken within twelve months to the First Comptroller. He superintends the collection of all debts due the Post-office Department, and all penalties and forfeitures imposed on postmasters and mail contractors for failing to do their duty; he directs suits and legal proceedings, civil and criminal, and takes all such measures as may be authorized by law to enforce the prompt payment of moneys due to the department, instructing United States attorneys, marshals, and clerks, on all matters relating thereto, and receives returns from each term of the United States courts of the condition and progress of such suits and legal proceedings; has charge of all lands and other property assigned to the United States in payment of debts due the Post-office Department, and has power to sell and dispose of the same for the benefit of the United States.

The Treasurer's office receives and keeps the moneys of the United States in his own office, and that of the depositories created by the Act of August 6th, 1846, and

pays out the same upon warrants drawn by the Secretary of the Treasury, countersigned by the First Comptroller, and upon warrants drawn by the Postmaster-
General and countersigned by the Sixth Auditor, and
recorded by the Register. He also holds public moneys
advanced by warrant to disbursing officers, and pays out
the same upon their checks.

The Registrar's office keeps the accounts of public receipts and expenditures, receives the returns and makes
out the official statement of commerce and navigation of
the United States, and receives from the First Comptroller
and Commissioner of Customs all accounts and vouchers
decided by them, and is charged by law with their safe
keeping.

The Solicitor's office superintends all civil suits commenced by the United States (except those arising in the
post-office department), and instructs the United States
attorneys, marshals and clerks in all matters relating to
them and their results. He receives returns from each
term of the United States courts, showing the progress
and condition of such suits; has charge of all lands and
other property assigned to the United States in payment
of debts (except those assigned in payment of debts due
the post-office department), and has power to sell and
dispose of the same for the benefit of the United States.

The Light-House Board, of which the Secretary of the
Treasury is *ex-officio* president, but in the deliberations of
which he has the assistance of naval, military and scientific conductors.

United States Coast Survey. The Superintendent, with
numerous assistants, employed in the office and upon the
survey of the coast, are under the control of this depart-

ment. A statement of their duties will be found in a future chapter.

The new rooms of the Internal Revenue Department are very beautiful. They run the entire length of the new wing of the Treasury, looking out on the magnificent marble court, with its central fountain below, the north entrance, the Presidential grounds and Pennsylvania avenue. They are covered with miles of Brussels carpeting, in green and gold. Their walls are set with elegant mirrors, hung with maps and pictures. There are globes, cases filled with books, cushioned furniture—all the accompaniments of elegant apartments, and one opening into the other, forming a perfect *suite*.

CHAPTER XXXIV.

WOMAN'S WORK IN THE DEPARTMENTS—WHAT THEY DO AND HOW THEY DO IT.

Women Experts in the Treasury—General Spinner's Opinion—A Woman's Logic—The Gifts of Women—Their Superiority to Men—Money Burnt in the Chicago Fire—Cases of Valuable Rubbish—Identifying Burnt Greenbacks—The Treasure Saved—The Ashes of the Boston Fire—From the Bottom of the Mississippi—Mrs. Patterson Saves a "Pile" of Money—Money in the Toes of Stockings—In the Stomachs of Men and Beasts—From the Bodies of the Murdered and Drowned—Not Fairly Paid—One Hundred and Eighty Women at Work—"The Broom Brigade"—Scrubbing the Floors—The Soldier's Widow—Stories which Might be Told—Meditating Suicide—The Struggle of Life—How a Thousand Women are Employed—Speaking of Their Characters—The Ill-paid Servants of the Country—Chief-Justice Taney's Daughters—Colonel Albert Johnson's Daughter—A Place Where Men are Not Employed—Writing "for the Press"—Miss Grundy of New York—The Internal Revenue Bureau—"Marvels of Mechanical Beauty"—Women of Business Capacity—A Lady as Big as Two Books!—In a Man's Place—A Disgrace to the Nation—Working for Two, Paid for One—How "Retrenchment" is Carried Out—In the Departments—Beaten by a Woman—The Post Office Department—Folding "Dead Letters"—A Woman who has Worked Well—"Sorrow Does Not Kill"—The Patent Office—The Agricultural Department—Changes Which Should be Made.

IN several branches of the Treasury service, women have risen to the proficiency of experts. This is especially true of them as rapid and accurate counters, as restorers of mutilated currency and as counterfeit detectors.

General Spinner says: "A man will examine a note systematically and deduce logically, from the imperfect engraving, blurred vignette or indistinct signature, that it is counterfeit, and be wrong four cases out of ten. A woman picks up a note, looks at it in a desultory fashion of her own, and says: 'That's counterfeit.' 'Why?' 'Because it is,' she answers promptly, and she is right eleven cases out of twelve." Yet this almost unerring accuracy is by no means the result of mere instinct, or of hap-hazard chance. It is the sequence of subtle perception, of fine, keen vision, and of exquisite sensitiveness of touch.

All women do not excel as counterfeit-detectors; nor can all become experts as restorers and counters of currency. But wherever a woman possesses native quickness, combined with power of concentration, with training and experience, she in time commands an absolute skill in her work, which, it has been proved, it is impossible for men to attain. Her very fineness of touch, swiftness of movement, and subtlety of sight give her this advantage. Thus when notes are defaced or charred beyond ordinary recognition, they are placed in the hands of women for identification.

After the great Chicago fire in 1871, cases of money to the value of one hundred and sixty-four thousand, nine hundred and ninety-seven dollars and ninety-eight cents, were sent to the United States Treasury for identification. They consisted of legal tenders, National State bank and fractional notes, bonds, certificates and coupons, internal revenue and postage stamps, all so shrivelled and burned, that they crumbled to the touch and defied unaided eyesight. All these charred treasures were placed in the hands of a committee of six ladies, for identification. What patience, practice, skill, were indispensable to the fulfilment of this task, it is not difficult to conjecture.

"After unpacking the money from the raw cotton in which it travelled, as jealously swathed as the most precious jewellery, the ladies separated each small piece with thin knives made for the purpose, then laying the blackened fragments on sheets of blotting-paper, they decided by close scrutiny the value, genuineness and nature of the note. Magnifying glasses were provided, but seldom used, except for the deciphering of coupon-numbers or other minute details. The pieces were then pasted on thin paper, the bank-notes returned to their respective banks, and the United States money put in sealed envelopes and delivered to a committee of four, who superintended the final burning. The amount of one million, two hundred and twenty-six thousand, three hundred and forty-one dollars and thirty-three cents was identified—over seventy-six per cent. of the whole."

A year later, Boston, from the ruins of its great fire, gathered the ashes of its money and sent it to the United States Treasury, begging identification and aid in restoration. Eighty-three cases came from that city, and these were so carefully packed that the labor of identification was greatly lightened. Of the eighty-eight thousand, eight hundred and twelve dollars and ninety-nine cents, which they contained, over ninety per cent. of the whole was identified by the same six ladies, who saved so much to individuals and to the Government from the Chicago fire.

Besides money, a large amount of checks, drafts, promissory notes, insurance policies, and other valuable papers were identified by these same clear eyes and patient hands, and restored to their owners. The entire responsibility of the whole amount rested on them. The money was delivered to them, when it came, and on their reports

all remittances on it were made.   It took over six months
of constant labor to identify the money from these fires.

The names of this committee of six are Mrs. M. J.
Patterson, Miss Pearl, Mrs. Davis, Miss Schriner, Miss
Wright, and Miss Powers.   "Mrs. Patterson has been
engaged for seven or eight years on what are called
'affidavit cases'—cases where the money is too badly
mutilated to be redeemed in the regular way, and the
sender testifying under oath that the missing fragments
are totally destroyed, receives whatever proportion of the
original value allowed by the rules."

The most noted case that she ever worked on was that
of a paymaster's trunk that was sunk in the Mississippi,
in the *Robert Carter*.   After lying three years in the bottom of the river, the steamer was raised, and the money,
soaked, rotten and obliterated, given to Mrs. Patterson
for identification.   She saved one hundred and eighty-five
thousand out of two hundred thousand dollars, and the
express company, which was responsible for the original
amount, presented her with five hundred dollars, as a
recognition of her services.

All the money which she identifies passes from the
hands of this lady to a committee of three—two gentlemen, one from the Treasurer's and one from the Register's office, and a lady from the Secretary's office.   The
duties of these three persons are identical.   They re-count
the money, seal it with the official seal of the three
offices, and for so doing receive, per year, the gentlemen
each eighteen hundred dollars, the lady twelve hundred
dollars—one more illustration of the sort of justice between the work of men and women, which prevails in
the Treasury service !

23

The identification and restoration of defaced and mutilated notes is a very difficult and important operation. From the toes of stockings, in which they have been washed and dissolved; from the stomachs of animals, and even of men; from the bodies of drowned and murdered human beings; from the holes of vice and of deadly disease, these fragments of money, whose lines are often utterly obliterated, whose tissues emit the foulest smells, come to the Treasury, and are committed wholly to the supervision and skill of women.

Let any just mind decide whether such labor does not deserve to be recognized and rewarded absolutely on its own merits. Such is its acknowleged value, that these Government experts have been allowed to go to distant parts of the country, to restore burnt money belonging to Adams' Express Company, because it was known that there was no one else in the land, who could perform this service.

The whole basement floor of the north wing of the Treasury is occupied by the busy counters of mutilated money. Here sit one hundred and eighty women counters, restorers and detectors. Side by side, we see the faded and the blooming face. Here is the woman, worn and weary—born, more than likely, to ease and luxury—thankfully working to support herself and her children; and at the very next table, a maiden, whose fresh youth, care has not yet worn out—each working with equal thankfulness, to support herself, and besides, perhaps, father and mother, brother, sister or child.

The time of toil, for one who must earn her living, is not long; indeed, the hours are fewer than the average hours of ordinary labor. She does not complain of them;

she is grateful for her chance. Yet her working-day is as long as her brother's. Her chance, alone, is less. For the same hours and the same toil, her stipend is one-fourth smaller than his smallest.

At three o'clock P. M., hats and shawls come down from their pegs, lunch-baskets come forth from their hiding-places, the great corridors, and porticoes, and broad streets are thronged with homeward-wending workers. For the space of half an hour, the Treasury-offices and halls seem deserted, and then—Lo! the Broom Brigade! Cobwebs, dust and dirt, no longer dim the granite steps, the tessellated floors, the marble surfaces of the Treasury-building, as they used to do, years ago. Congress has provided a Broom Brigade, with fifteen dollars a month, to pay each member—and here they come, the sweepers, the dusters and the scrubbers—ninety women!

Three years ago, was established the present efficient system of daily cleaning of the Treasury, exclusively under feminine control, with what perfect result, all who remember the Treasury as it was, and see it as it is, can bear witness.

These ninety women-workers are under the exclusive control of a lady custodian. The organization, supervision, general control, payment, etc., of this small army of sweepers, brushers and scrubbers, all devolve on her. She is a fair and stately woman, wearing a crown of snow-white hair, her soul looking out of eyes clear and bright, yet of tender blue. Her face tells its own story of sorrow out-lived, and of deep human sympathy. Did it tell any other, she would not be the right woman in the right place. No woman who has not suffered, who is not in profound sympathy with every form of human poverty and want, could of right reign over an army of women toilers, sweeping, scrubbing for bread. At 4 P. M., each day, ninety women enter a little room on the basement floor of the Treasury, there to exchange their decent street dress for the dusty garments of toil. As they ascend the broad stairs and disperse—broom, duster, or scrubbing-brush in hand—to make the beautiful offices and broad halls fresh and bright for the next coming day, the lady who guards and guides them all—who knows the history of each one—what stories she might tell!

Here is a little woman whose husband was killed in the Union army, leaving her nothing but his memory, his small pension, and a pair of brave hands to support herself and three little ones. Here are two bright little colored girls. They are students in Howard's University, and come every day after school, the long way to the Treasury, to earn a part of the money which is to insure their education. Here is a young woman whose keenly lined, sorrowful face is a history. "Months ago she came to the silver-haired lady in the custodian's room, and asked for work of any kind. The possibility to grant her request did not then exist, and again and again, with little hope, she came. At last she applied when some necessitous vacancy in the ranks of workers rendered it possible for the lady to assign her at once to a place of employment; and gladly she gave it, for the petitioner was wan and despairing. After work and the departure of the throng, she again sought the lady, to thank her on her knees 'for saving her life.' She said, 'I had made up my mind to take my life if you refused me; I had reached the end of every thing.' Then followed the oft-repeated story —deception, desertion, desperation, and the one last struggle to live"—to live honestly by honest, albeit the lowliest toil.

"Many a soldier's widow, struggling with smallest fortune, has occasion to be thankful for the fifteen dollars earned here every month, although the walk and work seem insufferable at times. Many a soldier's orphan is sustained by the stroke of brush and broom, making hall and stair and wall brightly clean to the step and sight of coming visitors from far and near, and the same shining polish which some strangers may admire, on the perspected marble floors and wrought pilasters, is a source and means of maintenance to humble homes when a death, desertion, and (O ! sadly often) drunkenness has removed the head and protector, and in which life means only toil and sorrow. Every one of these ninety women has her own story of trouble, and want, and endurance, which made up her past, and won for her, her niche in this scheme of labor."

Near a thousand women, from the toilers of the tubs under its roof, to the Brush-and-Broom Brigade in its basement, are employed in the Treasury. Their labor ranges from the lowliest manual toil, to the highest intellectual employment. In the social scale they measure the entire gamut of society. In isolated instances, women of exceptional character may still hold positions in the Treasury, and in so large a number, and under an unjust system of appointment, it would be strange if no such case could be found. But so powerful is the public sentiment roused against such appointments, it is impossible that they should be longer permitted, if known. The deepest wrong which their presence ever inflicted, was the unjust suspicion which they brought upon a large body of intelligent, pure women. The truth is, there is not an-

other company of women-workers in the land which numbers so many ladies of high character, intelligence, culture,
and social position.

The country is not aware to what an extent its most
noble public servants have died poor, nor how many of
their wives and daughters have sought the Government
Civil Service as the means of honorable self-support.

Until within a short time, when the friends of their
father raised a fund for their support, the daughters of
Chief-Justice Taney were employed in the Treasury. The
fair young orphan daughter of Robert J. Walker, once Secretary of the Treasury, now supports herself by service in
the Internal Revenue. Governor Fairchild, of Wisconsin,
found his beautiful wife, the daughter of a distinguished
public man, occupying a desk in the Treasury. Mrs.
Mary Johnson, daughter of Colonel Albert, who for a long
series of years was head of the Topographical Bureau, has
been for ten years a clerk in the Treasury. Her husband
was Consul at Florence, where he died. Her father passing away soon after, she found herself alone, with two
young sons to rear and educate. She became a Government clerk, or, as that title is now officially denied
to a woman, "a Government *employé.*" Her sons are
growing up to honor her, one having entered the Naval
School at Annapolis. Mrs. Tilton, sister of General Robert Ould, is an "*employé*" in the Internal Revenue. The
widow of Captain Ringgold is also there.

The Quarter-master-General's Office, which is a division
of the War Department, has been almost exclusively set
apart for the widows, daughters, and sisters of officers of
army or navy, killed or injured in the war. Almost without exception, the "*employés*" of this office are gentle-

women. It is filled with elegant and accomplished women,
some of whom are remarkable for their literary and scientific attainments.   These ladies now occupy offices provided in a plain building on Fifteenth street.   Their rooms
are smaller and much more private than those of the
Treasury opposite.   Their work is the copying, recording,
and registering of the letters of the department.   No men
are employed in these offices.   Their superintendent is a
lady, who has entire supervision of the ladies and the labor
of this division.   She is the widow of a naval officer who
died in the service, a descendant of Benjamin Franklin,
and occupies now, as she has all her life, the highest social
position.   She has children to support, and carries heavy official responsibilities—her duties are identical with those
of the head of any other bureau—she receives only the
stipend of the lowest male clerk, twelve hundred dollars.
Elizabeth Akers Allen (Florence Percy), whose deep and
tender lyrics call forth such universal response, held a position in this office until her last marriage.

Women of education and the finest intellectual gifts are
to be found in every department.   No inconsiderable number attempt to bring their meagre nine hundred dollar
salary up to the most ignorant man *employé's* twelve hundred, by writing for the press, or pursuing some artistic
employment outside of office hours.

The Treasury boasts of a number of more than ordinary women correspondents, whose letters have attracted
wide attention by the really important information which
they have imparted, concerning internal workings of Departmental life and service.   Foremost among these, is
Miss Austine Snead (Miss Grundy, of the New York
World).   Miss Snead is the only and fatherless daughter

of an accomplished gentleman. She is a "Class-child" of Harvard College, a loyal Kentuckian whom, with her youthful and lovely mother, the vicissitudes of war drifted to the one work-shop of the Nation open to women. The loss of her position, by change of administration, forced her to turn to the chance of journalism, and in the branch of the profession which she entered, she rose at once to the foremost rank. Mrs. Snead, formerly a famous *belle* of Louisville, Kentucky, is one of the most patient, faithful, and accurate counters in the redemption division of the Treasury, and is beside, weekly correspondent of the *Louisville Courier Journal.* Both are women who wear industry, integrity, and honor as their jewels, far dearer to them than all the lost treasures of Fortune's more prosperous days.

The Internal Revenue Bureau, a branch of the Treasury Service, and occupying beautiful apartments in the Treasury Building, employs a large number of women. Copying, recording, filing of letters, and keeping accounts, make the chief work of this division. It demands a high order of clerical ability, and the books kept by these ladies are marvels of mechanical beauty.

The complications and immensity of the Internal Revenue Service, make this one of the busiest offices in the entire Department. It contains from forty-five to fifty women—*employés.* Beside those who execute the exquisite copper-plate copying, there are many whose whole duty is "head work." This consists of examining, sorting, and filing the different daily communications received at the office.. These are of one hundred and fifty varieties, concerning internal revenue, taxes, etc., subjects usually supposed not to be particularly lucid to the average feminine mind. Many are employed in examining, approving, and recording reports of surveys of distilleries, and other important papers; and such is the estimate placed on their business capacity, as thus applied, that their opinions on the papers are accepted without question.

At one of these desks sits a lovely sylph-like creature, whose bird-like hands always reminds me of Charlotte Brontë's. She is scarcely bigger than the two big books which she handles and "keeps"—and to see her at them, perched upon a high stool, *is* "a sight." Born and reared in affluence, fragile in constitution, and exquisitely sensitive in organism, she is yet intellectually one of the best clerks—no "*employés*" in the Bureau. Years ago, she was placed at this eighteen hundred dollar desk, which a man-clerk had just vacated. She has filled it, performing its duties for seven or eight years, for the woman's stipend of nine hundred dollars. When the new Civil Service Rules first went into operation, she was awarded twelve hundred dollars per annum, for her service from that date. To have awarded her the remaining six hundred dollars, which was paid the man at the same desk, for doing the same work, would have been an equality of justice, from which the average official masculine mind instinctively recoiled.

Apropos of the preponderance of favor with which this same official masculine mind is able to regard and reward itself, is the case of a lady in another division. She has mathematical genius, and is one of the best practical mathematicians in the Treasury Department. Many of the statistical tables, for reports to Congress, are made out by her. Members of Congress, on the most important committees, do not disdain to come to her for assistance in making out their reports. Near two years ago, a man-clerk, in the same room with this lady, (who received his appointment through political favoritism,) became so dissipated, that he was totally unfitted to fulfil the duties of his desk, and he was carried by his friends to an inebriate asylum. Since that time, this lady, in addition to the arduous duties of her own desk, has performed all the labor accruing to that of the absent inebriate. She whose official existence as a clerk is denied by the legislators who employ her, has performed steadily, for many months, the labor of two men-clerks. How much does she receive for so doing? Nine hundred dollars a year. The eighteen hundred dollars, which she earns at one desk, is paid to the drunkard in whose name she earns it !

The Government, who support this man for being a drunkard, forces a woman to do his work for nothing, or lose the chance of earning the pittance paid to her in her own name. This lady, broken in health by her long-continued and overtaxing toil, sees what before her? Surely not recognition or justice from the Government which she serves and honors, while it, through selfishness and injustice, disgraces itself.

Of the forty-five ladies in the Internal Revenue Bureau, there is but one, and she fifty years of age, who has not more than herself to support on the pittance which she is paid. Nevertheless, whenever a spasmodic cry of "retrenchment" is raised, three women are always dismissed from office, to one man, although the men so greatly outnumber the women, to say nothing of their being so much more expensive.

"One of the greatest advocates of economy took work from a woman whose pay was the invariable nine hundred dollars per year, to give it to a man, who received for doing it, sixteen hundred dollars. No complaint was made of her manner of doing the work, but the head of the division said that she could count money, and he had not enough work for the men. Nothing was said of dismissing the superfluous male clerks. The work given the manly mind, in this instance, was the entering of dates of redemption opposite the numbers of redeemed notes. A child of ten years could scarcely have blundered at it. The same date was written sometimes for two weeks at a time."

The lady at the head of the woman's division of the Internal Revenue Bureau, has filled the position, with marked efficiency, for ten years, and upon the adoption of the new Civil Service Rules, she was authorized to receive eighteen hundred dollars per annum.

The lady who is one of the librarians of the library of the Treasury, is an accomplished linguist, a very intellectual woman. She was appointed by Mr. Boutwell, and received sixteen hundred dollars.

There are some very important desks filled by ladies in the Fifth Auditor's office. Into their hands come all consular reports. To fulfil their duties efficiently, they must possess a knowledge of banking, as well as of mathematics.

Before the Civil Service Rules were vetoed, several ladies competed in one, two, and three examinations. Thus several won, by pure intellectual test, twelve hundred dollars, sixteen hundred dollars, eighteen hundred dollars, and one or two, I believe, a twenty-two hundred dollars position.

In the office of the Comptroller of the Treasury, are

some very important desks filled by ladies. One young lady in this office has charge of the correspondence with the national banks and engraving companies. This involves a complicated routine. The desk was formerly filled by a man who received fourteen hundred dollars. It was taken from him because he was two hundred letters behind date. The work which has been in charge of this lady for six or seven years, at nine hundred dollars per annum, is always even with the day.

Another young lady, in this office, prepares an abstract of the circulation issued and returned by national banks, by means of which an immediate answer can be given, when information is asked, as to the outstanding circulation of any particular bank. Another laborious task, performed in this office by a lady, is the preparation of an abstract of the number of notes of each denomination and issue, work requiring great intellectual exactness and care.

In the Post Office Department, there are forty-seven women who address "returned letters," i. e., letters which have miscarried, and which are to be returned, if the signature, or anything inside the letter, gives a clue to whom it is to be sent. There are ten women who fold "dead letters," and three who translate foreign letters.

The lady in charge of the women clerks in the Dead Letter Office, is the daughter of an officer high in rank in the army, now dead. Her grandfather was the President of a New England college. Mrs. Pettigru King, whose father was the Governor of South Carolina, and a member of the United States Senate, herself a woman of remarkable talents, was long employed in the Dead-Letter Office. Sitting among many younger women, her hands flying as swift as any of theirs—the daily task, that of re-directing two hundred letters, usually completed by her before that of any one else—we see a fair, round-faced, blue-eyed woman, whose sudden, bright glance and rapid movements at once fix our attention. She looks to be about fifty; she is in reality over seventy years of age. She and her history combined, probably make as remarkable a fact as the Dead-Letter Office contains. She is the widow of a clergyman. When the war broke out, her only son became hopelessly insane. "As he could not go to the war, I went myself," she said. As the Assistant-Manager of the United States Sanitary Committee for an entire State," she raised, in money, ten thousand dollars, and collected and distributed ninety thousand hospital articles. She was in the field, in the hospital, and travelling between certain large cities, till the close of the war. Just as she finished her great work, she fell and broke one of her limbs. This confined her to her room for six months. In the meantime, her daughter's husband died, leaving her with three little children, and no income. Soon after, the mother lost what little she had, and the entire family were left penniless. After an unsuccessful attempt at the widow's forlorn hope, "keeping boarders," mother and daughter came to Washington, and sought for positions in the Departments. "Friends tried to dissuade us," said the old lady. "They told us that we must not come here, to mingle with such people as they thought were in the Departments. We have *not* seen them. I have been three years in the Post Office Department, and my daughter in the Treasury, and we have met none but respectable women."

Three winters ago, by act of Congress, she was allowed

to place her insane son in the Lunatic Asylum here, free of charge, leaving her at liberty to assist her daughter in the support of her young family. Notwithstanding her war services, and the names of twenty prominent men in her native State attached to her papers, it took her six months to obtain, for herself and daughter, the chances to labor which she sought. "Sorrow does not kill," she says, and as we look into her beaming eyes, we say it does not even extinguish the brightness of a soul forever young,—and yet this lady, in a few eventful years, "lived through sorrow enough to break any heart less stout than hers."

In the Patent Office, fifty-two women clerks are allowed by law. A few women are employed in copying Pension Rolls in the Pension Office, who have a room provided for them in the Patent Office. Ten or twelve women have work given them from the Patent Office, which they do at their homes. This work, as well as that done in the Office, consists chiefly of the drawing of models. Every model of all the tens of thousands received in the Patent Office, from the beginning to the present day, has thus been re-produced and preserved. Glazed transparent linen is placed over the engraved lines, and through this, with ink and stencil, the most intricate and exquisite lines are drawn. To do this work perfectly, a lady must be something of an artist and draughtswoman. Magnifying glasses are used, and even with their aid, the work is most trying, and often destructive to the eyesight. The salary fixed for this work is ten hundred dollars per annum. Those who take their work home, and are paid by the piece, make as much as those who give the work will allow. Here, of course, is a large opportunity for favor-

itism and injustice. Thus favorites are often allowed to
do twice their share, while others get barely work enough
to subsist.

The Agricultural Department affords temporary employment for numbers of women, for two or three months
of the year, and two have permanent positions there.
The temporary work is the putting up of seeds for universal distribution, and occasionally copying is given out.
Of the two ladies who find constant employment there,
one is the assistant of Professor Glover, in taking charge
of the Museum. She is the widow of a western editor,
and at one time had exclusive control of a public journal
(an agricultural one,) herself. She is a woman of large
intelligence, a proficient in botany and natural history,
which fact gave her, her present position, and enabled
her to fill it with credit to herself. The other lady employé is a taxidermist, who prepares the birds and insects
for the Museum. The officers of this Department regard
her as a proficient in her profession. She is a German,
has been connected with the Department over six years,
and has a room provided for her in the beautiful agricultural building.

Woman's work in the Government Printing-Office, remains yet to be noticed, but enough has been mentioned,
to prove its value in other branches of the Civil Service.
It would be strange if so large a hive held no drones. It
is doubtless true, that while many women are not only
qualified, but actually perform the duties of the highest
class desks, for an unjust pittance, many more do not
even earn their nine hundred dollars per annum. There
could be no more striking proof of the inequality and
injustice which prevail in our Civil Service, than the

fact that such persons, men and women, are appointed by men in power, really to be supported by the Government, and receive from that Government, for inefficiency and idleness, all, and more, than is paid often to the most intellectual, the most efficient, the most devoted of its servants.

CHAPTER XXXV.

WOMEN'S WORK IN THE TREASURY.

The Scales of Justitia—Where They Hang and Where They Do Not Hang —The Difference Between Men and Women—Reform a " Sham !"—The First Women-Clerks—A Shameful and Disgraceful Fraud—What Two Women Did—Cutting Down the Salaries of Women—The First Woman-Clerk in the Treasury—Taking Her Husband's Place—Working "*in Her Brother's Name*"—A Matter of Expediency—The Feminine Tea-Pot—The Secretary Growls at the Tea-Pots—The Hegira of the Tea-Pots—Thackeray's Opinion of Nature's Intentions—Blind on One Side—In War Days—General Spinner Visits Secretary Chase—"A Woman can Use Scissors Better than a Man "—Profound Discovery !— " She 'll do it *Cheaper* "—" Light Work "—" Recognized "—Besieged by Women—Scenes of Distress and Trouble—Hundreds of Homeless Women—After the War—How the Appointments were Made—Creating an Interest—The Advantages of the " Sinners "—Infamous Intrigues—The Baseness of Certain Senators—Virtue Spattered with Mud—A Disgrace to the Nation—Secret Doings in High Places—New Civil Service Rules— Sounding Magnanimous—Passing the Examination—The Irrepressible Masculine Tyrants—The New Rules a Perfect Failure—Up to the Mark, but not Winning—An Alarming Suggestion—Men *versus* Women—Tampering with the Scales—How Much a Woman Ought to be Paid—Opinion of a Man in Power—Interesting Description of an Average Representative—" Keeping Women in Their Place "—Getting up a Speech on Women—The Man who Stayed at Home—Generosity of the " Back-Pay " Congress—What Women Believe Ought to be Done.

ON the carved cornices which surmount windows and mirrors in the spacious Office of the Secretary of the Treasury may be seen, equally balanced above its keys, the scales of Justitia. Would that they symbolized the equal justice reigning through the minutest division of the great departments of the Government service.

24

Weighted with human selfishness, perhaps this is impossible. Majestic in aspect, great in magnitude, in energy and action, they will never be morally grand till they are established and perpetuated in absolute equity. In that hour the scales of Justitia will hang in equal balance above the head of the masculine and feminine worker. Whatever *their* difference, there will be no disparity in the equity which shall measure, weigh and reward equal toil. To-day the departments of Government teem with kindness and favoritism to individual women. What they lack is justice to woman. This they have lacked from the beginning. What a comment on human selfishness is the fact, that with all the legislation of successive Congresses, the employment of women in the departments of the Government is to-day as it was in the beginning—perpetuated in favoritism and injustice. Civil Service Reform, as carried on, is a mockery and a sham. Nowhere has its hollow pretence been so visible— so keenly felt—as in its utter failure of simple justice to the woman-worker in the public service.

From the beginning, when her work has been tacitly recognized and rewarded as a man's, her sex has been proscribed. The first work given to women from the Government was issued from the General Land Office, as early, if not earlier, than President Pierce's administration, and consisted of the copying of land warrants. This work was sent to their homes. They received it in the name of some male relative, and for that reason were paid what he would have received for doing it, viz., twelve hundred dollars per annum. One lady supported a worthless husband (the nominal clerk) and her two children in this way, doing all his work for him. Another supported herself, her two nephews, and educated them out of the same salary.

During Mr. Buchanan's administration, this work was taken out of feminine hands, to a very large extent, and the few allowed to retain it were paid only six hundred dollars. Somewhere in this era the first woman clerk appeared in the Treasury. She was a wife who, during her husband's illness, was allowed to take his desk and to do his work, for his support and their children's. This she continued to do until her second marriage; but it was *in her brother's name*. She copied and recorded, did both well, and was paid—not because she did well, but because she did her work in the name of a man—sixteen hundred dollars per annum. Thus, while this lady performed the work of a man, and performed it in his name, as a woman her presence at the desk was a subterfuge, and her official existence ignored.

Without recognition or acknowledgment, the woman-clerk system in the Treasury Department is an outgrowth of expediency. Like many another fact born of the same parentage, it soon proved its own right to existence, and refused to be extinguished.

By the time that Secretary McCulloch made his advent, the feminine tea-pot had invaded every window-ledge. The Secretary complained of the accumulation of tea-pots in the Treasury of the nation. They vanished, and ceased to distill the gentle beverage for the woman-worker at her noonday lunch. "Nature meant kindly by woman when it made her the tea-plant," Thackeray says. The presence of her tea-pot was made a mental and moral sign, by political philosophers, that woman was unfit for Government service. Nobody ever heard that the costly cigars and tobacco which filled the man clerk's "noöning," to the exhilaration of his body and soul, was a like sign of his inability to perform prolonged service without the aid of stimulants.

In war days, when tens of thousands of men were withdrawn from civil labor, and when one day's expense to the Government equalled a whole year's in the time of Washington, General Spinner went to Secretary Chase and said: "A woman can use scissors better than a man, and she will do it cheaper. I want to employ women to cut the Treasury notes." Mr. Chase consented, and soon the great rooms of the Treasury witnessed the unwonted sight of hundreds of women, scissors in hand, cutting and trimming each Treasury-note sheet into four separate notes. This was "light work;" but if anybody supposes it easy, let him try it for hours without stopping, and the exquisite pain in his shoulder-joints and the blisters on his fingers will bear aching witness to his mistake.

Washington was full of needy women, of women whom the exigencies of war had suddenly bereft of protection and home. In her appointment at that hour, political differences went for nothing. Every poor woman who applied to the good General was given work if he had it. A pair of scissors were placed in her hands, and she was told to go at it. She had no official appointment or existence. During 1862, these women were paid six hundred dollars per annum out of the fund provided by Congress for temporary clerks. A year or two later the working existence of these women was recognized in the annual appropriation bills.

After that it did not take long to spread through the land that the Government Departments in Washington

offered work to women. The land was full—fuller than
ever before of women who needed work to live. Necessity, exaggeration, romance and sorrow, combined as
propelling motives, and the Capital was soon overrun
with women seeking Government employment. Then,
more conspicuously than to-day, the supply far ex-
ceeded the demand. The disappointment, the suffering,
the sin which grew out of this fact, can never be measured.

The war had torn the whole social fabric like an earth-
quake. Society seemed upheaved from its foundations—
shattered, and scattered in chaos. Nowhere was this so
apparent as in Washington. Women seeking their husbands; women, whose husbands were dead, left penniless
with dependent children. Young girls, orphaned and
homeless, with women adventurers of every phase and
sort, all, sooner or later, found their way to Washington.
The male population was scarcely less chaotic. Men, restrained and harmonized through life by the holiest influences of home, found themselves suddenly homeless,
herded together in masses, exposed to hardships, danger
and undreamed-of temptations. "Let us eat and drink,
for to-morrow we die," seemed to be blazoned on the
painted sign-boards of the dens of drink and sin, and on
the debauched and brazen faces of the stranger men and
women who jostled each other on the crowded thorough-
fares.

While thousands escaped unharmed the moral pestilence
which brooded in the air, tens of thousands more were
touched with its blight, and fell. Men and women who
would have lived and died innocent, in the safe shelter of
peace and home, grew demoralized and desperate amid the

rack and ruin of war. In the hour when human nature needed every sacred safeguard, it found itself bereft of the sweetest and best that it had ever known. This was especially true of the hundreds of homeless women in the Capital seeking employment. Congressional appropriations made woman's Government-employment at once a Congressional reward. Very soon, every woman's appointment to work was at the mercy of some Member of Congress. Political or war-service might secure a man his, but what had the woman but her bereavements, or her personal influence ? For the sake of the former, noble men, in many instances, sought and found honest employment for noble women, for women who had given their husbands, sons and fathers, their own heart's blood, to their country, asking nothing in return but the chance to work for their own bread and their children's.

In order to secure any Government position, the first thing a woman had to do was to go and tell her story to a man—in all probability a stranger—who possessed the appointing power, her chance of getting her place depending utterly on the personal interest which she might be able to arouse in him. If he was sufficiently interested in her story, and in her, to make the official demand necessary, she obtained the coveted place, no matter what her qualifications for it, or her lack of them might be. If she failed to interest him, by no possibility could she secure that place, unless she could succeed in winning over to her cause another man of equal political power. If the men who held her chance for bread were good men, and she a good woman, well; if they were bad men, and she a weak woman, not so well. In either case, the principle underlying the appointment was equally wrong.

It was this unjust mode of appointment which, in so many instances, especially through the years of the war, placed side by side, with pure and noble women, the women-adventurers and sinners, whose presence cast so much undeserved reproach upon the innocent, and who caused the only shadow of disrepute which has ever fallen upon woman's Treasury-service. Even in the worst days this class formed the exceptions to a host of honorable and noble women, and yet the shameful fact cannot be wiped out that men, high in political power, because they had that power, made womanly virtue its price, and were meanly base enough to use the Civil Service of their country to pay for their own disgraceful sins. Because this was possible, pure women, working day by day to support themselves and their children, were covered with the shadow of unjust suspicion, while women, unworthy and profligate, were allowed the same positions, with equal honor and equal pay.

There could be no greater moral injustice to woman than to place her employment under the Government on such a basis. It put the best under ban, while it drew those whose steps pointed downward swiftly along the inevitable descent. There was but one redress that the State could offer to its daughters, that of making their chance equal to that of its sons. Then, if they failed, the failure would be their own; if they succeeded, they would not be defrauded by the Government they served.

The new Civil-Service Rules, whatever their impracticability in other ways, seemed to offer to the women-workers of the Government this redress. If education and fitness were to be made the standard of Departmental Service, alike for women as men, then the reign of favor-

itism and might must end. An idle woman, the pet of
some man in power, would no longer receive all that was
paid a woman filling the desks of two men. The woman
who had proved, by years of efficient service at a man's
desk, that she was more than equal to the performing of
his duties, would cease to receive for doing them the pittance of the veriest idler in the lobbies, and no more.

It sounded well; magnanimous men and true women,
yearning only for justice, and that it might be earned and
won without ado, took heart. Educated women from
North and South, East and West, flocked to the Capital
to compete in impartial intellectual examination with
men. Many of these were teachers—all women to whom
self-support, or the support of others, were indispensable.
The number of women who have passed the highest competitive examinations, is remarkable. Their life-long pursuits and intellectual training made it impossible that,
in this regard, they should prove second to men. The
number so great, that all could receive appointments was
not probable.

In the face of so many new professions of equality of
chance in the public service for women, the astonishing
fact is, that while women pass the highest examinations
with honor, it is men, with scarcely an exception, who
pass into the highest places. With a mocking outcry of
"justice and equality," uttered to appease the universal
demand, selfishness and might still prevail in all departmental appointments. Political and · personal influence
appoint women to-day, just as they did before one woman
was summoned to compete in intellectual examination
with men.

"You were fools to expect a twelve-hundred-dollar

clerkship because you passed the examination of that class," said a high appointing officer of the Treasury to two ladies, one who had come from a far Western, the other from a far Eastern State. Both ladies passed the highest competitive examination—both, after months of wearing anxiety and struggle, with the wolf at the door, received—a nine-hundred-dollar clerkship. Did they receive even that on the high merit of their competitive examination? Not at all; had their appointment depended on that, they would not have received one at all. Sick and worn out, they received it at last on the special plea of two men in office, each having political power in his respective State.

With such results, I ask, what is a competitive examination to women but a shame to the power that treacherously offers it? The man who passes such an examination cannot receive less than a twelve-hundred-dollar clerkship; the woman who passes triumphantly the severest intellectual test offered by the Government, cannot receive more than a nine-hundred-dollar position. Why? So many women came to Washington and proved, by actual mental examination, that they were fully competent to fill the highest civil offices in the departments, its officials became alarmed. " Taken on their attainments, they will push out the men," they exclaimed, in alarm. Then straightway they fell back, as men in power always do, to carry their own ends on unjust legislation. They based their decision on the Act of Congress of four years ago, which fixed the salary of all women employed in the Government Departments at nine hundred dollars per annum.

The result of all the loud hypocritical outcry of civil

equality to women is, that hereafter, no matter how high the competitive examination which she passes, no matter what the services which she renders, no woman is to receive more than nine hundred dollars per year for any appointment received after a certain date ; and no man, no matter how low the labor which he performs, be it only as a messenger to run through the halls, is to receive less than twelve hundred dollars per annum.

Cast down your scales, O, Justitia, let them shiver to atoms on its marble floor for hanging in equal balance above the keys of the Treasury of the United States. They are a mocking lie. Beneath these desecrated symbols sits the Secretary of the Treasury, and to him a few shrinking, yet daring, women have appealed. "Four hundred dollars a year is enough for any woman to be paid for her work," replies this accidental potentate, borne from obscurity to power solely by the "boosting" of a friend, who lifted him from his unthought-of "bench" in Massachusetts, with no guarantee of fitness from his past, to the chiefship of the Treasury of the Nation. "Four hundred dollars is enough for any woman to receive for her work, and more than she could earn anywhere else," replies this man.

This one remark, pitted against the facts recorded in this chapter, proved the man who made it as too narrow-minded and unjust, too pervaded with the caste and selfishness of sex, to be fit to hold the appointing power over hundreds of women, in culture and intellectually more than his peers. No man whose spring of action is "might is right" has a right to rule.

To-day nothing could be more humiliating to a high-spirited, intelligent, honorable woman, than to sit in the gallery of the Hall of Representatives and be compelled to listen to a debate on woman's work and wages going on below. Yet if she never heard the words uttered by men who claim to be the representatives of the people, and who make the laws which define her rights and decide her rewards, she could never realize how selfish, ungenerous, and unjust is the average man who assumes to represent woman, and to legislate for her welfare. These men, on the average, are fairly good husbands and indulgent fathers. They are anything but tyrants, personally, to the women of their families. But their personal relations do not prevent them from placing a very low estimate upon the powers, performance, place and prospects of women in general. Their caste of sex infiltrates through every word they utter.

The man who is "bound to keep woman in her place," before he makes a speech to that effect, rushes into the Congressional Library, and asks Mr. Spofford to give him every book which will help him to prove that woman is a weak and inefficient creature. He then proceeds to "cram" himself with a crude mass of statements, which he extracts pell-mell out of a heap of books. This unassimilated and impracticable load he delivers, a few days later, to Congress, to the galleries, and to the *Globe*—to prove that—no matter what her qualities or qualifications, moral or mental—being a woman, for that fact alone, she must not be a clerk, but an "*employé ;*" and no matter what she has done or is capable of doing in the service of the Government, for that service she must receive but nine hundred dollars, and the sum be fixed by law.

There are honorable exceptions—a few men in Congress who, in the broadest and best sense, are the friends of woman. They form a small minority. The majority, after having made woman's very existence as a Government-worker to depend on their own personal favoritism or caprice, stand up in Congress and cast stones at the very class which they have themselves created. In nine cases out of ten, these men staid at home while others fought their country's battles. And now they reward the widows and orphans of soldiers and sailors by giving them a reluctant chance to earn their bread on half-pay. They do it under sufferance, while these legislators withhold just remuneration, sneer at their work, and defame their characters.

The Forty-second Congress, which, in its most hurried moments, could take time to vote to its members an increase of salary from five thousand to eight thousand' a year, rejected without debate a proposition to give women-clerks in the departments equal compensation with men, for the same labor. What added proof is required to show that the law-making power of our land is fast becoming a monied monopoly—a legislature for the rich— an ignorer of the poor. "Eight thousand dollars every twelve months, by dint of close economy, will keep my wife and daughters in silks and velvets; will give them a phæton by the sea, and make beautiful their paths upon the mountain tops! What to me are the wives and daughters of the poor? What care of mine the widows and orphans of men who perished in their country's service, if they do support themselves and their children by working for this just Government, which I help to make, for nine hundred dollars a year! while I pay at least twelve hundred to the laziest masculine lout who dawdles with papers across the Treasury floors?"

Yet there was scarcely a Member of that Congress that would not repel with jest or sneer the mere mention of woman's demand, in the face of such injustice, to legislate for herself. If you would avert this catastrophe, gentlemen, show that you are capable of just legislation; prove that the power of franchise does not always beget oppression to the disfranchised. I point to the practical working of the new Civil-Service Rules, to your own greedy grasp of additional thousands, with the refusal to grant three meagre hundreds to working women, to prove that woman has no hope of justice in man's representation. Represent her interests with half the eager avidity which marks your devotion to your own, and she will never ask to represent herself. But no matter what her individual distaste to public responsibility, nothing is more apparent to the wide-visioned, thoughtful woman than that, in a republic, the only possibility of obtaining personal justice lies in political equality.

CHAPTER XXXVI.

MR. PARASITE IN OFFICE—HOW PLACE AND POWER ARE WON.

Government Official Life—Its Effects on Human Nature—Keeping his Eye Open—The Sweet and Winning Ways of Mr. Parasite—In Office—The Fault of "the People" and "my Friends"—Shrinking from Responsibilities—Pulling the Wool over the Eyes of the Innocent—Writing Letters in a Big Way—The "Dark Ways" of Wicked Mr. P——— —A Suspicious Yearning for Private Life—The Sweets of Office—A Little Change of Opinion—A Man Afflicted with Too Many Friends—Forgetting Things that Were—John Jones is not Encouraged—Post-offices as Plentiful as Blackberries—Receiving Office-seekers—"The Worst Thing in the World for You"—Dismissing John—Over-crowded Pastures—John's Own Private Opinion—The "Mighty Messenger"—Government-Servants—Peculiar Impartiality of the Man in Office—What the Successful Man Said —I Change My Opinion of Him—A Certain Kind of Man, and Where He can be Found.

GOVERNMENTAL official life has one effect upon those whom it benefits, which is anything but creditable to human nature.

Mr. Parasite wants a high place in the governmental service, and circumstances favor his getting it. While there is any doubt about it, he does not disdain to use any influence within his reach to make it certain. How lovely he is to everybody whose good word or ill word may "tell" for or against him. How affable he is to every mortal, from the lowliest outspoken man in his home town, to the influential writer, whose powerful pen he wishes to propitiate. Mr. Parasite glides into his place

THE LOBBY OF THE SENATE.

INSIDE THE CAPITOL.—WASHINGTON.

with grace and resignation. " The people, the people, you know, and my friends—*they* forced it upon me. They quite overrate my fitness, quite. I shrink from such responsibilities, such arduous labors; but, if my country needs me, if my constituents *demand* my services, I feel that I have no right to refuse, no right to consult my personal ease, although the desire of my heart is for the peaceful quiet of private life."

Strange to tell, when an accommodating people are about to grant him the desire of his heart, Mr. Parasite suddenly starts up alert, and touches the springs of a most powerful enginery. He writes personal letters by thousands; he has his friends—i. e. agents—at work for him everywhere, whispering with this one, arguing with that one, and urging his claims incessantly upon the appointing power. But who, that did not know it, could believe it.

Chance to light upon Mr. Parasite about this time, and mention the subject of his possible appointment or election to him as one in which he is naturally interested. Lo! amid all others, Mr. Parasite alone is indifferent. "Of course, it would be a compliment, a re-election or re-appointment. He would prize it much as a mark of confidence from the people, or the Government; but really, so far as personal desires go, private life."

Private life still fills the measure of his yearning. " Retirement " is still the goal of his desire. This is but the weakness; the crime of Mr. Parasite is revealed further on. The long suspense over, safely ensconced in that official chair, while its cushions are a new delight, its honors are fresh, its powers unwonted, perhaps a consciousness of gratitude remains with Mr. Parasite. It's a pleasant office, very. Carpeted, cushioned, curtained, pictured, secluded. It is pleasant, very. This ever-acknowledged honor of official state, messengers flying at your bid, doors swinging noiselessly at your approach, hats springing into air as you pass by, *lorgnettes* lifted by fair hands in great assemblies, the crowd peering and shouting, "There goes the great Mr. Parasite!" Sweet, also, are the newly-found uses of official power—sweeter even than to die for one's country. The privileges of patronage, the consciousness of power over the fate of others, the uses of power in ministering to self—first sought and last relinquished—of all the gifts of office.

While all these retain the charm of newness, a sense of gratitude may remain with Mr. Parasite towards those who led and lifted him to his high estate. Rarely strong in any man, the sense of gratitude with continued office is sure to die out. When he first enters, and the memory of fresh services remains with him, he may feel, at least faintly, that he owes something to somebody besides himself; but the longer he remains, the surer he is that all is his by right, all due to his own exalted merit. There comes a time when it seems as if that cushioned chair, that luxurious office, those muffled doors, those cringing messengers, were all made especially for him and to do him service. With a growing sense of security in his position, comes, perhaps, an unconscious indifference toward those who, in the beginning, helped to lift him toward it. There is no intentional ingratitude, only it is so easy for some natures to forget others when they cease to need them.

Then, too, official place, even in a republican government, hourly feeds in a man his love of power, and his sense of personal importance. It feeds the vanity and self-satisfaction of poor human nature, when its fellows are dependent upon it even for the smallest favors. Few meet this test and survive it their noblest selves. It is astonishing how soon Mr. Parasite forgets that, a short time since, he was a seeker of favors himself, and is sure to be again, before old age strands him amid things gone by in the long-deferred haven of private life.

While a feeling of dependence on others survives, an emotion of gratitude lingers, Mr. Parasite will try to treat other applicants for office as he desired to be treated a few short months since himself. But these emotions were never known to live through a single stress of a single term of office.

Poor Mr. Parasite is very much beset! Every hour in the day somebody wants something that somebody believes is in Mr. Parasite's power to bestow. It may be flattering, but it is also wearing, tearing, exasperating, and even maddening, sometimes, to a man to be deemed the dispenser of so much power and patronage. He cannot give everybody all that everybody may ask—of course not. This is not all his sin. His sin is this: He comes in time (usually in a marvellously short time) to regard every one seeking the patronage of his office as a mendicant on his personal bounty, rather than as a member of one class with himself. Because he gained the highest honor, he forgets that he got it on the very same principle that John Jones, who, armed with credentials from his minister and doctor, so humbly sues for the post-office of Mudtown. He listens to the sister pleading for her brother, the wife for her husband, the father for his son, the poor man for himself, and because it is little each asks, despises each accordingly, lectures each on the folly of

25

wanting any Government place whatever. The one
thing that he cannot remember, and which it is most delightful to forget, is that he was ever in John Jones'
place himself.

To be sure, he did not sue for the Mudtown post-office.
He wanted a foreign ministry, a home secretaryship, to
be a Senator, or, at least, a Governor. He begged or bar-
tered for these Government-gifts precisely as John does
for his post-office. Both are equally office-seekers; but
there is such disparity between John's little Alpha and
the Omega of Mr. Parasite's desires, the latter does not recognize in this seeker of small things his remotest cousin.
Comparatively few dare demand ministries and secreta-
ryships, while post-offices and their ilk are as plentiful
as blackberries, and their pickers equally so—so plentiful
that Mr. Parasite leans back in his cushioned chair, on his
official tripod, and wonders *which* John Jones it will be
next, and what *he* will want; and, when one of the
innumerable Johns, waiting outside, is admitted by a
mighty messenger, whose official state is more overwhelming even than his master's, the suppliant quakes
to the bottom of his boots in the presence of the powerful potentate, Mr. Parasite.

"What do *you* want?" says the potentate, in a tone
which implies in advance, "You can't have it."

"Only the Mudtown post-office," says John, "or—or
anything that I can get."

"Impossible; I have nothing—nothing for you," says
the potentate, in a remote and superior tone, which indicates, as only a tone can, that he, the potentate, needs
nothing at present himself. And who can imagine that
he ever did? "Why on earth do so many of you come

for Government employment? Don't you know it is the worst thing in the world for you? You had better go to work. Do anything, rather than to hang upon the Government."

Thus *one* John is dismissed, to go and browse in the closely-cropped and over-crowded pastures of the inefficient and ne'er-do-well mediocrity.

Several days later, when John rebounds from the shock imparted by Mr. Parasite's grandeur, its momentum sends him pat against a fact. "Why, he is a hanger-on to the Government himself." Yes; and so, in one sense, is every office-holder, from the President down to the mighty messenger who condescends to shut and open doors. It implies no discredit to be a server of the Government; but it reveals a very ignoble side of human nature, when the favored holder rebuffs the lowliest seeker as a being from another race, in any essential quality the antipodes of himself.

A man who has just been lifted by his friends from one high place to another, has long boasted, while in power, "that he would not help a friend sooner than an enemy." I had a certain admiration for him till I knew that he said this, and proved it by his practice. There is something true and grateful and noble lacking in a man's nature, when he turns from his friend as he would from an enemy, doing nothing for either; always taking, and never giving; always seeking, yet sneering at others who seek; always subsisting on Government bounty and place himself, while he wounds, ignores, and sometimes insults the unfortunates who wish to do likewise and can't.

This is Mr. Parasite, and he lives, reigns and flourishes, as parasites only can, in every department of governmental state.

CHAPTER XXXVII

THE DEAD LETTER OFFICE—ITS MARVELS AND MYS-
TERIES.

THOUGH injured in comparison by the higher site and
loftier walls of the Patent-Office opposite, the Post-
Office, in itself, is one of the most beautiful public buildings in Washington. It occupies the entire block situated
on Seventh and Eighth streets west, and E and F streets
north. Like the Treasury and Patent-Office, it incloses
a grassy court-yard on which its inner offices look out.

The architecture of the Post-Office is a modified Corinthian, and is regarded by critics as the best representation of the Italian palatial ever built upon this continent. It was designed chiefly by F. A. Walter, at that time architect of the Capitol, an artist who has left monuments of architectural beauty behind him in marble which, seemingly, can never perish. On the Seventh street side there is a vestibule, the ceiling of which is composed of richly ornamented marbles, supported by four marble columns ; the walls, niches and floors are of marble, polished and tessellated. This is the grand entrance to the General Post-Office Department. The F street front affords accommodation to the city Post Office. It has a deeply recessed portico in the centre, consisting of eight columns grouped in pairs, and flanked by coupled pilasters supporting an entablature which girds the entire work. The portico is supported by an arcade which furnishes ample convenience for the delivery of letters, and the hurrying crowds which come after them. The Corinthian columns of this portico are each formed of a single block of marble, and each in itself is a marvel of architectural grace. The entrance for the mail wagons, on Eighth street, consists of a grand archway, the spandrels of which bear upon their face, sculpture representing Steam and Electricity, while a mask, representing Fidelity, forms the key-stone.

The Postal Service of the country is the oldest branch of the Government. As early as the year 1792, a proposition was introduced into the General Assembly of Virginia, to establish the office of Postmaster-General of Virginia and other parts of America. The proposition became a law, but was never carried into effect. In 1710, during the reign of Queen Anne, the British Parliament established a General Post-Office for all Her Majesty's dominions. By this act, the Postmaster-General was permitted to have one chief letter office in New York, and other chief letter offices at some convenient place or places in each of Her Majesty's provinces or colonies in America. When the colonies threw off their allegiance to the Crown, especial care was given to preserving, as far as possible, the postal facilities of the country. When the Federal Constitution was adopted, the right was secured to Congress " to establish Post-Offices and Post-Roads." In 1789, Congress created the office of Postmaster-General, and defined his duties. Other laws have since been passed, regulating the increased powers and duties of the Department, which is now, next to the Treasury, the most extensive in the country.

The Postmaster-General, the head of the Department, is a member of the President's Cabinet, and is in charge of the postal affairs of the United States. The business of the various branches of the Department is conducted in his name and by his authority. He has a general supervision of the whole Department, and issues all orders concerning the service rendered the Government through his subordinates. During the first administrations of the Government, the Postmaster-General was not regarded as a Cabinet Minister, but simply as the head of a Bureau. In 1829, General Jackson invited Mr. Barry, the gentleman appointed by him to that office, to a seat in his Cabinet. Since that time, the Postmaster-General has been recognized, as *ex-officio*, a Cabinet Minister.

The first Postmaster-General was Samuel Osgood, of Massachusetts. The present Postmaster is Marshall Jewell, of Hartford, Connecticut.

The subordinate officers of the Department are three

Assistant Postmaster-Generals, and the Chief of the Inspection Office. The Appointment Office is in charge of
the First Assistant Postmaster-General. To this office are
assigned all questions which relate to the establishment
and discontinuance of post-offices, changes of sites and
names, appointment and removal of postmasters, and *route*
and local agents, as, also, the giving of instructions to
postmasters. Postmasters are furnished with marking and
rating-stamps and letter-balances by this Bureau, which is
charged also with providing blanks and stationery for the
use of the Department, and with the superintendence of
the several agencies established for supplying postmasters
with blanks. "To this Bureau is likewise assigned the
supervision of the ocean-mail steamship-lines, and of the
foreign and international postal arrangements."

The Contract-Office is in charge of the Second Assistant
Postmaster-General. To this office is assigned the business of arranging the mail service of the United States,
and placing the same under contract, embracing all correspondence and proceedings affecting the frequency of
trips, mode of conveyance, and time of departures and
arrivals on all the *routes ;* the course of the mail between
the different sections of the country ; the points of mail
distribution ; and the regulations for the government of
the domestic mail service of the United States. It prepares the advertisements for mail proposals, receives the
bids, and takes charge of the annual and occasional mail
lettings, and the adjustment and execution of the contracts. All applications for the establishment or alteration
of mail arrangements, and the appointment of mail messengers, should be sent to this office. All claims should
be submitted to it for transportation service not under

contract, as the recognition of said service is first to be obtained through the Contract-Office as a necessary authority for the proper credits at the Auditor's-Office.

From this office all postmasters at the ends of *routes* receive the statement of mail arrangements prescribed for the respective *routes*. It reports weekly to the Auditor all contracts executed and all orders affecting accounts for mail transportation; prepares the statistical exhibits of mail service, and the reports of the mail lettings, giving a statement of each bid; also of the contracts made, the new service originated, the curtailments ordered, and the additional allowances granted within the year.

The Finance-Office is in charge of the Third Assistant Postmaster-General. To this office is assigned the supervision and management of the financial business of the Department not devolved by law upon the Auditor, embracing accounts with the draft offices and other depositories of the Department; the issuing of warrants and drafts in payment of balances, reported by the Auditor to be due mail contractors and other persons; the supervision of the accounts of offices under orders to deposit their quarterly balances at designated points; and the superintendence of the rendition by postmasters of their quarterly returns of postages. It has charge of the Dead-Letter Office, of the issuing of postage stamps and stamped envelopes for the prepayment of postage, and with the accounts connected therewith.

To the Third Assistant Postmaster-General all postmasters should direct their quarterly returns; those at draft-offices, their letters reporting quarterly the net proceeds of their offices; and those at depositing-offices, their certificates of deposit. To him should also be directed the weekly and monthly returns of the depositories of the Department, as well as applications and receipts for postage stamps and stamped envelopes, and for dead letters.

The Inspection-Office is in charge of a Chief Clerk. To this office is assigned the duty of receiving and examining the registers of the arrivals and departures of the mails, certificates of the service of *route*-agents, and reports of mail failures; noting the delinquencies of contractors, and preparing cases thereon for the action of the Postmaster-General; furnishing blanks for mail registers and reports of mail failures, providing and sending out mail bags and mail locks and keys, and doing all other things which may be necessary to secure a faithful and exact performance of all mail contracts.

All cases of mail depredation, of violations of law by private expresses, or by the forging and illegal use of postage stamps, are under supervision of this office, and should be reported to it. All communications respecting lost money-letters, mail depredations, or other violations of law, or mail locks and keys, should be directed to "Chief Clerk, Post-Office Department."

All registers of the arrivals and departures of the mails, certificates of the service of *route*-agents, reports of mail failures, applications for mail registers, and all complaints against contractors for irregular or imperfect service, should be directed, "Inspection Office, Post-Office Department."

Benjamin Franklin was appointed General Deputy Postmaster of the Colonies, in the year 1753, with a salary between him and his confederates, of £600, if they could get it. This experiment brought him in debt £900, and his success in expediting the mails, which he dwells upon with so much satisfaction in his writings, will create a smile in these days of electricity, steam, and "young-American" speed. In the year 1754, he gave notice that the mail to New England, which used to start but once a fortnight, in winter, should start once a week, all the year, "whereby answers might be obtained to letters between Philadelphia and Boston in three weeks, which used to require six weeks!"

Franklin was removed from his office by the British Ministry; but in the year 1775, the Congress of the Confederation having assumed the practical sovereignty of the Colonies, appointed a committee to devise a system of post-office communication, who made a report recommending a plan on the 26th of July, which on the same day was adopted, and Doctor Franklin unanimously appointed Postmaster-General, at a salary of $1,000 per annum. The salary of the Postmaster-General was doubled on the 16th of April, 1779, and on the 27th day of December, of the same year, Congress increased the salary to $5,000 per annum.

An Inspector of Dead Letters was also appointed, at a salary of $100 per annum, who was under oath faithfully and impartially to discharge the duties of his office, and enjoined to take no copies of letters, and not to divulge the contents to any but Congress, or to those who were appointed by Congress for that purpose. Dr. Franklin, on the 7th of November, 1776, was succeeded as Postmaster-General by his relative, Richard Bache, who remained in office till the 28th of January, 1782, when he was succeeded by Ebenezer Hazard, who was the last head of the General Post-Office under the Confederacy.

In 1790, there were but seventy-five post-offices in the United States, and but eighteen hundred and seventy-five miles of post *routes*.

The General Post-Office, in 1790, was located in New York, and Samuel Osgood, of Massachusetts, was the first Postmaster-General under the Federal Government. His conception of the duties of his office were, doubtless, very humble, as he recommended "that the Postmaster-General should not keep an office separate from the one in which the mail was opened and distributed; that he might, by his presence, prevent irregularities, and rectify any mistakes that might occur;" in fact, put the Postmaster-General, his assistant, and their one clerk, in the city post-office, to see that its mails were assorted and made up correctly.

The salary of Mr. Osgood was $1,500 per annum. Timothy Pickering was appointed by Washington, August 12, 1791, at an increased salary of $2,000. Joseph Haloshan was the last Postmaster-General appointed by Washington. He was commissioned April 22, 1795, at a salary of $2,400 per annum. The office was located in Philadelphia, in the year 1796, and was established at Washington when the Federal Government was removed there. In 1802, the United States ran their own stages between Philadelphia and New York, finding .coaches, drivers, horses, etc., and cleared in three years over $11,000, by carrying passengers.

That sultry morning of August 25, 1814, when Admiral Cockburn and his drunken crew, eager for fresh destruction, marched from Capitol Hill to the War Office, which they burned, and from it down F street to treat the Post-Office to the same fate, they found it on the site where its

marble successor now stands, and under the same roof the
Patent-Office.   Says Charles J. Ingersoll, in his rambling
history :

" Dr. Thornton, then Chief of the Patent-Office, accompanied
the detachment to the locked door of the repository, the key
having been taken away by another clerk watching out of night.
Axes and other implements of force were used to break in;
Thornton entreating, remonstrating, and finally prevailing on
Major Waters, superintending the destruction, to postpone it
till Thornton could see Colonel Jones, then engaged with Admiral Cockburn in destroying the office of the *National Intelligencer*, not far off on Pennsylvania avenue.   Colonel Jones
had declared that it was not designed to destroy private property, which Dr. Thornton assured Major Waters most of that in
the Patent-Office was.   A curious musical instrument, of his own
construction, which he particularly strove to snatch from ruin,
with a providential gust soon after, saved the seat of government from removal, for want of any building in which Congress
could assemble, when they met in Washington three weeks
afterwards.   Hundreds of models of the useful arts, preserved
in the office, were of no avail to save it; but music softened
the rugged breasts of the least musical of civilized people.
Major Waters agreed, at last, to respite the patents and the
musical instrument till his return from Greenleaf's Point, where
other objects were to be laid in ruins."

But with the explosion of the magazine at Greenleaf's
Point, and the tornado, both of which made unexpected
havoc with the lives of the British vandals, and their
withdrawal under cover of night, they never came back
to the Patent and Post-Office, to destroy it.   It was, I
believe, the only public building in the capital which
escaped their torch.   It was, however, destroyed by fire,
December 15, 1836.

One of the most precious treasures, now in the possession of the Post-Office Department, is the original ledger of Doctor Benjamin Franklin, Postmaster-General, 1776, which upon its title-page bears the following record:

" This book was rescued from the flames, during the burning of the Post-Office Building, on Thursday morning, Dec. 15, 1836, by W. W. Cox, messenger of the office of the Auditor of the Treasury for the Post-Office Department."

This ledger is now on file in the office of the Auditor of the Treasury for the Post-Office Department. Scorched and worn, it tells the story of time and fate. It embraces all the accounts of all the post-offices of the United States for the years 1776–77–78. These are all recorded in the handwriting of Doctor Franklin, and do not cover one hundred and twenty pages. The growth in the postal service may be partly measured by the fact that its money record, kept by Benjamin Franklin, running through eleven years, is equalled, at the present time, by the accounts of two days. When the philosopher was at the head of the Post-Office Department, there were eighty post-offices in the Confederation; there are now thirty-two thousand post-offices in the United States, with the number constantly increasing.

The Dead-Letter Office embodies more personal interest than any other in the Post-Office Department. It is a spacious room, unique in outline, many-windowed and well ventilated. It is surrounded by a wide gallery, supported by spiral columns. An open iron staircase connects it with' the lower office. It is set apart for the woman's work of this division. They are far out-numbered by the men below, and yet in this narrow gallery they are sadly crowded.

Spacious as the Post-Office is, in going thereto, the same conclusion is forced upon one, which is apparent in every public building, that it is already too small for the vast and rapidly increasing demands of the public service. The gentlemen which you see at work below have nothing to complain of in lack of light or air, but the ladies above say that their little gallery is the escape valve to all the poisoned air below; that their heads are so near the roof there is no chance for ventilation, and that sudden death, among their number, has been caused by the air-poison which pervades this gallery. The ladies need more room for a new office; indeed, already they have over-flowed the gallery and are packed closely in the halls.

Meanwhile, in an imposing-looking apartment beneath them, sit their brethren, on either side of the long table, opening the "dead-letters" which they are to re-direct. I believe there are fourteen clergymen, sitting at a single table, opening these letters. Preference is given to gentle-men of this profession, broken in health or fortune, as it is taken for granted that if they have lived to that age and fate, without ever having committed a dishonest act, it is most unlikely that they ever will—and that the treasure-letters are perfectly safe in their keeping. Moreover, their profession is also in their favor. They must have been unworldly-minded, says the reasoner, or they would never have chosen to be clergymen. Nearly all are elderly men, and among the number are a few old ones,—one, who has been in this office over fifty years, a brother of its one time Postmaster-General, Amos Kendall—hair white as snow—back bent over the table—hands trem-bling as he uses his knife—it is his life to go on opening his quota of daily letters, for the pittance of $1,200 per year.

"If he were refused the privilege," said an officer, " he would die at once."

In this office, from the thirty thousand post-offices in the United States are received, annually, about three million five hundred thousand dead-letters; unmailable letters, three hundred and sixty thousand; blank letters, three thousand.

It seems impossible that three thousand persons, in a single year, should post letters without a single letter traced on their envelopes; nevertheless, this is true.

In one corner of this office stand two men, by an open door, whose business it is to receive the dead-letters as they ascend to the office. They come up on an elevator—tied up in immense bags. As they are tossed out on the floor, one would suppose that they contained coffee for merchandise, rather than heart-messages and treasures gone astray. The bags are immediately opened and the letters transferred to the assorting table, where they are classified by clerks. The foreign letters are separated from the domestic, and any irregularity in their transmission is noted. They are then counted, numbered and tied up into packages of one hundred each, and thrown into bins, whence they are withdrawn in the order of the date of their reception, and transferred to the opening table to be *hari-karied* by our clergymen.

Letters containing nothing, if possible, are returned to their writers. If they cannot be, they are thrown into the waste-basket. This waste-paper is not burned but sold—and averages to the Government a revenue of about $4,000 per year. With all his extravagances, this is but one of numerous ways by which Uncle Sam manages to turn an economical penny out of the carelessness and misfortunes of nephews and nieces.

Letters containing anything, of the smallest value, are saved and registered under their different heads. Money, jewels, drafts, money-orders, receipts, hair, seeds, deeds, military-papers, pension-papers, etc., are all recorded and returned, if possible. A " money letter " has five different records before it leaves the Dead-Letter Office, and is so checked and counter-checked as to make collusion or abstraction almost impossible, in case any soul who surveyed it were fatally tempted.

When the opener of a letter finds money, he immediately makes a record of it. The next morning, the head of " the Opening Table " records in a book each letter found and recorded by each opener the day before. The letters are then taken from a safe, in which they were locked the night previous, and their contents recounted, to make sure of absolute correctness, before leaving the Opening Table. The money-letters, with the record of that day, are then handed over to the head of the Money Branch, where the letters recorded by the head of the Opening Table are certified and receipted. They are next indexed and delivered to the several clerks of the Money Branch, each receipting every letter he has recorded on the Index Book. He then records the letter and sends it to the writer, through the postmaster of the place where the party lives. The owner, on receiving the money, receipts for the same on a blank accompanying the letter, which he sends back to the Dead-Letter Office. The letters are again re-examined by two clerks, to see if the amounts are correct, who conjointly scrutinize and seal the letters. They are then registered to the different distributing offices, with all the precautionary checks of a registered letter. In time, the letter or a receipt from the owner, through the postmaster, is returned. If a receipt is received, it is recorded, with date, as a final disposition of the letter.   If the money is returned, it is so noted and recorded on a separate record kept for the purpose, that record showing, perpetually, how much money is on hand.   If not claimed at the end of three months, the money is deposited in the Treasury of the United States, subject to the application of the owner. By this minute and exhaustive routine, every money-letter, and every cent which they contain, is absolutely accounted for—traced, refunded, and held.

Drafts, deeds, checks, power-of-attorney and wills are recorded, and sent through postmasters to their owners, they returning receipts for the same.

Foreign letters are assorted, the amounts due this and other countries recorded, and a system of accounts kept, showing, by a list returned with the letters, a correct statement.   Foreign letters are returned weekly, to England, Germany and the Netherlands.   The liberal postage recently adopted by these countries has opened so large a correspondence, it involves more frequent returns.

The Property-Branch is of a most miscellaneous character.   It involves the recording and returning of jewellery, and of almost every other article under the sun. Many of these it is impossible to return.   These accumulate in such vast piles, it is necessary to dispose of them at auction, at least, as often as once in four years.

At each sale, a complete catalogue of the articles is presented, and the proceeds are deposited in the United States Treasury.

A room, leading from the Dead-Letter Office, lined with closed closets to its lofty ceiling, is the receptacle of

26

all these stranded treasures. When the custodian unlocks their doors and you behold what is shut within, you are lost in wonder as to what must be the conceived capacity of the Post-Office in the minds of your compatriots. Before your eyes, crammed into shelves, you see patch-work quilts, under garments, and outer garments; hats, caps, and bonnets; shoes and stockings; with no end of nicknacks and keepsakes; "sets" of embroidery, baby-wardrobes, watches, and jewels of every description—though the greater proportion is of the "fire-gilt," "dollar-store" description. Many really beautiful pictures are retained, because not sufficiently prepaid. Some of these, sent as gifts, are left by the chosen recipients to be sold at auction—the postage often amounting to far more than the value of the picture. Many motley articles peer forth from their hiding-places ignominiously "franked," yet retained, the frank not being sufficient legal-tender to insure their triumphal passage to the place of final destination. Among these is an iron apple-parer.

Many of these cheap treasures were precious keepsakes from the hearts which fondly sent them—under very un-intelligible superscriptions—to sweethearts whom they never reached. Some are tokens from beyond the seas, which came from a far-off land only to find the one sought—dead or living—gone, without a clue.

During the war, tens of thousands of photographs were thus sent astray. The husband, the father, the brother, the son, under whose name they came—alas! when they reached his regiment, he was not—the heaped-up trench, the unknown grave, the unburied dead—somewhere amid them all—he slept, and the memento of the love that lived for him, came back to this receptacle of the nation, and here. it is! On a stand near the window, is an immense open book lined with photographs, all the photographs of soldiers. With a tender hand, the Government gathered these pictures of its lost and unknown sons and garnered them here, for the sake of the living, who might seek their lost. Turning over the pages, we see many empty spaces, and find that friends coming here and turning over the pages of this book have identified the faces of loved ones who perished in the war. Many of these are photographs of a poor character, (whose transient chemicals are already fading out,) which were taken on the field, and sent, by soldiers, home to mothers, wives, sisters and sweethearts. The chances of war are sufficient to account for their going astray of their objects and for their return here—where more than one tear-blinded woman has sought and found them, at last.

To return to the dryer details of the Dead-Letter Office, we find that all letters held for postage, all blank, unmailable, and hotel letters pass through a like process with the dead-letter, with the exception of the unmailable letters, which come directly from the office with written lists, which are checked to see if the letters are all with the lists. These the opener counter-checks, marking the contents both on letter and list, to show that it was received and doubly opened. These lists, with their letters, are sent to the Return Branch. Here they are returned to their writers, and their lists are made to show the disposition of every letter. These lists are carefully filed and subject to re-perusal. The Return Branch, which is composed entirely of ladies, sends average dead-letters back to their writers at the rate of seven thousand a day. In this branch we find the application-clerk whose duty it is to trace letters, and to send such information to persons applying for letters as the records may show. In case of the loss of a valuable letter, the Department spares no pains in its efforts to trace and find it.

The Postmaster-General, in one of his recent reports, says of this branch of the Postal Service:

"In the examination of domestic dead-letters, for disposition, 1,736,867 were found to be either not susceptible of being returned, or of no importance, circulars, etc., and were destroyed after an effort to return them—making about 51 per cent. destroyed. The remainder were classified and returned to the owners as far as practicable. The whole number sent from the office was 2,258,199, of which about 84 per cent. were delivered to owners, and 16 per cent. were returned to the Department; 18,340 letters, containing $95,169.52, in sums of $1 and upward, of which 16,061 letters, containing $86,638.66, were delivered to owners, and 2,124, containing $7,862.36, were filed or held for disposition; 14,082 contained $3,436.68, in sums of less than $1, of which 12,513, containing $3,120.70, were delivered to owners; 17,750 contained drafts, deeds, and other papers of value, representing the value of $3,609,271.80—of these 16,809 were restored to the owners, and 821 were returned and filed; 13,964 contained books, jewellery, and other articles of property, of the estimated value of $8,500—of these 11,489 were forwarded for delivery and 9,911 were delivered to their owners; 125,221 contained photographs, postage-stamps, and articles of small value, of which 114,666 were delivered to owners; 2,068,842 without inclosures. Thus of the ordinary dead-letters forwarded from this office, about 84 per cent. were delivered, and of the valuable dead-letters (classed as money and minor) about 89 per cent. were delivered. The decrease of money-letters received (about 3,000) is probably owing to the growing use of money-orders for the transmission of small sums."

In August, 1864, Hon. Montgomery Blair appointed

Dr. C. F. Macdonald, now the Superintendent of the Money-Order Department, and J. M. McGrew, now Chief Clerk of the Sixth Auditor's office, commissioners to visit Quebec and examine the workings of the Money-Order System which has been in operation in Great Britain and Canada for several years.

The system, as used by the British Government, was modified and simplified by the commissioners, and on the 8th of November, 1864, the Money-Order System of the United States was inaugurated, with 138 offices authorized to issue and pay.

During the part of the fiscal year commencing November 8, 1864, and ending June 30, 1865, there were 74,277 money-orders issued, amounting to $1,360,122.52; during next fiscal year ending June 30, 1866—138,297, amounting to $3,977,259.28; during next fiscal year ending June 30, 1867—474,496, amounting to $9,229,327.72; during next fiscal year ending June 30, 1868—831,937, amounting to $16,197,858.47; during next fiscal year ending June 30, 1869—1,264,143, amounting to $24,848,058.93; during next fiscal year ending June 30, 1870—1,675,228, amounting to $33,658,740,27; during the next fiscal year ending June 30, 1871—2,151,794, amounting to $42,164,118.03; during next fiscal year ending June 30, 1872—2,573,349, amounting to $48,515,532.72.

During the present fiscal year, which expired June 30, 1873, the number of orders issued will reach 3,000,000, and the amount will be over $50,000,000.

The above figures, in themselves, contain the history of the money-order system from its beginning to the present time. During the war one letter was received at the

Dead-Letter Office which contained $12,000. Rarely now does any sum inside of an envelope amount to $50. As a rule, any sum over $5 is sent by money order—at least by all persons who have any reasonable idea of what is absolutely safe.

CHAPTER XXXVIII.

THE DEPARTMENT OF THE INTERIOR—UNCLE SAM'S DOMESTIC ARRANGEMENTS.

Inadequate Accommodation in Heaven—Defects of our Great Public Buildings—The Public Archives—Valuable Documents in Jeopardy—Talk of
Moving the Capital—A Dissension of a Hundred Years—Concerning
Certain Idiots—A Day in the Patent Office—The Inventive Genius of
the Country—Aggressions of the Home Department—A Comprehensive
Act of Congress—Seven Divisions of the Department of the Interior—
The Disbursing Division—Division of Indian Affairs—Lands and Rail-
roads—Pensions and Patents—Public Documents—Division of Appoint-
ments—The Superintendent of the Building—The Secretary of the In-
terior and his Subordinates—Pensions and their Recipients—Indian
Affairs—How the Savages are Treated—Over Twenty-one Million of
Dollars Credited to their Little Account—The Census Bureau—A Rather
Big Work—The Bureau of Patents—What is a Patent?—A Self-support-
ing Institution—A Few Dollars Over—The Use Made of a Certain Brick
Building—Secretary Delano—An Objection Against Him—How Wick-
edly he Acted to the Women Clerks—" The Accustomed Tyranny of
Men "—Cutting Down the Ladies' Salaries—Making Places for Useful
Voters—A Sweet Prayer for Delano's Welfare—Something about Del-
ano's Face.

IT has always been a mystery to me how Heaven could
continue large enough for all the people who are trying to get into it, that is, if the human race is to keep on
being born.

I am equally puzzled about the internal spaces of our
great public buildings. When designed, they were supposed to be ample for centuries to come; but with the
constant creation of new bureaus, and even of depart-

ments, with the fast and never-ceasing accumulations of records in every branch of the Government service, not a public building in Washington is now large enough to hold the archives, or even the *employés* belonging to its own department. Already the city is filled with temporary buildings, in which the overflow of the various departments have taken refuge. Even now, every public building needs a duplicate as large as itself to hold its treasures, and to carry on fitly the intricate machinery of its routine service. The constant cry of " Capital moving " has not only prevented this, but has caused the precious records of the departments to be packed into precarious and insufficient store-houses.

The public archives should all be stored in fire-proof buildings. The destruction of the titles to all the lands in the country sold by the Government would involve a loss greater than the cost of all Washington city. And yet, as they are stored at present, any morning you may hear that there is nothing left of them but ashes.

What madness to talk of moving the Capital! What idiots to breed another dissension of a hundred years as to where another Capital shall be, instead of making the most and best of the majestic one, bought at such cost, that already is!

Well, a day in the Patent-Office has caused this outburst. This building was built for the protection and display of the inventive genius of the country. But that genius finds itself fearfully " cabined and confined," and almost crowded out by the elephantine proportions of the Home Department, which needs, almost beyond any other, a vast building of its own, all to itself. At first a single room was demanded for the Secretary of the Interior. The needs of his department were such, he has gone on annexing room after room of the noble Patent-Office, till its "inventive genius" finds itself crowded into a very small corner of the majestic building built with the proceeds of its own industry.

March 3, 1849, Congress passed an act to establish the Home Department, and enacted that said new executive branch of the Government of the United States should be called the Department of the Interior, and that the head of said Department should be called Secretary of the Interior, and that the Secretary should be placed upon the same plane with other Cabinet officers.

This act transferred to the Secretary of the Interior the supervisory power over the office of the Commissioner of Patents, exercised before by the Secretary of State; the same power, over the Commissioner of the General Land-Office, held previously by the Secretary of the Treasury; the same over the Bureau of Indian Affairs, which had been under the supervision of the Secretary of War; the same over the acts of the Commissioner of Pensions, who had previously reported to the Secretary of the Navy; also over the marshals and orders of taking and returning the census, previously managed by the Secretary of State; the same over accounts of marshals, clerks and officers of courts of the United States, previously exercised by the Secretary of the Treasury. The same act relieved the President of the duty of supervising the acts of the Commissioner of Public Buildings, placing that gentleman under the directions of the Interior Department; giving the Secretary control over the Board of Inspectors and the Warden of the Penitentiary of the District of Columbia.

Thus, you see, the Department of the Interior was made up, at the beginning, of slices cut from each one of the other departments of the Government. Subsequent acts of legislation have added new duties to the Home Department. The Department of Justice; the Department of Metropolitan Police; the accounts of marshals and clerks of the United States Courts, and of matters pertaining to the judiciary; the discontinuance of the office of Commissioner of Public Buildings, and the assignment of his duties to the Chief Engineer of the Army, with the duties and powers heretofore exercised by the Secretary of State over the Governors and Secretaries of the various territories. All have been transferred to the Department of the Interior. Admission of indigent insane persons, resident in the District of Columbia, to the Insane Asylum, also to the Columbia Institution for the deaf and dumb, and to the National Deaf-mute College, and of blind children to the Columbia Institution, all are only obtained through the Secretary of the Interior.

The office of the Secretary of the Interior is divided into seven divisions, as follows:

The "Disbursing Division," through which all moneys, appropriated for the entire service of the department, pass.

The Division of the Indian Affairs; having charge of matters pertaining to the Indian office, and the various Indian tribes.

The Division of Lands and Railroads; having charge of matters pertaining to the General Land-Office, and the construction, &c., of land-grant railroads.

The Division of Pensions and Patents; having charge of matters pertaining to those offices.

The Division of Public Documents; having charge of the distribution of the public documents and the Department Library.

The Division of Appointments; having charge of all matters pertaining to the force of the department, the preparing, recording, etc., of Presidential appointments under the Interior Department.

The Superintendent of the building; having charge of all repairs, the oversight of the laboring force, heating apparatus, etc.

. The head of the Department is the Secretary of the Interior. His subordinates are the Commissioners of the Public Lands, Patents, Indian Affairs, and Pensions, and the Superintendent of the Census. The Secretary is charged with the general supervision of matters relating to the public lands, the pensions granted by the Government, the management of the Indian tribes, the granting patents, the management of the Agricultural Bureau, of the lead and other mines of the United States, the affairs of the Penitentiary of the District of Columbia, the overland-*routes* to the Pacific, including the great Pacific Railways, the taking of the Census, and the direction of the acts of the Commissioner of Public Buildings, the Insane Hospital for the District of Columbia, and the Army and Navy, is also under his control.

The first Secretary of the Interior was Thomas Ewing, of Ohio, appointed by President Taylor; and Columbus Delano, of Ohio, is the present Secretary.

The General Land-Office was established as a branch of the Treasury Department by act of Congress, approved April 25, 1812, which authorized the appointment of a Commissioner, at a salary of $3,000 per annum, and the employment of a Chief Clerk, and such other clerks as might be necessary to perform the work, at an annual compensation not to exceed, in the whole, $7,000.

By the act of July 4, 1836, the office was reorganized and the force increased. The number of clerks now employed is one hundred and fifty-four; and even this force is not sufficient to meet the requirements of a constantly growing business. Upon the creation of the Interior Department, in 1849, the Land-Office was placed under its jurisdiction.

The Commissioner of the General Land-Office is charged with the duty of supervising the surveys of private land claims, and also the survey and sale of the public lands of the United States. At present this supervision extends to seventeen surveying districts and ninety-two local land-offices.

The following table exhibits the progress of surveys and the disposal of public lands since the fiscal year, ending June 30, 1861:

Fiscal Year ending June 30.	Surveying districts.	Land Offices.	Cost of Survey.	Number of Acres Surveyed.	Number of Acres Disposed of.
1862	9	58	$219,000 00	2,673,132	1,337,922.00
1863	11	54	151,840 00	2,147,981	2,966,698.00
1864	10	53	172,906 00	4,315,954	3,238,865.00
1865	10	53	170,721 00	4,161,778	4,513,738.00
1866	10	61	186,389 88	4,267,037	4,629,312.00
1867	12	62	423,416 22	10,808,314	7,041,114 00
1868	13	68	325,779 50	10,170,656	6,665,742.00
1869	12	66	497,471 00	10,822,812	7,666,151.00
1870	17	81	560,210 00	18,165,278	8,095,413.00
1871	17	83	683,910 00	22,016,607	10,765,705.00
1872	17	92	1,019,378 66	29,450,939	11,864,975.64

This shows an increase of the number of surveyors' general from nine to seventeen, and land-offices from fifty-eight to ninety-two, and an increase in the annual survey from 2,673,132 acres to 29,458,939 acres, and an increase in the number of acres disposed of from 1,337,-932 to 11,864,975.64, for the year ending June 30, 1872.

The Land-Office audits its own accounts. It is also charged with laying off land-grants' made to the various railroad schemes by Congress. The mines belonging to the Government are also in charge of this office.

The Commissioner of Pensions examines and adjudicates all claims arising under the various and numerous laws passed by Congress, granting bounty-lands or pensions for military and naval services rendered the United States at various times. The Rebellion greatly increased the pension list.

The Commissioner of Indian Affairs has charge of all the matters relating to the Indian tribes of the frontier. The Government has at sundry times purchased the lands of various tribes residing east of the Mississippi River, and has settled the Indians upon reservations in the extreme West. For some of these lands a perpetual annuity was granted the tribes; for others, an annuity for a certain specified time; and for others still, a temporary annuity, payable during the pleasure of the President or Congress. The total sum thus pledged to these tribes amounts to nearly twenty-one and a half millions. It is funded at five per cent., the interest alone being paid to the tribes; this interest amounts to over two hundred thousand dollars. It is paid in various ways—in money, in provisions, and in clothing. The Commissioner has charge of all these dealings with the savages.

Prior to Act of Congress of June 30, 1834, organizing the " Department of Indian Affairs," Indian matters were managed by a Bureau, with a superintendent in charge, under the direction and control of the War Department, and under the organization, the department or office continued with the War Department, until March 3, 1849, when Congress created the Department of the Interior, and gave the supervisory and appellate power, exercised by the Secretary of War in relation to the acts of the Commissioner of Indian Affairs, to the Secretary of the new department.

A "Commissioner of Indian Affairs" was first authorized by Act of Congress, dated July 9, 1832, and the same law required the Secretary of War to prescribe a new set of regulations as to the mode in which the business of the Commissioner should be performed.

E. Herring was the first Commissioner, and his successors have been as follows: C. A. Harris, appointed in 1836; T. H. Crawford, 1838; Wm. Medell, 1845; O. Brown, 1849; L. Lee, 1850; G. W. Monypenny, 1853; J. W. Denver, 1857; C. E. Mix, 1858; A. B. Greenwood, 1859; W. P. Dole, 1861; D. N. Cooley, 1865; L. V. Bogy, 1866; N. G. Taylor, 1867; E. S. Parker, 1869; F. E. Walker, 1871; and E. P. Smith, 1873.

The Indian Department comprehended, under the new regulations provided for by the law of July 9, 1832, four superintendencies, thirteen agencies, and thirteen sub-agencies, having charge of about two hundred and fifty thousand Indians, inhabiting some of the States west of the Mississippi, and also what was then held to be ".Indian Country," defined by the first section of the law of June 30, 1834, regulating trade and intercourse with

Indian tribes, to be "all that part of the United States west of the Mississippi and not within the State of Missouri and Louisiana, or the Territory of Arkansas, and, also, that part of the United States east of the Mississippi River and not within any State to which the Indian title has not been extinguished."

By subsequent acquisition of territory from Mexico, the area of Indian country became greatly extended, with a consequent large addition to the Indian population within the jurisdiction of the Indian Department. In the beginning of the current year, the Department consisted of eight superintendencies, seventy agencies and special agencies, and three sub-agencies. At present there are four superintendencies, four having been abolished by act of Congress, February 14, 1873, providing in lieu thereof five Indian Inspectors, whose duty it is to visit every superintendency and agency, and examine into the affairs of the same, as often as once or twice a year, and to report their proceedings; sixty-eight agencies, nine special agencies and three sub-agencies, with an Indian population, approximately, of 300,000, exclusive of those in Alaska, estimated at between 50,000 and 75,000.

In the Indian service there is also a Board of "Indian Commissioners," nine in number, authorized by act of Congress, approved April 10, 1869, men eminent for their intelligence and philanthropy, who serve without compensation, the object of the Commission being to co-operate with the President in efforts to maintain peace among the Indians, bring them upon reservations, relieve their necessities, and to encourage them in attempts at self-support.

The Census Bureau is now a permanent branch of the

Department of the Interior.   It is in charge of a super-intendent, and is assigned the duty of compiling the statistics which constitute the Census of the Republic.   This enumeration is made every ten years.   Some idea of the magnitude of the task may be gained from the fact that the tabulation and publication of the census of 1870 were not completed in January, 1873.

The Bureau of Patents is a part of the Department of the Interior, but is in all its proportions and features so vast and imposing, that it is almost a separate department, as, indeed, it must become erelong.   It is in charge of a Commissioner of Patents, who is appointed by the President of the United States, by and with the advice and consent of the Senate.   It is intrusted with the duty of granting letters patent, securing to the inventor the control of and the reward from articles beneficial to civilization.   It was formerly a part of the Treasury Department, and is one of the best known branches of the Government.

Patents are not, as some persons suppose, monopolies, but are protections granted to individuals as rewards for, and incentives to discoveries and inventions of all kinds pertaining to the useful arts.   This Bureau is allowed to charge for these letters of protection only the cost of investigating and registering the invention.   It is a self-supporting institution, its receipts being largely in excess of its expenditures.

If you have traced the many Bureaus of the Interior Department thus far, you have come to the conclusion that it needs a public building all to itself, and that it should be an immense one.   A large brick building opposite the Patent-Office, on G street, is already exclusively occupied by the Bureau of Education.

The present Secretary of the Interior is Hon. Columbus Delano, of Ohio, a man who has been long in public life, first as Member of Congress from Ohio, then as Commissioner of Internal Revenue, now as Secretary of the Interior. I have but one objection to make to Mr. Delano in the position which he now holds. He found twelve-hundred-dollar-positions in his department filled, as they had been from the beginning, by women. He degrades them to nine-hundred-dollar-clerkships, to make place for his voters. Judging by the course he pursues, we may believe that he is of the same opinion as the Secretary of the Treasury, that "four hundred dollars per year are enough for any woman to earn," unless she should be a Delano! I hope that Ohio will reward him by not giving him the desire of his heart and making him Senator, till he practices justice as the supreme virtue of a public servant.

Columbus Delano has a face which nature never weakened by cutting it down to absolute fineness, but added to its power by leaving it a little in the rough. Iron-gray hair, shaggy eyebrows beetling over a pair of straight-forward, out-looking gray eyes, make the more prominent features of a face which you willingly believe in as that of a strong and honorable man.

27

CHAPTER XXXIX.

THE PENSION BUREAU—HOW GOVERNMENT PAYS ITS SERVANTS.

The Generosity of Congress to Itself—How Four Hundred Acts of Congress were Passed—How Pensions have Increased and Multiplied—Sneering at Red-Tape—The Division of Labor—Scrutinizing Petitions—A Heavy Paper Jacket—The Judicial Division—Invalids, Widows, and Minors—The Examiner of Pensions—The Difficulties of his Position—Unsatisfactory Work—How Claims are Entertained and Tested—What is Recorded in the Thirty Enormous Volumes—How many Genuine Cases are Refused—One of the Inconveniences of Ignorance—The Claim-Agent Gobbles up the Lion's Share—An Extensive Correspondence—How Claims are Mystified, and Money is Wasted—The "Reviewer's" Work—The "Rejected Files"—The "Admitted Files"—Seventy-Five Thousand Claims Pending—Very Ancient Claimants—The Bounty Land Division—The Reward of Fourteen Days' Service—The Sum Total of what the Government has Paid in Pensions—How the Pensions are Paid —The Finance Division—The Largest and the Smallest Pension Office— The Miscellaneous Branch—Investigating Frauds—A Poor "Dependent" Woman with Forty Thousand Dollars—How "Honest and Respectable" People Defraud the Government—The Medical Division—Examining Invalids—The Restoration-Desk—The Appeal-Desk—The Final-Desk—The Work that Has Been Done—One Hundred and Fifty Thousand People Grumbling—Letter of an Ancient Claimant—The Wrath of a Pugnacious Captain.

COMPARED to the generosity with which it rewards itself, Congress doles out most scanty recompense even to the Government's most faithful and long-suffering servants. Nevertheless, that it does not neglect or ignore them altogether, the annals of the Pension Bureau accurately attest.

The first Act promising pensions to those disabled by war, was passed in the next month after the Declaration of Independence, August 26, 1776. On September 16, 1776, specified grants of land were promised to those who should enter the service, and continue to its close; and in case of their death, to their heirs.

Under these early enactments, the mode prescribed by law, to decide who were entitled to pensions, was to leave the State Legislatures to decide who should justly receive pensions. Having decided, the State Legislatures paid the pensioners, and were reimbursed by the general Government.

Afterward, this method gave way to another, requiring the Judges of district, and circuit-courts, to decide the equity of the demand, and to pay it, as had formerly been done, by the Legislatures of the several States. These payments were not made, however, until after the lists reported by the Judges had been verified by comparison with the rolls on file in the War Department, when they were reported by the Secretary of War to Congress, and placed on the pension-lists, by a resolution of that body. This mode was found to be too slow in detecting frauds, and February 25, 1793, an Act was passed, prescribing rules to be observed by the courts in the investigation of claims, and providing that the evidence upon which the decision was based should accompany the report. This Act prevailed, with slight modifications, until March 3, 1819, when an Act was passed, authorizing the Secretary of War to place on the pension-rolls, without reporting the lists to Congress.

This authority was exercised by the Secretary of War, until March 2, 1833, when a distinct Bureau of the Government was established for the adjustment of pension

claims.   It was provided for in the section of a bill, which
made an appropriation for the civil and diplomatic expense of the Government, for the year.   This section said:
"A Commissioner of Pensions shall be appointed by the
President and the Senate, who shall receive a salary of
twenty-five hundred dollars, which is hereby appropriated."   This office was perpetuated for many years by
biennial enactments, the last providing that it should continue until further legislation on the subject.

Since the passage of the first Act, by the old Congress in
1776, there have been over four hundred distinct Acts relating to pensions for military and naval services, and for
bounty-land rewarding such services, enacted by Congress.
Instead of the small pension-lists transmitted by the
courts of the country, through the Secretary of War to
Congress, the tens of thousands of pension-claims, presented to the Government, under the various laws which
relate to them, now require the constant services of more
than three hundred clerks in the Pension Bureau, supervised by the Commissioner of Pensions.

It is the dual duty of this Bureau, to protect private
interests, and to secure the enforcement of the law.   The
claims are infinite and often conflicting; the provisions of
law manifold; and people unfamiliar with the immense
demand upon such an office, sneer or smile, or weep over
the length of the "red-tape" routine, through which its
cases are so often "long drawn out."   Persons waiting
outside the Bureau, can not comprehend the requirements
or exigencies of a business demanding the employment
of so large a force of actors, or touching the springs of
so many public and private interests.   Says one who
knows: "Far better the delays of red tape, than the inex-

tricable confusion, and total inability to transact business, which would be the inevitable result of a business system less minute and stringent."

The Pension Bureau is divided into four divisions, viz: the Mail Division, the Judicial, the Financial, and the Miscellaneous.

The Mail Division is charged with the receiving, reading, distributing to the proper desks, all the mail. Every original application, every piece of additional evidence, every communication, of whatever nature, is stamped with the date of receipt, and, with the exception of letters of inquiry, they are entered on the records, which show from whom received, when received, and to whom delivered.

" It requires careful examination of the papers, a thorough knowledge of the office, and the closest analysis, to determine the proper destination of each communication. Many writers are obscure, many misstate their business, through ignorance or carelessness, and to quickly comprehend the import of all papers, requires a keen eye and a ready mind.

"Persons communicating with the Office, should remember this, and to insure a correct distribution of their mail, should, in all cases, indorse upon the outside of the envelope, the number of the claim referred to, the name of the claimant, and the nature of the claim.

"In this Division, claims are also prepared for the files, by having a heavy paper jacket placed round them, upon which is indorsed the Act under which it is filed, the description of the party claiming, their address, also the address of the attorney, if one appears in the claim."

The Judicial Division is charged with an application of

the law to the evidence, and the determining of the right of the applicant to the pension. This office is divided into three grand divisions—invalid, widows, and minors. The first embraces all claims preferred by surviving soldiers; the second, all claims based upon the service and death of soldiers and sailors; the third, those of minors.

An Examiner of Pensions does not sit upon a bed of roses—or, if he does, it is full of thorns. So various and minute are the provisions of law, applicable to the cases under his consideration, so numerous are the rulings of the office, and the decisions of the Heads of Departments, and of the Bureau, with the opinion of the Attorney-General added, all bearing upon this claim, it demands the most exhaustive examination, the keenest discrimination, and the most wise judgment, to reach a final just conclusion. And when his conclusion is reached, it is not final.

In the Judicial Division, are filed all pending claims. These files are arranged with reference to the initial letter of the soldier's surname, and are divided into sections proportioned to the magnitude of the letter of the alphabet. Upon the receipt of jacketed claims from the mail division, the first step is to see if the party, making application, ever filed a claim before, and this is ascertained by examining the "original records."

These records fill thirty enormous volumes, and contain three hundred and eighty-three thousand applications that have been filed under the act of July 14, 1862. All entries are made therein with reference to the first three letters of the soldier's surname, and only by this subdivision of names, affording two thousand eight hundred combinations, can convenient reference to any given claim be had; and even when so divided, the examination of the greater combination requires considerable labor. For instance, in two hundred thousand entries under W. I. L., there will be three thousand two hundred and fifty entries; and under S. M. I. you will find two thousand seven hundred and fifty Smiths. If the result of this examination affords no evidence of a prior application by the same person, after noting all other applications based upon the service of the same soldier, the claims are numbered in numerical order and placed upon the record, which includes a full description thereof, and the recorded claims are then placed in the files, to await examination in the order of their receipt.

When they are reached, the examiner's duties begin. He first searches for such recorded evidence as can be found in any of the Departments of the Government. From these he notes all omissions, and points unsupported, and calls upon the claimant, or his attorney, for corroborative evidence of the statements made in the declaration. He is guided in his requirements by the hundreds of rulings applicable to the smallest details of the various kinds of claims. All the evidence furnished in response must comply with the minutest demand of the law; the law of evidence as applied in courts, and the express requirements of the law under which the pension is claimed, are both brought to bear in the consideration of the points to be met, and the testimony offered in proof.

You will not be astonished to be told that very often they are not met, or that in thousands of just cases the testimony is unequal to the gradgrind requirements of the law. A want of a knowledge of the provisions of the law—more than of willful knavery—is the great acknowledged difficulty with which the Office has to contend. Many a poor sinner, who lost his leg or arm, or carries a bullet in him, received in his country's battles, knows all about the minus members, the battles, and the bullet, and not an atom about "the provisions of the law," or the inextricable windings of official red-tape. Because his knowledge is of so one-sided a character, he finds it no easy matter to get the governmental reward for that buried leg or arm; and by the time all "the requirements of the law" have been slowly beaten into his brains, the greater portion of his pension is pocketed by the claim-agent who showed him how to get it.

All these provisions and safeguards of the law are said to be necessary, to protect the Government against fraudulent claims. Perhaps they are; but that makes them no less hard, or ofttimes unjust "to the soldier and widow" who, in writing a letter, are as ignorant as babies of "the requirements of the law." Under these requirements, and with the utter ignorance of common people of technical terms, and judicial statements, it is not strange that "a large percentage of the evidence offered, is imperfectly prepared." A great deal more is deficient in substance, or suspected of fraud.

The correspondence from this Division, stating objections, requiring further proof, and elucidating doubtful points, amounts to hundreds of letters a day. The long delay inevitable, is said to be the fault of the system. "*Ex-parte* evidence is the criminal." "Were means afforded for a cross-examination of all applicants and witnesses, these difficulties and delays would disappear. One-half of the amount now taken from the pockets of pensioners, to compensate agents for procuring their pensions, would pay the entire cost of such a system, to say nothing of the thousands of dollars paid from the Treasury upon fraudulent claims, that would be saved."

When the examiner has ended his researches, he prepares a brief of the evidence, on which he bases his admission, or rejection, of the claim. . He closes it with a statement of his decision, showing from what date, and at what rate admitted, or, if rejected, the cause therefor, and signs his name, as examiner.

This action is entered in a record. The case is taken from out the file of pending claims, and is placed in the hands of a clerk, who is called the "Reviewer." He is selected for this task, for his superior judgment, and for his familiarity with the law, and the rules of office. He "begins again," goes over the entire action of the examiner, goes through the entire evidence, in order to be able to approve, or disprove, the examiner's decision. If he approves, the case passes on to the Chief of the Division, for *his* approval, which, except in unusual cases, is *pro forma*. From his desk the case goes to the Certificate Section, for issue. There it receives its certificate and approved brief, decorated with which it departs to the Commissioner's desk, there to receive his final and crowning signature, and the grand seal of the Department. If the claim is a rejected one, and its rejection receives the approval of the receiver, it is cast into the outer darkness of the "rejected files." Here it is subject to an appeal to the Secretary, and may be borne forth again to the light, upon the presentation of new and material evidence.

After the triumphant claim has received its certificate, it is treated to a new coat of a wrapper, upon whose back a certificate-number, and its history, is endorsed. It is then entered upon the admitted records. After it has been reported to the Pension Agent, Finance Division, to the Third .Auditor of the Treasury, and to the Second Comptroller, it is placed on the "admitted files."   •

Seventy-five thousand pending claims are now on file in these two divisions. They are slowly reduced in number, and the receipt of new claims equals the disposal of the old ones. This statement does not include the adjustment of claims filed under the act of February 14, 1871, granting pensions to survivors of the war of 1812, who served sixty days, and to their widows. Their claims have been organized into a separate division, in which a force of fifty clerks has been constantly employed since its organization, May, 1871. This division is known as the "1812 Division," and strenuous efforts are made to reach very early decisions in all its cases, the extreme age of the applicants making it necessary—if their pension is to reach them "this side of Jordan."

In this division, the claims are carried through their entire process, from the application to the placing of the pensioner's name on the rolls.

The Bounty-Land Division forms a part of the Judicial branch.   Herein all claims for bounty-land, filed under the act of March 3, 1855, which is the latest general provision, are adjusted. The *modus operandi* of obtaining land-grants is nearly identical with the process of obtaining a pension.

Under the act of 1855, all persons who served fourteen days, either in the army or navy, are entitled to one hundred and sixty acres, and those who were actually engaged in battle, though their services were less than fourteen days, are entitled to the same.

Under the various laws governing these land grants, warrants representing 73,932,451 acres have been issued, which, estimated at $1.25 per acre, amounts to $92,415,- 563.75, which, added to $313,170,412.77 that has been paid since the beginning of the Government, as pension, makes a total expenditure of $405,585,976.52, which has been paid in gratuities to the defenders of the Republic.

Where the Judicial Branch ends in the certificate of a pension, the Financial Branch begins. The rolls reported by those divisions are entered in the agency registers, which are arranged to show payments for several years, and the agents' quarterly accounts of disbursements are compared with these registers, and errors noted.

There are now upon the United States pension rolls the names of 232,229 pensioners, who are paid quarterly through fifty-seven pension agents. When we remember that the accounts of all these agents, for these tens of thousands of names, are adjusted and reported within the short space of three months, it is not difficult to realize the amount of labor involved.

The Finance Division is charged with all correspondence with the pension agents, to suspend and resume payments, to drop from the rolls (in which case the auditor and controller must also be notified), the payment of accrued pensions to heirs and legal representatives; restorations, under the act of July 27, 1868, where a pension has been unclaimed for three years; the transfer of payments from one agency to another; the issue of duplicate certificates in lieu of those lost or destroyed. All these, and many, many other things are required at the hands of the gentlemen employed therein. The act of June 8, 1872, granted increase to pensioners of the first, second and

third grades; and this Division, after the passage of the
Act and before the quarterly payment of September
4, following, received, examined and issued 9,237 certificates granting the increase. Of the agencies disbursing
pension-money, there are ten whose payments exceed
$100,000,000 per annum.   Of these, Boston is the largest,
paying out more than $1,800,000. The smallest amount
paid by any agency is that at Vancouver, Washington
Territory, which disburses less than $2,500 per annum.

The Miscellaneous Branch covers many features too
minute to be brought into this sketch. Among the more
important is its Special Service Division.   This is occupied
with the investigation of all claims in which fraud is suspected.   It prosecutes and convicts all persons whose
guilt is proved. Congress annually appropriates a considerable sum to pay the expenses of such investigations,
which tends largely to lessen fraudulent practices against
the Government. By means of this fund the Office is
enabled to keep a large number of special agents employed, who are charged with the investigation of all suspected frauds perpetrated within their respective districts.

This division requires clerks who are thoroughly familiar
with all laws which the Office is called upon to execute, as
well as a general knowledge of the criminal laws of each
State.   Its efforts are : first, to secure the pensioner in
all his rights; second, to prosecute all persons where it is
thought a conviction can be had; and third, to secure a
return to the Government of all money unlawfully obtained. The amount saved in reducing pensions illegally
rated, in dropping from the rolls those found not to be
entitled, and in sums refunded, largely exceed the cost of
the work, while the effect upon the public is beneficial in

deterring others from criminal practices. Cases have been found which were allowed on the clearest proof of dependence upon the part of mothers of soldiers, where an investigation proved that that same dependent mother owned property in her own right to the amount of forty thousand dollars!

Such cases are not confined to the classes usually engaged in unlawful acts. Nothing is more remarkable than the number of persons—in the average transactions of life deemed honest and honorable—who are ready and eager, under one pretext or another, to " gouge " and defraud the revenues of the Government; and these persons are by no means confined to the seekers of pensions, but may be found every day in the highest class that can reach the hard-earned treasure of the National Treasury.

The Medical Division of the Pension Bureau acts conjointly with the Invalid Division in deciding the degree of disability of claimants for original, and the increase of invalid pensions. This division is supervised by medical gentlemen thoroughly trained in their profession. All invalid claims, after having been briefed by the examiner, and before passing into the reviewer's hands, are referred to this division. The Examining Surgeon makes a personal examination of the applicant, and from his medical testimony, endorsed by the Chief of the Medical Division, the Chief of the Invalid Division bases his final opinion and action.

The Restoration Desk is devoted to all claims, which are to be restored to the rolls, of parties who have been dropped for cause—principally those who were residents of the States in rebellion at the beginning of the late war. These are only placed upon the rolls upon incontestible proof of loyalty.

The Appeal Desk is the recipient of all cases in preparation for reference to the Secretary, where an appeal from the action of the Office is taken.

The Final Desk is the extensive one of the Commissioner of Pensions.

From the beginning to the end of this busy Bureau, charged with the comfort, the very subsistence of so many bereaved and disabled fellow-creatures, the Commissioner must see all things, anticipate all wants, supply all needs; upon him rests the entire administration of this vast and potent Bureau. His position is not easy or his burden light.

To fill so important a trust with honor, a Commissioner needs not only clear judgment and business training, but should also be a man of positive administrative talents, large information, thorough education, and broad, comprehensive mind.

These qualities are all possessed in a pre-eminent degree by the present Commissioner of Pensions.

General J. H. Baker was born in Lebanon, Ohio, 1829. He is the son of a Methodist clergyman, and was graduated from the Wesleyan University, Delaware, Ohio, taking the Latin honors of a large class in 1852. He was Secretary of the State of Ohio during Chief-Justice Chase's term as Governor of that State. He moved to Minnesota, and was Secretary of the State when he resigned to take command of the Tenth Minnesota Volunteers. He served with distinction in the Indian expedition under General Sibley, and, on his return, was ordered South. At St. Louis he was placed in command of the post, and soon after was made Provost-Marshal General of the Department of Missouri. At the close of the war he became

Register of Public Lands in Missouri, and, resigning this position, in 1868 he returned to Minnesota, was candidate for the United States Senate, and defeated by a very small majority. In 1871, he was appointed Commissioner of Pensions.

General Baker is a tall, commanding looking gentleman, with dark hair, complexion and eyes. He is of nervo-motive temperament, quick, prompt, energetic in action, yet courteous and genial in his bearing to a very marked degree.

Since the passage of the Act of July 4, 1862, nearly 400,000 claims for pensions have been filed in and considered by the Pension Office. Of course, in the examination of so vast a number of cases, errors have been committed, matters of fact misinterpreted, and in many instances, through carelessness, ignorance and neglect, injustice has been done.

The clerks of this office have always compared favorably, both in industry and capacity, with those of other Bureaus; but, among so large a number, worthless and inefficient ones will be found, and the still greater evil of employing men who, though capable, take no interest in their official duties, and, through the want of that spur to well-doing, fail to make themselves of value to the Government, and render aid to those whom the Office was organized to protect and assist. The percentage of claims affected by these causes, small though it may have been, would amount to thousands in the aggregate, and these, distributed throughout the country, would give an enlarged color to their complaints, and lead the people to believe that the evil was general and unusual in its extent. When we add to this class of complainants the

150,000 who, in some shape, have had claims before the office for increase, arrears, etc., and which, not coming within the law under which they filed, were rejected, and who, not understanding what the law did provide, but deriving their information from unscrupulous agents who would not or could not instruct them in the matter, they feel seriously aggrieved, and loudly complain. Two dependent mothers, equally poor, and who were alike aided by their respective sons, reside in the same village. They apply for a pension for the services and deaths of their sons. The records of the War Department show that one of the soldiers died of a disease contracted in the service and in the line of duty, and that the other soldier died of a disease, though contracted in the service, yet it *did not* originate while he was in the line of duty. These are distinctions which neither this poor woman nor the community can understand. Yet the claim last described must be rejected, as it is barred by the law. The whole community cries out about the great injustice practiced by the Pension Office, while, in fact, the *law* is responsible, and *not* the office.

Again, invalid pensioners, suffering from a partial or total disability, are strongly urged, by their *pecuniary interests*, to believe that they are entitled to a total or special rating. They apply for increase, and are referred to an examining surgeon for a personal examination, and a report as to nature and degree of disability. The surgeon fails to conform to the applicant's estimate as to the extent of his disability, and the claim for increase is rejected, and here is another case of " great injustice."

Biennial examinations of all invalid pensioners are required, except in cases of permanent disability. At such

times the surgeon finds they are partially or entirely recovered from the disability that existed at the date of last
examination, and notwithstanding the firm conviction of
the pensioner that he is just as much disabled as ever, he
is reduced or dropped. He at once joins the army of
grumblers, and complains of injustice.

The office acknowledges its imperfections, but respectfully declines to admit the correctness of a tithe of the
grievances reported. There is some show of injustice in
the delay frequently experienced in the settlement of
claims, and yet the Office is responsible to a slight degree
only. As heretofore intimated, the *system* is largely ac-
countable for this. The suspicion, warranted by experience, attaching to every piece of testimony received,
and necessitating a close scrutiny and reconciliation of the
slightest discrepancies before final action can be had.
The hundreds of points going to make up a case must be
found in proofs, and the affidavits offered, three times out
of five, fail to cover the point.

Here is another cause for complaint. "The Pension
Office called three times for the same evidence." It must
be admitted that, some years ago, there was an entire
neglect of correspondence. "Letters of inquiry," asking
condition of claim and countless questions, arrived by
thousands. Examiners were ambitious to pass (admit or
reject) a large number of claims, during the month, and
these letters proved nothing, and required time and labor
to answer them, and were cast aside. This has all been
changed by the present Commissioner, and these letters are
confided to clerks who engage in nothing but correspondence, and who are required to keep their desks up to
date ; and in this connection it is proper to add that a mag-

28

ical change has been made in the style and completeness
of the letters. Some years ago, a fac-simile of the Commissioner's signature was stamped upon the out-going mail.
Now, each letter is subjected to a careful review by the
Chiefs of Divisions, and goes thence to the Commissioner's
room for his signature and a frequent review by him; and
the occasional return of a letter, with a sharp reminder,
suffices to keep the letter writers on the alert. And this
idea of a careful surveillance is not confined to correspondents, but it has been carefully impressed upon the whole
force by frequent illustrations. By judicious, yet not
burdensome reports, and by frequent reference thereto
by the Commissioner, which is forcibly brought to the
knowledge of a careless clerk, the *employés* have been
taught that no trifling will be allowed.

It has also been realized by the *employés* of this Bureau that merit *is* noted, and *de*merit will insure dismissal. It is the policy of General Baker to hold his
subordinates strictly responsible for the proper performance of their individual duties, and to look to those having charge of others to secure the desired results, or to
report the delinquent. The result of two years' growth
in this direction has been gratifying. The increased industry of the Office, the improvement resulting from a
thoughtful and careful performance of its duties, and the
elevation of the standard which all seeking appointments
must come up to, and a careful weeding-out of the inefficient ones, are rapidly tending to secure commendation
from those having business with the Bureau, rather than
censure.

An aged claimant for a pension, who served in the war
of 1812, residing in Illinois in December, 1871, wrote to

the Office as follows: "Oh! can it be true that I am going to get $100? That news is too good! I'm so hungry, and I love coffee so, but I can't get any! All I have to eat is corn-bread and sour milk. I can't believe that I am to get so much money, but I pray God it may be true." It is needless to say that this claim was made "special," and the octogenarian had "coffee" for his Christmas breakfast.

A Captain B., of Havre-de-Grace, Maryland, a claimant for pension under Act of 1871, for services in the War of 1812, had his claim rejected, it appearing that he served less than sixty days, as required by that Act; whereupon the Captain grew wrathy, and wrote as follows:

"N. B.—Any man that will say that I was not a Private soldier in Capt. Paca Smith's company before the attack of the British on the City of Baltimore, and during the attack on said City in Sept., 1814, and after the British dropped down to Cape Henry, I say he is a dastard, a liar, and a coward, and no gentleman, or any man that will say that I got my Land-warrant from the Hon. Geo. C. Whiting, for 160 acres of Land, for 14 days' services in Capt. Paca Smith's company, is the same, as stated above, and I hold myself responsible for the contents of this letter; and if their dignity should be touched, a note of honor directed to Capt. Wm. B——, Havre-de-Grace, Harford Co., Md., shall be punctually attended to.

"Wм. B——."

CHAPTER XL.

TREASURES AND CURIOSITIES OF THE PATENT OFFICE —THE MODEL ROOM—ITS RELICS AND INVENTIONS.

The Patent Office Building—Grace and Beauty of its Architecture—Four " Sublime " Porticoes—A Pretty Large Passage—The Model Room— " The Exhibition of the Nation "—A Room two hundred and seventy Feet in Length—The Models—Recording our Name—Wonders and Treasures of the Room—Benjamin Franklin's Press—Model Fire-Escapes—Wonderful Fire-Extinguishers—The Efforts of Genius—Sheep-Stalls, Rat-Traps, and Gutta Percha—An Ancient Mariner's Compass—Captain Cook's Razor—The Atlantic Cable—Original Treaties—The Signatures of Emperors—An Extraordinary Turkish Treaty—Treasures of the Orient— Rare Medals—The Reward of Major Andre's Captors—The Washington Relics—His Old Tent—His Blankets and Bed-Curtain—His Chairs and Looking-Glass—His Primitive Mess-Chess and old Tin Plates—The Old Clothes of the " Father of His Country "—Military Relics of Well-known Men—Original Draft of the Declaration of Independence—Washington's Commission—Model of an Extraordinary Boat—Abraham Lincoln as an Inventor—The Hat Worn on the Fatal Night—The Gift of the Tycoon— The Efforts of Genius—A Machine to Force Hens to Lay Eggs—A Hook for Fishing Worms out of the Human Stomach—The Library of the Patent Office.

THE lawful fees for issuing patents having accumulated into a considerable fund, Congress added an appropriation, and directed that the whole amount should be invested in a new building to be called the Patent Office.

From that double fund has arisen the majestic structure which, next to the Capitol, is the most august building in Washington. The southern front of the Treasury is of superlative beauty, and from several other points its architectural grace cannot be surpassed; but its whole effect is marred by the dingy, unbroken outline of its Fifteenth-street side.　The advantage of the Patent-Office is, that from any point which you choose to survey it, it impresses you as supremely grand.　Occupying two blocks, or an entire public square, standing upon a prominence, it spreads and towers into space incomparable in mass and majesty.　You may approach it from four opposite directions, and on each side you lift your eyes to four sublime porticoes towering before you.　They are supported by double rows of Doric columns, eighteen feet in circumference, made of gleaming crystallized marble.　The entire building is of pure Doric architecture, strong, simple and majestic.　Its southern front is an exact copy of the Pantheon at Rome, and the eastern portico is modelled after that of the Parthenon at Athens.

The length of the building, from Seventh to Ninth streets, is 410 feet, and its width, from F to G streets, 275 feet.　Its original design was made by Mr. William P. Elliot, at that time surveyor of the City of Washington. The plan was largely executed by Mr. Mills, architect of Public Buildings; while the grand northern portico has been consummated under the superintendence of Mr. Edward Clark, the present architect of the Capitol.

We enter the eastern door of the basement-story, into a spacious passage running from east to west, the whole length of the building.　Through it, large-wheeled machines can be drawn.　On each side of this hall are rooms for the deposit of fuel, large and heavy models and department offices.　In the centre springs a semi-circular stone staircase, with three flights of steps, which ascend to the second, third and last story.　The corridor in the first story is like the one that we entered below, and on each side of the hall, doors open into commodious apartments for the accommodation of the commissioners, examiners, clerks, etc.

Ascending the stone staircase, we come to the Model Room—*par excellence*, the Exhibition Room of the nation. For architectural simplicity and space, and the purpose for which it was designed, it is unsurpassed in the whole world. Standing here, we look down a vista two hundred and seventy-four feet in length, and its perspective is enchanting to the sight. A double row of stone columns supports a succession of brick arches, finely proportioned, and-corresponding in depth with the rooms below. The floor is paved with tessellated stone, and the light streams in from numerous windows on each side.

The models and other articles are arranged in glass cases on each side of the room, leaving ample space in the centre for promenading. There are two rows of cases, one above the other—the upper row being placed within a light gallery of iron, reached by iron stairways, and extending entirely round the east, north and west halls. The ceiling is supported by a double row of pillars, which also act as supports to the galleries, and both the walls and ceiling are finished in marble and frescoes.

Entering, we find a large register, with pens and ink, at the right of the door, in which we may record our name and the date of our visit, if we please.

The first case on the right of the entrance contains Benjamin Franklin's press, at which he worked when a journeyman-printer in London. It is old and worm-eaten, and is only held together by means of bolts and iron plates, and bears but little resemblance to the mighty

THE MODEL ROOM, PATENT OFFICE. — WASHINGTON.

This room contains the fruits of the inventive genius of the whole nation. More than 160,000 models are here deposited.

machines by which the printing of to-day is done. Then come models of "fire-escapes," some of which are curiosities and well worth studying. The impression left by the majority, however, is that if they constitute one's only hope of escape, in case of fire, an old-fashioned headlong leap from a window may just as well be attempted at once.

Near by are the models of those inventive geniuses who have attempted to extinguish conflagrations by discharging a patent cartridge into the burning mass. The guns, from which the cartridges are thrown, are most remarkable in design.

Then follow tobacco-cutting machines, of various kinds, all sorts of skates, billiard-table models, ice-cutters, billiard-registers, improved fire-arms, and toys, of different designs, among which is a most ingenious model of a walking-horse. Having reached the end of this row of cases, we cross over to the south side of the hall. The first cases contain models of cattle and sheep-stalls, vermin and rat-traps, and are followed by a handsome display of articles in gutta percha, manufactured by the Goodyear Company.

In the bottom of one of the cases is an old mariner's compass of the year 1604, presented by Ex-Governor Wise, of Virginia, then United States Minister to Brazil, in the name of Lieutenant Sheppard, U. S. N. The ticket attached to the compass is written in the bold, running hand of the ex-rebel statesman. Near by is a razor which belonged to the celebrated navigator, Captain Cook. It was recovered from the natives of the island upon which he was murdered, and is hardly such an instrument any of those who behold it would care to use. A piece of the Atlantic cable is just below it.

Several of the cases following contain the original treaties of the United States with foreign powers. They are written upon heavy sheets of vellum, in wretchedly bad hands, and are worn and faded. All, save the treaties with England and the Eastern nations, are written in French, and are all furnished with a multiplicity of red and green seals; the first is the treaty with Austria, and bears the weak, hesitating signature of Francis I. The signature of Alexander I., attached to the first Russian treaty, has more character in it. The treaty of peace with England, in 1814, which ended our second war with that power, bears the signature of the Regent, afterwards George IV. The treaty of 1803, with the Republic of France, is signed "Bonaparte," in a nervous, sprawling hand. Bernadotte's smooth and flowing hand adorns the first treaty with Sweden.

The original treaty with Turkey is a curious document. It consists of a number of long slips of parchment, covered with columns of Turkish characters. Near by it hangs a bag, in which it was conveyed to this country. The bag is its legal covering, or case, and is provided with a huge ball of red wax, by way of a seal. Next to it is the first treaty of alliance with France—the famous one of 1778— which gave the aid of the French king to the cause of the suffering and struggling States of the new republic. It is signed by the unfortunate Louis XVI. The "Louis" is written in a round, phlegmatic hand; but the lines are delicate, as if the pen did not press the paper with the firmness of a strong will. The French treaty, of 1822, bears the autograph of Louis XVIII.; and that of 1831, the signature of Louis Phillippe. Don Pedro I., Emperor of Brazil, has affixed his hand to the Brazilian treaty, and the name of Ferdinand (the last, and least) is affixed to that of Spain.

In the glass cases with the treaties are several Oriental articles,—a Persian carpet and horse-cover, presented to President Van Buren, by the Imän of Muscat; and two magnificent rifles, presented to President Jefferson, by the Emperor of Morocco. These rifles are finished in the highest style of Eastern art, and are really beautiful. In the same cases are collections of medals, some of European sovereigns, and others of American celebrities. Among them is a copy of the medal, awarded by Congress, to the captors of Major André. Near these are several splendid Eastern sabres, presented by the great All Pacha, the Bey of Egypt, to Captain Perry and the officers of the U. S. ship-of-war, *Concord*, at Alexandria, (Egypt,) in 1832.

The next cases contain the Washington relics, which are amongst the greatest treasures of the nation. They consist of the camp-equipage, and other articles used by General Washington, during the Revolution. They are just as he left them at the close of the war, and were given to the Government, for safe keeping, after his death. Here are the tents which constituted the head-quarters, in the field, of the great soldier. They are wrapped tightly round the poles, just as they were tied when they were struck for the last time, when victory had crowned his country's arms, and the long war was over. Every cord, every button and tent-pin is in its place, for he was careful of little things. His blankets and the bed-curtain, worked for him by his wife, and his window-curtains, are all well preserved. His chairs are perfect, not a round being broken; and the little square mirror in his dressing-case is not even cracked. The wash-stand and table are also well kept. His knife-case is filled with plain horn-handle knives and forks, which were deemed "good enough for him," and his mess-chest is a curiosity. It is a plain wooden trunk, covered with leather, with a common lock, the hasp of which is broken. It is divided by small partitions of thin wood, and the compartments are provided with bottles, still stained with the liquids, tin plates, common knives and forks, and other articles pertaining to such an establishment.

In these days of luxury, an ordinary sergeant would not be satisfied with so simple and plain an establishment. His cooking utensils, bellows, andirons, and iron money-chest, all of which went with him from Boston to York-town, are in the same case, from the side of which hangs the suit of clothes worn by him upon the occasion of his resignation of his commission as Commander-in-Chief, at Annapolis, in 1783. A hall lantern, and several articles from Mount Vernon, a "travelling secretary," Washington's sword and cane, and a surveyor's compass, presented by him to Captain Samuel Duvall, the surveyor of Frederick county, Maryland, are in the same case, as are also a number of articles taken from Arlington House, and belonging formerly to the Washington family.

A coat worn by Andrew Jackson, at the battle of New Orleans, and the war-saddle of the Baron De Kalb, a bayonet used by one of Braddock's soldiers, and found on the fatal field upon which that commander met his death-wound, together with the panels from the state-coach of President Washington, make up the collection. The original draft of the Declaration of Independence, with the signatures of the Continental Congress attached, is framed and placed near the Washington case. It is old and yellow, and the ink is fading from the paper. Near it hangs Washington's Commission as Commander-in-Chief of the American army, bearing the characteristic signature of John Hancock, President of the Continental Congress.

In the same case is a plain model, roughly executed, representing the frame-work of the hull of a Western steamboat. Beneath the keel is a false bottom, provided with bellows and air-bags. The ticket upon it bears the memorandum, "Model of sinking and raising boats by bellows below. A. Lincoln, May 30, 1849."

By means of this arrangement, Mr. Lincoln hoped to solve the difficulty of passing boats over sand-bars in the Western rivers. The success of his scheme would have made him independently wealthy, but it failed, and, twelve years later, he became President of the United States. During the interval, the model lay forgotten in the Patent Office, but, after his inauguration, Mr. Lincoln got one of the *employés* to find it for him. After his death, it was placed in the Washington case.

The opposite case contains another memento of him— the hat worn by him on the night of his assassination.

In a couple of cases, filled with machinery for making shoes, we see a number of handsome silk robes and Japanese articles, of various kinds, presented to Presidents Buchanan and Lincoln, by the Tycoon of Japan. The remainder of the hall is filled with models of machines for making leather harness and trunks, models of gas and kerosene oil apparatuses, liquor distilleries, machines for making confectionery, and for trying out lard and fat. Also, methods of curing fish and meat, and embalming the dead. A splendid model of a steel revolving tower, for harbor defence, stands near the door, and is one of the most conspicuous ornaments of the room. The other halls are devoted exclusively to models of patented machinery, and other inventions. The cases above and below are well filled; models of bridges span the spaces between the other cases, and those of the larger machines are laid on the floor of the hall.

Models of improved arms, clocks, telegraphs, burglar and fire alarms, musical instruments, light-houses, street cars, lamps, stoves, ranges, furnaces, peat and fuel-machines, brick and tile-machines, sewing-machines, power-looms, paper-making machinery, knitting-machines, machines for making cloth, hats, spool cotton, for working up hemp, harbor cleaners, patent hooks-and-eyes, buttons, umbrella and cane-handles, fluting-machines, trusses, medical instruments of gutta percha, corsets, ambulances and other military establishments, arrangements for excluding the dust and smoke from railroad cars, railroad and steamboat machinery, agricultural and domestic machinery of all kinds, and hundreds of other inventions, line these three immense halls. Among the most remarkable is a machine to force a hen to lay eggs, and a silver worm hook, invented to fish worms out of the human stomach.

A large library, of great value, is attached to the Patent Office, containing many volumes of the highest scientific value. Under judicious arrangement, a collection already rich and ample is forming, of every work of interest to the inventors, and that new, increasing, important class of professional men—the attorneys in patent cases. Upon its shelves may be found a complete set of the reports of the British Patent Commissioners, of which there are only six copies in the United States. The reports of French patents are also complete, and those of various other countries are being obtained as rapidly as possible. A system of exchanges has been established, which employs three agents abroad; and, in addition to various and arduous duties, the librarian annually dispatches several hundred copies of the reports.

CHAPTER XLI.

THE BUREAU OF PATENTS—CRAZY INVENTORS AND WONDERFUL INVENTIONS.

Patent-Rights in Steamboats—Origin of Copyright and Patent-Laws—Congress Settles the Matter—A Board of " Disinterested, Competent " Persons—Destruction of the Patent-Office by Fire—The New Building—The Corps of Examiners—The Commissioner's Speech—Twenty Thousand Applications *per annum*—Fourteen Thousand Patents Granted in One Year—Wonderful Expansion of Inventive Genius—" The Universal Yankee "—Second-hand Inventions—Where the Inventions Come from—Taking Out a Patent for the Lord's Prayer—A Patent for a Cow's Tail—A Lady's Patent—Hesitating to Accept a Million Dollars—How Patentees are Protected—The American System—What American Inventors Have Done, and What They Have n't—The First Superintendent—The Present Commissioner—Exploits of General Legett—His Efficiency in Office—The Inventor Always a Dreamer—Perpetual Motion—The Invention of a D. D.—His Little Machine—" Original with Me "—Silencing the Doctor—A New Process of Embalming—A Dead Body Sent to the Office—Utilizing Niagara—A *Generous* Offer—An Englishman's Invention—Inventors in Paris—How to Kill Lions and Tigers in the United States with Catmint—A Fearful Bomb-shell—Eccentric Letters—Amusing Specimens of Correspondence.

WITH the settlement of the English colonies in America came a great many English customs and laws, and among those adhered to was that of granting patents or passing special Acts for the protection of inventors.

In 1728, the Legislature of Connecticut granted the exclusive right of practicing the business or trade of steel-making, provided the petitioners improved the art to any good and reasonable perfection within two years. In 1785, the State of Maryland passed an act giving to one James Rumsey the exclusive right to construct, employ and navigate boats of an improved construction, to run against the current of rapid rivers. In 1787, an act was passed vesting the exclusive right of propelling boats by steam and water for a limited time. In this year a number of acts were passed to protect inventions of machines for ruff-carding-belts, grinding flour, &c., and in 1789, one for the protection of a hand fire-engine in New Hampshire was enacted.

The founders of the Constitution saw the advantages to be derived from protecting the useful arts and sciences, and we find in Article 1, Section 8, the authority and power given Congress " to promote the progress of science and the useful arts by securing, for a limited time, to authors and inventors, the exclusive right to their respective writings and discoveries," etc.; "to make all laws which shall be necessary and proper for carrying into execution the foregoing powers." Accordingly, Congress, in 1790, immediately after the ratification of the Constitution, found it necessary and thought it beneficial to enact a statute which authorized the issue of a patent to inventors and discoverers of any useful manufacture, engine, machine, and those who should devise any improvement thereon not before known or used.

The application, consisting of a clear description of the invention, was at that time made to the Secretary-of-State, and the Attorney-General of the United States. If such application was found to be new, a patent was issued by authority of any two persons enumerated, attested by the signature of the President of the United

States, who granted to the inventor the exclusive right of making, constructing, using, or vending to others to be used, the invention or discovery, for the term of fourteen years.

As the nation increased in power and talent, this Act was modified as the necessities of the time required. Abuses crept in, the most noted of which was the granting and issuing of a great many patents without any record being kept to indicate that such patents were ever granted. This was caused by lack of organization and want of proper assistance. The Executive and Members of the Cabinet, having other duties to perform, neglected the proper examination of applications, and the system degenerated into as bad a one as the English.

This Act, with the amendment, was, in 1836, swept from the statute books, and the Patent-Office was established on a surer basis, with an organization of a Commissioner, Chief Clerk, an Examiner, a Draughtsman, and some five clerks to conduct the examination and issues of applications. As the decisions of the Commissioner, who was then presumed to examine all applications, was not always impartial and right, an appeal was allowed to a Board composed of three disinterested and competent persons, who were appointed by the Secretary of State, as occasion required.

The Patent-Office Building, which was at that time situated on the present site of the General Post-Office, was completely destroyed by fire in December, 1836, and all models, drawings and records were consumed. Congress appropriated money, and issued circulars directed to all who were thought to be interested in the restoration.

The majority of the patentees sent in duplicates of their papers and models, but many were never heard from, and for this reason the office is unable to present a complete record of the grants. After the fire, the business of the Office was conducted in the City Hall building until the present building was erected for the Patent-Office, a few years later. In 1849, the Office was placed under the supervision of the Secretary of the Interior or Home Department, where it now remains.

The fostering of invention encouraged home manufactures, one of the results most eagerly sought, after the war with Great Britain. So active became the inventive genius and so prolific of results, that Congress was compelled, from time to time, to increase the examining corps, and the little band of seven persons, who occupied the contracted rooms in the City Hall, has expanded into a corps of eighty examiners and assistants, more than two hundred clerks and other officials, all under the control of a Commissioner and an Assistant-Commissioner.

The grant of one thousand patents in 1836, when the office was first regularly organized, has enlarged into one hundred and sixty thousand at the present time. And the latter number is scarcely two-thirds of the number of applications. With this enormous increase followed a corresponding labor and intricacy in examining so large a number of applications, but so perfectly has the system been developed, that very few mistakes are made in the way of wrongfully granting patents.

Hon. S. S. Fisher, United States Commissioner of Patents, before the American Institute, New York City, September 28, 1869, made an eloquent address concern-

29

ing the American system of granting patents, from which I make the following extracts:

"The great Patent Act of 1836 established what is now distinctively the American system in regard to the grant of letters-patent.

"In the Patent-office, under the act of 1836, the Commissioner and one examining-clerk were thought to be sufficient to do the work of examining into the patentability of the two or three hundred that were offered; now sixty-two examiners are over-crowded with work, a force of over three hundred *employes* is maintained, and the applications have swelled to over twenty thousand per annum. This year the number of patents granted will average two hundred and seventy-five per week, or fourteen thousand a year.

"In England and on the Continent all applications are patented without examination into the novelty of the inventions claimed. In some instances the instrument is scanned to see if it cover a patentable subject matter, and in Prussia some examination is made into the character of the new idea; but in no case are such appliances provided, such a corps of skilled examiners, such a provision of drawings, models, and books, such a collection of foreign patents, and such checks to prevent and review error, as with us. As a result, an American patent has in our courts a value that no foreign patent can acquire in the courts of its own country.

. . . .

"The foreign patents of American inventors, that have been copies of patents previously granted in this country, are the best that are granted abroad. Many an English or French invention that has been patented without difficulty there, has been stopped in its passage through our office by a reference to some patent previously granted in this country. In spite of our examination which rejects over one-third of all the applications that are made invention has been stimulated by the hope of protection; and nearly as many patents will issue in the United States this year as in the whole of Europe put together, including the British Isles. But a few days ago I took up a volume of Italian patents, when I was amused and gratified to find on every page the name of the universal Yankee, re-patenting there his American invention. He is, I suspect, much the best customer in the Patent Office of United Italy.

" We are an inventive people. Invention is by no means confined to our mechanics. Our merchants invent, our soldiers and our sailors invent, our school-masters invent, our professional men invent, aye, our women and children invent. One man, lately, wished to patent the application of the Lord's Prayer, repeated in a loud tone of voice, to prevent stammering; another claimed the new and useful attachment of a weight to a cow's tail, to prevent her from switching it while milking; another proposed to cure worms by extracting by a delicate line and tiny hook, baited with a seductive pill; while a lady patented a crimping-pin, which she declared might also be used as a paper-cutter, as a skirt-supporter, as a paper-file, as a child's pin, as a bouquet-holder, as a shawl-fastener, or as a book-mark. Do not suppose that this is the highest flight that the gentle sex has achieved. It has obtained many other patents, some of which have no relation to wearing apparel, and are of considerable value.

" Every inventor supposes that he has a fortune in every conception that he puts into wood and iron. Stealing tremblingly and furtively up the steps of the Patent Office, with his model concealed under his coat, lest some sharper shall see it and rob him of his darling thought, he hopes to come down those steps with the precious parchment that shall insure him a present competency and enrich his children. If he were offered a million in the first flush of his triumph, he would hesitate about touching it without sleeping over it for a night. Yet fourteen thousand millions would be a pretty heavy bill to pay from a treasury not over full. No commission could satisfy the inventor, and no price that we could afford to pay would take the place of the hope of unlimited wealth, which now lightens his toil. . . . . We say, we cannot pay you in money, we will pay you in time. A new thought developed, explained, described, put on record for the use of the nation—this is the one side. The right to the exclusive benefit of this new thought, for a limited time, and protection in that right, this on the other. This is the patent system. A fair contract between the inventor and the public.

"The inventor's best security is to take out a patent.

"To secure this fair dealing, we have on the one side the Patent Office, with its examiners, its drawings, its models, its books and its foreign patents, to scan and test the invention.

On the other side we have the courts of law to protect the inventor and punish the thief. It is impossible that these instrumentalities should do their work imperfectly. This is the American system. Under its protection great inventions have been born, and have thriven. It has given to the world the steamboat, the telegraph, the sewing-machine, the hard and soft rubber. It has reconstructed the loom, the reaping-machine, and the locomotive. It has won from the older homes of the mechanic arts their richest trophies, and like Columbus, who found a new world for Castile and Leon, it has created new arts in which our nation has neither competitive or peer."

The first Superintendent of the Patent Office was Doctor W. Thornton, a gentleman of great attainments, who held his position for many years. The present Commissioner of Patents is General Mortimer D. Leggett, born of Quaker parents, in the State of New York, fifty years ago. At an early age, he went with his parents to the Western Reserve, Ohio. He received an academical education, studied law, was admitted to the bar, and at twenty-eight, was established in a flourishing business in Warren, Ohio. Jacob D. Cox, late Secretary of the Interior, studied law with General Leggett, and ultimately became his partner under the firm name of Leggett &

Cox. General Leggett afterwards filled the position of Professor of Pleadings and Equity Jurisprudence, in the Ohio Law College, which he occupied till 1857, and later was called to become the Superintendent of Public Schools in the city of Zanesville, which his management made pre-eminent among the schools of the West. At the beginning of the war, he entered the field at the head of the Seventy-eighth Ohio. This regiment received its first baptism in the snow and sleet of Fort Donelson, and was under fire there.

The executive and administrative ability of Colonel Leggett, as shown in the discipline and condition of his regiment, attracted the attention of General Grant, who made him Provost-Marshal of the post. He did his work so well, that he was repeatedly chosen again, and by the warm commendation of his chief, was made Brigadier-General. At the battle of Shiloh, and the siege of Corinth, General Leggett held advanced posts. In the siege of Vicksburg, General Leggett commanded the first brigade of Logan's Division—the brigade which, for its gallant service, was honored by being designated for the coveted distinction of marching first into the captured works. Soon after, he received command of this division, and was made Major-General, and with it, made with Sherman, the famous " march to the sea."

There are many young men who live to say—that the most genial, beneficent, and valuable influence, exerted upon them during the toilsome campaign, and the dangerous periods of idleness in camp-life, was that of General Leggett, who ever inspired patience by his unfailing good humor, persistent fidelity to temperance, both by precept and lofty example. He made many a dreary march seem like a picnic excursion ; and his quick, fearless, yet sympathetic glance, often inspired the sinking heart at the moment of danger. Beyond this, he was a true soldier, in caring anxiously for the comfort of his soldiers, in enforcing rigid discipline, and in stimulating officers and men to excel in drill and all service.

At the close of the war, General Leggett became Superintendent and Business Manager of the engine works at Zanesville and Newark, Ohio, the largest establishment of the kind in the West, where he remained, till he was called by the friend who remembered his brave services in the peril of war,—to the administration of one of the most important branches of the Government service in time of peace. He has already inaugurated one of the most potent movements toward the encouragement of the useful arts, ever made in this country—viz.: the publication in popular form, and at low rates, of the Patent Office drawings and specifications.

General Leggett has a clear red-and-white complexion, wide, open laughing blue eyes, and an aspect of fresh health which amounts to youth. His frame and brain are cast in herculean mould. He is a man of muscle, as well as mind—the former having been toughened by long geological foot-tramps through the mountains of Virginia, as well as by the exposures of war, and of an all-time active life.

The official chair of General Leggett has not proved too much for his better self, as it does for so many. He meets all who approach him with a smile and kind word, apparently not forgetting that in a republic the potentate of to-day may be the suppliant of to-morrow, and that at any rate, but one man at a time can be a Commissioner of Patents. He brings to his official administration and decisions the same untiring industry, intelligence and integrity; the same broad views, clear insight and devotion to duty, which in every previous sphere that he has filled have made his whole life an honorable success.

With all its comprehensive cares, one side of the Commissioner's official life tends to jollity, good digestion, and long life. In no other position in the world, probably, could a man discover how many crazy people there are outside of the lunatic asylum. The born inventor is always a dreamer. For the sake of his darling thought, he is willing to sacrifice himself, his wife and children, every thing but the "machine" growing in his brain and quickening under his eager hand. How often they fail! How often the precious thought, developed into form, is only a mistake—a failure.

Sometimes this is sad—quite as often it is funny. The procession which started, far back in the ages, with its machine of "Perpetual Motion," long ago reached the doors of the American Patent Office. The persons found in that procession are sometimes astonishing. A doctor of divinity, well-known at the Capital, and not suspected of studying any machinery but that of the moral law, appeared one day in the office of the Commissioner.

"I know I've got it," he said.

"What, sir?"

"PERPETUAL MOTION, sir. Look!" and he set down a little machine. "If the floor were not in the way, if the earth were not in the way, that weight would never stop, and my machine would go on forever. I know this is original with me—that it never dawned before upon any other human mind."

So enthusiastic was the doctor, it was with difficulty he could be restrained from depositing his ten dollars and leaving his experiment to be patented. The Commissioner, quietly, sent to the library for a book—a history of attempts to create Perpetual Motion. Opening at a certain page, he pointed out to the astonished would-be inventor, where his own machine had been attempted and failed, more than a hundred years before. The reverend doctor took the book home, read, digested, and meditated thereon—to bring it back and lay it down before the Commissioner, in silence. No one has ever heard him speak of Perpetual Motion since.

It would take a large volume, to record all the preposterous letters and inventions received at this office. A very short time since, a man sent a letter to the Patent Bureau describing a new process of embalming which he had originated. It was accompanied by a dead baby—"the model" which he requested should be placed in one of the glass cases of the Exhibition Room. He considered himself deeply injured when his request was refused.

A letter was recently received by the Commissioner of Patents, from a man in Portsmouth, England, offering this Government the benefit of an invention of his own for utilizing water-power, so as to force the water to a great height when confined in reservoirs constructed for the purpose. He offers the invention free of all charge, because, he states, that it pains him to see "such mighty power as there is at the Niagara wasted." In addition, he offers his own services at the *low* rate of £1,000 per annum, to build and operate the invention. He says in his letter, that "if the mighty great power in Niagara was accumulated, it would move a great deal." He also states that he "has a good plan for a velocipede and a bicicle, that he thinks would be a good thing for this country," but admits that "people in England don't like it."

Referring again to his water-power, he claims that if this Government would build the road, he can take ships across the isthmus of Panama "in a box, water and all."

The Commissioner recently received the following communication from the Legation of the United States :

PARIS, Dec. 3, 1872.

"SIR:—A very large number of inventions and discoveries are submitted to this Legation, with the request that we shall transmit them to Washington. Most of them are, as you may suppose, worthless. We have had, for instance, serious plans proposed for the extermination of all the lions and tigers in the United States by the use of catmint, the *modus operandi* being to dig an immense pit, and fill it with this herb. The well-known love of the feline race for catmint will naturally induce the lions and tigers to jump into the pit and roll themselves upon it; whereupon concealed hunters are to appear and slaughter the ferocious animals.

"Another plan is for the destruction of grasshoppers upon the plains by the use of artillery; it being perfectly well known that concussion kills insects.

"A third is for the capture of a besieged city by the use of a bomb which, upon exploding, shall emit so foul a smell that the besieged will rush headlong from the walls, and fall an easy prey to the besiegers."

The President of the United States receives many letters of like character, which are by him transmitted to the Bureau of Patents. I append verbatim copies (including orthography) of three which represent many thousands more of equal intelligence received at this Department of the Government.

AUGUST 31st 1872

MR. U. S. GRANT Sir it is with pleasure I take this opportunity Of writing to You I Am well at Present Hoping those few lines will find you enjoying Good health And prosperity I am doing all I can for you in this locality and I hope and expect you will be our next President Of the United States I would like to have an Office of Siveliseing the Indians What Salary will you give me per Annum please Write to me and let me no in fact I am in need of A little money at present Will you please send me 600 or 1000 dolors to—— —— Sumthing Aught to be done for the poor Indean And I beleave that I can sivelise them. If you will give me 200 or 300 per month it will doo.

MARCH 13 1873

HON. SIR PRESEDENT OF THE UNITED STATES OF AMERICA I announce to you that I am inventing Perpetual Motion I have once had my paterns stolen or I should had the machine in running order before this and I have altered my plan so that it carrys a shaft and wheel and when constructed on a large plan it will move machinery, And being on a new plan and different from all others and I am sure of success which I hope to place before the world soon. Though in consequence of poor health and not having the means to work with it will take some months longer to accomplish it I might write you the plan but I am not sure that you will receive this And now I wish to ask a few questions which I hope you will answer by writing as soon as you receive this

1st has there been a patent granted or applied for on perpetual motion

2nd has the Government a bounty offered to the inventor

3d when the Machine is in perfect running order and shure that it will go without stoping will you and a man from the

Patent Office come on and grant me a patent and fetch me the bounty if there is one.

4th is there eney way that I can have time to get the machine completed before others can apply for a Patent

Please write soon and address ———

MAY 1872

HON FRIEND—*Solicitor of Patents* I have invented a secret form of writing expressly for the use of our gov in time of warfare the publick demands it, It is different from any other invention known to the publick in this or any gov. It consists simply of the English alphabet and can be changed to any form that the safety of our gov. demands it no higherglyphicks are employed but it is practicable and safe I propose to sell it to our gov for the sum of one million dollars I will meet any committee appointed to investigate the matter. If you will give me your influence in Congress and aid in bringing a sale of the invention about to our gov or any other I will reward you with the sum of ten thousand dollars ($10,000) It is no illusion or a whim of the brain but is what I represent it to be scientific practicable and safe, Wishing to hear from you on the subject I remain

` Yours most truly ———

CHAPTER XLII.

THE WAR DEPARTMENT.

THE first recorded legislation of importance upon the military affairs of the nation, is the Act of Congress, of the twenty-seventh day of January, 1785, entitled "An Ordinance for ascertaining the Powers and Duties of the Secretary of War."

By this Act the duties of the Secretary are defined; and amongst them is a provision requiring him to visit, " at least once a year," " all the magazines and deposits of public stores, and report the state of them, with proper arrangements, to Congress."

Immediately after the confederation of the States, by

the adoption of the Constitution, this legislation was superseded by an Act of Congress, approved on the seventh day of August, 1789, defining the duties of the department, which was again modified by the fifth Congress, in the Act of the thirtieth day of April, 1798, "To establish an Executive Department, to be denominated the Department of the Navy." Of the efficiency of this department, and its services to the Republic, there can be no better testimony than that which has been extorted from history, in the following words: "The United States, from the peace of Independence, in 1783, achieved by war, and merely acknowledged by treaty, have always (?) lost by treaty, but never by war."

This sentiment, which is not as true now of our relations with Great Britain as in 1814, contains within it a compliment to the Department which, with limited means, and encountering the natural jealousy of civism, has so administered its scanty finances that the army has been made not only a defence for the frontiers, but a recognized national force, equal to the direst emergency, a nucleus around which, in any peril, the strength and bravery of the Republic may safely rally.

By the Act of the fourteenth of April, 1814, the Secretaries of War and of the Navy were placed in custody of the flags, trophies of war, etc., to deliver the same for presentation and display in such public places as the President may deem proper. Although many trophies, which a monarchical power would have jealously preserved, have been lost, or at least detached from their proper resting-place, there are still enough in both departments to stir the patriotic emotions of all who take the trouble to inquire for them.

The war of the Rebellion greatly increased these tro-
phics. The Rebel flags taken in battle, and in surrender,
and the Union flags, re-captured from the Confederates,
now occupy large apartments in two buildings belonging to the War Department; and are all placed under
the supervision of the Adjutant-General. In "Winder's
Buildings" hundreds of these flags are deposited, and
many hundreds more in the Adjutant-General's office on
Seventeenth street. The front and back rooms on the
lower floor of the latter house are exclusively devoted
to their preservation. A polite "orderly" is in waiting,
with a record-book, which gives the name and history
of every flag in the building. The front room is devoted to the Union colors which were re-taken from the
rebels. The back room is filled with Confederate flags
of every device and hue. Here is the first Confederate
flag adopted—an ugly rag, thirteen stars on a blue field,
with white and red bars. Its motto: "We will collect
our own revenues. We choose our own institutions."

The colors of the Benjamin Infantry, organized April
24, 1861, bear the inscriptions: "Crown for the brave."
"Strike for your altars and your fires."

An Alabama flag, of white bunting, with broad cross-
bars of blue, sewed on by women's hands, is inscribed:
"Our Homes, our Rights, we entrust to your keeping,
brave Sons of Alabama."

"*Sic Semper Tyrannis,*" says a tattered banner of fine
silk, presented in the first flush of rebellion-fever, with
the confidence of assured victory, "by the ladies of
Norfolk, to the N. L. A. Blues." Again, says Virginia:
"Our Rights we will maintain." "Death to Invaders
covered with blood." "Death or Victory," cries the

BLOOD-STAINED CONFEDERATE BATTLE FLAGS, CAPTURED DURING THE WAR.

Sketched by permission of the Government from the large collection in possession of the War Department, at Washington.

1. Black Flag.
2. Alabama Flag.
3. Palmetto Flag.
4. State and Regiment unknown. [Captured at the Battle of Gettysburg, by the 80th Regiment of New York Volunteers.]
5. State Colors of North Carolina.

Zachary Rangers—and again: "Tyranny is hateful to the gods."

With the exception of the State colors, the Union flags bear fewer mottoes. Many are fashioned of the finest fabrics, touched with the most exquisite tints. They need no florid and sensational sentence. Enough, that they bear the potent and silent stars of indissoluble union:

> " When Freedom, from her mountain height,
> Unfurled her standard to the air,
> She tore the azure robe of night,
> And set the stars of glory there ;
> She mingled with the gorgeous dyes
> The milky baldrick of the skies,
> And striped its pure celestial white
> With streakings of the morning light ;
> Then, from his mansion in the sun,
> She called her eagle-bearer down,
> And gave into his mighty hand,
> The symbols of her chosen land."

Beside this Flag of the Republic, the Black Flag, borne at Winchester, with its hideous yellow stripe, and hellish sentence, "No Quarter," needs no comment. From floor to nave, they droop everywhere, faded, tattered, bullet-riddled, the flags of Freedom, and the ensigns of Slavery, defiant, yet doomed. On one side of the apartment, cases, divided into minute boxes, rise to the ceiling. Each one is large enough to take a flag tightly rolled. Over all hangs a curtain ; and here these rags, which have outlasted the wasting march, the sore defeat, wait to tell their story in silence to coming generations.

The War Department is now divided into the following Bureaus :

Secretary's Office: The Secretary of War is charged, under the direction of the President, with the general control of the military establishment, and the execution of the laws relating thereto. The functions of the several Bureaus are performed under his supervision and authority. In the duties of his immediate office he is assisted by a chief clerk, claims-and-disbursing clerk, requisition-clerk, registering-clerk, and three recording-clerks.

The Adjutant-General's Office is the medium of communication to the army of all general and special orders of the Secretary-of-War relating to matters of military detail. The rolls of the army, and the records of service are kept, and all military commissions prepared in this office.

The Quartermaster-General's Office has charge of all matters pertaining to barracks and quarters for the troops, transportation, camp and garrison-equipage, clothing, fuel, forage, and the incidental expenses of the military establishment.

The Commissary-General's Office has charge of all matters relating to the procurement and issue of subsistence-stores in the army.

The Paymaster-General's Office has the general direction of matters relating to the pay of the army.

The Surgeon-General's Office has charge of all matters relating to the medical and hospital service.

The Engineer's Office, at the head of which is the Chief Engineer of the army, has charge of all matters relating to the construction of the fortifications, and to the Military Academy. At present, the Washington Aqueduct is being built under its direction. The Bureau of

Topographical Engineers, at the head of which is the Chief of the Corps, has charge of all matters relating to river and harbor improvements, the survey of the lakes, the construction of military works, and generally of all military surveys.

The Ordnance Bureau, at the head of which is the chief of ordnance, has charge of all matters relating to the manufacture, purchase, storage, and issue of all ordnance, arms, and munitions of war. The management of the arsenals and armories is conducted under its orders.

The present building, still used for the War Department, is utterly inadequate to its necessities. Already its Bureaus are scattered in several transient resting-places. In a few years they will be again concentrated in the magnificent structure now going up, for the combined use of the State, War and Navy Departments.

With the present War Department building will be obliterated one of the oldest land-marks of the Capital. All through the war of the Rebellion, it seemed to be the temple of the people, to which the whole nation came up, as they did to the temple at Jerusalem. What fates hung upon the fiats which issued from its walls! Hither came mother, wife, and daughter, to seek their dead, and to supplicate the furlough for their living soldier. What times those were, when the very life of the nation seemed suspended upon the will of the great War Secretary. I cannot look at the trees which arch the avenue between the War Department and the President's house, without thinking of those days when Lincoln took his solitary walk to and fro to consult with Stanton, his step slow, his eyes sad, over-weighted with responsibility and sorrow. And going down Seventeenth street, who that

30

ever saw him can fail to recall the image of Stanton as he paced up and down before the door of the War Department for his half-hour's exercise, when he held himself a prisoner within its walls.

All will soon be gone—the old familiar places as well as the old familiar faces. The grating of the trowel, cementing stone on stone, the ceaseless click of the hammer foretell how speedily the august stone structure, with graceful monoliths and turreted roof stretching over the vast square, will take the place of the old War Department.

The exigencies of war not only augmented the business of the War Department to gigantic proportions, but they created important Bureaus which have survived to flourish in times of peace; of these, none are so interesting, both to scientists and to citizens, as those connected with the medical history of the war. It may not be universally known to the public, but the medical profession has long been aware that the immense collection of cases and treatment, recorded in the field and hospital experiences of the late war, was being examined, condensed, tabulated, and the valuable conclusion, deducible therefrom, prepared for publication, under the direction of the Surgeon General of the army.

During the past few years "circulars" or detached portions of the work, of special interest, have been issued, and this spring two quarto volumes, being the first parts of the first two volumes of the entire work, have been given to the world.

Part I. of Volume I. is devoted to *medical* history, and has been compiled by Dr. Woodward, an assistant-surgeon of the army. This is a volume of eleven hundred

Wevill—N.Y.

THE NEW BUILDING NOW BEING CONSTRUCTED FOR DEPARTMENTS OF STATE, ARMY, AND NAVY.—WASHINGTON.

pages, and is divided into two parts and an appendix. The parts give the statistics of disease and death, respectively, of white and colored troops. The appendix consists of reports and statements of medical officers and their superiors.

Part I. of Volume II. commences the *surgical* history, and is the work of Dr. Otis, also an assistant-surgeon of the army, and well known as the curator of the Army Medical Museum. It contains nearly eight hundred pages, and is illustrated by numerous photo-lithographs of gunshot wounds, stumps of amputated limbs, and various other injuries of the human body—all evidences of the cruelties of war.

The merit of the conception of this vast undertaking, is due to the former Surgeon-General, Dr. Hammond, now the distinguished physician of New York city.

In 1862 he devised the form and routine for copious and precise returns of hospital treatment, and under his energetic supervision, Dr. Brinton of the volunteer corps, and Doctors Woodward and Otis, commenced the "Medical and Surgical History of the War of the Rebellion."

The work was ably continued by Dr. Barnes, the present Surgeon-General, and the result of all these labors is, so far, seen in the two volumes described, for the publication of which an appropriation was made by Congress in June, 1868. It is supposed that the entire work will reach six, and perhaps eight, such parts, and it certainly will be, when completed, a noble evidence of the liberality with which the Government provided for its sick and wounded soldiers, who fought for its preservation, and of the patriotism of the men who suffered in supporting such Government.

Brevet Major-General Joseph K. Barnes, Surgeon-General of the United States Army, was born in Pennsylvania, and appointed Assistant-Surgeon United States Army from that State, June, 1840, and stationed at the United States Military Academy, West Point, N. Y., until November of that year. He served in the Florida war against the Seminole Indians to 1842 ; at Fort Jesup, La., to 1846 ; in the war with Mexico to 1848 ; at Baton Rouge, La., and in Texas the same year, at Baltimore, Md., to 1851 ; in Missouri, to 1854 ; again at the United States Military Academy, West Point, N. Y., to 1857 ; in California and at Fort Vancouver, W. T., to 1861; at the head-quarters of General Hunter, Western Department and Department of Kansas to 1862.

He was promoted to be surgeon in the United States Army, August, 1856; Lieutenant Colonel and Medical Inspector, February, 1863 ; Colonel and Medical Inspector-General, August, 1863 ; and was assigned duty as Acting-Surgeon-General, United States Army, in the same month; appointed Brigadier-General and Surgeon-General, United States Army, August, 1864 ; Brevetted Major-General, United States Army, for faithful and meritorious services during the war.

Another medical report, perhaps equal in value to the Surgeon General's, has issued from the medical branch of the Provost-Marshal-General's Bureau, under the supervision of Dr. J. H. Baxter.

Dr. Jedediah H. Baxter, Lieutenant-Colonel and Chief Medical-Purveyor, United States Army, was born in Strafford, Orange County, Vt., May 11, 1837. He was graduated at the University of Vermont, both in the academical and medical departments, and in 1860 served as assistant professor of anatomy and surgery in that University. He was house surgeon in "Bellevue Hospital" at the "Seamen's Retreat," Staten Island, and on "Blackwell's Island."

He entered the Twelfth Regiment of Massachusetts Volunteers in April, 1861, was commissioned assistant-surgeon of the Regiment, May 13, 1861, and promoted to be surgeon, June 19, 1861. Served as post surgeon at Fort Warren, Boston Harbor, until July 26, 1861, when, with his regiment, he was mustered into the United States service and ordered to join the forces then forming under Gen. N. P. Banks at Sandy Hook, Md., opposite Harper's Ferry. He was Acting-Brigade-Surgeon, until April 4, 1862, when, promoted to Brigade-Surgeon of Volunteers, he was ordered to report for duty to Gen. Geo. B. McClellan, and served on the staff of that officer during the Peninsular campaign, as Medical Director of Field-Hospitals and the transportation of sick and wounded of the Army of the Potomac.

Disabled from field service by the "peninsular fever," he was ordered to hospital duty in Washington, D. C., August 1, 1862, and was in charge of Judiciary Square United States General Hospital until September, 1862, when he was ordered to superintend the building of Campbell United States General Hospital, Washington, D. C., of which Hospital, when completed, he was placed in charge, where he remained until January 5, 1864, when he was relieved and ordered to report for special duty to the Provost-Marshal-General of the United States, who assigned him to duty as "Chief Medical Officer of the Provost-Marshal-General's Bureau." In this capacity he served, having the management of all medical matters pertaining to the recruitment of the army, until the close of the war, hav-

ing been Brevetted Lieutenant-Colonel of the United
States Volunteers in March, 1865, and Colonel of the
United States Volunteers in January, 1866.

When the Provost-Marshal-General's Bureau was abolished, he was placed on special duty by an Act of Congress, in preparing a report of the medical statistics of
the Provost-Marshal-General's Bureau. On July 20, 1866,
he was commissioned Assistant-Medical-Purveyor, United
States Army, with the rank of Lieutenant-Colonel and
was Brevetted Colonel "for faithful and meritorious services during the war." He was promoted to the position
of Chief Medical Purveyor of the United States Army,
March 12, 1872, in which position he has supervision of
the purchase and distribution of all hospital and medical
supplies required for the use of the army.

On being called to the charge of the medical branch
of the Provost-Marshal-General's Bureau, Dr. Baxter soon
perceived that, in the several Acts of Congress devolving
upon the Provost-Marshal-General the duty of recruiting
by voluntary enlistment, conscription and substitution,
the vast armies called out to suppress the rebellion, lay
the means of obtaining such a view of the physical state
and military capacity of the nation as had never before
and might never again be obtained. After an examination of such material as had already accumulated under
the limited operation of the draft and recruiting Acts, he
prepared and issued to the surgeons of the enrolling
boards, in the several congressional districts, blank forms
and instructions designed to afford the means of tabula-
ting from the reports of individual examinations of recruits, drafted men and substitutes, the statistics illustrating the relations between disease and nativity, residence,

age, complexion, height, and size, social condition and occupation in the sex on which the principal physical burdens of life fall.

The accumulating records of the medical department of the army could be utilized for the benefit of military surgery and hygiene by showing the varying facts of disease and wounds among soldiers, and the records of pension applications and the regularly recurring examinations of invalid pensioners would give the results of non-fatal wounds and disease upon the disabled soldier returned to civil life. But Dr. Baxter saw that a separate and important field of study and action was left to his own bureau, if its current records could be reduced to a system of fulness, accuracy and uniformity. This was successfully done, and the results will soon be before the public. From advance sheets of the volume, many interesting facts have been drawn for this article. The work is based on the reports made of the medical inspection of about 605,000 persons subject to draft, and minuter descriptions of the fuller examination of 508,735 recruits, substitutes and drafted men.

Of the whole number examined, a little over 257 in each thousand were found unfit for military service. The largest number found disqualified through any specific class of diseases were those affected by diseases of the digestive organs, the ratio of unfitness to the whole number examined being a little more than sixty in a thousand. Fifty nativities are embraced in the report, the ratio of unfitness in each thousand being, for American whites, 323; American colored, 225; Canadians, 258; Irish, 337; Germans, 400; Scandinavians, 294; English, 325; and Scotch, 308.

From these ratios it will be seen that the Negroes, Canadians and Scandinavians were the healthiest, and the Germans and Irish the unhealthiest. The relative position assigned to the negro by these figures is not in accord with the general opinion upon the subject, but the healthiness of unskilled occupations and his simple method of life in the South accounts for the fact. The report also shows that a larger proportion of civilians are fit for military duty in this country than in Great Britain or France, and probably Germany, though the figures to prove the proposition in the latter case are not at hand.

Of the recruits, conscripts and substitutes under twenty years of age, the ratio of rejection and exemption was 268 in the thousand, including those too young for service; between twenty and twenty-five years, the ratio was 245; between twenty-five and thirty, the ratio was 330; it was 411 between thirty and thirty-five; between thirty-five and forty it was 462, and over forty years it was 607 in a thousand, including all rejected for dotage.

This table bears out the common experience that infirmities grow with age. Of the native whites, 663 in a thousand were of light complexion; of Canadians, 661 in a thousand; of English, 705; of Irish, 702; and of German, 694—indicating, by the lower ratio of fair complexion, a greater admixture of races in this country than in the parent countries. Of persons of light complexion, 385 in the thousand were unfit for service, while the dark complexions show the healthier ratio of 332 in each thousand. The average height of Americans is found to be 5 feet 7½ inches, of Canadians 5.5, 5.1, of Irish and Germans 5.5, 5.4, of Scandinavians and English 5.6, 0, and of French one-fifth of an inch lower than the last named.

All under five feet were rejected or exempted, as the case might be; and the rejections under 5 feet 1 inch were 582 in the thousand, between 5.1 and 5.3 they were 443, between 5.3 and 5.5 they were 322, between 5.5 and 5.7 they were 303, between 5.7 and 5.9 they were 313, between 5.9 and 5.11 they were 326, between 5.11 and 6.1 they were 350, and they were 358 in all over 6 feet 1 inch. The healthiest persons were those of the average height of 5 feet 7 inches.

The chest measurements, at moment of respiration, averaged 33.11 inches for Americans, 32.84 for Irish, 33.56 for Germans, 33.01 for Canadians and 32.93 for English. The detailed statistics of height and size bear out the statement that, as a rule, only healthy foreigners migrate from the Old to the New World and healthy natives from the old to the new States; both conclusions are quite reasonable, when the anticipated and real hardships of migration are considered.

Considering the figures relating to occupation, it is found that the ratio of unfitness for army life was 409 in a thousand among persons engaged in in-door pursuits, and only 349 in a thousand, in persons of out-door callings.

Taken by trades and professions, it appears that of journalists 740 in a thousand were disqualified, physicians 670, clergymen and preachers 654, dentists 549, lawyers 544, tailors 473, teachers 455, photographers 451, mercantile clerks 416, painters 392, carpenters 383, stone-cutters 376, shoe-makers 362, laborers 358, farmers 350, printers 335, tanners 216, iron-workers 189. The average ratio of disability among professional men was 520 in a thousand, merchants 480, artisans 484, and unskilled laborers 348 only.

The journalists, doctors and clergymen were the unhealthiest professional men, and teachers and musicians the healthiest.   Brokers were the unhealthiest of the mercantile class, and shop-keepers and peddlers the healthiest.   Iron and leather-workers were the healthiest of the artisans; in the first occupation, partly, because only robust men can follow it.   Paper-makers, tailors and upholsterers appear to have been the unhealthiest trades. Of unskilled occupations, so-called, for the purposes of this work, miners and mariners were the healthiest, and watchmen, bar-keepers and fishermen the unhealthiest. Explanation is found in the case of watchmen, in the number of old and broken-down men following that vocation.   The ratio of single men found disqualified was 393 in a thousand, and of married men 447 in a thousand; the difference, however, being no argument against marriage, as the latter class embraces a larger proportion of men beyond middle age.

Congress has provided liberally for the publication of Dr. Baxter's medical statistics of drafts and recruitments, and the volume will contain shaded maps and diagrams, to aid in exhibiting and contrasting the results of his unique studies of the physical status of the nation.

CHAPTER XLIII.

THE ARMY MEDICAL MUSEUM—ITS CURIOSITIES AND WONDERS.

Ford's Theatre—Its Interesting Memories—The Last Festivities—Assassination of President Lincoln—Two Years Later—Effects of "War, Disease, and Human Skill"—Collection of Pathological Specimens—The Army Medical Museum Opened—Purchase of Ford's Theatre—Its Present Aspect—Ghastly Specimens—Medical and Surgical Histories of the War—The Library—A Book Four Centuries Old—Rare Old Volumes—The Most Interesting of the National Institutions—Various Opinions—Effects on Visitors—An Extraordinary Withered Arm—A Dried Sioux Baby!—Its Poor Little Nose—A Well-dressed Child—Its Buttons and Beads—Casts of Soldier-Martyrs—Making a New Nose—Vassear's Mounted Craniums—Model Skeletons—A Giant, Seven Feet High—Skeleton of a Child—All that Remains of Wilkes Booth, the Assassin—Fractures by Shot and Shell—General Sickles Contributes His Quota—A Case of Skulls—Arrow-head Wounds—Nine Savage Sabre-Cuts—Seven Bullets in One Head—Phenomenal Skulls—A Powerful Nose—An Attempted Suicide—A Proverb Corrected—Specimen from the Paris Catacombs—An " Interesting Case "—Typical Heads of the Human Race—Remarkable Indian Relics—" Flatheads "—The Work of Indian Arrows—An Extraordinary Story—A " Pet " Curiosity—A Japanese Manikin—Tattooed Heads—Representatives of Animated Nature—Adventure of Captain John Smith—A " Stingaree "—The Microscopical Division—Medical Records of the War—Preparing Specimens.

THE building in which Abraham Lincoln was assassinated will always retain a deep and sad interest in the mind of the American people. It was well that it should be consecrated to a national purpose. None could be more fit than to make it the repository of the Pathological and Surgical results of the war.

From the dark hour of the great martyr's death, the light and music of amusement never again animated these dark halls. But in two years from the day of the tragedy, its doors were opened to the people, to come in and behold what war, disease, death, and human skill had wrought.

In obedience to an order from the War Department, issued in 1862, thousands of pathological specimens had accumulated in the office of the Surgeon-General. An ample and fit receptacle was needed for their proper care and display. And April 13, 1867, the old Ford Theatre, on Tenth street, between E and F, was opened as the Army Medical Museum.

Congress had already purchased the building of Mr. Ford, and used it for a time as the receptacle for the captured archives of the Confederate Government. Before it was opened as the Army Museum, its interior had been entirely remodeled, retaining nothing of the original building but the outside walls. It has been made fire-proof, and is exclusively devoted to the uses of the Museum. The third story is the Museum hall, lined on its four sides with pictures and glass cases filled with ghastly specimens, beside many more in the interior of the room.

Over a square railing, in the centre of the hall, you look down upon the second story, and through that to the first. The lower floor is filled with busy clerks, sitting at tables, writing out the medical and surgical histories of the war.

The second floor, which is reached by light spiral stairs from the first, is largely devoted to the very valuable Medical and Surgical Library, which has been collected

THE MAIN HALL OF THE ARMY MEDICAL MUSEUM.—WASHINGTON.

since the opening of the Museum. It now numbers thirty-eight thousand volumes, some of which are rare books of extreme value. One of these was among the earliest of printed volumes. The art of printing was first used to give to the world religious and medical books. This treasure of the Medical Museum was published at Venice, in 1480, and is the work of Petrus de Argelata. It is bound and illuminated in vellum. Another choice book, is a copy of Galen, which once belonged to the Dutch anatomist, Vierodt, and copiously annotated by him. These, and many other valuable books, have been bought by the agents of the Museum, abroad, while many others have been received as contributions from physicians, and scientific societies interested in the growth of this national institution.

Louis Bagger, in a late number of *Appleton's Journal,* speaks of the Army Medical Museum as one of the most interesting, but least visited, of all the national institutions in Washington. It cannot fail to be one of the most absorbing spots on earth to the student of surgery or medicine; but to the unscientific mind, especially to one still aching with the memories of war, it must ever remain a museum of horrors. Its many bones, which never ached, and which have survived their painful sheaths of mortal flesh, all cool and clean, and rehung on golden threads, are not unpleasant to behold. But those faces in frames, eaten by cancer or lost in tumors, which you look up to as you enter, are horrible enough to haunt one forever (if you are not scientific) with the thought of what human flesh is heir to.

No! the Museum is a very interesting, but can never be a popular place to visit. I doubt if a sight at the Sioux

pappoose, and a bit of John Wilkes Booth's spinal mar-
row, or a piece of General Sickles' leg, will be sufficient
compensation to the average unscientific mind, to go
twice to look at those terrible tumors and elephantiasis in
gilt frames and glass jars. It is enough to make one feel
as if the like were starting out all over you. But that's
because you are not scientific.

The first " specimen " which confronts you on entering is
a withered human arm, with contracted hand and clinched
fingers, mounted on wires in a glass case on the window-
ledge. The sharp bone protrudes where it was shot off
near the shoulder joint; every muscle is defined; the skin
looks like tanned leather. It is not pleasant to look at. A
thrilling story has been printed about this arm. I am
sorry it is not wholly true. The one I have to tell will
not please you as well, for it is not nearly as exciting.

We were told that the shock of the cannon-shot, which
took off this arm, carried it up into a high tree, where, a
year or two after, its owner, a Gettysburg hero, revisiting
the battle-field, discovered his lost member lodged in the
branches, brought it down and bore it hither as a trophy.
The soldier *did* find his arm (I am telling the true story);
but he found it in a corn-field. By what mark he knew
it I am not informed, but he declared it to be his arm,
and brought it to the Museum as a first-class "sensational
specimen."

In the next window we find another one—the Sioux
baby. Poor little baby! It is not a Modoc—though not
much better—it did not live to slay our brethren, so we
are sorry as we look at it—for its once black locks are
bleached red, and its nose is gone. It was found in a
tree near Fort Laramie. I have seen Sioux babies alive

upon their native soil, and can testify from personal observation that this little pappoose-mummy is extraordi-
narily well dressed. Hannah of old did not sew more
buttons on the coat of her little Samuel in the Temple,
than this poor savage mother did on the plains of Wyoming. It is of blue flannel, profusely ornamented with
round tin buttons, and many beads on its broad collar.
On its neck it wears a string of white delf beads, and
there is something cunning and dainty in the tiny em-
broidered moccasins upon its feet. In a case there is another pappoose still less agreeable to contemplate. It is a
little Flat-head Indian. Its head is so very flat no doubt
it died in the process of compression. This melancholy
child also wears a white necklace, and was found *buried*
in a tree.

Passing on, we are arrested by a table surrounded on its
outer edge by plaster casts of soldiers who have under-
gone famous and difficult surgical operations. It is gratifying to know that, if you lose your nose by some other
collision beside that of a cannon ball, you can have
a new one set on made out of your cheek. The new
nose will grow to the root of the old one, and the hole in
your cheek will fill up and the scar heal. To be sure it
will hurt you frightfully ; but you *can* have a new nose
made, and you yourself supply the material. If you
don't believe it, come to the Army Medical Museum and
see ! Here is the head of the poor fellow with his nose
shot off—and here is another with the new nose grown
on.

In the centre of the table are some of Vassear's mounted
craniums, purchased for the museum by order of the
Surgeon-General. These craniums, with the skeletons in

the cases, are mounted after Blanchêne's method, which
allows every portion to be taken apart and put together
again.   This cranium on the table is as white as crystal;
it is mounted on gold, and tiny blue and crimson threads
of silk trace from chin to head-top the entire nerve system.   It is a work of exquisite art as well as of science,
and in no sense repulsive.   The glass cases just in the
rear contain skeletons mounted by the same method.
One is the skeleton of a giant, in life seven feet high,
prepared by Auzoax and mounted by Blanchêne's method.
It is as white as snow, and its brass or gold joints (we
will call them gold) are bright and flexile.   Another, of
a child of some six years, shows the entire double sets
of first and second teeth.   The first, not one tooth gone,
and above, in the jaw, the entire row of second teeth
ready to push the first ones out.

Amid the thousands of mounted specimens in glass
cases, which reveal the freaks of bullets and cannon-shot,
we come to one which would scarcely arrest the attention of a casual observer.   It is simply three human
vertebræ mounted on a stand and numbered 4,086.   Beside it hangs a glass phial, marked 4,087, filled with alcohol, in which floats a nebulæ of white matter.   The official catalogue contains the following records of these
apparently uninteresting specimens :

" No. 4,086.—The third, fourth and fifth cervical vertebræ.
A conoidal carbine ball entered the right side, comminuting the
base of the right lamina of the fourth vertebræ, fracturing it
longitudinally and separating it from the spinous process, at the
same time fracturing the fifth through its pedicles, and involving
that transverse process.   The missile passed directly through
the canal, with a slight inclination downward and to the rear,

emerging through the left bases of the fourth and fifth laminæ, which are comminuted, and from which fragments were embedded in the muscles of the neck. The bullet, in its course, avoided the large cervical vessels. From a case where death occurred in a few hours after injury, April 26, 1865."

" No. 4,087.—A portion of the spinal-cord from the cervical region, transversely perforated from right to left by a carbine-bullet, which fractured the laminæ of the fourth and fifth vertebræ. The cord is much torn and is discolored by blood. From a case where death occurred a few hours after injury, April 26, 1865."

Such are the colorless scientific records of the death wounds of John Wilkes Booth. All that remains of him above the grave finds its perpetual place a few feet above the spot where he shot down his illustrious victim.

It has been recorded elsewhere that the fatal wounds of Wilkes Booth and his victim were strikingly alike. " The balls entered the skull of each at nearly the same spot, but the trifling difference made an immeasurable difference in the sufferings of the two. Mr. Lincoln was unconscious of all pain, while his assassin suffered as exquisite agony as if he had been broken on a wheel."

In the surgical division which contains the above specimens we find illustrations from living and dead subjects of almost every conceivable fracture by shot and shell.

On a black stand, bearing the number 1,335, we see a strong white bone shattered in the middle. The official statement concerning it is: " The right tibia and fibula comminuted in three shafts by a round shell. Major-General D. E. S., United States Volunteers, Gettysburg, July 2, amputated in the lower third of the thigh by Surgeon T. Sim, United States Volunteers, on the field.

31

Stump healed rapidly, and subject was able to ride in carriage July 16; completely healed, so that he mounted his horse, in September, 1863. Contributed by the subject"—who is General Daniel E. Sickles.

One of the cases in this division is filled with skulls which show gunshot wounds from arrow-heads and thrusts from tomahawks and sabres. One of the latter, No. 970, shows nine savage sabre cuts. It is the skull of an Araucanian Indian, killed by Chilian troops. Near it is the skull of another Indian, riddled by six or seven bullet-shots received from American troops or trappers.

The Museum contains eight craniums, which illustrate the wonderful fact of an unbroken external skull, while the vitreous table is perforated or dented. One of these shows slight discoloration on the outside of the head without fracture or depression, while inside, the bone is broken. The seven other specimens illustrate the same phenomena. In this case we see craniums in which bullets are imbedded and broken. We see one where a conical bullet split in two in entering the head at the temple, one half going inside, caused instant death, while the other half struck the face outside. Here we see a minié-bullet split on the bones of the nose. Another case is of an attempted suicide—who died a natural death. He fired a pistol in his mouth, whose bullet passed through the jugular vein, but not through the head. It stopped short, embedded in the bone, where it remained as a stopper to the blood from the perforated artery, and the man who tried to kill himself, lived seventeen years to be sorry for doing so.

Two specimens in this collection deny the assertion that "when a man breaks his neck that is the last of

A WITHERED ARM

ib and bones complete. Amputated by a cannon shot on the battle field of Gettysburg.
carried the severed limb up into the high branches of a tree, where it was subsequently
mpletely air and sun-dried.

All that remains Above Ground
OF
JOHN WILKES BOOTH.

Being part of the Vertebræ penetrated [A] by
the bullet of Boston Corbett. Strange freak of fate that these
remains of Booth should find a resting place under the same roof,
and but a few feet from the spot where the fatal shot was fired.

A SIOUX PAPPOOSE

1 Infant, found in a tree near Fort Laramie, where it had been buried (?) according to
m of the tribe.

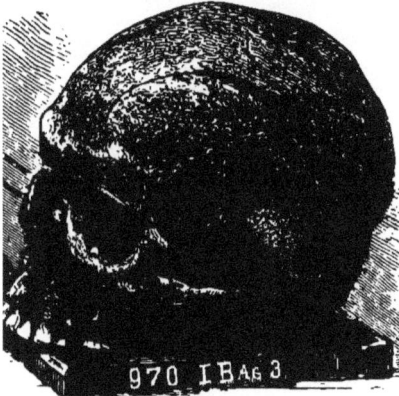

SKULL OF LITTLE BEAR'S SQUAW,

Perforated by seven bullet holes. Killed in Wyoming Territory.

SKULL OF AN INDIAN,

Showing nine distinct sabre wounds.

SKULL OF A MAN

Who received an arrow wound on the head, three gun-shot flesh wounds, one in the
arm, another in the breast, and a third in the leg. Seven days afterwards he was
admitted to the hospital at Fort Concha, Texas [where he subsequently died], after
having traveled above 160 miles on the barren plains — mostly on foot.

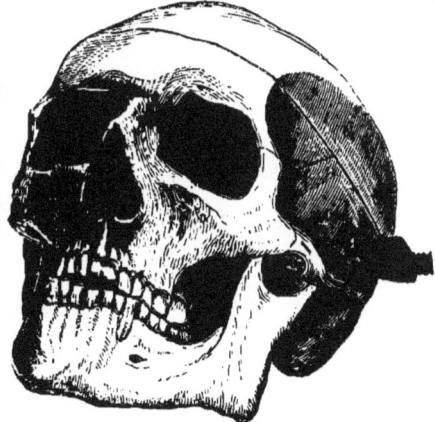

SKULL OF A SOLDIER

at Spottsylvania — showing the splitting of a Rifle ball, one
ing buried deep in the brain, and the other between the scalp
kull. He lived twenty-three days.

APACHE INDIAN ARROW-HEAD

Of soft hoop-iron. These arrows will perforate a bone without causing the slightest
fracture, where a rifle or musket ball will flatten; and will make a cut as clean as the
finest surgical instrument.

CURIOSITIES

FROM THE ARMY MEDICAL MUSEUM, WASHINGTON.

him." One of these is a skull taken from the Catacombs in Paris. It has a few vertebræ attached to the neck. One of these shows a distinct dislocation where it was broken from the head, and where it had grown closely together again. The other is a home specimen, which shows no less distinctly where the broken neck again formed the connection with the head. There is also in this section of the museum a piece of human cranium, about the size of a silver dollar, cut from the head of a soldier wounded at Petersburgh, Va., June 14, 1864. The following is the official history of this "interesting case:"

"The subject was admitted to Mount Pleasant General Hospital, Washington, D. C., on June 24, with the report that the progress of the case had been so far eminently satisfactory. After admission he was found to be insensible, and a few hours subsequently convulsions supervened in rapidly recurring paroxysms. Twelve ounces of blood were taken from the temporal artery without apparent benefit. A trephine was then applied to the seat of fracture, and upon the removal of a bottom of bone, a portion of the inner table was found slightly depressed. This was elevated, and the patient, soon after, regained consciousness. On the 28th of June, the wound in the scalp became erysipelatous, and before the inflammation subsided there was extensive loss of substance of the integuments and pericranium denuding a large portion of the parietal bone. Necrosis ensued, and embraced the whole thickness of the bone. In September, 1864, a portion of the parietal, three inches by four, had become so much loosened that it was readily removed. After this, cicatrization went on rapidly; and at the date of the last report, December 2, 1864, the wound had contracted to an ulcer less than an inch in diameter. The patient's mental faculties were impaired somewhat, the ward-physician thought, but not to a great extent."

This specimen was contributed by Assistant-Surgeon E. A. McCall, United States Army. A colored drawing was made representing the parts prior to the separation of the exfoliation, (No. 74, surgical series of drawings, Surgeon General's office.)

We see suspended in a case the bone of an arm from the shoulder to the elbow. A musket ball having shattered it, it was necessary to take it out or amputate the arm. The surgeon chose the former. The bone with all its splinters was removed. The photograph of its owner is set up under it, while the living original may come and look at it any moment he chooses, he being one of the *attachés* to the Museum. He says that he can use the injured arm as readily as the other. The muscles and integuments have taken the place of the lost bone, and are strong enough to enable him to lift a two-hundred-pounds' weight without difficulty.

Another case of great interest to the medical profession, is that of a soldier of Company C, Eighth New Jersey Volunteers, who was wounded in the battle of the Wilderness, May 5, 1864. The specimen on exhibition is a piece of the hip-bone, about four or five inches long. This shattered bone was excised, May 27, 1864, and the patient was discharged from the hospital, April 17, 1865, perfectly cured, and able to use the mutilated limb without its portion of thigh-bone. In 1868, he was well, could walk without a cane, and was employed as a hod-carrier. He now receives a Government pension of fifteen dollars a month.

At the right of the main entrance, stands the Cranio-logical Cabinet. It contains a thousand or more speci-mens of the craniæ of different human races. Beside the skull of the Caucasian, we see that of the African, each of the highest order of its kind. The long line contains a "sample" of nearly all the typical heads of the human race.

The collection contains a large number of Indian skulls of opposite tribes, taken from tumuli, and gathered from other sources. There are none to which the scientific man points with more interest, than to the skulls of the Flat-head Indians. These are perfectly flat on the top, forming a right angle with the forehead. Here is the head of a baby, who probably died in the process. Boards are tightly bound to infants' heads, from birth, till they cease to grow. One would suppose that this would lessen the brain-capacity. But as it can not grow in front, it avenges itself by pushing far out on the sides. Thus the Flat-head Indian's head is as wide as it is flat, and in defiance of phrenology, he is not only as bright, but brighter in his wits, than many of his neighbors.

Here are Indian arrows, taken from the dead bodies of our soldiers on the plains. The arrowheads are made of barrel-hoops, and so sharp, they can pierce any skull. One is shown, still sticking through a portion of the shoulder-blade of a buffalo. The point of the arrow is outside of the bone, the arrow-tip having passed through the body of the buffalo, and through the bone, opposite the side that it entered. A rifle-ball would be flattened where an Indian arrowhead penetrates without hin-drance. The cut of an arrowhead is as clear and clean as if made by the most acute surgical instrument. The fatal force with which an arrow is driven from an Indian bow, is illustrated in the following fact: Here, in the Museum, is the piece of a door of a stage which was attacked by Comanches near Bellos River, Texas, September 1, 1870. The wood, about an inch and a half thick, is pierced by an Indian arrowhead, the point appearing on the outside.

Of the two passengers in the stage at the time of the occurrence, one was killed and the other escaped. The stage guard consisted of three soldiers—one was killed instantly, another escaped, the third was wounded. He received an arrow wound in the head, and three gunshot flesh-wounds, one in the arm, another in the leg and one in the breast. In this condition he travelled one hundred and sixty miles across the plains, on foot. Seven long days it took him to reach the post-hospital at Fort Concha, Texas. When admitted, mentally, he was clear and bright. But on September 19, he died.

The skull of this unfortunate man, preserved in the Army Museum, shows an arrowhead firmly embedded in the petrous portion of the right temporal bone—a wound in itself, it would seem, sufficient to prove instantly fatal.

One of the pet curiosities of the Museum is a Japanese manikin—ess—we will call it, as it is supposed to represent the creature feminine. The heart is a red apple and the liver (very properly) a yellow one. The stomach looks like a lean pomegranate. The lungs are represented by five green oak leaves. These organs are lumped together, the lungs being below all the rest. The Japanese idea of anatomy seems to be quite as muddled as its powers of perspective.

A case near the front window, contains three Maori

heads from New Zealand. They are all tattooed with the black juice of the betel-nut. Any thing more hideous than their empty eye-sockets, their striped cheek bones and ghastly white teeth cannot be imagined.

Along the windows at the opposite end of the great hall, may be seen skeletons of all kinds of animals, birds, fishes and reptiles. Here are skeletons of the horse, the buffalo, the grizzly bear, the elk, the walrus, and the ray. One of these last, caught in James river, has been presented to the Museum.

Those who have read the early history of Virginia may remember that it chronicles the fact that once when Captain John Smith, of wonderful memory, was one day bathing in the James River, he received a sudden shock, and many days elapsed before he recovered from it. It was supposed that he was struck by a 'stingaree.'

The 'stingaree' is a corruption of the stinging ray— and such a specimen is shown in the Museum. The ray is a fish of the cartilaginous species, not having the vertebrated form. It has wings, each measuring about fourteen inches across the widest part; and it has a very long tail, in which is implanted a sting, which resembles in its effects a shock of electricity, and produces temporary paralysis. The ray darts in among a shoal of fishes, electrifies them, and then proceeds to devour them.

The microscopical division of the Museum on the library floor is of great value. It affords facilities for the study of natural history and comparative anatomy equal to the medical schools of Paris. This department contains a series of photographical publications of enlarged photographic pictures of the specimens, mounted on cardboard and bound in Russia leather. A set of this series,

also a complete set of bound photographs of all the specimens contained in the surgical department of the Museum, with a sketch of the case attached, has been presented to all the governments and large public libraries of
Europe. In return, these European governments and
libraries have sent complete sets of like publications of
their own. Several hundred volumes, handsomely bound,
include these foreign gifts to the Army Medical Museum
at Washington.

The primary object of the Army Medical Museum is
to illustrate minutely the wounds and diseases of our late
war, while the medical and surgical histories of the war,
now being written under the supervision of the Surgeon-
General, will show the processes of treatment and their
results. Dr. J. J. Woodward, assisted by Dr. Otis, both
of Pennsylvania, are charged with the writing of this
history. Doctor Woodward is writing the medical history, and Doctor Otis the surgical history of this important national report. Five thousand copies of each will
be issued by Congress. The first volumes of both histories have already come from the bindery of the Public
Printer in handsome form. The first of the medical volumes is chiefly occupied with tabular statements of the
diseases which prevailed, and the numbers dying of each,
during the entire period of our civil war. The coming
volumes will treat of these diseases, the treatment pursued, and will give photographs of the organs affected in
each disease.

The Museum proper is divided into four departments,
Surgery, Medicine, Anatomy, and Comparative Anatomy.
These are all placed in the hall of the third story. We
reach this by an outer iron stair-case, whose walls on

either side are lined with sketches and plans of the battle-fields of Gettysburg and Antietam, in black walnut frames. Entering the long hall, we are confronted at once by the ghastly victims in the frames opposite, and the eyes are quickly withdrawn to glance up and down along the polished glass cases which line the walls. Above some of these cases droop the flags and standards, the swords and sabres which have survived the war. Models of ambulances, stretchers, and hospital tents, also have a place on the top of these cases.

More than four-fifths of the specimens in the Museum have been presented to it, or exchanged for duplicate objects, quantities of which are stored in the attic, ready for exchange. The Army Medical Museum belongs to the nation, and as its existence and object have been widely published, it is in daily receipt of new specimens. It has become an object of personal interest and pride to the medical fraternity of the country, each one of whom is invited to become a contributor to its pathological treasures. In a late official report, the Surgeon-General thus refers to the subject, which is of interest to all medical persons:

"It is not intended to impose upon medical officers the labor of dissecting and preparing the specimens they may contribute to the Museum. This will be done under the superintendence of the curator. In forwarding such pathological objects as compound fractures, bony specimens, and wet preparations generally, obtained after amputation, operation, or cadaveric examination, all unnecessary soft parts should first be roughly removed. Every specimen should then be wrapped separately in a cloth, so as to preserve all spiculæ and fragments. A small block of wood should be attached, with the number of the specimen and the name of the medical officer sending it inscribed in lead-pencil; or a strip of sheet-lead, properly marked with the point of an awl, may be employed for this purpose. In either case, the inscription will be uninjured by the contact of fluids. The preparation should be then immersed in diluted alcohol or whisky, contained in a keg or small cask. When a sufficient number of objects shall have accumulated, the cask should be forwarded to the Army Medical Museum, in Washington, D. C. The expenses of expressage will be defrayed in Washington. The receipt of the keg or package will be duly acknowledged by the curator of the Museum."

When the first Army Medical Museum report was issued, January 1, 1863, the collection begun in August, 1862, numbered over thirteen hundred in all. Since then the collection has grown to the following proportions. In 1873 it contains over sixteen thousand objects. In the surgical department alone, there are over six thousand. In the medical department over eleven hundred. In the anatomical department over nine hundred. In the department of comparative anatomy over one thousand. In the microscopical department over six thousand. A library and photograph-gallery belong exclusively to the Museum. The side rooms and lower stories are used as the laboratories and work-rooms for preparing and mounting the specimens for exhibition. The Army Medical Museum is a great beginning—and yet only a beginning of one of the most unique, precious and important, pathological collections in the world.

CHAPTER XLIV.

"OLD PROBABILITIES" AT HOME—THE WEATHER BUREAU.

THERE is no theme, not excepting marriage, birth, and death, that is more absorbing than " the weather." It has made and unmade kingdoms, it has brought triumph in battle, and terrible defeat, it has brought woe and death; but that was before the day of "Old Probabilities," or the Weather Bureau.

It is your own fault now, if your wedding-day is wet and gloomy, or if the rain pours into the open grave of the best-beloved. If you follow the weather report, you will know days before what the weather, in all probability, will be, and the report seldom fails. Even ten years ago, who would have thought that he could so soon find in the newspaper the almost unfailing prophecy of the skies of the coming day! Think of the millions of anxious faces which have turned sky-ward since the earth began! What eager and ignorant eyes have peered upward, to descry the portents of the unseen, yet brooding storm. Ignorance has already given place to knowledge, to a scientific forecasting of the elements, to a fore-statement of the conditions of earth and air.

This wonderful fact, in its influence, penetrates not only to the finest fibre of social happiness, but influences all the civilizations of the earth. Although the changes of the atmosphere have seemed the most apparent of all the workings of nature, and have been more closely watched, and more constantly commented on by mankind, than all others taken together, after the lapse of fifty centuries, the desultory observer is unable to predict certainly the weather of a single day.

The value of accurate scientific knowledge on a subject which affects vitally the agricultural and commercial interests of the world, as well as the physical health and spiritual happiness of mankind, cannot be overestimated.

By a joint resolution of Congress, approved February 9, 1870, the Secretary-of-War was authorized and required to provide for taking meteorological observations at the military stations in the interior of the continent, and at other points in the States and Territories of the United States, and for giving notice on the northern lakes, and on the sea-coast, by magnetic telegraph and marine signals, of the approach and force of storms.

This special service was intrusted to the immediate supervision and control of General Albert J. Meyer. The following record of his services, in the United States Army, can but slightly indicate his peculiar fitness for the position which he now holds.

Brevet Brigadier-General Albert J. Meyer, Colonel and Chief Signal Officer, United States Army, was born in New York, and appointed Assistant-Surgeon, United States Army, from that State, September, 1854. He served on the Texas frontier, in the Rio Grande Valley, and at Fort Davis, Texas, to 1857; on special duty, signal service, 1858 to 1860. He was appointed Major and Chief Signal Officer, United States Army, July, 1860. In the Department of New Mexico to May, 1861 ; on staff of General Butler, Fort Monroe, Va., June, 1861; organized and commanded Signal Camp, Fort Monroe, Va.; *Aide-de-Camp* to General McDowell at first battle of Bull Run, Va.; Chief Signal Officer on staff of General McClellan, and commanded Signal Corps, Army of the Potomac, to October, 1862; charge of Signal Office, Washington, D. C., to November, 1863.

He was appointed Colonel and Chief Signal Officer, United States Army, March, 1863; member of Central Board of Examination for admission to Signal Corps from April, 1863; on *reconnoissance* of the Mississippi River, between Cairo, Ill., and Memphis, Tenn., December, 1863, to May, 1864; Chief Signal Officer, Military Division of West Mississippi, May, 1864; Colonel and Chief Signal Officer, United States Army, July, 1866. He was brevetted Lieutenant-Colonel, United States Army, for gallant and meritorious services at the battle of Hanover Courthouse, Va.; Colonel, United States Army, for gallant and meritorious services at the battle of Malvern Hill, Va.; and Brigadier General, United States Army, for distinguished services in organizing, instructing, and commanding Signal Corps of the army, and for its especial service at Altoona, Ga., October 5, 1864.

General Meyer graduated at Geneva College, New York, 1847, A. B. and A. M., and took the degree of M. D., at the University of Buffalo, in 1851. He is the author of a manual of signals for the United States Army and Navy.

Upon his appointment as Chief of the Signal Service, of the United States Army, General Meyer at once inaugurated a systematic plan; he established stations at all points, decided by competent authorities to be important and practicable. These he provided with plain, efficient instruments, and keen, trained observers, whose duty it was to report three times daily, at intervals of eight hours. These reports, made in abbreviated cypher, were conveyed by telegraph. With the delivery of the reports at Washington, and at other important posts to which they were sent, began the practical workings of the " Weather Bureau " in the Signal Service of the United States. January 15, 1871, the stations on the Atlantic Coast, with others, were added to the list reporting.

One of the most important practical functions of the Bureau, is that of giving warning of approaching storms to vessels at the ports on the lakes. The unfortunate *Metis* received such a warning before it started on its last disastrous voyage. It gave no heed, and in consequence went to wreck, and scattered its victims thick as snow-flakes on the engulfing waters of the Sound. The velocity of a storm being accurately observed at any one of the stations, it was easy to predict with accuracy the time of its arrival at any given point lying in its path; while the lightning wing of the telegraph bore this knowledge instantaneously to the threatened point.

The first telegraphic warning given thus was sent and bulletined at the several ports along the lakes, November 8, 1870.

The system was soon carried still nearer perfection by the adoption of cautionary signals. The first of these was displayed at Oswego, N. Y., October 26, 1871. Near this time, without any cost to the United States, the Bureau obtained a considerable extension to its area of observation.

In time the Canadian Government made a considerable appropriation to establish a similar system in the Dominion. Professor Kingston, chief of the Meteorological Bureau of Canada, requested of General Meyer an exchange of reports. Arrangements for such an exchange were duly made, and the first reports from Toronto were forwarded to the United States, November 13, 1871. Reports were also exchanged with the director of the Observatory at Montreal. The Canadian reports are made synchronously with those of the United States and in the same cypher. The stations of the Dominion are van-posts to the United States, giving warning of storms moving downward from the north.

By the Act of Congress, approved June 10, 1872, it was made the duty of the Secretary-of-War to provide such stations, signals and reports as might be found necessary for the benefit of the commercial and agricultural interests throughout the country. In response to an invitation made by the Chief Signal Officer, eighty-nine agri-

cultural societies and thirty-eight boards of trade and
chambers of commerce have appointed meteorological
committees to coöperate and correspond with the Signal
Bureau.   The observing stations now number eighty-five.
New stations are constantly being added.   The station at
Mount Washington is six thousand two hundred and
ninety feet above the level of the sea.   Other mountain-
stations are to be established for the purpose of making
observations upon the varying meteorological phenomena
of different altitudes.   These observations are sometimes
made in a balloon.

To obtain reports of observations at sea, to some extent, the coöperation of ship-captains and of officers at
the head of exploring expeditions has been obtained.   A
constant interchange of correspondence is also maintained
with foreign meteorological societies.   Five hundred tri-
daily reports are constantly sent abroad.   The same exchange with foreign governments will be arranged as
soon as possible.

Besides weather-reports, a system of observation on
the changes in the depth of waters in the principal Western rivers is already established.   Great pains are taken
with the reports on this subject, which are made to protect the river commerce from ice and freshets, and the
lower river _levées_ from breakage and overflow.   The observations on the weather embrace those on atmospheric
pressure, temperature, humidity of the air, force, direction and velocity of the wind, and the amount of rain-fall.
For these purposes each station is carefully provided with
appropriate instruments by the central office.

The Signal Corps is composed of a commanding officer
with the rank of brigadier-general, several commissioned

officers, and a certain number of sergeants and enlisted men. The sergeants are required to be proficient in spelling, the ground-rules of arithmetic, including decimal fractions, and the geography of the United States, and are required to write a legible hand. They are examined in these branches before being admitted into the service. They are also subjected to a medical examination, and only men of sound physical condition are accepted. They are regularly enlisted into the military service of the United States, and are subject to the regulations for the government of the army.

Immediately upon admission to the corps, each sergeant is sent to Fort Whipple, in Virginia, opposite Washington, where he is taught the duties of his profession, which are "chiefly those pertaining to the observation, record and proper publication and report, at such times as may be required, of the state of the barometer, thermometer, hygrometer, and rain-gauge, or other instruments, and the report by telegraph or signal, at such times as indicated, and to such places as may be designated by the chief signal officer, of the observations as made, or such other information as may be required." The text-books used in the school at Fort Whipple, are Loomis's "Text Book of Meteorology," Buchan's "Hand Book of Meteorology," Pape's "Practical Telegraphy," and the "Manual of Signals for the United States Army." Instruction in the use of the instruments is also given, and the sergeant is taught to operate the telegraph. He is required to make daily recitations, and when he is considered prepared, by his instructor, he is ordered before an examining board, and is subjected to a rigid examination. If he is found properly qualified, he is assigned to a signal station in some

32

part of the country, and is allowed an enlisted man to assist him in his duties.

There are eighty-five signal stations, located in various parts of the Union, from the Atlantic to the Pacific, and from British America to the Gulf of Mexico. Each of these is supplied with a full set of the instruments necessary for ascertaining the condition of the weather, etc., and is in charge of an observer-sergeant, who is required to make observations three times a day, by means of his instruments, which are adjusted to a standard at Washington. These observations are made at 8 A. M., at 4 P. M., and at midnight. Each post of observation is furnished with a clock which is regulated by the standard of Washington time, so that the observations are taken precisely at the same moment all over the United States.

The result of each observation is immediately telegraphed to the Signal Office at Washington, the Government having made arrangements with the telegraph companies to secure the instant transmission of these messages. The reports are limited to a fixed number of words, and the time of their transmission to a fixed number of seconds.

The signal stations, as at present located throughout the country, have been chosen or located at points from which reports of observations will be most useful as indicating the general barometric pressure, or the approach and force of storms, and from which storm warnings, as the atmospheric indications arise, may be forwarded, with greatest dispatch, to imperilled ports.

The work of the observers at the stations is simple. It is limited to a reading of their instruments at stated times, the transmission to Washington of the results of these observations, and of information of any meteorological facts existing at the station, when their tri-daily report is telegraphed to Washington. The work of the officers on duty at the Signal Office in Washington, is of a higher character, and demands of them the highest skill and perfect accuracy. The reports from the various stations are read and recorded as they come in, and from them, the officer charged with this duty prepares a statement of the condition of the weather during the *past* twenty-four hours, and indicates the changes most likely to occur within the *next* twenty-four hours. These statements are prepared shortly after midnight, and are at once telegraphed to the various cities and important ports of the Union, in time for their publication in the newspapers the next morning.

Professor Maury, of the Signal Office, thus sums up the working of the service:

" Each observer at the station writes his report on manifold paper. One copy he preserves, another he gives to the telegraph-operator, who telegraphs the contents to Washington. The preserved copy is a voucher for the report actually sent by the observer; and, if the operator is careless, and makes a mistake, he cannot lay the blame on the observer, who has a copy of his report, which must be a *fac-simile* of the one he has handed to the operator. The preserved copy is afterward forwarded by the Observer-Sergeant to the office in Washington, where it is filed, and finally bound up in a volume for future reference.

" When all the reports from the various stations have been received, they are tabulated and handed to the officer, (Professor Abbe,) whose duty it is to write out the synopsis and deduce the ' probabilities,' which in a few minutes are to be telegraphed to the press all over the country. This is a work of thirty minutes. The bulletin of 'probabilities,' which at present is all that is undertaken, is made out thrice daily, in the forenoon, afternoon, and after the midnight reports have been received, inspected, and studied out by the accomplished gentleman and able meteorologist, who is at the head of this work. The 'probabilities' for the weather for the ensuing day, so soon as written out by the Professor, are immediately telegraphed to all newspapers in the country who are willing to publish them for the benefit of their readers."

Copies of the telegrams of "Probabilities" are also instantly sent to all boards of trade, chambers of commerce, merchants' exchanges, scientific societies, etc., and to conspicuous places, especially sea-ports, all over the country.

While the professor is preparing his bulletins from the reports just furnished him by telegraph, the sergeants are preparing maps which shall show, by arrows and numbers, exactly what was the meteorologic condition of the whole country when the last reports were sent in. These maps are printed in quantities, and give all the signal stations. A dozen copies are laid on the table with sheets of carbon paper between them, and arrow-stamps strike in them (by the manifold process) the direction of the window at each station. The other observations as to temperature, barometric pressure, etc., etc., are also in the same way put on them. These maps are displayed at various conspicuous points in Washington, e. g., at the War Department, Capitol, Observatory, Smithsonian Institute, and the office of the chief signal-officer. They serve also as perfect records of the weather for the day and hour indicated on them, and are bound up in a book for future use.

Every report and paper that reaches the Signal Office

is carefully preserved on a file, so that, at the end of each year, the office possesses a complete history of the meteorology of every day in the year, or nearly 50,000 observations, besides the countless and continuous records from all of its self-registering instruments.

When momentous storms are moving, observers send extra telegrams, which are dispatched, received, acted upon, filed, etc., precisely as are the tri-daily reports. One invaluable feature of the system, as now organized by General Meyer, is that the phenomena of any particular storm are not studied some days or weeks after the occurrence, but while the occurrence is fresh in mind. To the study of every such storm, and of all the "probabilities" issued from the office, the chief signal-officer gives his personal and unremitting attention. As the observations are made at so many stations, and forwarded every eight hours, or oftener, by special telegram from all quarters of the country, the movements and behavior of every decided storm can be precisely noted; and the terrible meteor can be tracked and "raced down" in a few hours or minutes.

An instance of this occurred on the 22d of February, 1871, just after the great storm which had fallen upon San Francisco. While it was still revolving round that city, its probable arrival at Corinne, Utah, was telegraphed there, and also at Cheyenne. Thousands of miles from its roar, the officers at the Signal Office in Washington indicated its track, velocity, and force. In twenty-four hours, as they had fore-warned Cheyenne and Omaha, it reached those cities. Chicago was warned twenty-four hours before it came. It arrived there with great violence, unroofing houses and causing much destruction.

Its course was telegraphed to Cleveland and Buffalo, both of which places, a day after, it duly visited. The President of the Pacific Railroad has not more perfectly under his eye and control the train that left San Francisco, to-day, than General Meyer had the storm just described.

While the observers now in the field are perfecting themselves in their work, the chief signal-officer is training other sergeants at the camp of instruction (Fort Whipple, Virginia), who will go forth hereafter as valued auxiliaries. It has been fully demonstrated by the signal-officer that the army of the United States is the best medium through which to conduct most efficiently and economically the operations of the Storm Signal-Service. Through the army organization the vast system of telegraphy for meteorological purposes can be, and is now being most successfully handled. "Whatever else General Meyer has not done," says the New York *World*, "he has demonstrated that there can be, and now is, a perfect net-work of telegraphic communication extending over the whole country, working in perfect order, by the signal-men, and capable of furnishing almost instantaneous messages from every point to the central office at Washington.

Away up on G street we see the scientific home of both old and young "Probabilities." We see it from afar, for its high Mansard seems to be stuck full of boys' kites and wind-mills, playing and flying with the winds. It looks like a gigantic play-house. Any mortal, scientific or otherwise, would pause before this ancient house with an infantile roof, and wonder what child of larger growth amused himself playing with all the vanes and anemometers on its roof. It is painted a pearly drab. Fresh and fair, it has the effect of a youthful wig on an old man's head, or a girl's spring hat perched upon the head of a wintry old lady. Inside, the house looks less like a Skimpole in brick, and really takes on a cheerfully serious air.

On the first floor, we find two large offices, and a cozy little library, which stows away one thousand books, or more, on Meteorology, and its kindred themes. In its eastern hall, hang three great weather-maps, on which the state and changes of the weather at all the stations, for the past twenty-four hours, are indicated by established symbols. The second and third stories are occupied by the telegraphic corps. To this the station-work proper is assigned. In one room is the telegraphic apparatus, connecting with the many lines over which weather-reports are received from all over the country. After translation from the cypher into every-day speech, the reports are combined, and the weather-bulletin prepared. On this floor, also, the weekly mail-reports, from the widely-scattered stations, are received, examined, corrected, and filed for future use. Here, tucked away in a little room, we find "Acting Probabilities"—Professor Abbe, the unerring " weather-man," who makes ready the synopsis each day prepared for the Associate Press Agents, Postmasters, etc.

We are sure, also, somewhere, to come in contact with " Old Probabilities " himself, supervising all. Like Professor Abbe, strange to say, he is a young man. General Meyer looks soldierly, and trig. He has fair face and hair, closely-cut whiskers, a rather small head, and a pair of inquiring, wise-looking eyes. The entire top floor is devoted to " local observations, and the gentlemen who play with the wind-mills and high-flying kites, upon the roof." Among the instruments used here, are Hough's barograph, a self-registering tide gauge; Addie's London barometer, which is acknowledged as the standard barometer; Gibbon's electric self-recording anemometer and anemoscope, the inventions of Lieutenant Gibbon, of the Signal-Service. The working force of the office is divided into three reliefs, each of which is on duty eight hours out of the twenty-four.

Any night, one sitting by this window, at a late hour, may see a slender youth shooting past toward the Signal-Service Bureau. This is "Young Probabilities," and he is dressed in white. He is going to forecast the midnight portents for the next day.

The positive advantage of the midnight probabilities is that they relate to the weather of the coming day, and appear at the breakfast table to tell Dick and Dolly what, and what *not* to do. The number of weather-maps issued daily from the central office is 600; from St. Louis 200; from New York 200; from Philadelphia, Chicago and Cincinnati 100 each, making a daily issue of 1,300. All of these are lithographed and printed at the central office.

"During the year 1872, 16,064 weather bulletins and 107,888 maps were issued from the office, and 2,920 reports furnished to the press. The work of the office has been recently extended by the publication of the probabilities based upon the midnight reports, which are widely distributed through the joint agency of the Signal Bureau and the Post-Office Department. Four hundred copies are issued from the Washington office, 1,000 from New York, 1,500 from Cincinnati, 800 from Detroit, 1,500 from Chicago, and 1,000 from St. Louis, and it is expected that the number will be still further increased during the year.

"OLD PROBABILITIES." INSTRUMENT ROOM.

The printed copies are sent by mail to each post-office within a radius of one hundred miles of the several points of distribution, to which the matter is telegraphed from the central office."

"The practical value of the observations on our western rivers is strikingly illustrated by the report of the observer at Memphis, Tenn., who states that captains and pilots of boats generally decide by the reports of the Signal Bureau, on the board on the *levée* at that port, whether the depth of the water above is sufficient to permit them to ascend the upper Mississippi or the Ohio. Before these reports were published, boats arriving during the night lost from six to ten hours in waiting for the telegraphic reports in the morning papers.

"A curious illustration of the legal value of the reports is furnished by the observer at Shreveport, La., who was summoned as a witness in a murder case, as to the condition of the river and the direction of the wind at the time of the supposed murder. These circumstances formed an essential part of the proof in the case.

" Perhaps few people would have supposed that the reports of the Bureau could have any relation to the practice of medicine, yet it is said to be a fact that many intelligent physicians avail themselves of the records of the stations in recommending to their patient an equable and agreeable climate. An observer at Indianapolis reports that several are accustomed to note the readings of the barometer every morning and evening, and one of them assured him that he modified his prescriptions according to barometric changes, believing that such changes have a direct effect upon the condition of his patients.

"Among the most important of the advantages connected

with operations of the Weather Bureau are those arising from the continuous registering of atmospheric conditions, which will enable the scientific inquirer to determine, from the records of the office, the degree of temperature, barometric pressure, moisture of the air, the amount of rainfalls, the direction of the wind at various points for long periods of time. Having these data for various sections, agriculturists, microscopists, and mycologists will be enabled to determine in advance the probabilities as to the prevalence of particular classes of fungi in any district, and thus to indicate the adaptation of such districts for the cultivation of the grains, vegetables, or fruits which are liable to be affected by fungoid diseases.

"The signal service is not without its humorous side, an instance of which is furnished by the observer at Fort Gibson, Indian Territory. The establishment of the station at that point, early last spring, chanced to be followed by a long-continued period of unusually wet and stormy weather. This the Indians attributed to the observer, whom some person of waggish propensities had represented to them as the man that regulated the weather. After bearing their supposed persecution with exemplary fortitude for some weeks, their patience finally gave way, and they held an indignation meeting, at which it was seriously proposed to tear down the station. It was ultimately determined, however, to consult their agent; and upon his representing to them the true state of affairs, they reconciled themselves to the 'weather-witch,' and wisely resolved to wait peacefully for better times."

CHAPTER XLV.

THE NAVY DEPARTMENT—THE UNITED STATES OB-
SERVATORY—THE STATE DEPARTMENT.

Primitive Arrangements—The Navy in Early Days—The Department of the Navy Established—The Secretary's Office—The Navy-Yards and Docks—The Bureau of Construction—The Bureau of Provisions and Clothing—Equipment of Vessels—Bureau of Ordnance and Hydrography—The Naval Observatory—The Bureau of Medicine—Interesting Statistics—The Navy Seventy Years Ago—The " Day of Small Things " —Instructions of the Great Napoleon—Keeping Pace with England— The Glories of Foote, Ferry, Porter and Farragut—Scene from the Observatory—Peeping Through the Telescope—The Mountains in the Moon—The Largest Telescope in the World—Making Mathematical Notes—A Passion for Star-gazing—Casting Horoscopes—Gazing for Pastime—" For the Sake of Science "—The Chronometers of the Government—Comparing Notes—The Test of Time—Chronometers on Trial—The Wind and Current Charts—The Good Deeds of Lieutenant Maury—" The Habits of the Whale "—The Equatorial—A Self-acting Telescope—The Transit Instrument—The Great Astronomical Clock— Telling Time by Telegraph—Hearing the Clock Tick Miles Away— The Transit of Venus—Great Preparations—A Trifle of Half-a-Million of Miles—The Department of Foreign Affairs—The Secretary of State —A Little Secret Suggestion—The Diplomatic Bureau—The Consular Bureau—The Disbursing-Agent—The Translator—The Clerk-of-Appointments — Clerk-of-the-Rolls — The Clerk-of-Authentications — Pardons and Passports—The Superintendent of Statistics.

THE first intention of the fathers of the American Republic was to provide for a chief clerk, under whose direction contracts might be made for munitions of war, and the inspection of provisions necessary for carrying on war by land or sea.

As the maritime warfare of the United States increased in the brilliancy of its victories, the necessity for a separate organization to control its officers, and to provide for the feeding, equipment, and payment of its sea-faring warriors gradually became apparent; but it was not until the thirtieth day of April, 1798, that Congress was sufficiently apprised of this necessity to pass and secure the approval of an "Act to establish an Executive Department, to be denominated the Department of the Navy," and on the twenty-second day of June of the same year an Act was passed granting the franking privilege to the Secretary of the Navy.

Subsequent legislation has dealt more with the *morale* of the navy than with the functions of the department; reference to various other Acts is therefore omitted.

As organized in 1860, the department consists of the following officials: The Secretary; Chief-Clerk; Bureau of Navy-yards and Docks; Bureau of Provisions and Clothing; Bureau of Ordnance and Hydrography; and the Bureau of Medicine and Surgery.

The division of labor is as follows:

Secretary's Office: The Secretary has charge of everything connected with the naval establishment, and the execution of all laws relating thereto is intrusted to him, under the general direction of the President of the United States, who, by the Constitution, is Commander-in-chief of the Army and Navy. All instructions to commanders of squadrons and commanders of vessels, all orders of officers, commissions of officers, both in the navy and marine corps, appointments of commissioned and warrant-officers, orders for the enlistment and discharge of seamen, emanate from the Secretary's office. All the duties of the different Bureaus are performed under the authority of the Secretary, and their orders are considered as emanating from him. The general superintendence of the marine corps forms also a part of the duties of the Secretary, and all the orders of the commandant of that corps should be approved by him.

Bureau of Navy-yards and Docks: Chief-of-the-Bureau, four clerks, one civil-engineer and one draughtsman. All the navy-yards, docks and wharves, buildings and machinery in navy-yards, and everything immediately connected with them, are under the superintendence of this Bureau. It is also charged with the management of the Naval Asylum.

Bureau of Construction, Equipment, and Repair: Chief-of-the Bureau, eight clerks, and one draughtsman. The office of the Engineer-in-chief of the Navy, who is assisted by three assistant-engineers, is attached to this Bureau. This Bureau has charge of the building and repairs of all vessels-of-war, purchase of materials, and the providing of all vessels with their equipments, as sails, anchors, water-tanks, etc. The Engineer-in-chief superintends the construction of all marine steam-engines for the navy, and, with the approval of the Secretary, decides upon plans for their construction.

Bureau of Provisions and Clothing: Chief-of-Bureau and four clerks. All provisions for the use of the navy, and clothing, together with the making of contracts for furnishing the same, come under the charge of this Bureau.

Bureau of Ordnance and Hydrography: Chief-of-Bureau, four clerks, and one draughtsman. This Bureau has charge of all ordnance and ordnance stores, the manufacture or purchase of cannon, guns, powder, shot, shells, etc., and the equipment of vessels-of-war, with everything connected therewith. It also provides them with maps, charts, chronometers, barometers, etc., together, with such books as are furnished to ships-of-war. The United States Naval Observatory and Hydrographical Office at Washington, and the Naval Academy at Annapolis, are also under the general superintendence of the Chief of this Bureau.

Bureau of Medicine and Surgery: Chief-of-Bureau, one Passed-Assistant-Surgeon United States Navy, and two clerks. Everything relating to medicines and medical stores, treatment of sick and wounded, and management of hospitals, comes within the superintendence of this Bureau. .

The following statistics may be interesting to some of our readers: In 1806, the number of seamen authorized by law was 925, to which number 3,600 were added in 1809. In 1812, Congress authorized the President to employ as many as would be necessary to equip the vessels to be put in service, and to build as many vessels for the lakes as the public service required. In January, 1814, there were in actual service seven frigates, two corvettes, seven sloops-of-war, two block-ships, four brigs, and three schooners, for sea, besides the several lake-squadrons, gunboats, and harbor-barges, three ships-of-the-line, and three frigates on the stocks. The whole number of men and officers employed was 13,339, of which 3,729 were able seamen, and 6,721 ordinary. The marine corps, as enlarged in 1814, was 2,700 men and officers. The commissioned naval officers combatant were 22 captains, 18 commanders, 107 lieutenants, 450 midshipmen.

In 1814, Secretary Jones reported to the Senate that
there were three 74-gun and three 44-gun ships building,
six new sloops-of-war built, twenty barges and one hundred and twenty gun-boats employed in the Atlantic
waters, thirty-three vessels of all sizes for sea, afloat or
building, and thirty-one on the lakes. Even in 1813,
the energy of this department had led the first Napoleon to issue the following instructions to his Minister of
Marine :

"You will receive a decree by which I order the building, at
Toulon, at Rochefort, and at Cherburg, of a frigate of American
construction. I am certain that the English have had built a
considerable number of frigates on that model. They go better,
and they adopt them; we must not be behindhand. Those
which you will have built at Toulon, at Rochefort, and at Cherburg, will manoeuvre in the roads, and give us to understand
what to think of the model."

Since then, in defence of the nation, the American
Navy has won victories which placed it in the front rank
of the navies of the world. Mobile, with the names of
Foote, Terry, Porter and Farragut, do not pale before
any victories or names of earth.

A soft midsummer night, we stood upon the roof of
the United States Observatory. Beneath us was Braddock's Hill, where, generations gone, the young surveyor
dreamed ; and stretching far on to its guardian Capitol,
the city which he foresaw—a verity now—its myriad
lights twinkling through the misty distance. To our
right was Georgetown ; beyond Arlington Heights, and
House ; before us the Potomac, winding on to Alexandria ; above us the fathomless heavens, the waxing moon

and silent stars. Professor Harkness moved an axle; the great revolving dome turned round and parted; the great telescope was pointed to the opening, and the broad seam of sky visible between. We mounted the perch, and there were the mountains in the moon! their jagged edges, their yawning craters, yet only for a moment; for earth and moon are swift travellers. In a moment Madame Moon had outstripped our point of vision, and we had to pursue her.

Just before us was the unfinished dome of another observatory, wherein will soon be placed the largest telescope in the world. Beside us two other open domes, and upward pointed telescopes, told of other star-gazers below. We descended. There, in a dimly-lighted room, stood a solitary man peering through a telescope, its divining face uplifted to the narrow field of stars visible through the open dome. Hush! An observation! The solitary man whose face we now see is aged, and his hair white, with swift and silent step turns from his telescope to his desk, to make his mathematical notes.

"He need not do this unless he chooses," says Professor II. "He was long ago promoted above this work. But a man who has formed a passion for star-gazing and observation never gets over it." The room was dim and silent. enough to have been given up to the presence of death. One felt as if some momentous operation were going on. The stars and the star-gazer both were felt. I shrank silent, into a corner, till that horoscope was cast, and the path of that far-away world measured to its minutest fraction. In the opposite wing we found another star-gazer. Was he gazing for pastime? Not at all.

He was gazing for the Government and the sake of science.

Thus, while the nation sleeps, its servants keep watch not only of the weather, but of remotest worlds.

The chronometers belonging to the Government are kept in a room set apart for that purpose. These instruments are purchased by the Navy Department, with the understanding that they are to be tested in the Observatory for one year. They are placed in the chronometer room, and are carefully wound and regulated. They are examined daily, and compared with the great Astronomical Clock of the Observatory, and an accurate record of the movements of each one is kept in a book prepared for that purpose.

The temperature of the room is also examined daily, and recorded. These minute records enable the officers of the Observatory to point out the exact fault of each imperfect chronometer. Thanks to this, the maker is enabled to remedy the defect, and the instrument is made perfect. At the end of the year, the instruments found to be unsatisfactory are returned to their makers, and those which pass the test are paid for. The returned instruments are usually overhauled by the makers, and the defects remedied. They are then sent back for a trial of another year, at the end of which time they rarely fail to pass.

There are usually from sixty to one hundred chronometers on trial at the Observatory, and the apartment in which they are kept is one of the most interesting in the establishment.

The researches connected with the famous " Wind-and Current-Charts," begun and prosecuted so successfully

33

by Lieutenant Matthew F. Maury, whose services were lost to the country by his participation in the Rebellion, are conducted here, and also those connected with "The Habits of the Whale," and other ocean phenomena.

The Equatorial, which is the largest telescope in the Observatory, is mounted in the revolving dome which rises above the main building. It has a fourteen-feet refractor, and an object-glass nine inches in diameter. Its movements are most ingenious, being regulated by machinery and clock-work. Its powers are so great, that it renders stars visible at midday, and, if directed at a given star in the morning, its machinery will work so accurately, that it will follow with perfect exactness the path of the star, which will be visible through it as long as the star is above the horizon. The Meridian and Mural Circles are in one of the rooms below.

The Transit-Instrument is placed in the west wing of the building, under a slit twenty inches wide, extending across the roofs, and down the wall of the apartment on each side, to within four or five feet of the floor. It was made by Estel & Son, Munich, and is a seven-foot achromatic, with a clear aperture of 5.3 inches. The mounting consists of two granite piers, seven feet high, each formed of a solid block of that stone, let down below the floor and imbedded in a stone foundation eight feet deep, and completely isolated from the building. Midway between the piers, and running north and south, is the artificial horizon composed of a slab of granite ten feet long, nineteen inches deep, and thirteen inches broad; it rests on the foundation, and is isolated from the floor, with the level of which the top of it is even, with a space all round it of half an inch. In the middle of this slab, and

in the nadir of the telescope, there is a mortise, nine inches square and ten inches deep, in which the artificial
horizon is placed to protect it from the wind during the
adjustment for collimation, or the determination of the error of collimation of level, and the adjustment for stellar
focus, verticality of wires, and the other uses of the colli-
mating eye-piece.

The great Astronomical Clock, or "Electro-Chrono-
graph" is placed in the same room with the Transit-Instrument, and is used in connection with it to denote side-
real time. It was invented by Professor John Locke, of
Cincinnati, and is one of the most remarkable instruments
in the world. By means of an electrical battery in the
building, the movements of this clock can be repeated by
telegraph in any city or town in the land to which the
wires extend. With the wires connected with it, its ticks
may be heard in any part of the country, and it will record the time so accurately that an astronomer in Port-
land or New Orleans can tell with exactness the time of
day by this clock. It also regulates the time for the city.
There is a flag-staff on top of the dome, upon which a
black ball is hoisted at ten minutes before noon, every
day. This is to warn persons desiring to know the exact
time to examine their watches and clocks. Just as the
clock records the hour of twelve, the ball drops, and thus
informs the city that it is high noon.

The officials of the Naval Observatory have nearly completed the plan of operation for observing the transit of
Venus, which will occur in December, 1874. Eight parties of five persons each will be dispatched; four to stations in the Southern Hemisphere, and the others to the
Northern. Those going south of the Equator will leave

New York next spring in a naval vessel, specially prepared and fitted for their accommodation, while others will probably proceed to their stations by mail-steamer. The posts in the Southern Hemisphere will be on the Kerguelen Islands, Auckland and Van Diemen's Land. In the northern station they will be located at Yokohama, Nangasaki, Shanghai, and near the Siberian border.

After the transit, the observers in the Southern Hemisphere will be collected by a Government ship, transported to Japan, and sent home by mail-steamer. The whole expedition will probably occupy a year at least. Each party will include astronomers and photographer, with a complete equipment and apparatus for obtaining perfect observations and a record of the transit. Prof. Harkness will have charge of the parties and observations in the Southern Hemisphere, and Prof. Newcomb of those in the Northern. The object of the observation, for which Congress has appropriated $150,000, is to determine more accurately the distance between the earth and the sun, and the Professors at the head of the expedition expect to be able to settle the distance within half a million of miles.

In July, 1789, Congress organized a "Department of Foreign Affairs," and placed it in charge of a secretary, who was called the "Secretary of the Department of Foreign Affairs." He was required to discharge his duties "conformably to the instructions of the President," but as his powers were derived from Congress, he was required to hold himself amenable to that body, to attend its sessions, and to "explain all matters pertaining to his province." In September, 1779, Congress changed the title of the department to the "Department of State," and made a definite enumeration of the duties of the Secretary.

The head of the Department is the Secretary-of-State. His subordinates are: an Assistant Secretary-of-State, a Chief-Clerk, a Superintendent of Statistics, a Translator, a Librarian, and as many clerks as are needed. The Secretary receives a salary of $8,000 per annum. He conducts all the intercourse of this Government with the governments of foreign countries, and is frequently required to take a prominent part in the administration of domestic affairs. He countersigns all proclamations and official documents issued by the President. If popular rumor be correct, the Secretaries-of-State have frequently written the messages and inaugurals of the Presidents, and thus have kept those august personages from making laughing-stocks of themselves.

The duties of the office require the exercise of the highest ability, and the Secretaries-of-State have usually been among the first statesmen of our country. The first incumbent of the office was Thomas Jefferson, and the present Secretary is the Hon. Hamilton Fish, of New York.

The Diplomatic-Bureau is in charge of, and conducts all the official correspondence between the Department and the ministers and other agents of the United States residing abroad, and the representatives of foreign powers accredited to this Government. It is in this Bureau that all instructions sent from the Department, and communications to commissioners under treaties of boundaries, etc., are prepared, copied, and recorded; all similar communications received by the Department are registered and filed in this Bureau, and their contents are entered in an analytical table or index.

The Consular-Bureau has charge of all correspondence

and other business between the Department and the consuls and commercial agents of the United States. Applications for such positions are received and attended to in this Bureau. A concise record of all its transactions is ·kept by the clerk in charge of it.

The Disbursing-Agent has charge of all correspondence and other business relating to any and all expenditures of money with which the Department is charged.

The Translator is required to furnish translations of such documents as may be submitted to him by the proper officers of the Department. He also records the commissions of the consuls and the vice-consuls, when not in English, upon which exequaturs are based.

The Clerk of Appointments and Commissions makes out and keeps a record of all commissions, letters of appointment, and nominations to the Senate; makes out and keeps a record of all exequaturs, and when in English, the commissions on which they are issued. He also has charge of the Library of the Department, which is large and valuable.

The Clerk of the Rolls and Archives has charge of the "rolls," by which are meant the enrolled acts and resolutions of Congress, as they are received by the Department by the President. When authenticated copies thereof are called for, he prepares them. He also prepares these acts and resolutions, and the various treaties negotiated, for publication in the newspapers and in book form, and superintends their passage through the press. He distributes through the United States the various publications of the Department, and receives and answers all letters relating thereto. He has charge of all treaties with the Indian tribes, and all business relating to them.

The Clerk of Authentications is in charge of the Seals of the United States and of the Department, and prepares and attaches certificates to papers presented for authentication; receives and accounts for the fees; and records the correspondence of the Department, except the diplomatic and consular letters. He also has charge of all correspondence relating to territorial affairs.

The Clerk of Pardons and Passports prepares and records pardons and remissions of sentences by the President; and registers and files the papers and petitions upon which they are founded. He makes out and records passports, and keeps a daily register of letters received, other than diplomatic and consular, and the disposition made of them. He also has charge of the correspondence relating to his business.

The Superintendent of Statistics prepares the "Annual Report of the Secretary of State and Foreign commerce," as required by the acts of 1842 and 1856.

CHAPTER XLVI

THE GOVERNMENT PRINTING-OFFICE — HISTORY OF A "PUB. DOC."

Another Government Hive — The Largest Printing Establishment in the World — Judge Douglass's Villa — The Celebrated "Pub. Doc." — "Making Many Books" — The Convenience of a "Frank" — The Omnipresent "Doc." — A Weariness to the Flesh — An Average "Doc." — A Personal Experience — What the Nation's Printing Costs — "Not Worth the Paper" — A Melancholy Fact — Two Sides of the Question — Invaluable "Pub. Docs." — Printing a Million Money-Orders — The Stereotype Foundry — A Few Figures — The Government Printing-Office — A Model Office — Aiding Human Labor — Working by Machinery — The Ink-Room — The Private Offices — Mr. Clapp's Comfortable Office — The Proof-Reading Room — The Workers There — The Compositors' Room — The Women-Workers — Setting Up Her Daily Task — A Quiet Spot for the Executive Printing — The Tricks and Stratagems of Correspondents — A Private Press in the White House — The Supreme Pride of a Congressional Printer — Rule-and-Figure Work — The Executive Binding-Room — Acres of Paper — Specimens of Binding — The "Most Beautiful Binding in the World" — Specimen Copies — Binding the Surgical History of the War — The Ladies Require a Little More Air — Delicate Gold-Leaf Work — The Folding-Room — An Army of Maidens — The Stitching-Room — The Needles of Women — A Busy Girl at Work — "Thirty Cents Apiece" — Getting Used to it — The Girl Over Yonder — The Manual Labor System — The Story of a "Pub. Doc." — Preparing "Copy" — "Setting Up" — Making-Up "Forms" — Reading "Proof" — The Press-Room — Going to Press — Folding, Stitching, and Binding — Sent Out to "the Wide, Wide World."

GETTING into the airy little Boundary car at Fifteenth street, it soon brings us far out on H street to another busy Government hive — the largest printing establishment in the world.

As late as 1859, the Government Printing-Office stood upon the suburbs. "Judge Douglass's Villa" was then one of the mile-stones which marked the road thither, leading through grassy fields to the youngest *faubourg* of the capital. Closely-built metropolitan blocks already stretch far beyond it, and the great Public Printing-Office no longer stands on the "edge" of the city.

There is nothing so plenty in Washington, not even Congressmen, as the "Pub. Doc." We see it everywhere, and in every shape. Piles on piles of huge unbound pamphlets, cumber and crowd the narrow lodgings of the average Congressman, waiting the superscription, and formerly the "frank," which was to convey each one to ten thousand dear constituents. They cram every available nook, "up stairs, down stairs, and in my lady's chamber." They are patent receptacles for the dust, which defies extermination. They overflow every public archive, and, falling down and running over, demand that greater shall be builded. Thousands on thousands have no covers, and tens of thousands more are clad in purple and fine linen. The average Public Doc. is a weariness to flesh and spirit. You get tired of the sight—so many, so many! And as for the knowledge which it contains, it may be of infinite value to mankind, but the pursuit of it through endless tables, reports, briefs and statements is a weariness to the soul. I have tried it and know. If I had not, you might never have known how many of these "Pub. Doc's" are printed by the Government, what for, and at what cost.

Well, I will give you a few items in figures, as they appear on the books of the office. Of all executive and miscellaneous documents and reports of Committees, there were printed in the Government Printing-Office, last year, one thousand six hundred and twenty-five copies for the Senate, and one thousand six hundred and fifty for the House, also eight hundred and twenty-five copies of bills and resolutions for the Senate and House each.

Statement showing the cost of Public Printing done in the Government Printing-Office in the year 1872:

Department.	Printing and Paper for same.		Total cost of printing and paper.	Blank books, binding, ruling, etc.	Aggregate cost of printing, paper and binding.
	Printing.	Paper.			
State Department................	$8,445 45	$4,244 40	$12,689 85	$11,416 55	$24,106 40
Treasury Department............	141,933 17	65,809 27	207,742 44	115,119 06	322,861 50
Interior Department............	128,414 53	37,593 76	166,008 29	59,789 71	225,798 00
War Department................	45,171 69	29,049 83	74,221 52	68,184 57	142,406 09
Navy Department................	52,156 77	12,302 95	64,459 72	23,541 68	88,001 40
Judiciary Department...........	38,303 02	1,219 37	39 522 39	2,951 02	42,473 41
Post-Office Department..........	81,301 63	46,817 28	128,118 91	39,247 44	167,366 35
Department of Agriculture.......	9,828 29	7,599 77	17,428 06	4,362 39	21,790 45
Office of Congressional Printer...	1,077 43	185 54	1,212 97	290 45	1,503 42
Total......................	506,631 98	204,772 17	711,404 15	324,902 87	1,036,307 02

Tens of thousands of public documents are published here whose intrinsic value is not worth the paper they are printed on. After witnessing the manual labor expended on them, it is melancholy to reflect that, with it all, they are often less valuable than the unsullied paper would be.

While this is true of an immense number of "bills" and documents, and reports of contested election cases printed in this building, it is equally true that thousands of others are published here which are of extreme value not only to the Government but the world.

It is through the presses of the Government Printing-House that the public is informed what the Government is doing for science and for philanthropy. It prints all the reports of the Smithsonian Institution; Professor Hayden's reports of yearly United States Geological Surveys, including his very interesting and valuable reports on Wyoming, Montana, Nebraska, and the famous Yellowstone Valley. The Medical Reports of the War; Surgeon-General Barnes' Medical and Surgical History of the War; and Chief-Medical-Purveyor Baxter's Report of the Medical Statistics of the Provost-Marshal-General's Bureau; Reports on the Diseases of Cattle in the United States; on Mines and Mining; Postal Code and Coast-Survey Reports; Reports of Commission of Education; of the Commissioner of the United States to the International Penitentiary Congress at London; Reports of the Government Institution for Deaf and Dumb and the Insane, etc.

These make a very small proportion of the really interesting and valuable reports issued yearly by the Government.

When we remember that many of these works are accompanied by copious maps and illustrations, and that the processes of photolithographing, lithographing and engraving are all executed within these walls, you can form some estimate of the value of its services to the country.

The demands made upon it by each single department of the Government is immense. The Post-Office will send in a single order for the printing of one million money-orders; and the other departments cry out to have their wants supplied in the same proportion.

The Stereotype Foundry, under the same roof, long ago vindicated itself in the facts of convenience and economy. The following is a correct exhibit of the product of its labor for the year ending September 30, 1872 :

Value of plates, &c., manufactured, at trade-prices, $35,371 08
Amount expended for labor and material consumed, 16,516 80
                                                    _____
          Net saving to the Government, . . . $18,854 28

The Government Printing-Office, from an external view, is a large, long, plain brick building of four stories, with a cupola in the centre, and flag-staffs at either end, from which the National banner floats on gala days. If we enter from II street, a large open door on the side reveals to us at once the power-press room, with its wheels and belts; its women-workers and its mighty engine. This engine of eighty-horse power, swings its giant lever to and fro, with the accuracy of a chronometer. The boiler which supplies its steam-power is placed in a separate building, so that in case of explosion the danger to human life would be lessened. This boiler also supplies steam for heating the entire main building, and for propelling a " donkey engine," which performs the more menial labor of pumping water.

This is not only the largest, but is one of the model printing-houses of the world. Its typographical arrangements are perfect, and in each department it is supplied with every appliance of ingenious and exquisite mechanism to save human muscle and to aid human labor. In the press-room, stretching before and on either side of the majestic engine, we see scores of ponderous presses, their swiftly-flying rollers moving with the perfect time of a watch—at each revolution clinching the unsullied sheet of paper which, in an instant more, it tosses forth a printed page.

When Benjamin Franklin tugged away at the little printing-press now exhibited at the Patent-Office, an enormous amount of human muscle was needed to perform press-work; but now, without effort and without fatigue, the tireless engine supplies the material power, while women do the work. On the lower floor of the main building we find the wetting room, filled with troughs and all the liquids for dampening the immense supply of paper, beside the hydraulic presses for smoothing it. On this floor also is the "ink room," with its vast supplies of "lamp-black and oil" always ready for the rollers.

Ascending to the second story we come to the business and private offices of the Government Printer—his clerks, telegraph-operators, copy-holders, and proof-readers. Mr. A. M. Clapp, a man of clear intellectual out-look, of benign expression and venerable years, occupies a pleasant parlor for an office, furnished with plain desk, chairs, a mirror, engravings and a Brussels' carpet; it opens into a *suite* of rooms occupied by the Chief-Clerk, the Paymaster and the Telegraph-Operator.

On the other side of the hall, we pass the open door of the proof-reading room. This is comfortably filled with men, young and old. The copy-holder and the proof-reader sit side by side, before a table or desk. The copy-holder has in his hands the original manuscript, from which he slowly reads, while the proof-reader listens, proof-sheets and pencil in hand, erasing each error in print as he detects it, from the lips of the copy-holder.

The proof-reader is paid $26, the copy-holder $24 per week.

Ascending a few steps, we come into the composition room, occupying the central and larger portion of the second story. It contains sixty or more windows, is spacious and well-lighted, and yet, especially in the winter, when the windows are closed and the heat necessarily intense, the fumes from the chemicals render the work very unhealthy, especially to some constitutions. Long rows of double stands reach the entire length of the apartment.

At every one of these stands a patient worker—he must be patient if he is a faithful type-setter. Here are men past their prime, young men, boys and one woman. There have been three. One left her stand for a husband, another—Miss Mary Green—left hers to become the editor of a real-estate journal in Indianapolis, Indiana. The third, in neat calico dress and apron, stands beside a window, "setting up" her daily task. The pay of women in this room is the same as that of the men, viz., $24 per week.

A portion of this floor is shut in for the executive printing. This was made necessary by the fact that before it was done, the country found out what was in the president's message before it was published. Such tricks and stratagems were used by "correspondents" to discover in advance what was in the president's message, that one president had a press, types and workmen brought into the White House, that he might have his message confidentially printed, and "keep it to himself" till he was ready to give it to the world.

The supreme pride of these congressional printers is their "rule-and-figure work." Confused tables of Commercial statistics, astronomical calculations, and abstracts of Government estimates, are marshalled into columns with the precision of a well-trained brigade.

The executive binding-room is fitted up with powerful machines for trimming the edges of books, shears for cutting pasteboard, etc. Here stands a man who does nothing, from the beginning to the end of the year, but cut book-covers. In another room are " ruling machines," exquisite pieces of mechanism, which trace, in a year, acres of paper with the delicate red, blue or black lines which rule with mathematical accuracy the blank-books of the Government.

The third floor is almost exclusively devoted to binding. Some of the most beautifully bound books in the world here issue from the hands of the Government bindery. There are always specimen-copies of scientific and other important reports, which are bound in Turkey morocco, finely marbled and exquisitely gilded. The first volume of the Surgeon-General's Medical and Surgical History of the War, on the day of our visit, was receiving this artistic finish, of delicate gold leaf, stamped upon the rich, dark-green morocco.

The furnaces for heating the stamps, for gilding, are heated by gas, which is considered safer, cleaner and healthier than charcoal. Still the ladies employed in this gold-leaf work suffer for want of air. The hottest summer day the windows have to remain closed, as the lightest zephyr may ruffle fatally the mimosa edges of the tremulous foil.

In the folding-room, on this floor, we find an army of maidens, whose deft and flying fingers fold the sheets, and make them ready for the binder. In the new wing beyond we come into the "stitching-room." Here also the busy fingers and needles of women fly. Long rows of women, chiefly young girls, sit at tables beside wire frames, which hold down and mark the piled-up folios.

Standing beside a young slender girl, she seemed to have the St. Vitus' dance. Every muscle and nerve in her body flew. The very nerves in her face twitched with the quick intensity of her movement; while her fingers stuck the needle and drew the thread with the persistency of a perpetual motion.

"You should be paid good wages to work like this," I said.

"It is because I am paid so little that I have to work like this," she answered, not relaxing an atom.

"How much?"

"Thirty cents a-piece."

"How many can you stitch a day?"

"Well, if I work like this all day, nine."

"But I should think it would kill you to work like this all the time."

"I've been doing it for four years, and I'm not dead yet."

I did not inform her that she looked as if she soon would be, but asked, "Doesn't such constant, quick action give you pain?"

"Yes, in my shoulders, but I've got used to it."

"Does any one else in this room stitch as fast as you do?"

"Only one," said a smiling girl who rested with her needle in her mouth to admire her dextrous companion. "There is only one other who can work as fast as she; it is that girl, over yonder."

There are no drones in this busy hive. The whole routine is based upon the manual labor system. The Government *employé*, man or woman, in the Government Printing-Office, instead of from 9 A. M to 3 P. M., as in all other departments, works from 8 A. M. to 5 P. M., and for smaller pay, proportionally, than is received in any other public Bureau.

Having told you the story of a Dollar, I will now tell that of a "Pub. Doc."—hoping that the next time you feel inclined to kick it for the dust it gathers, and the room it takes up, you will forgive it these misfortunes, for the sake of the many busy and patient human hands which fashioned it.

First, it appears in the room of the Government Printer in the shape of a huge pile of manuscript. Perhaps it is in copper-plate hand, "plain as print;" perhaps, as is more likely, it is a bundle of unsightly hieroglyphics written on "rags and tags" of paper of all sorts and sizes. However it looks, in due time it appears in the composing-room, accompanied with the directions of the Government Printer. It is received by the foreman, who divides it into portions, or "takes," and it is now "copy."

This copy is put in the hands of compositors, who place it, every word and figure, into what is called a "composing stick." When these are filled with the set-up type, they are emptied on wooden boards called "galleys." Here the type is divided into pages, each one of which is tied round with twine so that it can be carried away by a practiced hand. These pages are now arranged on the imposing-stones, either by fours or by eights, or by twelves, as the work is to be printed in quarto, in octavo, or in duo-decimo form. The pages are so regulated that when the

34

printed sheet is folded, they will read consecutively, and they are then wedged tightly in a "chase," or frame of iron. These pages of type thus placed are called "forms."

A rough impression of a form having been printed, it is given to the proof-reader, who, with the copy-holder, notes all errors with printers' marks. The compositor next receives these corrected pages; re-sets all wrong letters with the right ones. When he has finished, he takes a second proof impression, called a revise, which the proof-reader compares with the first one, to see if all the errors have been accurately corrected. This process of revising is repeated four times, when the form is at last ready for the press.

It is then lowered by steam-power into the press-room. The form is laid upon a smooth iron table, called "the bed of the press," where it is treated to a good beating. It is levelled by a block of wood called a planer, and pounded with a mallet, that no aspiring type may stick its nose above its fellows, and mar the perfect level of the printed page.

Meanwhile, a sufficient quantity of paper has been taken from the public store-house to the wetting-room. There it has been dampened, quire by quire, turned and laid in piles under the crushing pressure of an hydraulic-pump, worked by steam-power. When taken out the paper is ready for the press.

The rollers are brought from the room in which they are cleaned and kept, and set in the press. The ink fountain is filled. Sheet on sheet of spotless paper is placed aloft. The young woman who is to "tend" mounts to her perch. The steam-power is applied, and the printing begins.

The maiden takes in her hand a single snowy sheet, and spreads it on the inclined plane before her. It is caught by steel fingers and clutched into the abyss beneath. There it passes swiftly over the pages of type just moistened with ink from the rollers, which were previously coated by revolving cylinders. When the sheet is directly above the type, its flight is for an instant stayed, and by a potent mechanical movement the impression is given, and the sheet is printed. Onward it moves transfigured, till, by the puff of a pair of bellows, it is thrown upon a frame-work which throws it, smooth and fresh, upon a table on the opposite side of the table, and by this time another is on its way. Swiftly almost as thought it is tossed above it. In a briefer time than the process is traced, the unsullied sheets above have been transmuted into printed pages piled upon the table below.

Only one side of a sheet is printed at a time; thus each one goes through the press twice before it leaves the press-room. Each sheet has its own special care. It is carried into the drying-room with a pile. Each one takes its place on a large frame which is pulled out on hanging rollers. When one of these frames is covered with damp sheets it is pushed into the drying-machine, which is made of ranges of steam tubes, which keep a high temperature, while the vapor is carried off by a system of ventilation.

When the sheets are dried, the frames are pulled out, and the printed sheets are taken from them to be pressed. Each printed sheet is put between two sheets of hard, smooth pasteboard, and its high piles of alternate layers are subjected again to the intense power of the hydraulic-press. It comes forth from that embrace smooth, clear, complete.

From the pressing-room the sheets are taken to the fold-ing-room in the third story, conveyed thither by an ele-vator lifted by steam. Here they are folded by the swift hands of girls. Hundreds are busy at it. Looking down the long room and seeing them work is a sight worth quite a journey to see. The folded pages then pass to the fingers of the eager stitchers. These pages are now a book in need of a binding. Thus it comes into the bindery for its black cotton cloak, or its coat of cloth of gold, according to its station and lot in life.

This, good friends, is the story of a Pub. Doc. from its birth to the hour when it starts on its first journey out into " the wide, wide world."

CHAPTER XLVII.

THE SMITHSONIAN INSTITUTION—THE AGRICULTURAL BUREAU.

A Singular Bequest—Strange Story of James Smithson—A Good Use of Money—Seeking the Diffusion of Knowledge—Catching a Tear from a Lady's Cheek—Analysis of the Same Tear—The Attainments of a Philosopher—A brief Tract on Coffee-Making—James Smithson's Will—A Genealogical Declaration—Announcing a Bequest to Congress—Discussions and Reports—Praiseworthy Efforts of Robert Dale Owen—The Bequest Accepted—The Board of Regents—The Plan of the Institution—Its Intent and Object—Changes Made by the Regents—*Ex-Officio* Members of the Institution—"The Power Behind the Throne"—The Secretary—The Smithsonian Reservation—The Smithsonian Building—Its Style of Architecture—Inside the Building—Injuries Received by Fire—Loss of Works of Art—The Museum—Treasures of Art and Science—The Results of Thirty Government Expeditions—The Largest Collection in the World—Valuable Mineral Specimens—All the Vertebrated Animals of North America—Classified Curiosities—The Smithsonian Contributions—Comprehensive Character of the Institution—Its Advantages and Operations—Results—The Agricultural Bureau—Its Plan and Object—Collecting Valuable Agricultural Facts—Helping the Purchaser of a Farm—The Expenses of the Bureau—The Library—Nature-Printing—In the Museum—The Great California Plank—Vegetable Specimens—International Exchanges.

AN Englishman, of the name of James Smithson, gave all his property to the United States of America, to found at Washington, under the name of the Smithsonian Institution, " an establishment for the increase and diffusion of knowledge among men."

But few are aware of the singularity of the bequest. Such a donation, from a citizen of Europe, would be re-

markable under any circumstances; but it was much
more singular coming from an Englishman, endued with
no small degree of pride of country and lineage, if we
may judge from the pains he takes, in the caption of his
will, to detail his descent from the nobility. He is not
known to have ever visited the United States, or to have
had any friends residing here.   Mr. Rush informs us that
he was a natural son of the Duke of Northumberland,
his mother being Mrs. Macie, of an ancient family in
Wiltshire, of the name of Hungerford; he was educated
at Oxford, where he took an honorary degree.   In 1786,
he took the name of James Lewis Macie, until a few
years after he left the University, when he changed it to
Smithson.   He does not appear to have had any fixed
home, living in lodgings when in London, and occasionally, a year or two at a time, in the cities on the continent, as Paris, Berlin, Florence, and Genoa; at which
last place he died.   The ample provision made for him
by the Duke of Northumberland, with retired and simple habits, enabled him to accumulate the fortune which
passed to the United States.   He interested himself little
in questions of government, being devoted to science, and
chiefly to chemistry.   This had introduced him to the
society of Cavendish, Wollaston, and others, advantageously known to the Royal Society in London, of which
he was a member.

In a paper relative to one of the publications of the
Smithsonian Institution, read before a scientific society at
Dublin, it is stated, on the authority of Chambers' Journal, that he had gained a name by the analysis of minute
quantities, and that "it was he who caught a tear as it
fell from a lady's cheek, and detected the salts and other
substances which it held in solution."

In a notice of his scientific pursuits, by Professor Johnson, of Philadelphia, there are enumerated twenty-four papers, or treatises by Smithson, published in the Transactions of the Royal Society, and other scientific journals of the day, containing articles on mineralogy, geology, and more especially mineral chemistry. In the Annals of Philosophy (Vol. 22, page 30) he has a brief tract on the method of making coffee. The small case of his personal effects, which is to be preserved in a separate apartment of the Institution, consists chiefly of minerals and chemical apparatus.

The will indicates a degree of sensitiveness on the subject of his illegitimacy. He starts with a declaration of pedigree :

I, James Smithson, son of Hough, first Duke of Northumberland, and Elizabeth, heiress of the Hungerfords of Audley, and niece of Charles the Proud, Duke of Somerset, now residing in Bentinck street, Cavendish Square, do make this my last will and testament, ...

" To found at Washington, under the name of the Smithsonian Institution, an establishment FOR THE INCREASE AND DIFFUSION OF KNOWLEDGE AMONG MEN."

The bequest was first announced to Congress by President Jackson, in 1835. Long discussions and reports followed ; first, upon the propriety of accepting the trust ; and next, upon the kind of institution to be established ; in the course of which the ablest minds in the country, in and out of Congress, gave expression to their views. The report of Mr. Adams was particularly eloquent. The objection to receiving the bequest was based mainly upon the alleged absence of constitutional power, but partly upon policy.

The discussion as to the kind of institution which wouldl best fulfil the testator's intention, extended through a series of years, and led to almost every possible proposi-- tion. I shall not attempt to give even an outline of these debates, which finally culminated in the adoption of a somewhat mixed scheme, allowing of almost anything.. To Robert Dale Owen, of Indiana, is mainly due the credit of finally pressing the bill to a vote. The Act re-- quired that there be provided a hall or halls for a library,. a museum, a chemical laboratory, necessary lecture-- rooms, and a gallery of art.

The Board of Regents, in whose hands the control of the institution is vested, drew up the following general plan, upon which the operations of the institution have been conducted, this plan being, in their judgment, best calculated to carry into effect the wishes of the founder:

To Increase Knowledge: It is proposed—first, to stimulate men of talent to make original researches, by offering suitable rewards for memoirs containing new truths; and, second, to appropriate annually a portion of the income for particular re- searches, under the direction of suitable persons.

To Diffuse Knowledge: It is proposed—first, to publish a series of periodical reports on the progress of the different branches of knowledge; and, second, to publish occasionally separate treatises on subjects of general interest.

Details of Plan to Increase Knowledge by Stimulating Re- searches: First, facilities to be afforded for the production of original memoirs on all branches of knowledge. Second, the memoirs thus obtained to be published in a series of volumes, in a quarto form, and entitled Smithsonian Contributions to Knowl- edge. Third, no memoir, on subjects of physical science, to be accepted for publication, which does not furnish a positive addi- tion to human knowledge, resting on original research; and all

unverified speculations to be rejected. Fourth, each memoir presented to the institution to be submitted for examination to a commission of persons of reputation for learning in the branch to which the memoir pertains, and to be accepted for publication only in case the report of this commission is favorable. Fifth, the Commission to be chosen by officers of the Institution, and the name of the author, as far as practicable, concealed, unless a favorable decision be made.   Sixth, the volumes of the memoirs to be changed for the transactions of literary and scientific societies, and copies to be given to all the colleges and principal libraries in this country.   One part of the remaining copies may be offered for sale, and the other carefully preserved, to form complete sets of the work to supply the demand for new institutions.   Seventh, an abstract, or popular account, of the contents of these memoirs, to be given to the public through the annual reports of the Regents to Congress.

By Appropriating a Part of the Income, Annually, to Special Objects of Research, under the Direction of Suitable Persons: First, the objects, and the amount appropriated, to be recommended by Councillors of the Institution.   Second, appropriations in different years to different objects; so that, in course of time, each branch of knowledge may receive a share.   Third, the results obtained from these appropriations to be published, with the memoirs before mentioned, in the volumes of the Smithsonian Contributions to Knowledge.   Fourth, examples of objects for which appropriations may be made: 1. System of extended meteorological observations for solving the problem of American storms; 2. Explorations in descriptive natural history, and geological, magnetical, and topographical surveys, to collect materials for the formation of a physical atlas of the United States; 3. Solution of experimental problems, such as a new determination of the weight of the earth, of the velocity of electricity and of light; chemical analyses of soils and plants; collection and publication of scientific facts accumulated in the offices of Government; 4. Institution of statistical inquiries with reference to physical, moral, and political subjects; 5. Historical researches, and accurate surveys of places celebrated in American history ; 6. Ethnological researches, particularly with reference to the different races of men in North America ; also, explorations and accurate surveys of the mounds and other remains of the ancient people of our country.

Details of the Plan for Diffusing Knowledge : First, by the publication of a series of reports, giving an account of the new discoveries in science, and of the changes made from year to year in all branches of knowledge, not strictly professional. These reports will diffuse a kind of knowledge generally interesting, but which, at present, is inaccessible to the public. Some reports may be published annually, others at longer intervals, as the income of the Institution or the changes in the branches of knowledge may indicate. Second, the reports are to be prepared by collaborators eminent in the different branches of knowledge. Third, each collaborator to be furnished with the journals and publications, domestic and foreign, necessary to the compilation of his report ; to be paid a certain sum for his labors, and to be named on the title-page of the report. Fourth, the reports to be published in separate parts, so that persons interested in a particular branch can procure the parts relating to it without purchasing the whole. Fifth, these reports may be presented to Congress for partial distribution, the remaining copies to be given to literary and scientific institutions, and sold to individuals for a moderate price.

By the Publication of Separate Treatises on Subjects of General Interest: First, these treatises may occasionally consist of valuable memoirs translated from foreign languages, or of articles prepared under the direction of the Institution, or procured by offering premiums for the best exposition of a given subject. Second, the treatises should, in all cases, be submitted to a commission of competent judges, previous to their publication.

" The only changes made in the policy above indicated have been the passage of resolutions, by the Regents, repealing the equal division of the income between the act-

ive operations and the museum and library, and further providing that the annual appropriations are to be apportioned specifically among the different objects and operations of the Institution, in such manner as may, in the judgment of the Regents, be necessary and proper for each, according to its intrinsic importance, and a compliance in good faith with the law."

The Act of Congress, organizing the Institution, makes the President and Vice-President of the United States, the Cabinet Ministers, the Chief-Justice of the United States, the Cabinet Ministers and the Mayor of Washington, members *ex officio* of the Institution. The Board of Regents charged with the control of the Institution, consists of the President of the United States, the Mayor of Washington, three Senators of the United States, three members of the House of Representatives, who are *ex officio* Regents, six persons, not members of Congress, two of whom must be citizens of Washington, and members of the National Institute of that city, and the other four citizens of any of the states of the Union, no two of whom are to be chosen from the same state. The Board of Regents make annual reports of their conduct of the Institution to Congress.

The real "power behind the throne" is the Secretary of the Institution, who is executive officer. He has charge of the edifice, its contents, and the grounds, and is given as many assistants, as are necessary to enable him to conduct the varied operations of the Institution. The property of the Institution is placed under the protection of the laws for the preservation and safe keeping of the public buildings and grounds of the City of Washington.

Upon the organization of the Institution, Congress sett apart for its use a portion of the public ground lying westward of the Capitol, and between it and the Potomac River. Fifty-two acres comprised the grant, which was known as the "Smithsonian Reservation." They were laid out under the supervision of Andrew Jacksom Downing. He died while engaged in this work, and hiss memory is perpetuated by a memorial erected in the grounds in 1852, by the American Pomological Society;, and consisting of a massive vase resting on a handsome pedestal, with appropriate inscriptions, the whole being of the finest Italian marble.

The building is situated near the centre of the groundss as they originally existed, the centre of the edifice being immediately opposite Tenth Street west. It is constructed of a fine quality of lilac-gray freestone, found in the new red sandstone formation, where it crosses the Potomac, near the mouth of Seneca Creek, one of the tributaries of that river, and about twenty-three miles above Washington. The stone is very soft at first, and is quarried with comparative ease. In its fresh state, it may be worked with the chisel and mallet; but it hardens rapidly upon exposure to the air and weather, and will withstand, after a time, the severest usage.

The structure is in the style of architecture belonging to the last half of the twelfth century, the latest variety of rounded style, as it is found immediately anterior to its merging into the early Gothic, and is known as the Norman, the Lombard, or Romanesque. The semi-circular arch, stilted, is employed throughout, in door, windows, and other openings.

The main building is 205 feet long by 57 feet wide,

and to the top of the corbel course, 58 feet high.   The east wing is 82 by 52 feet, and to the top of its battlement, 42½ feet high.   The west wing, including its projecting apsis, is 84 by 40 feet, and 38 feet high.   Each of the wings is connected with the main building by a range which, including its cloisters, is 60 feet long by 49 feet wide.   This makes the length of the entire building, from east to west, 447 feet.   Its greatest breadth is 160 feet.

The north front of the main building has two central towers, the loftiest of which is 150 feet high.   It has also a broad, covered carriage-way, upon which opens the main entrance to the building.   The south central tower is 37 feet square, 91 feet high, and massively constructed. A double campanile tower, 17 feet square, 117 feet high, rises from the north-east corner of the main building ; and the south-west corner has an imposing octagonal tower, in which is a spiral stair-way, leading to the summit.   There are four other smaller towers of lesser hights, making nine in all, the effect of which is very beautiful, and which once caused a wit to remark that it seemed to him as if a " collection of church steeples had gotten lost, and were consulting together as to the best means of getting home to their respective churches."

The building was much injured by fire in January, 1865.   The flames destroyed the upper part of the main buildings, and the towers.   Although the lower story was saved, the valuable official, scientific, and miscellaneous correspondence, record-books, and manuscripts in the Secretary's office, the large collection of scientific apparatus, the personal effects of James Smithson, Stanley's Collection of Indian Portraits, and much other val-

uable property were destroyed. Fortunately, the Lii-
brary, Museum, and Laboratory were uninjured. The
fire made no interruption in the practical workings of
the Institution, and in a comparatively short space of
time the burned portions were restored.

The museum occupies the ground-floor, and is the principal attraction to a large portion of the visitors. It iis
a spacious hall, containing two tiers of cases, in which are
placed the specimens on exhibition. Access to the upper
tier of cases is had by means of a light iron gallery,
which is reached by stair-ways of the same materiall.
The Official Guide to the Institution, thus describes the
Museum :

Under these provisions, the Institution has received
and taken charge of such Government collections in min--
eralogy, geology and natural history, as have been made
since its organization. The amount of these has been
very great, as all the United States geological, boundary;,
and railroad surveys, with the various topographical,,
military, and naval explorations, have been, to a greater
or less extent, ordered to make such collections as would
illustrate the physical and natural history features of the
regions traversed.

Of the collections made by thirty Government expedi--
tions, those of twenty-five are now deposited with the
Smithsonian Institution, embracing more than five-sixths
of the whole amount of materials collected. The princi--
ple expeditions thus furnishing collections are the United
States Geological Surveys of Doctors Owen, Jackson, and
Evans, and Messrs Foster and Whitney ; the United States
and Mexican boundary survey ; the Pacific Railroad sur--
vey ; the exploration of the Yellowstone, by Lieutenant

Warren; the survey of Lieutenant Bryant; The United States naval astronomical expedition; the North Pacific Behring's Strait expedition; the Japan expedition, and Paraguay expedition.

The Institution has also received, from other sources, collections of greater or less extent, from various portions of North America, tending to complete the Government series.

The collections thus made, taken as a whole, constitute the largest and best series of the minerals, fossils, rocks, animals, and plants of the entire continent of North America, in the world. Many tons of geological and mineralogical specimens, illustrating the surveys throughout the West, are embraced therein. There is also a very large collection of minerals of the mining regions of Northern Mexico, and of New Mexico, made by a practical Mexican geologist, during a period of twenty-five years, and furnishing indications of many rich mining localities within our own borders, yet unknown to the American people.

It includes also, with scarcely an exception, all the vertebrate animals of North America. The greater part of the mammalia have been arranged in walnut drawers, made proof against dust and insects. The birds have been similarly treated, while the reptiles and fish have been classified, as, to some extent, have also been the shells, minerals, fossils, and plants.

The Museum hall is quite large enough to contain all the collections hitherto made, as well as such others as may be assigned to it. No single room in the country is, perhaps, equal to it in capacity or adaptation to its purposes, as, by the arrangements now being perfected, and denoted in the illustration, it is capable of receiving twice as large a surface of cases as the old Patent-Office hall, and three times that of the Academy of Sciences of Philadelphia.

The Smithsonian Contributions are the work of men residing in every part of the United States. Does an individual think he has the data upon which to base an important discovery, he communicates his plans to the Institution. His suggestions are referred to men in other places, who have made that branch an especial subject of study, and who are not advised of the author's name. If they report favorably upon it, the author is furnished with facilities for pursuing and describing his investigations. Does he want some book not to be found in the library nearest his home? The Institution purchases it and loans it to him, to be returned to the library. His work, when finished, may be invaluable to a scientific man, but is not in sufficient demand to warrant any publisher in issuing it. The Institution prints it, with the proper illustrations, and gives the author the privilege of using the plates in order to print a copyright for sale. Those published by the Institution are sent to every great library and to every scientific body in the world; and those bodies, in return, send back all their publications. Thus, already, a most valuable library has been collected, containing books hardly to be found collected together anywhere else in the United States.

Thirty years ago, the merely nominal sum of $1,000 was, at the instance of the Commissioner of Patents, Hon. H. L. Ellsworth, devoted by Congress for the purposes of Agriculture. For two years before, this patri-

TROPICAL FRUITS.

INSIDE THE GOVERNMENT CONSERVATORY.—WASHINGTON.

otic gentleman had been distributing seeds and plants gratuitously, and for nine years, during his entire term of office, he continued his good work. His successors in the Patent-Office kept up the practice ; but it was not until 1862 that the Department of Agriculture was formally organized.

It now nominally belongs to the Department of the Interior, but in every essential is a distinct department in itself.

The beautiful building built expressly for it, and dedicated exclusively to its uses, terminates one of the finest vistas running out from Pennsylvania avenue. It stands within the grounds of the Smithsonian Institution, surrounded by spacious conservatories and wide blooming gardens—every plant and tree indigenous to our country—from the luxuriant tropical vegetation of the Southern States, to the dwarfed and hardy foliage of our northern borders, may be found in its grounds. A division is devoted to horticulture, and the propagation and acclimatization of new and foreign species. Studies in ornamentation, in the best means of hybridizing, budding, pruning and grafting, in treating diseases of plants and trees, are thoroughly pursued in the experimental gardens. Seeds of new varieties and of superior quality, as soon as they are obtained, are freely distributed throughout the country, on application to the Commissioner of Agriculture.

The Department maintains, at least, one correspondent in every county of the United States, through whom statistics of quality and quantity of crops, and other facts, are forwarded to Washington, to be there distributed by means of the monthly and yearly reports. Spe-

35

cialists are also employed to prepare for these reports instructive articles on suitable topics. Questions from agriculturists are freely answered and the fullest possible information afforded. The purchaser of a farm situated in a region with which he is unacquainted, has only to inquire, and the department will tell him the crops likely to prove remunerative in the special locality, advise him regarding cultivation, and warn him of obstacles to be surmounted, and the best means of overcoming them. A chemist will analyze the soil, report as to its properties and the value of fertilizers to be used thereon; a botanist will give every particular regarding the natures and diseases of plants, and will point out in what families to seek needed products, and what effect a change of soil will have upon them. An entomologist will give advice regarding the insects which destroy vegetation, and as to the best mode for their extermination.

As compared with the other national bureaux, the expense of this department is remarkably small. The cost of the library and museum was $140,000, and the conservatories were built at an expense of but $52,000 more. The library contains a valuable collection of agricultural literature in several languages. Volumes of rare pictures are arranged on long tables; one work, a present from Francis Joseph I., Emperor of Austria, entitled "Nature-Printing," containing representations of ferns so exquisitely printed that it is difficult to believe them unreal.

In the museum are specimens of fibrous products, cereals of this and other countries, stuffed birds and plaster-casts of fruits from all the different sections of the United States, arranged so as to show at a glance the products

THE DOME AND SPIRAL STAIR CASE, RARE PLANTS AND FLOWERS.

INSIDE THE GOVERNMENT CONSERVATORY.—WASHINGTON.

of each region and the specific changes caused by transportation. On the walls of the fruit-cabinet are hung diagrams showing the character and habits of the different insects that prey upon fruit and fruit trees; and in glass cases are preserved the native birds that feed upon destructive insects, and should be protected by the kind treatment of the agriculturist.

The halls of this beautiful building are laid with imported tiles, its ceilings are exquisitely frescoed, and many of its walls hung with wood-paper in rich blending tints. The museum filling the main hall of the second floor is furnished with lofty, air-tight walnut cases.

The great California plank which once stood in one of the underground halls of the Patent-Office, has been wrought into a massive table which stands in the Museum. It is seven feet by twelve, and looks like a billiard-table without the cloth, and is finely polished. The legs and frame are made of Florida cedar. The top of the table is composed of the plank; it looks like solid mahogany without knot or blemish. Much attention has been given to the cultivation of the fibrous grasses which, in China, are woven into fine and durable cloth. Specimens of these grasses, and of the cloth which they make, in its various stages of manufacture, are on exhibition in the cases of the museum. A number of acres have been set apart in the grounds for the cultivation of these grasses. The shade-trees of our entire country are to be represented in these grounds. Already over one thousand four hundred native varieties have been planted.

Through the Smithsonian Institute the Department has been put into communication with leading foreign agricultural societies, and the result has been, not only an exchange of reports, but of almost every known specimen of flower-seeds, seeds of shrubs, vegetables and fruits. The display of flowers in the agricultural grounds is already something wonderful, and soon will equal any like display in the world.

TROPICAL PLANTS AND FLOWERS.

INSIDE THE GOVERNMENT CONSERVATORY.—WASHINGTON.

CHAPTER XLVIII.

OLD HOMES AND HAUNTS OF WASHINGTON.

THE oldest home in Washington is the cottage of David Burns.

You remember *him*, he was Washington's " obstinate Mr. Burns." Well, he owned nearly the entire site of the future Federal city, an estate which had descended to him, through several generations of Scottish ancestors. It was perfectly human and right that he should make the most and best of his precious paternal acres. Long before quarrelling Congresses had even thought of the District of Columbia as a site to contend over as the future Capitol, the cottage of David Burns had gathered on its lowly roof the moss of time.

After the lapse of nearly a century it stands to-day as it stood then, only the moss on its roof is deeper, and the trees which arch above it, cast a longer and deeper shadow. It was a mansion in that day of small beginnings. Yet it is but a low, sharp-roofed cottage, one story high, with a garret; its doors facing north and south, one opening upon the river, with no steps, but one broad flag-stone, now settled deep within its grassy borders. Besides the garret, there cannot be more than four rooms in the house; a dining-room, sitting-room, and two sleeping-rooms; the kitchen, after the Maryland and Virginia fashion of the present day, was probably a detached building. The farm-house no doubt equalled its average neighbors, scattered miles apart across the wide domain of open country.

Before Washington came to negotiate for the future site of the Federal city, the society of Davy Burns was probably composed of plain farmer folk like himself. It was at a later time, when the farmer was transformed into a millionaire, and his only daughter had grown into the fairest *belle* and richest heiress in all the country round, that the long, low rooms of the one-story farm-house were filled with the most illustrious men of their generation.

At the time of the sale of his estate to President Wash-

THE NATIONAL CAPITOL,

As seen from Pennsylvania Avenue.

THE VAN NESS MANSION, AND DAVY BURNS' COTTAGE.

ington, David Burns' only daughter was not more than twelve or thirteen years of age.

With a prescience of her future lot, he proceeded to give her every advantage of education and society at that period accessible to a gentlewoman of fortune. The Rector of St. John's Church, who preached her funeral sermon in 1832, said: "She was placed by her parents in the family of Luther Martin, Esq., of Baltimore, who was then at the height of his fame as the most distinguished jurist and advocate in the State of Maryland, and with his daughters and family she had the best opportunity of education and society."

At eighteen, Marcia Burns returned to the home of her parents — the lowly farm-house on the banks of the Potomac. Then, and at a later day, when the flush and enchantment of youth had fled, the vision of Marcia Burns is altogether lovely. Beside the attractions of fortune, she seemed to possess in an eminent degree the highest qualities of the feminine nature. It was of Marcia Burns that Horatio Greenough wrote:

> "'Mid rank and wealth and worldly pride,
> From every snare she turned aside.
>
> .   .   .   .
>
> She sought the low, the humble shed,
> Where gaunt disease and famine tread;
> And from that time, in youthful pride,
> She stood Van Ness's blooming bride,
> No day her blameless head o'erpast,
> But saw her dearer than the last."

The return of the only child and heiress of David Burns, in the first beauty of young womanhood, soon.

filled the paternal cottage with illustrious society, and with many suitors for her hand and heart. The Keys, the Lloyds, the Peters, the Lows, the Tayloes, the Calverts, the Carrols, all visited here. Washington, Jefferson, Hamilton, Burr, with many other famous then, not forgotten now, were guests at the Burns cottage. Thomas Moore was entertained beneath its roof, and slept in one of the little rooms "off" the large one on the ground floor.

The favored suitor was John P. Van Ness, the son of Judge Peter Van Ness of New York, celebrated as an anti-Federalist, a Revolutionary officer, and a supporter of Aaron Burr against the Clinton and Livingston feud.

When John Van Ness wooed and won Marcia Burns, he was thirty years of age, a Member of Congress from New York, "well-fed, well-bred, well-read," elegant, popular and handsome enough to win his way to any maiden's heart, unassisted by the accessories of fortune, which, in addition, were bountifully his. In Gilbert Stuart's picture we see him with powdered wig and *toupee*, light-brown hair and side whiskers, perceptive forehead, aquiline nose, finely-curved lips and chin, a small mouth, with clear, hazel eyes, which could look their way straight to many hearts.

The portrait of the heiress of David Burns may be seen to-day in Washington, not in any hall of wealth or fashion, but in the Orphan Asylum, which she founded and endowed, to whose children she was a mother. It looks down upon us, a Madonna face, with intellectual, spiritual brow, dewy eyes, and a tender mouth.

Marcia Burns married John P. Van Ness at the age of twenty. Her only brother dying in early youth, she inherited the whole of her father's vast estate. For a few years after her marriage she lived at the old cottage.

Her husband then built a two-story house on the corner
of Twelfth and D streets.   Later, he began the house,
which, still standing in the centre of Mansion Square, is one
of the most unique of all the historic houses of Washington.   It was designed, as were so many famous Washington houses, by Latrobe, and cost between $50,000 and
$60,000 more than half a century ago.   Its marble man-
tel-pieces, wrought in Italy, with their sculptured Loves
and Vestas, still remain, models of exquisite art.   It is
finished with costly woods, and about its door-knobs are
set tiles inlaid with Mosaics.   Its great portico, facing
north, is modelled after that of the President's house.
This stately brick mansion, amid the trees, standing a
few rods back from the Burns' cottage, presents to it an
absolute contrast.

This costly home was ready for the family when the
only daughter and child of General and Mrs. Van Ness
returned, in 1820, from school in Philadelphia.   Thither
Marcia Burns brought *her* daughter.   The bond between
the two is said to have been more intimate and profound
than that of simply mother and daughter.   The daughter was the cherished companion of the mother, who
cultivated an intelligent interest in public affairs, who
loved poetry, and wrote it, and who, amid all the pomp
of wealth and state, never forgot, or allowed her child to
forget, that the fashion of this world passeth away.

Ann Elbertina Van Ness married Arthur Middleton of
South Carolina, son of a signer of the Declaration of
Independence.   But, in November, 1822, in less than
two years from her return from school, this only child,
this youthful bride, this heiress of untold wealth, with
her babe in her arms, was carried to the grave.

From that hour, her mother, Marcia Burns, who, in the world, had never been of it, renounced its vanities entirely. The cottage in which she was born, in which her parents lived and died, nestling under the patriarchal trees, just outside the windows of her stately home, had ever remained the object of her veneration and affection. In this humble dwelling, over whose venerable roof waved the branches of trees planted by her dear parents, she selected a secluded apartment, with appropriate arrangements for solemn meditation, to which she often retired, and spent hours in quiet solitude and holy communion.

The offering to God which she made beside the grave of her daughter, was the City Orphan Asylum of Washington. She became a mother to the children, saved, sheltered, and trained for heaven beneath its roof. She did not wait for these orphans to come to her door. Night and day she sought them out. In her portrait, still hanging in this asylum, she is sitting with three little girls, clinging to her for protection, one with its head in her lap.

Her last sickness was long and painful. A few days before her death, with a few Christian friends gathered about her bed, she celebrated the holy Sacrament; then, with perfect serenity, awaited the final call. Her last words to her husband, placing her hand upon his head, were: "Heaven bless and protect you. Never mind me." She died September 9, 1832, aged fifty years.

She was the first American woman buried with public honors. At the time of her death, General Van Ness was Mayor of Washington. Meetings of condolence were held by citizens in different places. As the funeral procession began to move, a committee of citizens placed a second silver plate upon her coffin, inscribed :—

" The Citizens of Washington, in testimony of their veneration for departed worth, dedicate this plate to the memory of Marcia Van Ness, the excellent consort of D. P. Van Ness.. If piety, charity, high principle and exalted worth could have averted the shafts of fate, she would still have remained among us, a bright example of every virtue. The hand of death has removed her to a purer and happier state of existence; and, while we lament her loss, let us endeavor to emulate her virtues."

The procession passed between the little girls of the Orphan Asylum, who stood in lines, till the coffin was placed at the door of the vault, when they came forward, strewing the bier with branches of weeping-willows, and singing a farewell hymn.

The last earthly house which received the body of Marcia Burns was more magnificent than any she had ever inhabited. Years before, General Van Ness had reared a Mausoleum, which still remains, one of the purest examples of monumental art on this continent. It is a copy of the Temple of Vesta, and could not be built at the present time for a sum less than thirty-four or thirty-five thousand dollars. In the vault, beneath its open dome, Marcia Burns was laid beside her child. This magnificent temple of the dead was recently removed and rebuilt, precisely as it was in the Oak Hill Cemetery, Georgetown. The cells of its deep vault now hold nearly all of the dust left of the Burns and Van Ness alliance.

General Van Ness lived to the period of the Mexican war, passing away at the age of seventy-six, after having enjoyed every honor which the citizens of Washington

could bestow upon him.   He sued the Government of the
United States for violating its contract with the original
proprietors of Washington in selling to private purchasers
lots near the Mall.   Roger B. Taney was his lawyer, and
yet he lost his suit.   He gave an entertainment to Congress every year up to the time of his death, and wonder-
heads declare that his six horses, headless, still gallop
around the Van Ness Mansion, in Mansion square, annually, on the anniversary of that event.

Some twenty-five years ago, this old mansion and estate
was bought by its present proprietor, Thomas Green, Esq.,
a Virginia gentleman.   The last time that it came prominently before the public, was during the assassination con-
spiracy, when an irresponsible newspaper sent the report
flying, that its great wine-vault was to have been used as
a place of incarceration for Mr. Lincoln, before he was
conveyed across the river.   In those mad days no magnate waited for proof, and the result was that Mr. Green
and his gentle wife, who,—as her husband remarked—
"was as innocent as an angel," were shut up in our small
bastile, the old Capitol prison.   Here both were held for
more than thirty days, when after having vindicated their
honor beyond the possibility of reproach, the Government somewhat ashamed of itself, let them depart to the
shelter of their patriarchal home.

On buying the estate, Mr. Green with that veneration
for old, sacred associations which pre-eminently marks
the Virginian,—instead of tearing down the old Burns'
cottage as "nothing to him" or as a blot upon his fair
estate, went immediately to work to preserve it.   Without changing it in any way, he re-roofed it, made it rain-
proof, whitewashed it, and left it with its trees and mem-

ories. What Mr. Green has preserved, let not the Board of Public Works destroy! In this case, gentlemen, let your "grade" go—and the cottage of "the obstinate Mr. Burns," the first owner of this great Capital, and the oldest house in it—remain.

It was a June evening that we last passed the gate and the lodge of the old Van Ness estate, at the foot of Seventeenth street. The high brick-wall which shut in this historic garden, is mantled with ivy and honeysuckle. Old fruit trees, apple, pear, peach, apricot, plum, cherry, nectarine, and fig trees, all in their season, lift their crowns of fruitage to the sun within these old walls. Following a winding avenue, we pass through grounds above which gigantic aspen, maple, walnut, holly, and yew trees cast deep, cool shadows in the hottest summer days. As we approach the house we see that the drive before the northern portico is encircled with an immense growth of box. Before the low windows of the eastern drawing-room, stretch wide *parterres* of roses of every known variety. In June it is literally a garden of roses— and the early snow falls upon them, budding and blooming still in the delicious air. Oranges ripen on the sunshiny lawn which surrounds the house, and masses of honeysuckle which climb the balustrades of the southern portico pervade the air with sweetness, acres away.

This southern portico used as a conservatory in the winter, is a counterpart, on a smaller plan, of the south veranda of the President's house. It has the same outlook only nearer the river. To the right, the dome of the observatory swells into the blue air, and, before it, the Potomac runs up and kisses the grasses at its feet. Lovers' walk, shaded by murmuring pines, as such a walk should be, runs on through the grove down to a mimic lake, where, in mid-water, is a tiny island with shadowy trees and restful seats.

I stray down this walk with Alice,—golden-haired and poet-eyed. We wander across under the patriarchal trees and come out on the river-side of the old Burns cottage. Its sunken door-stone, its antique door-latch, its minute window-panes, all are just the same as when Marcia Burns, beautiful and young, received within its walls her courtly worshippers; just the same as when Marcia Burns, smitten and childless, knelt alone by its desolate hearth, to commune with the God and Father of her spirit, and to dedicate herself to His service for ever.

Beside us, eight lofty Kentucky coffee-trees soar palm-like towards the sky. Through their clustering crowns the full moon peers down upon us; upon the cottage, so fraught with the memories of buried generations; upon the white walls of the mansion, so rich in recollections of the illustrious dead of a later past,—and she transfigures both cottage and hall in her hallowing radiance, as, with lingering steps, I say to gentle host and hostess, and to Alice,—golden-haired and poet-eyed,—" Farewell."

The Octagon House, now used as an office by the Navy Department, stands on the corner of Eighteenth street and New York avenue. It was built near the close of the last century by Colonel John Tayloe, one of the most famous men of his time, and is still owned by his descendents. Colonel Tayloe was a friend of Washington, who persuaded him to invest some of his immense fortune in the new Federal city. He was educated at Cambridge,

England, and during his life in Washington, four of his former class-mates were sent as Ministers to the United States.

Colonel Tayloe had an income of seventy-five thousand dollars a year. He had an immense country estate at Mount Airy, Virginia, and both there and in Octagon House, entertained his friends in princely state. He kept race-horses, and expended about thirty-three thousand dollars every year in new purchases. He owned five hundred slaves, built brigs and schooners, worked iron-mines, converted the iron into ploughshares,—and all was done by the hands of his own subjects. After the burning of the White House, Mr. and Mrs. Madison lived in the Octagon House for a year, and held these elegant draw-ing-rooms and gave costly dinners. The Octagon House has long had the reputation of being haunted. "It is an authenticated fact, that every night, at the same hour, all the bells would ring at once. One gentleman, dining with Colonel Tayloe, when this mysterious ringing began, being an unbeliever in mysteries, and a very powerful man, jumped up and caught the bell wires in his hand, but only to be lifted bodily from the floor, while he was unsuccessful in stopping the ringing. Some declare that it was discovered, after a time, that rats were the ghosts who rung the bells; others, that the cause was never dis-covered, and that finally the family, to secure peace, were compelled to take the bells down and hang them in dif-ferent fashion. Among other remedies, had been previ-ously tried that of exorcism, but the prayers of the priest who was summoned availed nought."

In 1805, Washington city was an old field, covered everywhere with green grass and many original trees of the forest. There were no streets made. The President's house was unfinished, and Lafayette square, opposite, was still called the "Burns Orchard." One corner of it was used as a burial-ground of St. John's Church. Where General Jackson's statue is now rearing in the air on a frantic horse, then stood a clump of cherry trees, under which John Gardner's school-boys used to make themselves sick eating green cherries. As the boys of this school never allowed the green apples or any other fruit in this orchard to ripen, and for that reason were in a perpetually griped condition all summer, their school-master, much against their wishes, and that of the militia who paraded under the trees, obtained permission of President Jefferson to cut the orchard down.

As an open "reservation," the square was long a landmark of the departed joys and stomachaches of the boys of a former generation. In course of time Dowing laid out the graceful walks and grassy plats which make it now a perfect *bijou* of beauty. He planted the trees which to-day arch high in mid-air, and spread so deep and grateful a shade above the weary multitudes who seek rest and a touch of nature's healing upon its wayside seats. It is altogether beautiful and soul and sense-reviving, in the spring, when its many-flowering shrubs pervade the air with fragrance, and no less delicious in the autumn, when it flames a mosaic of gorgeous landscape set in the dusty square, its many tinted leaves warm and red as gems raining about your feet.

August 11, 1848, a resolution of Congress authorized the Jackson Monument Committee to receive the brass guns captured by Jackson at Pensacola, to be used as material for the construction of a monument to that distinguished patriot. Clark Mills was appointed to execute the statue. President Fillmore chose its site in the centre of the square, opposite the President's House, where it was inaugurated January 8, 1853, the anniversary of Jackson's victory at New Orleans, in 1815. As I am inadequate to describe such a work of art, I give the guide-book description :—

" General Jackson is represented in the exact military costume worn by him, with cocked-hat in hand, saluting his troops. The charger, a noble specimen of the animal, with all the fire and spirit of a Bucephalus, is in a rearing posture, poised upon his hind feet, with no other stay than the balance of gravity, and the bolts pinning the feet to the pedestal. The work is colossal, the figure of Jackson being eight feet in height, and that of the horse in proportion. The whole stands upon a pyramidal pedestal of white marble, seven feet in height, at the base of which are planted four brass six-pound guns, taken by the hero at New Orleans. The cost of the statue to the Government, including the pedestal and iron railing, was $28,500."

Around this peaceful spot, where the militia beat their *reveille,* and the school-boys munched green apples and cherries, and gathered nuts in days of yore, human life in all its passion of pleasure, tragedy and pain, now pressed close. One of the saddest tragedies of the square is associated with the Decatur House. It is said that three powers rule the world—Intellect, Wealth, and Fame. Wearing this triple crown, Stephen Decatur came home to the wife whom he worshipped, saying: "I have gained a small sprig of laurel, which I hasten to lay at your feet." He bought the lot on the corner of Sixteenth and H streets, and employed Latrobe to design a commodious and elegant mansion. In this house the

home-life of Decatur begun with the most dazzling aug-
uries. Its walls were hung with the trophies of his
glory: the sword presented by Congress for burning the
Philadelphia; another from Congress for the attack on
Tripoli; a medal from Congress for the capture of the
Macedonian; a box containing the freedom of New York;
the medal of the Order of Cincinnati; swords from the
States of Pennsylvania and Virginia, and the City of
Philadelphia; and services of plate from the cities of
Baltimore and Philadelphia. All these were but leaves
on the sprig of laurel which he laid at the feet of the
beloved one.

Mrs. Decatur was accomplished, intellectual, and pas-
sionately devoted to her heroic husband. Not yet forty-two
years of age, he had scaled the very summit of fame, and
already rested after the toilsome ascent. His mornings
were given to the fulfilment of his duties as Navy Commissioner, and his leisure was spent with the best in the
society of Washington, made up of the highest in the
land for station, character, and intelligence.

The *salon* of Mrs. Decatur, which, to-day, is larger
than can be found in any other private house in Washington, was a focal point for all that was dazzling in the
social life of the capital. There are those still living
who remember the brilliant assembly gathered here only
the night before his death. Mrs. Decatur, who had no
prescience of the anguish awaiting her, at the request of
friends, played on the harp, on which she was a skilful
performer. Commodore Decatur, conscious of the por-
tentous appointment which awaited him the coming morning, abated not one jot of the wonted charm of his manner,
staying in the parlors till the last guest had gone.

At dawn of the next day he arose, left the sleeping wife and household, crossed Lafayette Square, walked to Beale's Tavern, near the Capitol, breakfasted, proceeded to Bladensburg, where the duel was fought at nine o'clock. Mortally wounded, he was brought back to his happy home, where he died the night of the same day. He tried to avert the duel, saying to Commodore Barron: " I have not challenged you, nor do I intend to challenge you ; your life depends on yourself."

He was followed to the grave by the President of the United States and the most illustrious men of his time. " The same cannon which had so often announced the splendid achievements of Decatur now marked the periods in bearing him to the tomb. Their reverberating thunder mournfully echoed through the metropolis, and also vibrated through a heart tortured to agony." A vast concourse of citizens, marching to a funeral dirge, followed the dead hero to Kalorama.

Mrs. Decatur, within the walls of her home, for three years shut herself away from all the world. Afterwards the Decatur house was rented to Edward Livingston, then Secretary-of-State. Here Cora Livingston was married to Dr. Barton, who is remembered not only as a diplomat, but as the editor of an extensive and valuable collection of Shakespeare's works. Here Sir Charles Vaughan, the British Ambassador, lived, and by his wit and affable manners and hospitality, made the house again a centre of elegant society. Martin Van Buren, while Secretary-of-State, occupied the Decatur House. The brothers King, both Members of Congress from New York, lived here. One was the father of the much-admired Mrs. Bancroft Davis, a portion of whose girlhood

was passed under its roof. Mr. Orr, while Speaker of
the House, was its tenant, and dispensed hospitalities to
thousands in its grand *salon*. From Madison to Grant,
every President has been entertained within its walls.

Madame de Staël says: "The homes and haunts of
the great ever bear impress of their individuality."
Jean Paul Richter declares: "No thought is lost." If
this be true, how affluent of eloquence, wit and mirth
these historic halls must be! They are ready to revive more than the splendor of past days. For a number of years the house, rented to the Government, has
been used for offices. But within twelve months it has
been purchased by General Edward Fitzgerald Beale,
who has rehabilitated it, without remodelling it, for his
own family residence. The ample halls and grand *salon* remain unchanged in proportions, while fresh frescoes,
historic devices, French windows and marble vestibule,
give to the antique mansion the aspect of modern elegance.

General Beale is the grandson of Commodore Thomas
Truxton, one of the first six captains appointed by General Washington in the early navy to guard the commerce of the United States. Commodore Decatur was a
favorite midshipman and lieutenant under Truxton; and
the grandson of his early commander, in this home of
Decatur's heart, is now preserving every possible souve-
nir of the sea. The Decatur mansion has passed into
fitting hands. Its present owner made his gallant record
under Commodore Stockton, and, in imperilling his life
for others, has maintained the illustrious escutcheon
transmitted him by his ancestors. When the gay season
begins, light and music, warmth and cheer, wisdom,

beauty and grace will again make these old halls glad. "Memnon-like, the old walls will again give forth sweet sounds." A new generation will repeat the festivities of the generation gone to dust.

A few rods further on we came to the famous Stockton-Sickles House. Just now it shrinks, shabby and small, below its lofty modern neighbors. It is a white stuccoed house, two stories, with basement and attic, with high steps and square central hall, after the fashion of old times. It was called the Stockton House because Purser Stockton, who married a relative of Commodore Decatur, owned and lived in it. Afterwards, it was occupied by Levi Woodbury, the father of Mrs. Montgomery Blair, who lived here both while Secretary of the Treasury and of the Navy. It was also rented by Mr. Southard, of Georgia, the father of Mrs. Ogden Hoffman. When Mr. and Mrs. Sickles lived in it, it is said that the trees in Lafayette square were so small that the waving of a handkerchief from one of the windows could be distinctly seen at the club house opposite, on the other side of the square. This was the signal used between the first betrayed, then tempted and ruined wife, and the man of the world, to whom seduction was at once a pastime and a profession.

The trunk of the tree against which Key fell when shot by Sickles, may still be seen near the corner of Madison place and Pennsylvania avenue.

A few steps further on, in the middle of the block, stands the famous club-house which has witnessed more of the vicissitudes and tragedy of human life than any other house on the square, excepting, perhaps, the White House. The Club-House is a large, square, three-storied

red brick house, built for his own use by Commodore
Rogers, of the Navy.   After his death, it became a fashionable boarding-house, then a club-house.   To one of
its rooms Barton Key was borne after being wounded by
Sickles.   While Secretary-of-State, Mr. Seward occupied
the house for eight years, and during that time it was the
centre of most elegant hospitality.   In the assassination
of Mr. Seward, it witnessed its crowning tragedy.   In its
rooms Mr. Seward and his son languished for months,
while slowly recovering from the almost death-blows
dealt by Payne.

After their recovery, the lovely and only daughter of
Mr. Seward here slowly faded from earth.   This young
lady was, in a very remarkable degree, the chosen companion and confidante of her father.   She not only sym-
pathized profoundly in his pursuits, she shared them with
him.   I believe she witnessed, with unavailing cries, the
attempted assassination of her father.   At least, she
never recovered from the shock received at that time.
With her, passed from earth one of the loveliest spirits
which ever shed its pure light upon the social life of the
Capital.   Her death left Mr. Seward wifeless and daugh-
terless.   With everything to live for, she met death with
perfect faith and resignation.   Her beautiful life, with
her triumphant passage through death to a life still more
perfect, remained with him to his last moment the most
precious memory of her illustrious father.

With all its burden of tragedy and pathetic death,
with the departure of the Sewards, the old house did not
take on the shadow of gloom.   Its parlors never witnessed
gayer or more crowded assemblies than thronged them
the next winter, when occupied by General Belknap, the

Secretary-of-War. This was but for a single season. Another winter dropped its earliest snows on the new-made grave of the young wife and mother, the memory of whose gentle face and graceful presence and tender spirit, will only fade from the Capital with the present generation. It was the last flaming up of festivity in the old house. It has never been gay since Mrs. Belknap died.

The next year it waned into a boarding-house. Even that was not successful. People of sensibility do not wish even to board in a house so haunted with tragic memories of human lives. The house is now used for Government purposes. Its site is so superlative ; central to the most interesting objects of Washington, and facing the waving sea of summer-green in Lafayette square. In the march of change its place will soon be filled by some soaring Mansard mansion of the future. But when every brick has vanished, the memories of the old club-house and Seward mansion will survive while any chronicle of Washington endures.

Next to it stands the house of Mr. Benjamin Ogle Tayloe, a descendant of Mr. Tayloe, of Octagon House memory. Mr. and Mrs. Tayloe have occupied this stately house for many years. The reminiscences of Washington published by Mr. Tayloe for private circulation are among the most entertaining records ever written of the Capital.

Next to the Tayloe House, on the corner of Fifteenth and H street, stands the Madison House, in which, as a widow, Mrs. Madison so long held her court. No eminent man retired from service of the state ever had more public recognition and honor bestowed upon him by the

Government he had served than did this popular and ever-beloved woman. On New Year's day, after paying their respects to the President, all the high officers of the Government always adjourned to the house of Mrs. Madison, to pay their respects to *her*. In her drawing-room political foes met on equal ground, and for the time, public and private animosities were forgotten or ignored.

"Never" says "Uncle Paul" her colored servant, who had lived with her from boyhood, and who still lives, "never was a more gracefuller lady in a drawing-room. We always had our Wednesday-evening receptions in the old Madison House, and we had them in style." Mrs. Madison's turbans are as famous in Washington to-day as her snuff box. It is said that she expended $1,000 a year in turbans. She wore one as long as she lived—long after it had ceased to be fashionable. "These turbans were made. of the finest materials and trimmed to match her various dresses." Uncle Paul tells of one of her dresses of purple velvet with a long train trimmed with wide gold-lace with which she wore a turban trimmed with gold-lace and a pair of gold shoes. With a white satin dress, she wore a turban spangled with silver, and silver shoes." She sent to Paris for all her grand costumes. Her tea-parties and her "loo" parties are still dwelt upon with loving accents by her admiring contemporaries who still linger on the borders of a later generation.

After the death of Mrs. Madison, her house was purchased and occupied for many years by Commodore Wilkes, who captured Mason and Slidell. It still stands in perfect preservation and is rented year by year to chance tenants. Two years ago, it was occupied by the Secretary-of-War and its drawing-rooms again thronged with brilliant crowds.

On an opposite corner facing Vermont avenue we see
the brown walls, floating flag and gay equipages of Arlington Hotel.   Beside it, on the corner, is the red-brick
house with white shades, and Mansard roof, where, amid
rare pictures, books, works of art, and choice friends,
lives Charles Sumner.

A few rods further on, on the corner of H and Sixteenth streets, facing Lafayette square and peering out
toward the old Decatur mansion, we came to "Corcoran
Castle."   It is an imposing house, built of red-brick with
brown facings, divided from the street by an iron railing,
painted green, tipped with gilt, with an immense garden
at the back, covering an entire square.   The house is now
owned and has been greatly beautified by W. W. Corcoran, the famous Washington banker, but has had many
other occupants.   It was once owned by Daniel Webster
to whom it was presented by leaders of the party whom
he had served.   Great astonishment was expressed when
he afterwards sold it.   But as Daniel Webster was ever
an impecunious man, he probably was compelled to part
with his palace as Sheridan was so often compelled to part
with his.

Before and during the Mexican war, the British Minister, Mr. Packingham resided in it, kept open house and
made his parlors the rendezvous of the young people.   A
lady tells "of the young officers she saw taking part in
those brilliant life-pictures, who in a few short weeks
were lying with rigid, upturned faces, on Mexican battle-
fields."   The house was at one time occupied by General Gratios, whose daughter married Count Montholon.
During the war, when Mr. Corcoran resided abroad, he
gave his house in charge of the successive French Minis-

ters. During that time Madame de Montholon came back to the former home of her father. Within, the house is a delight to the eyes. Its picture-gallery is one of the finest in America, and holds amid many other treasures of art, Powers' Greek Slave. The whole house is a gallery of costly furniture and works of art.

In this home of grace, "Maggie Beck" a Kentucky *belle* of three seasons ago, who married a nephew of Mr. Corcoran, "received" her friends for the last time. The bride of a month, she was already the bride of death, and in her marriage robe, and veil and gleaming jewels, white, cold, and silent, she received the tears and lamentations poured upon her by agonized hearts. After an absence of years, hither Mr. Corcoran bore the dead body of his only child, and here, widowed and childless, shut himself in alone with his dead. The children of this daughter now make music in these stately halls. Age and childhood make the family life of Corcoran Castle.

A high brick wall shuts in this garden from the city. Its inner side is completely hung with ivy. Immense *parterres* of roses and flowers of every tint, conservatories, a *croquet*-ground, rustic summer-houses, fountains, a fish-pond, forest trees shading a closely-shorn lawn, all these make a garden perfect in seclusion and beauty in the very heart of the Capital.

One of the most famous of suburban Washington haunts is Kalorama, literally like Bellevue—"beautiful view." The ruins of Kalorama stand on a forest-shaded slope, a little more than a mile, perhaps, from the President's house. From Twenty-first street it is approached by an avenue planted closely on either side by locust trees. Under their green arch the titled and famous of an earlier generation passed; but in our own memory it is associated with the pestilence-laden ambulance, for during the war beautiful Kalorama was a small-pox hospital.

Below Kalorama, Rock Creek winds its shining thread between the hills. Looking up the creek, we see grassy glades, along which cattle feed, and a picturesque valley walled by embowering woods. Climbing a green, tree-shaded slope, we reach a *plateau* from which we look down upon two cities, Rock Creek still winding its silvery thread between. Opposite is Analoston Island, beyond the Virginia shore, and Arlington House peering through the trees of its crowning hill.

To the left lies Washington, guarded by the Capitol; before us, crumbling amid its guardian oaks, the ruins of Kalorama. It was built by Joel Barlow, once of "Columbiad" fame, in 1805. After spending several years abroad, where he espoused the cause of the French Republic, he returned to his own country and built a castle for himself overlooking its Capital. Before this, his "Columbiad" had been published with fine engravings, whose execution was superintended by Robert Fulton. On this poem he had spent the labor of the best years of his life. He believed without a doubt that it would be the national poem of the future. A copy of it graced every drawing-room. In what drawing-room is it visible now! Alas! for "Fame!"

Joel Barlow and Robert Fulton were intimate friends. In 1810 Fulton visited Kalorama, and it is declared that some of his first ventures in navigation were launched upon Rock Creek. History records that Fulton tested his torpedoes during this visit to Washington, and persuaded Congress to consider his navigation schemes. Mr. Barlow went to France as American Minister in 1812. He was taken ill while on his way to meet Napoleon, who had invited the American Minister to an interview with him at Wilna. Mr. Barlow died at Cracow, in Poland, where he solaced his death-bed by dictating a poem full of withering expression of resentment toward Napoleon for the hopes he had disappointed.

Mr. Barlow bequeathed Kalorama to his niece Mrs. Bomford. A romantic story is told of this lady. While with her first husband (whose name has deservedly perished) on the frontier, he being an officer in the United States Army, she was captured by Indians. For some reason known only to himself, her husband did not take the trouble to pursue her; but Lieutenant Bomford did. He organized a force of citizens and soldiers, and sallied forth in quest of the lady. He found her, and she rewarded him by marrying him after she had obtained a divorce from her indifferent lord.

Colonel and Mrs. Bomford resided at Kalorama for many years. During their residence here the Decatur-Barron duel took place, and the body of Decatur found a temporary resting-place in the tomb of the Barlows. This vault is still visible at the top of a small hill near the main entrance to the Kalorama grounds. With its low sharp roof and its plastered walls, it looks like an old spring-house. It bears an inscription to the memory of Joel Barlow, " poet, patriot, and philosopher," although he was buried, when he died, at Cracow, Poland.

When Mrs. Decatur left the Decatur mansion, she retired to Kalorama. And years after her husband's death she made it famous by the elegant entertainments which she gave there. There are gentlemen still in public life in Washington, who recall the elegant and costly dinners given by this lady at Kalorama.

This beautiful historic spot is now owned by a family named Lovett, who, it is said, intend in time to rebuild it.

Following Seventh street a mile or two beyond the city limits, we come to an unpretending country house, at some distance back from the road, surrounded by lawns, gardens and groves. It is a long, low house, before which runs a piazza, and behind which bubbles a famous spring. If it is morning, a pair of saddle-horses stand waiting their riders before the door. Presently they come out together, an ancient knight and lady, ready for a ten-mile ride on horseback. Eighty years and more have set their seal on the brows of each. The gentleman's frame bears the marks of extreme age; it is attenuated, yet shows few signs of decrepitude. His skin may look like parchment, but the eyes burn with unabated fires. The lady is tall, straight, and stately, with dark, keen eyes, and head erect, as befits the mother of the Blairs. She has a son more than sixty years of age, and yet she seems not to have lived so many years herself. More than fifty years ago, this couple, by wagons and on horseback, came through the woods from far Kentucky to seek their fortune in the new capital city. The struggling village has grown into a metropolis; sons and daughters to the fourth generation have blessed them; they have done their share in the making and unmaking of presidents and men in power; they have received their full meed of honor as well as of blame; their name has grown to fame; they have long outstripped the allotted years of man, and here they are, ready for their eight or ten miles' horseback ride this morning. This is Francis P. Blair, Senior, and his wife, and this their country home. Honored among suburban Washington haunts is " Silver Spring."

Almost any sunny day this ancient knight and lady, mounted on their two solid steeds, with a green bough in their hands in lieu of riding whips, she with a stately calash upon her head, may be seen jogging along Pennsylvania avenue toward the stately home of Montgomery Blair, which faces the War-Department. For more than two generations Mr. Blair has been a power in the land. He has had more or less to do with the making and unmaking of every president since the days of Jackson. The Nestor of the Washington Press, he was a powerful supporter of "old Hickory," and to-day retains, undiminished, the living love now bestowed upon the friend so long buried in the past. Mr. Blair, leaning on his long staff, may often be seen wandering through the unbowered ways of Lafayette square, which he so well remembers as the Burns' orchard. Here he never fails to gaze upon the bronze equestrian statue of his friend. Others may laugh at the pivoted horse, but " old Frank Blair " pronounces the statue to be the best likeness of Jackson now extant.

With the exception of the Burns' house, the oldest houses in the city are found on Capitol Hill. Here are houses whose antiquity alone make them remarkable amid the houses of America. For example, here is the old Duddington house, built by Daniel Carroll, who you may remember was so angry with Major L'Enfant for tearing down his first abode, in the way of a beloved street. The

present house, built at that time, stands jus in front of
the old site.   Going south-east from the Capitol, the tall
forest trees of Duddington are soon visible.   So completely do they screen the house, nothing is seen of it
until the visitor comes to the large entrance gate, directly
in front of the dwelling.   It is a double house, built of
red brick, with wings stretching out on either side.   The
grounds are beautiful in their very wildness, presenting
all the attributes of a primitive forest.   Outside is a
spring with an ancient covering of brick.   " This spring
was once a well-known resort, on the Duddington farm,
for the school-boys of the neighborhood, one of whom, an
aged man now, told me how pleasantly he used to pass
his noon recess there."

Nearly all the buildings in this part of the city can lay
claim to antiquity.   Many of them were built by Thomas
Low, of brick brought from England.   Thomas Low is an
historic name in Washington.   " The brother of Lord
Ellenborough, he belonged to one of the most distinguished families in England.   He amassed a large fortune
in India, at the time that Warren Hastings was Governor-
General.   He was a friend of Hastings, and warmly defended him.   Low brought with him to this country five
hundred thousand dollars in gold.   Soon after his arrival
he became acquainted with General Washington, who in-
duced him to invest largely in the wilderness which was
to be transformed into the ..capital of the nation.   The
investment was not profitable to Mr. Low.   The high
price set upon property caused the city to go up far in
the rear of his many new buildings.   He married Miss
Custis, the granddaughter of Mrs. Washington, and sister
of George W. Parke Custis.   His matrimonial venture

was not more satisfactory than his landed one. He parted from his wife, and at his death his five hundred thousand dollars had dwindled down to one hundred thousand. Mr. Low was so absent-minded, it is said he would forget his name when inquiring for letters at the post-office, and once locked his wife in a room, and not knowing what he had done, half a day passed before she obtained her liberty.

There is a row of two-story brick dwellings near Duddington which were built by Mr. Low, in one of which he lived. These houses bear the name of the " Ten Buildings." During Mr. Low's residence there, Louis Phillippe, then an exile, was his guest. In one of these the first copy of the *National Intelligencer* was printed, October 31, 1800. Another row of houses on New Jersey avenue, one block south of the Capitol, was also built by Thomas Low. Originally they were fashionable boarding-houses, and such men as Thomas Jefferson, Alexander Dallas and Louis Phillippe were entertained beneath their roof. They are now occupied by the Coast Survey. In this house the bill was drawn up and prepared for presentation to Congress, authorizing the establishment of a United States Bank. A house a little nearer to the Capitol, long occupied by John W. Forney, was built for the Bank of Washington, but never occupied for that purpose. Instead, the United States Supreme Court held its sessions in it for several years, and a house opposite was used as the Bank of Washington.

Opposite the eastern front of the Capitol may be seen a block of three houses, which for modern elegance will bear comparison with any in Washington. Any one who recalls the forbidding-looking edifice which used to occupy this site will find it difficult to identify this elegant block of private dwelling-houses with the Old Capitol Prison. Nevertheless the walls which once enclosed Wirz, Belle Boyd, "rebels" and sinners of every phase and degree beside no inconsiderable number of perfectly innocent prisoners, now surround the luxurious drawing-rooms of a supreme judge, a senator, and an advocate-general. This building which will ever remain most memorable as the Old Capitol Prison, was built for the temporary accommodation of Congress in 1815. Niles, *Register* of November 4, 1815 in an article entitled :—"The Capitol Rising from Its Ashes" thus speaks of this building:

"The new building on Capitol Hill preparing for the accommodation of Congress, is in such a state of forwardness, that it is expected to be finished early in November. The spacious room for the House of Representatives has been finished for several weeks. The Senate-room has been *plaistered* for some time."

Congress took possession of the new house, December 4, 1815. The first day a communication was received from the citizens who voluntarily erected the building for the temporary accommodation of Congress. The building cost $30,000; $5,000 of which had been expended on objects necessary for the accommodation of Congress, which would be useless when they vacated the house. Therefore the proprietors declared they would be satisfied with $5,000 in money, and a rent of $1,650 per annum with cost of insurance. Niles' *Register* went on to say:

"The spot where this large and commodious building was erected was a garden on the fourth of July last; the bricks of

37

which it is built were clay, and the timber used in its construction was growing in the woods on that day."

The building thus expeditiously erected, was used as the Capitol for several years. In front of this building, James Monroe was inaugurated with great brilliancy, March 4, 1817. In the winter of 1833–4, Luigi Persico occupied a room in this house as a studio. There in plaster stood the group, which now in marble occupies the south block in front of the main entrance to the Rotunda known as "Columbus and the Indian." Says the Hon. B. B. French:

"How well I remember the *artistic* enthusiasm with which he described to me his conception of Columbus holding up, with his right hand, the new world which he had discovered!

There he stands, in marble, to-day, with that same "new world," in the form of a huge nine-pin ball, or bomb-shell, elevated in his right hand, to the vast apparent admiration or fear of the crouching squaw at his side! What the squaw is there for, or what she is doing, has never yet been satisfactorily decided!"

The next mutation of this historic house was into the eminently Washingtonian one of a fashionable boarding-house. It was first kept by a Mrs. Lindenberger, afterwards by a Mr. Henry Hill, and was always a favorite abode of Southern Members of Congress. John C. Calhoun, while a Senator from South Carolina, died in this house. It was at one time occupied by the famous Ann Royal, who with her factotum Sally Brass used it as the publishing house of her feared and famous publications "The Huntress" and "Paul Pry."

Mrs. Royal inaugurated black-mailing journalism at an early day. She was the widow of a Revolutionary officer, who, reduced to the necessity of earning her living, chose a very malicious way of doing it. She kept what she called the Black Book, in which she recorded descriptions of the persons and characters of conspicuous residents of the city. She canvassed the city for subscribers to her publications, and whoever refused was threatened with a place in the Black Book. So fearfully and effectually was this threat carried out, but few had the temerity to refuse her requests. If such a daring mortal was found, the breakfast-tables of Washington were, the next morning, regaled with a portrayal whose impudence and audacity was only equalled by its shrewdness and sharpness. All who gave her money were sure of adulation, while those who refused it were equally sure of being defamed, without regard to truth.

She was feared by all mankind, from the highest functionary in the Government to the remotest clerk in the departments. " Few refused to comply with her demands, and clerks, who saw her approach, would not disdain to seek a friendly hiding-place." I believe she printed her papers with her own hands, and they were afterwards peddled about the town by her female man, Sally Brass.

During the War of the Rebellion this building perfectly swarmed with prisoners. Not only soldiers from the Rebel army, and undoubted culprits, but also hundreds of citizens, arrested on the faintest suspicion, were incarcerated within its walls. Any one suspected of having given comfort to the enemy, of having interfered with military discipline, or of having defrauded the Government in the remotest way, was hurried off to the Old Capitol Prison. It was a small American Bastile, and it

is well, perhaps, that its walls cannot tell all or aught
of the oppression and outrage which transpired within
them.   In its yard stood the just gallows whereon Wirz
was hung for the tortures which he inflicted on Union
prisoners at Andersonville.   Others were also executed
here during the war.

Soon after the close of the war, Mr. George T. Brown,
then Sergeant-at-Arms of the Senate, bought the property
and proceeded to transmute the Old Capitol Prison into
the three elegant mansions which now occupy its ground.

With this famous house must close my chapter on the
Historic Homes and Haunts of Washington.   To write
minutely of them all would require a volume.   Full detail is here impossible, but no one of the most famous
has been omitted.

CHAPTER XLIX.

MOUNT VERNON — MEMORIAL DAY — ARLINGTON.

The Tomb of Washington—The Pilgrims Who Visit it—Where George and Martha Washington Rest—The American Mecca—The Thought of Other Graves—The Defenders of the Republic—Eating Boiled Eggs—A Butterfly Visit—The Old Mansion-House—Patriarchal Dogs—Remembering a Feast—The Room in which Washington Died—The Great Key of the Bastile—The Gift of Lafayette—The Harpsichord of Eleanor Custis—The *Belle* of Mount Vernon—Moralizing—Inside the Mansion—Uncle Tom's *Bouquets*—Beautiful Scenery—Memorial Day at Arlington—The Soldiers' Orphans—The Grave of Forty Soldiers—. The Sacrifice of a Widow's Son—The Children's Offering—The Record of the Brave—A National Prayer for the Dead.

WE have newer and dearer shrines, even, than the tomb of Washington; yet, in these soft, summer mornings, many pilgrims turn their faces toward Mount Vernon.

Every morning a large company, including the young and the old, the refined and the vulgar, land at the little wharf below the home of Washington. Fathers and mothers come with their children and their lunch-baskets. Pretty girls come with venerable duennas, and young men come to look at them in spite of their keepers. Lovers come and go, maundering along the lanes, as lovers will. Relic-hunters come to break off twigs and pilfer pansies; newspaper people come, agog for an item; and, for the climax, we will believe that a few come solely to do reverence at the tomb of the Father of their country.

Passing up a wooded lane that winds over the hill, we reached the famed sarcophagus, which engravings have made familiar to many eyes that have never beheld it. Here, on their marble couch, amid the grassy slopes and tutelary trees of their ancient domain, rest the bodies of George and Martha Washington. Full of years and full of honors they laid down, and their tomb has been the Mecca of this continent. It never can be other than it is. Who would rob it of one hallowed memory? Yet, as I looked at its sculptured marble, I thought of many and many a nameless grave that I had seen by the road-side, and on the scathed fields of Virginia, parched by summer's sun, covered by winter's snow, unturfed, un-cared-for—the grave of the volunteer. Dear to me as this sepulchre of the great, is the grave of the lowliest soldier who perished for his country.

The nation will reverence always the grave of Wash-ington. But to this generation, and to the generations which shall come after, are committed many graves which cannot be held less dear. Let every city and every village in the land gather, as most precious jewels, the names of its dead who died for liberty. Set them in enduring marble; blazon them in the public places; let them greet the traveller on silent hill-tops, and in the peaceful vales; the names of our heroes, that we, our children, our children's children, to remotest time, may never forget the defenders of the republic, what they suffered and what they gained.

We ate boiled eggs and other good things within sight of the tomb of the Father of our Country—a very neces-sary proceeding before essaying to climb the hill. While we were eating, a bright blue butterfly came and paid

VIEW OF "THE CITY OF THE SLAIN." - ARLINGTON.

The remains of over 15,000 soldiers killed during the war, are buried in the Cemetery; — the name, regiment, and date of death of each is painted on a wooden headboard.

us a visit. It looked just as if one of the myrtles had danced up from the bank before us, and was palpitating in the sunshiny air. Miss Butterfly was the loveliest "blue" I ever saw.

From the tomb to the old mansion house is a pleasant walk over upland lawns and under sheltering trees. A few patriarchal dogs came forth to meet us, and that was all the welcome we received. Their tails were very limp, their ears very droopy, their legs very shaky, but they did their best to seem glad to see us, and that was more than anybody else did. One emaciated quadruped, I am sure, will remember to his dying hour the luncheon of beef and eggs of which he partook so peacefully yesterday, under an old tree within sight of Washington's dining-room.

I am thankful that Congress appropriated thousands of dollars to repair the Mount Vernon mansion. A mansion in its day, its rooms can bear no comparison with those of modern houses which make no pretensions. The dining-hall is the only one that can claim anything like stateliness or elegance of proportion. The parlors are the merest boxes, each containing one high window. The chamber in which Washington died commands an exquisite view, through the vistas of the grounds, down the Potomac. But, oh! what a cell, compared with the spacious apartments inhabited by the great generals of our own day. Mrs. Washington never occupied this room after the death of her husband. It was closed, and all in it kept sacred to his memory. She removed to the chamber above, and occupied it till her death. We went up. It is a mere garret. One little attic-window gives a meagre glimpse of the lovely landscape below. But in its best estate the room must have been very contracted, dreary, and without a convenience. No modern "Bridget" would be content to occupy for a week such a room as this in which Martha Washington lived and died.

The home of Washington, now the home of the nation, at last is open, kindly and genial. Here, in the hall, in its glass case, hangs the great key of the Bastile, presented to Washington by Lafayette, at the destruction of that prison in 1789.

Here what an opportunity to stand and gaze and moralize over the history of the brave men and beautiful women whose faces it shut into darkness! So thick gather the celebrated names, I must not mention one.

Here, in the grand dining-room, stands the quaint old harpsichord which General Washington presented as a wedding gift to his adopted daughter, the beautiful Eleanor Custis. It was made in Cheapside, Haymarket, London, and old ocean tossed it over to delight the heart of the *belle* of Mount Vernon. Here what another fine opportunity to "reflect" over the broken and rusty keys that once thrilled to the touch of beauty, and stirred with melody in the presence of the great, and made the old halls ring with the music of festivals! Only my reflections, like many other people's, have all come to me afterward, sitting here in my chair, thinking of that old harpsichord. When I looked at it, I doubt if I had a reflection at all. Staring at relics in the midst of a jostling crowd is not particularly conducive to reflection — at least not to emotion. Even the bedstead on which Washington died seems to lose half its sacredness being handled and commented on by a careless crowd.

In the dining-room, we see the famous marble mantel,

carved in Italy, and presented to General Washington by Samuel Vaugh. Its proportions are not grand, but its carving is exquisite, and it still retains its whiteness and polish.

The dining-room is a noble apartment of lofty proportions, extending through the depth of the house, its windows on front, back and sides overlooking the loveliest portion of the grounds. It is a sunshiny room, fit for family cheer. And (reflection third) what illustrious men and famous women have broken bread and tasted wine within its carved and mouldy walls in the days that are no more!

The east and west parlors, leading from the diningroom, are meagre, high-windowed rooms. Indeed, the whole house of the Father of his Country, though, doubtless, a princely mansion in its day, reminds a denizen of the present generation of the growth of architecture, and of modern convenience and elegance, quite as much as of anything else. Out on the veranda, where a venerable Uncle Tom drives a thrifty trade in the *bouquet* line, we find the real beauty of Mount Vernon — its prospect. Here, looking out upon terraced lawns and forest trees, and down the gentlest of slopes to the wide Potomac, flecked with milky sails, steamboats plying its waves, and pleasure-barques drifting and dozing with the spring-time gales, we see one of the softest and fairest of landscapes. A gentle sky; the blue air goldened with daffodils and fragrant with hyacinths, pleasant friends by my side. Thus I think of Mount Vernon.

Last Saturday was Memorial Day. With banners and bands, music and speech under the softest of May skies, and in its serenest airs tens of thousands of our soldiers' graves were decorated with flowers. Most lovely was Arlington that day ! No words could have been more eloquently fitting than those which were spoken; no music tenderer, nor fuller of precious memories, nor sweeter with suggestions of Heaven, than that sung under those patriarchal trees by fifty orphan children. And no sight could have been more touching than when these soldiers' orphans laid their flower-wreaths down upon ten thousand soldiers' graves. Yet the magnetism of the multitude was there. The tide followed the banners and the bands, the blooming maidens, the eloquent speech.

Miles out Seventh street, beyond Fort Stevens, there is a little cemetery where forty soldiers lie alone, who fell in defence of Washington. One of these was a poor widow's son. She had three ; and this was the last that she gave to her country. She, a poor widow, living far in northern Vermont, has never even seen the graves of her three soldier sons, whom she gave up, one by one, as they came to man's estate ; and who went forth from her love to return to it living no more.

To this little grave-yard on Seventh street one woman went alone with her children, carrying forty wreaths of May's loveliest flowers, and laid one on every grave. Forty mother's sons slept under the green turf; and one mother, in her large love, remembered and consecrated them all. She chose these because, with more than thirty thousand others in the larger cemeteries to be decorated, she feared the forty, in their isolation, might be forgotten. No others followed her ; and this mother, alone with her children, scattering flowers in the silence of love upon those unremembered graves, some way wears a halo which does not shine about the multitude.

THE TOMB OF "THE UNKNOWN."—ARLINGTON.

Erected by the Government to the memory of Union soldiers killed during the War.

We look on Arlington through softest airs. How beautiful it is! how sad it is! how holy! Again the tender spring grasses have crept over its sixteen thousand graves. The innocents, the violets of the woods, are blooming over the heads of our brave. In the rear of the house a granite obelisk has been raised to the two thousand who sleep in one grave. Four cannon point from its summit, and on its face it bears this inscription :—

" Beneath this stone repose the bones of two thousand one hundred and eleven unknown soldiers, gathered after the war from the fields of Bull Run, and the route to the Rappahannock. Their bodies could not be identified, but their names and deaths are recorded in the archives of their country, and its grateful citizens honor them as their noble army of martyrs. May they rest in peace."

The rooms and conservatories of the house are filled with luxurious plants, soon to be set out on the graves of this cemetery. Beauty and silence reign through this domain of the dead. There is a hush in the air, and a hush in the heart, as you walk through it, reading its names, pausing by the graves of its " unknown," thinking of the past. Far as the sight reaches, stretch the long columns of immortal dead. The beauty of their sleeping-place, the reverent care covering it everywhere, tells how dear to the Nation's heart is the dust of its heroes, how sacred the spot where they lie. In this let us not forget the still higher love which we owe them; let us attest it by a deeper devotion to the principles for which they died.

(Whole number of pages, with Illustrations, 651.)